Old Bread
New Wine

Old Bread
New Wine

A Portrait
of the Italian-Americans

Patrick J. Gallo

Nelson-Hall nh Chicago

Library of Congress Cataloging in Publication Data

Gallo, Patrick J
  Old bread, new wine.

  Bibliography: p.
  Includes index.
  1. Italian Americans—History.   I. Title.
E184.I8G344   973'.0451   80-20401
ISBN 0-88229-146-7

Manufactured in the United States of America

10   9   8   7   6   5   4   3   2   1

This book is dedicated to
my wife Grace and our beautiful children
Laura Ann, Andrew, and Daniela.

Contents

Preface

"Immigration, which was America's raison d'être," wrote Maldwyn Jones in *American Immigration*, "has been the most persistent and the most pervasive influence in her development."[1] Successive waves of immigrants have molded and transformed America. Given the importance of immigration and ethnicity, it is startling to learn that so many ethnic groups have been ignored by historians, political scientists, and sociologists. There remains a great need for detailed and intensive studies of all the ethnic groups in America. In *The Uprooted*, Oscar Handlin revealed a fundamental truth: "Once I thought to write a history of the immigrants in America. Then I discovered that the immigrants were American history."[2]

This book is an interdisciplinary study of an ethnic group, the Italian-Americans. I have relied upon materials from political science, history, sociology, and anthropology. The book is a broad portrait, not a caricature, of a proud and diverse people. I have also drawn upon my personal encounters and experiences to illustrate aspects of the Italian-American experience, in the hope that these personal references will add color, depth, texture, and life to the portrait. This is not to say I intend to take liberties with the canons of scholarship. I intend neither to romanticize nor to apologize, but to explain, describe, and analyze.

In any project of this nature, the author is necessarily indebted to a great many people. I have taught courses on the subject of Italians in America. My students have been a source of stimulation and inspiration.

Two organizations have had a major impact on me. The Italian-American Forum of New York City was a consciousness-raising activist group, where my encounters with people like Giulio Miranda helped challenge my assumptions and acted as important catalysts in creating new insights into the contemporary scene. Likewise, the passionate and talented group of scholars who constitute the American Italian Historical Association have stimulated my investigation and research.

I value the friendship and moral encouragement given to me by Dr. Rose Basile Green. She is not only an outstanding scholar, but a wonderful human being.

Anyone who writes about the Italian-American experience is especially indebted to Leonard Covello and Giovanni Schiavo. Leonard Covello, more than anyone else, understood the need for the study of Italians in the United States. Covello was an educator, a social reformer, and a social historian. His book, *The Social Background of the Italo-American School Child,* remains a classic study of an American ethnic group. Often a lone figure, he strove to convey the importance of Italian-American studies in particular, and ethnic studies in general, to an apathetic public. He was instrumental in the creation of many organizations devoted to the study of the Italian-American experience, including Casa Italiana at Columbia University, the Casa Italian Educational Bureau, and the American Italian Historical Association.

Giovanni E. Schiavo, a Sicilian journalist, is a prolific writer and researcher. He has produced a number of works, including: *Italian-American History, Italians in America Before the Civil War,* and *Italians in Chicago.* Schiavo's work was not systematic. Some might even dismiss it as ancestor worship. This criticism misses the important point that Schiavo was one of the most important forces in early Italian-American historiography. Leonard Covello and Giovanni Schiavo are the fathers of Italian-American studies. I acknowledge their pioneering efforts with gratitude and admiration.

Jeanne Berger, editorial assistant at Nelson-Hall publishers, made many invaluable suggestions. I am deeply grateful for all her assistance. And finally, I have my family to thank. Without the encouraging understanding, patience, and love of my wife, Grace, I would not have been able to complete this work. She bore with me as I thought aloud about every idea in the book. She contributed her thoughts and insights. My wife continues to be my constant safeguard against sham and compromise. My children have good-naturedly suffered through many months with a father whose ambitions may have exceeded his abilities. Any errors in this book are of course mine alone.

Acknowledgment

The author is grateful for permission to quote from the following works: Leonard Covello, *The Heart Is The Teacher* and *The Social Background of the Italo-American School Child;* Rose Basile Green and the publishers of *Primo Vino*, A. S. Barnes and Co., Inc. Cranbury, N. J. 08512, the poem "Primo Vino"; Giulio Miranda, "Out of the Closet—Some Echoes of Italian Unity Day."

1 From Columbus to Colombo

In August, 1962, a Spanish guide brought me to a room in the Alhambra Palace near Granada, Spain. I had just completed my first visit to my ancestral home in Italy. Throughout my travels in Europe I was warmed by the company of friends and relatives whom I had never seen before the day I landed in Rome. This experience made the guide's remarks all the more meaningful: "There is where King Ferdinand and Queen Isabella sat, and here," he pointed downward and his voice grew solemn, "is where Columbus stood as he pleaded his case for the great project."

"My God!" I said to myself. "I'm standing on the very spot where it all began." Indescribable emotion gripped me as I thought about the deep significance of Columbus and his discovery. A picture of Columbus came to mind. I saw a forty-year-old, ruddy-complexioned, red-haired man. His long face was accentuated by his blue eyes and aquiline nose. His eyes were those of a mariner; they had the look of a man who had scanned many horizons.

Christopher Columbus was born and reared in Genoa, one of the oldest and most renowned seafaring communities in Europe. Christopher's father, Domenico Columbo, was a middle-class wool weaver, as had been his father before him. Susanna Colombo, a wool weaver's daughter, gave birth to Christopher sometime between August and October 1451. Christopher adored his father, who, with little urging from his son, would close his shop and take the young boy fishing. Young Christopher had little schooling. As a result, he was unable to read or write until he went to Portugal in 1476.

His formal education as a sailor probably began at the age of ten when he first went to sea. At the age of twenty-five, Columbus was serving as a seaman on a vessel bound from Genoa to northern Europe. Since it contained valuable cargo, the ship was accompanied by an armed convoy. The fleet was attacked by a

1

French force off the southern Portugese coast. Columbus' ship was hit, and it sank. Columbus swam to Lagos in southern Portugal, not far from Cape Saint Vincent. Later, he learned his brother Bartholomew was living in Lisbon.

Christopher set out for Lisbon, the center of Renaissance exploration and discovery. Lisbon was also a cultural center, and Columbus did not escape its influence. There he learned modern languages and Latin. He acquired and read books that were to open new vistas to him.

Bartholomew was able to get his brother a job in the chartmaking company where he was employed. Shortly thereafter, the brothers started their own chart-making firm. In addition, Christopher gained valuable experience as a seaman, sailing under the Portuguese flag to such far-off places as Iceland, Ireland, and the Azores.

Exactly how and when he conceived of his great enterprise we do not know. His bold and daring goal was to reach the Indies— eastern Asia—by sailing westward from Europe.

Though people had talked about this idea hundreds of years before, nobody had yet attempted the journey. The ocean was reported to be too broad, winds were thought to be too uncertain for such a journey. Moreover, the fifteenth-century ships could not carry enough cargo to feed their crews for several months. While every educated person admitted it was theoretically possible to reach the Orient by sailing west, and many believed the earth to be a sphere, nobody had actually tested the east-to-west theory.

By the age of thirty-two, Columbus had considerable experience as a seaman. A superb mariner, he was confident he could convince anyone of the merits of his project.

Columbus appealed to his native city Genoa to support his project. A select committee was chosen from the finest academic minds in Genoa to evaluate the proposal. Although the committee was impressed, it finally declined to grant financial support. The committee contended that more preliminary exploration was necessary. Problems concerning the depths and temperatures of the oceans, the nature of the tides, the weather, and the prevention of scurvy and other diseases needed to be solved before such a voyage could be undertaken.

Nearly a year had passed since the time Columbus had first set foot in Spain before he was received by Queen Isabella in the Alcazar Palace in Cordova on May 1, 1486. A basis of understanding developed between Columbus and Isabella, even though she was to turn down his project more than once. After their first encounter, she appointed a special commission to evaluate his project. In 1490, the commission came to a deadlock. The only person who was convinced he could successfully complete the project was Columbus himself. Though the Queen opened the way for another application, he needed something to break the deadlock.

In December 1491, he appeared again at the court in Granada. A new commission was established and apparently approved the project, only to be overruled by the Royal Council. Reviewing the commission's findings, the council felt that Columbus' costs and demands were too extravagant. Rejected, Columbus started out for Seville. Meanwhile, Luis de Santangel, keeper of King Ferdinand's privy purse, interceded. The deadlock was broken, and the decision was reversed.

It took Columbus three months to prepare for the voyage. On August 3, 1492, he boarded the flagship *Santa Maria* and gave the orders to get under way. Such a ship was capable of sailing 3 to 5 knots in a light breeze, up to $9\frac{1}{2}$ knots in a strong gale, and sometimes even 12 knots.[1] Columbus' fleet of three ships was to average 142 miles per day for five consecutive days; their longest run, 182 miles, averaged 8 knots.[2] After a number of false landfalls, great flocks of birds passed over the three ships. On that day, October 7, 1492, Columbus decided to change course by following the birds rather than his chart.

On October 12, 1492, Rodrigo de Triana, lookout on the *Pinta*, spotted something which looked like a white cliff shining in the moonlight. Excitedly, he cried out, "*Tierra! Tierra!*" (Land! Land!) The great enterprise had reached its goal, or so Columbus must have thought. Dressed in the uniform of an admiral of the Spanish Navy, Columbus went ashore and, in the name of Ferdinand and Isabella, named the land San Salvador.

The original plan of reaching the Indies was never completed. What Columbus did not and could not know was that the continents of North and South America stood in his path. In spite of this fact, his was to be one of the most spectacular and far-reaching discoveries in human history. Columbus had been certain he had found the Indies. Ironically, people the world over now honor Christopher Columbus for discovering the Americas, something that he never knew he had done.[3]

Just before Columbus Day in 1965, Yale University released a map of Vineland (a portion of the coast of North America), which university officials claimed as "the most exciting carto-

graphic discovery of the century."⁴ The map, given to Yale by
an anonymous donor, was part of three fifteenth-century books.
The map was found in the back of the book now entitled *Tartar
Relation*, by Friar John, dealing with Plano Cartini's mission to
the Tartars in 1245. The map contained the legend on its face,
"By God's will after a long voyage from the island of Greenland
to the south toward the most distant remaining parts of the
western ocean sea, sailing southward amidst the ice, the com-
panions, Bjani and Leif Ericson, discovered a new land extremely fertile and even having vines, which island they named
Vineland."

The authenticity of the map came under immediate attack.
The legend, handwritten in Latin, was attacked for improper
word construction and other textual incongruities. In addition,
it was contended that the rendering of Greenland was surpris-
ingly accurate considering the primitive state of cartography in
1440, when the Yale map was believed to have been copied from
a still earlier map.

Nevertheless, Yale University officials, claiming eight years of
scientific testing, sold ten thousand copies of the map and the
related works at fifteen dollars each. In addition, they contracted
with the Book-of-the-Month Club to print an additional forty
thousand copies.

Then, in 1973, Yale University was rocked by the disclosure
that the map was a forgery. A newly devised chemical test revealed the ink used on the 11 by 16 inch parchment could not
have been produced prior to the 1920s.

Trying to recover from their initial embarrassment, university
officials hailed the chemical tests as a victory for scholarship and
science. This did not satisfy Francesco Guinta of the University
of Palmero, who noted that it appears to be "part of the process
to get rid of Columbus.... The Americans apparently would be
happier if their continent had been discovered by a Nordic
race."⁵ Underlying Professor Guinta's remark is a feeling shared
by many Italian-Americans and other ethnics that their cultural
and historical impact on the development of American society is
neither recognized nor appreciated.

I remember a lone individual at a recent Columbus Day
parade in New York City holding a placard which carried the
declaration, "Leif Erickson was here first," Another person,
obviously an Italian-American, exclaimed, "They are even trying
to rob us of that?" He shook his head in disgust.

An angry letter to the editor, which appeared in a local New
Jersey newspaper, expresses another side of this frustration.

As it comes time for the Academy Awards, I see that *The Godfather Part II* is up for an award.

I consider this picture part of the on-going stereotype of Italians as criminals.

May you be reminded that, when the master races of Northern Europe such as England, Germany, and Norway were still swinging from the trees, the Romans and the Italians were civilized and civilizing these people.[6]

Over the years, it has been claimed that American culture was rooted in Anglo-Saxon culture and traditions. Anglo-Saxons and other northern Europeans boasted, on setting foot on American soil, to be Americans. This prevailing cultural myth, that failed to decipher the identity of culture, was accompanied by a contempt for southern and eastern European peoples in the latter nineteenth century.

Aside from acknowledging the early centuries of Roman culture in Britain, the influence and impact of which steadily grow with each archaeological discovery, one must remember it was the Italian Renaissance that gave us Columbus and wove the scholarly fabric of Anglo-Saxon culture which gives richness to "American" thought. The high ideals of the Italian Renaissance were expressed in the historical thoughts of Bellarmini, Machiavelli, and other champions of human thought.

The great Italian cultural awakening brought about sophisticated concepts in human thought which influenced the newly independent America. The clue to this Italian genius is that it gave magic to thought, besides being functional and literary in value. As an example, the historian Polydore Vergil of Urbino, who spent five decades in England, deciphered the medieval chronicles of English history and reorganized them into a superior readable style, underlined by accuracy and the removal of myths. In his *Historia Anglica,* he gave the English a new historiography which was to serve as a model for the writing of their own history. And through the arts, Italians embarked on a fresh, spirited exploration which inspired da Vinci and Michelangelo to breathe life into the arts and reveal its secrets, secrets which Shakespeare later captured and translated into his tragedies.

The Renaissance was Italian in spirit and origin; in essence, it enriched Western culture with new ideas, manners, habits, and tastes which inspired new modes for the best minds of the world, including England.[7] Italian culture brought realism and relevance to its times and introduced a beautiful way of living that was emulated by English society. It was a life style that seeped into the American colonies but was credited to England.

Looking at the full sweep of American history, it becomes apparent that immigration has been America's *raison d'être*. With the exception of the American Indian, the United States is "a nation of immigrants." Its people are the recent sons and daughters of Europeans, Africans, and Asiatics, who have forged a culturally pluralistic society—a nation of subcultures—characterized by a unity of spirit and ideals, but with a diversity of origins and expressions.

We are justified in honoring Christopher Columbus for his discovery. No other sailor known had the persistence, the knowledge, the audacity, and the raw courage to sail thousands of miles into the unknown ocean until he found land. Permanent settlement and a new civilization were to follow Columbus' discovery. The preeminence of Columbus does not stem from his discovery alone, but in his hastening others along the same path by his promise and example.

The "Great Enterprise" of 1492 led to the "Great American Experiment" of 1787. The discovery of the New World was the beginning of the long course of events that allowed the establishment of the American heritage of freedom. And it all started with Columbus. The history of the Italian experience in America began with him.

Indeed, the roots of the Italian-American heritage lie very deep in American soil. Amerigo Vespucci, a later Florentine explorer, vividly described the distant lands discovered by Columbus. Vespucci sailed along the coast of South America and was probably the first European to sight what the Spaniards later called Cape Canaveral, now Cape Kennedy, on the eastern Florida coast. Cartographers thereafter came to use the name "America" (after Amerigo) on maps of the Western Hemisphere. Columbus discovered the new land and Vespucci gave his name to it.

In many ways, Columbus' spirit was written upon the new nation. As Samuel Eliot Morison has observed:

> To be sure, he had defects and faults, but they were largely the defects of the qualities that made him great—his indomitable will, his superb faith in God and in mission, his stubborn persistence despite neglect, poverty, and discouragement. But there was no flaw, no dark side, to the most outstanding and essential of all his qualities—his seamanship. As a master mariner and navigator, Columbus was supreme in his generation. Never was a title more justly bestowed than the one which he

most guarded—Almirante del Mar Oceano, Admiral of the Ocean Sea.[8]

All Americans *of Italian descent* are, in a sense, the children of Columbus. But, in the deepest significance of his discovery, *all* Americans are his children.

The View from Columbus Circle

We meet here not to rejoice, but rather to raise a unified voice of protest.

We have been defamed in the press, on television, and radio.

We have been degraded and discriminated against, and now, we say, Enough!

. . . . . .

We have been reduced to the status of second class citizens and we say, Never!

. . . . . .

Let this, our first Unity Day Rally, serve notice that the Italian-Americans will no longer tolerate that treatment. . . .

—from the program of the Italian-American Unity Day

On June 29, 1970, thousands of Italian-Americans poured into Circolo di Colombo (Columbus Circle) in New York City. Green, red, and white streamers decorated the Circle. Buttons declared openly, "Kiss Me/I'm Italian," "Italian Power," and "Italian is Beautiful." Others shouted, "Olive is Gorgeous!" The air was festive and exciting. What brought these people there on that hot day? The main catalyst seemed to have been Joe Colombo, Sr., founder of the Italian-American Civil Rights League. Colombo tapped an undercurrent of restless discontent which reached as far back as the arrival in America of the fathers, mothers, and grandparents of those who stood in Columbus Circle.

My good friend Giulio Miranda, an astute observer of the American scene, has said, "The love of Italian-Americans for the United States is like the outpouring of an adopted child for a foster father who has given him what he never received from his natural parent. To most of us, especially those who have not benefited from the enlightenments and disillusionments of higher education, it is inconceivable that we, or anyone else, should rebel against such a father."

If Colombo's followers were the most visible, they were by no means alone in their expressions of identity and feelings of re-

jection. To many Italian-Americans, Joe Colombo, a reputed
underworld figure, was an embarrassment. He was not their
leader. To many non-Italians, he fit the stereotype of an Italian-
American. Of Colombo, Michael Novak observed,

> He sensed that Poles, Sicilians, Italians, Greeks, Armenians,
> Coats, Serbs, Portuguese, Russians, Spaniards, Lithuanians, and
> others were losing their sharp lust to "become Americans." . . .
> One by one, hundreds and then thousands were deciding not to
> continue trying to become what they are not, can never be. . . .
> I watched Joe Colombo with fascination. He was (I thought)
> the wrong man for the job. But who else was doing it?[9]

Italian-Americans are not demonstrators by nature. Their
style, as revealed by Italian cultural history, was to accept hardship with stoic endurance. That style was shattered on this occasion. For a hundred thousand to come out and demonstrate
despite obviously questionable leadership indicates that many
more thousands were quietly in agreement (if not with the
leadership) with the issues. These issues included: discrimination; taxation; lack of urban services and programs; an acute
sense of powerlessness; lack of group mobility, self-image, and
identity; and negative societal images. There was a perception
that they, like their fellow ethnics, paid the largest percentage
of local and federal taxes only to get the least in return in terms
of goods and services. And they were tired of put-downs. As
Giulio Miranda notes, "No, a great many Italian-Americans do
not feel that things have changed very much since the days when
they were openly called Wop and Guinea. This is the real meaning of the uproar about the words *mafia* and *cosa nostra*. To
many it is just a new way of saying the same old thing."
Months before the first Italian-American Unity Day, I was
engaged in field work on a study dealing with Italian-American
political behavior.[10] I spent hundreds of hours talking with
many first, second, and third generation Italian-Americans in the
New York metropolitan area. I sensed an uneasiness, a seething
discontent. When I heard that a Unity Day would be held in
June, 1970, I predicted there would be a great response. My pre-
diction proved to be correct.
Some readers might be confused by the title of this chapter,
"From Columbus to Colombo." Some might be outraged by even
faintly associating the latter with the great discoverer. In no way
do I assert that Colombo ranks with the giants of the Italian-
American experience. Was Colombo sincerely interested in the
problems and issues confronting Italian-Americans? Was he us-

ing Italian-Americans to force the Federal Bureau of Investigation to back off from their investigations of him? Joe Colombo's motives are known only to himself. However, to discredit Joe Colombo totally is to confuse the medium with the message.

Something unique happened on June 29, 1970, in the Italian-American experience, either because of or in spite of Joe Colombo. He brought many Italian-Americans out of hiding and into confrontation with some large questions: Who are we? What made us what we are? Where are we going? For many Italian-Americans, this day was the beginning of the discovery of themselves.

2 Destiny

Near the Verrazzano Monument in Battery Park in New York City, there is a commemorative bronze plaque to Peter Caesar Alberti. On June 2, 1635, Alberti became the first Italian immigrant to arrive in New York State. He was one of the first of many millions who left their native Italy to live in, to work in, and to help establish the United States of America.

Alberti first settled in the area known today as the Wall Street section of New York City. Alberti later worked for a Dutch landowner, until, in 1641, he acquired land in Brooklyn. On August 24, 1642, he married Judith Jans Manje, the daughter of a prosperous Dutch settler. Sometime in the 1650s, Alberti died while defending his home during an Indian attack. Today, Alberti's descendents are scattered all over the United States.

Peter Alberti wasn't the first Italian to have come to North America. Individually and in groups, priests, soldiers, and adventurers followed explorers into the Spanish southwestern portion of what would later become the United States, many years before the Pilgrims arrived to settle the eastern seaboard. Many of them included Italians who made vital explorations, including Fra Marcos de Niza, Eusebio Francesco Chino, Girolamo Benzoni, Giovanni Gemelli-Careri, Allesandro Malaspina, and Enrico Tonti.

There were some Italians in the English colonies during the seventeenth century. Because of the great distance and the cost of the voyage, few Europeans emigrated. In 1622, a group of Venetian glassmakers came to Jamestown, Virginia. By 1632, a small number of Italians had also settled in Maryland and Georgia.

The first large group of Italians to come to America were Protestant Waldensians who settled in Delaware and New York in 1657. In 1768, more than a hundred Italians helped establish a colony in East Florida.

11

In the northern colonies, some Italian settlers were managing stores, operating hotels, and serving as carpenters and shoe- makers. Others were doctors, lawyers, and musicians.

From the early 1600s to 1880, there was no large-scale immi- gration of Italians to America. Much of the immigration con- cerned small groups or individuals and occurred in short peri- odic spurts. In Philadelphia, there were approximately two hundred Italians by 1850; the group grew to three hundred in 1870. Census figures show that forty-four thousand Italians lived in the United States by 1880. One quarter of that number were in New York. There were probably many more Italians in America prior to 1880, since immigration records were not of- ficially kept prior to 1820. Moreover, Italian names were Angli- cized due to social pressures, errors in recording names, or be- cause of personal preference. In addition, federal census figures were not accurate.

In 1850, there were approximately two hundred Italians living in San Francisco. The lure of the gold rush during the 1850s drew more Italians to the West Coast. By 1851, six hundred Italians had settled in San Francisco. The distance to California was as far as that from Italy to New York. Until 1869, when the first transcontinental railroad was completed, travelers to Cali- fornia had to journey several months to reach the West coast.[1]

These low figures should not hide the importance of these early Italian settlers to the history of America. During the Ameri- can Revolution, characters like Filippo Mazzei, William Paca, and Giuseppe Vigo played important roles. In addition, hundreds of Italians died for this country's independence, and they are par- ticularly important to our nation's history. Mazzei's ideas were more radical than those of most colonists. He held strong beliefs on religious freedom, and he believed that America could only be a true democracy by ending its domination by England. Many colonial leaders listened closely to him, especially Thomas Jeffer- son, who later translated a series of Mazzei's articles under the pseudonym Furioso. The doctrine, "All men are created equal," incorporated in the Declaration of Independence by Thomas Jefferson, was paraphrased from the writings of Philip Mazzei. Thomas Paine's pamphlet *Common Sense* contained ideas origi- nated by Mazzei. Mazzei was active in a variety of ways in help- ing the revolutionary cause.

In the development of American culture, Giuseppe Ceracchi, Constantino Brumidi, Lorenzo Papanti, Ferdinando Palmo, Lorenzo da Ponte, Carlo Bellini, and Antonio Meucci are just a few of the many Italian men and women who helped mold the emerging culture but who are omitted from the traditional historical accounts. Giuseppe Ceracchi was the most important Italian sculptor to come to America in the colonial period. Ceracchi introduced to America the portrait bust, the most significant form of American sculpture in the early nineteenth century.[2]

One dimension of the interaction of Italians with America which is often ignored is the immigration of political refugees between 1831 and 1860.[3] Though the political refugees were only a small portion of the total European immigration during these years, they are nonetheless important. The presence of the Italian exiles greatly influenced American opinion on the struggle for Italian National unification. In turn, the exposure to America and her way of life influenced the ideas of the refugees. The exiles were political activists drawn from all regions of Italy. They include such names as Garabaldi, Avezzana, Tinelli, Argenti, Albinola, Confalonieri, Maroncelli, and Foresti.

As a result of their stay in America, the cause of Italian unity gained in a variety of ways. While in the United States, the Italian expatriates never forgot Italy and worked ceaselessly for the cause of Italian Nationhood. They collected arms, raised money, conducted benefits, and in some cases returned to Italy to fight for independence. In these efforts, the regional distinctions which had separated them in Italy broke down once they arrived in America. They recognized themselves as Italians and not just as Neapolitans or Sicilians.

Many of the expatriates were befriended and assisted by an influential group of American men and women including William Cullen Bryant, Andrew Norton, Theodore Sedgwick, Catherine Sedgwick, George Ticknor, and Henry Theodore Tuckerman. These people formed the nucleus of an American group dedicated to Italian independence. They expressed their dedication to this ideal through public meetings and the press. The American group, through their interaction with the exiles, publicized the theme of Italian freedom and made it fashionable and meaningful to the American public.

The political refugees influenced public opinion and occasionally swayed American policy. Their presence also influenced the development of the Young America Movement in the Democratic party, which espoused the cause of the oppressed people of Europe.

The turning point in the history of Italian immigration to the United States was 1880. Every year thereafter, one would find thousands of Italians pouring off the immigrant ships. Nearly four million Italians had entered America between 1891 and 1920. The overwhelming majority came from southern Italy. In 1907, the high-water mark of this movement, 285,000 came. Thousands more were still on the way. By 1910, Italians accounted for about 10 percent of the foreign-born population.[4] The Italian population in San Francisco reached 45,000 in 1920, nearly 10 percent of the total foreign stock, making it the largest of the city's immigrant groups. This pattern was to continue in many cities and communities throughout the United States. Many more Italians came to the United States than "official" sources indicated. Based on average annual totals, Italians composed the largest single wave of immigrants in American history.

What many accounts of Italian immigration ignore is that the movement of Italians to the United States was part of a massive exodus to other regions of the world. In fact, the movement to other lands preceded the mass immigration to the United States and then coincided with it. From 1880 to the late 1890s, Italian immigration was directed toward the countries of South America (especially Argentina and Brazil), Switzerland, Germany, and Austria. Most of the movement within Europe in the 1880s was of a temporary nature and consisted for the most part of unskilled workers. The movement within Europe was to continue (with interruptions for World War I, the Fascist Regime, and World War II) throughout the nineteenth century and into the twentieth century.

The movement to destinations other than the United States during these years becomes clearer when we consider the fact that the United States absorbed only 17 percent (687,284) of all Italians who emigrated from Italy between 1885 and 1900. The remaining 4,100,415 went to other places. Between 1901 and 1906, the United States received 38.1 percent of all Italian immigrants. That figure was to increase to 39 percent, or 1,975,511 people, between 1904 and 1914, while an additional 5,065,501 persons headed for other destinations.[5] The flood of emigrants from Italy constituted one of the great voluntary movements of people in history.

The movement of Italians to South America differed in many respects from their immigration into Europe or Africa. Italians and other Europeans were encouraged to come to South American countries, whose inhabitants were eager to develop their nations. Immigrants were encouraged to migrate with enticing offers of free land and jobs. Often the government or individual businessmen paid for passage and provided homes, tax rebates, or tax-free property. In addition, the more favorable attitudes of the native South Americans toward new arrivals were such that the immigrants were able to make a quick adjustment. The Spanish language was similar to the Italian language. The Catholicism of South America was similar to that of Italy. In many respects, the land resembled the one that they had left. Moreover, the temperament of the Latin Americans as a group was essentially Mediterranean. The Italians in South America, particularly those in Argentina and Brazil, experienced more rapid upward social mobility than those in North America.

Prior to the mass migration, most of the Italians emigrated from the north of Italy. Contrary to the common myth, they were not in the main better educated or more economically advanced than the later southern Italians. Most of the northern immigrants came from the poorest agricultural regions of the Northeast. Records indicate that they bore a similar profile to their southern counterparts with regard to literacy levels and socioeconomic status.

Of the Italians who left their native country after 1880, the overwhelming numbers were drawn from the South. Nearly 27.4 percent of the Italians who came to the United States between 1876 and 1930 came from the Naples area, while 16.2 percent were from Abruzzi and Molise; 7.4 percent from Apulia; 5.8 percent from Basilicata; 13 percent from Calabria; and 29.9 percent were from Sicily.[6] Thus, the Italian-American subculture bears the heavy imprint of the southern Italian.

What caused so many Italians to leave their native land? What did they encounter when they arrived? The Italian experience must be seen in terms of a mutual interaction. Although many factors merged to uproot them from Italy and to attract them to America, the interaction of the poverty of the land with the history of Italy is crucial to understanding the great migration.

Speaking of the central mission of the Italian government immediately following the unification in 1870, Massimo d'Azeglio, a *Risorgimento* leader, mused, *"Fara l'Italia, bisogna fare gli Italiani"* (Having made Italy, we must now make Italians.).

Professor La Palombara has said of Italy more recently: "The striking truth about Italy is that, except at a superficial level, the leaders of the country have failed to 'make Italians.' "[7]

Italy did not emerge as a national state until 1870 for a variety of reasons. The first factor was the inheritance of its Roman past.[8] Classical Rome, in Italian history, does not stand for Italy but represents a much wider concept. It included in its empire a great diversity of lands and peoples. Roman law and language served as the means of unification of a vast domain. Even with

the fall of the empire, the ideal of universality lingered on. The
Holy Roman Empire was certainly neither holy nor Roman, but
neither was it national or imperial. The long connection between
its chief component parts, Germanic and Italian, was on the
whole to work to their mutual disadvantage. The Roman ideal
of universality, as it survived the many centuries, was to be a
major obstacle to the creation of an Italian people. While Rome
ruled a vast domain, it had been unable to rule the peninsula.
The pattern of jealousies, ambitions, feuds, and rivalries persisted long after Rome and its empire had vanished.[9]

The Roman Catholic Church was the second obstacle to
national integration. The Pope operated in a dual capacity following the fall of Rome—as a petty temporal leader and as a
representative of a universal idea. The Church became more
firmly entrenched in Rome with its claim to temporal power.

A third major obstacle was the communal tradition. In the
anarchy that characterized Europe following the fall of Rome,
the emergence of city life coincided with the revival of foreign
trade. Italian cities were the primary beneficiaries of this revival.
As Carrie notes:

> The communal tradition struck deep roots in Italy; it became
> in fact a much more real and strong living force than
> the remote and embalmed influence of old Rome herself...
> precisely because this was a force of such vitality and one that
> commanded intense loyalty, it led after a while to a process of
> crystallization that prevented the grasping of the broader hori-
> zon of a larger unity.[10]

Localism or parochialism is still in evidence in Italy today.
There frequently are hostilities between many cities. Several
years ago, violence erupted when a provincial capital was
changed from one city to another in southern Italy.[11]

A fourth impulse, which left its enduring marks on Italian
society, was the succession of foreign invasions.[12] Exploitation is
the hallmark of foreign domination. Italy, throughout its long
and illustrious history, has known foreign domination and exploitation. Perhaps the period of foreign domination most important to our discussion spanned the era from 1500 to 1860.

By 1500, Italy consisted of five principal states: Naples, Venice,
Milan, Florence, and the Papal States. Before 1500, Italy was independent and politically and culturally distinguished. Italy at
that time was to Europe what Europe was to the rest of the
world in 1914—small but politically influential.

Naples occupied one-quarter of the Italian Peninsula, with

one-fifth of the total Italian population of twelve million people living in Naples and its environs. Wealthier than Naples but half its size and with a population of about two-and-one-half million people stood Venice. Economically prosperous with large revenue sources was the Duchy of Milan. The Duchy was one-third the size of Naples and contained a million people. In central Italy stood the Republic of Florence, with half the area of Naples and with a population of 1.2 million.

In the post-Renaissance period of foreign domination, the spirit of the Renaissance disappeared, along with its liberating values and attitudes. In this era of foreign domination the autonomy of these five city states was all but ended. The first period of foreign rule in the post-Renaissance era was administered by Spain and lasted from 1500 to 1706.

The economic and social difficulties of southern Italy worsened under Spanish rule. The Spanish left southern Italy in a condition from which it never fully recovered. Spain developed and applied laws arbitrarily, but these arbitrary laws were never applied to the privileged and titled. The Spanish laws were directed to the oppression of the masses. Their laws established the rights of pre-emption, banishment, and coercion. In addition, the Spanish left southern Italy with a system of excessive and abusive taxation, which continued after their domination waned.

But the Spanish were to leave their mark in other ways. A conscious policy of the Spanish monarchs was to keep the nobles and peasants in conflict with each other. Fearing a political union between the two, the monarchs followed a divide-and-conquer policy. This provided the basis for future class conflicts. The defenseless masses were led to displace their aggression toward members of their own class and all persons in positions of power and authority—their oppressors.

Heavy taxes on the exportation of Italian silk virtually destroyed that industry. Through this tax system, entreprenurial initiative and experimentation were crushed. The Spanish rule led to yet another abusive practice. The right to tax could now be leased to third parties. As a consequence, the peasant now faced three levels of exploitation: from the monarch, the landowner, and the overseer.

In the 1700s, a new factor was introduced. The aristocracy moved to the cities in increasing numbers due to governmental intervention in the manors and the rise of malaria in the countryside. Landowners left their land to the overseers. This led to even greater exploitation with the rise of the absentee landlord. These circumstances left the peasants with no means of obtaining capital and perpetuated their backwardness. Increasingly, peasants were left without land. According to Antonio Genovesi, by the start of the eighteenth century it was estimated that fifty-nine out of sixty families lacked enough land in which to be buried.

The impact of Spanish rule can be seen in the creation of a titled aristocracy. Freedom of intellectual expression was restricted. Austerity was in evidence in the wearing of black. Women took a still more restricted social and intellectual role. The Spanish domination stifled intellectual life; social forms became more rigid.

The two centuries of Spanish domination have left permanent traces on the social behavior of Italy. From this period dates the usual form of polite address, the *lei* (literally "she") and awkward locution. Mussolini tried in vain to substitute the more natural *voi*.

The rule of the Austrians replaced that of the Spanish. Their domination spanned a century and a half. During that time they had partial control of half of Italy and total control over most of the rest. That rule extended from 1706 to 1796 and was interrupted by the French conquest of Italy only to be re-established from 1814 to 1850. During the first period, the Austrian rule played a progressive role, in that it had a liberating impact and promoted a partial awakening of the Italian educated classes.

During the second period (from 1814 to 1859), the Austrians played a completely reactionary role, restricting the changes that were advocated by a liberal and patriotic minority. Official reaction functioned through police repression and terrorism made possible by superior military strength. The Austrian regime also held complete control of education and all communications.

The rule of the French interrupted that of the Austrians. Following the spectacular campaign of 1796, led by the young Corsican general Napoleon Bonaparte, Napoleon's brother was placed on the throne in Naples. While French rule had some liberating aspects, very little was done for the masses of Italians in concrete terms. There was some minor land reform of the great estates.

The Napoleonic reforms which broke up the *latifondi* (large feudal estates) did little to resolve the problems of Italian agriculture. These problems included a lack of managerial knowledge, insufficiency of capital, bullheaded traditionalism, and a host of other factors which conspired against peasant success. The land passed back into the hands of the large owners and the estates grew bigger in size. In central and northern Italy the *mezzadria* system was prevalent. This was a system of land tenure in which the landowner provided capital and paid all expenses.

The peasant provided the labor, and the output was divided in half. Even the *mezzadria* pattern of Tuscany, though it provided great social stability, failed to answer the problems of agriculture. The masses were still overtaxed. In order to make ends meet, the peasants began to overuse and misuse the land. Under pressure of still higher taxes, land was sold cheaply to the propertied or surrendered as payment for debts.

With hundreds of years of foreign domination, the Italians developed a sign language. This form of communication, which is still part of the Italian character, was designed to undercut the ever watchful conqueror. The continued use of a sign language in Italy is evident to any observer of the Italian scene.

What is important about the history of foreign domination is that the country was never rescued from the necessity of relying on regimes, protectors, or guardians to prevent civil wars, revolutions, and invasions. Salvadori writes:

> It is difficult to say which of the two main developments of the sixteenth century in Italy—the Great Reformation or the establishment of Spanish domination—had the greater influence in molding the contemporary nation. The two developments helped each other. They combined to produce conformity, deviousness, docility; to create the conviction that governmental authority is beyond the reach of common people, that the hierarchical order is the natural order.[13]

Barzini makes the following observations about the impact of foreign rule on individual behavior:

> He is powerless to deflect the tides of history. He can only try to defend himself from their blind violence, keep his mouth shut, and mind his own business.[14]
>
> . . . . . .
>
> They behave with circumspection, caution, and even cynicism. . . . They know the world is an ugly and pitiless place and adapt themselves, without useless recriminations to its inviolable laws.[15]

In summary, the long history of the *Mezzogiorno* (southern Italy) is not a happy one. Foreign domination has played a significant role in determining the destiny of the southern peasantry. From the days of Magna Grecia, the South has endured the onslaughts of Romans, Arabs, Normans, Hohenstaufen Germans, Angiovene French, Florentines, Genovese, Venetians, and Aragonese Spaniards, to name but a few of the more important invaders. The one-time "breadbasket" of ancient Rome had been reduced, by the time of the *Risorgimento,* to an impoverished land and people despised and disowned by the rest of Italy.

By 1815, the five states of Naples, Venice, Milan, Florence, and

the Papal states were now consolidated. The former maritime
provinces of Genoa and Venice were denied their independence
by the monarchist Congress of Vienna. Genoa was given to Piedmont; and Venice, along with the Lombard plain north of the
Po, including Milan, became a kingdom within the Austro-
Hungarian Empire. After 1815, in the territory that is now Italy,
there were two native kingdoms—to the north, the Kingdom of
Piedmont, and to the south, the Kingdom of the Two Sicilies.
Sandwiched between was the Grand Duchy of Tuscany. Nationalists would eventually rally around the House of Savoy, the
ruling house of Piedmont. The failure to establish Italian unification in 1848 led more and more nationalists to turn to Piedmont, led in the 1850s by Count Camillo Benso di Cavour. The
eventual unification of Italy resulted from a combination of
liberal nationalism and Piedmontese expansionism. The *Risorgimento,* which lasted from 1815 to 1870, was a post-Napoleonic
movement aimed at the establishment of an independent Italian
state founded on free institutions.

The Italian unification movement was never a mass movement. It did not attract the average Italian, but rather the
northern middle and upper classes.[16] The Italy that emerged in
1870 was not the Italy desired by either Mazzini or Garibaldi.[17]
The nation began its life without the widespread participation
of the masses, with only the half-hearted support of the people
south of Rome, and with the opposition of the Catholic Church
which was outraged over the loss of its power.[18]

Still another obstacle to national integration was the centralized administration system imposed by Piedmont after 1870,
which denied Italians the experience with political participation
they sorely needed.[19] In exchange for a central government, the
South was left pretty much to itself. Piedmont was able to "buy"
the support of the southern "notables" who saw their region as a
place to exploit for personal gain and not as an area to develop.
Thus, the South began its experience in the new nation under a
policy of neglect and corruption typical of Bourbon administrators.[20]

Political unification did not bring cultural unity or major
economic improvements for the South. The North dominated
the central government, treating the South as an unwanted ap-
pendage. The North received the accessibility to a national
market. A growing industrialization in the South was stifled
when the central government did not protect these new industries with the necessary protective tariffs. Moreover, in comparison to the North, the South paid taxes in disproportionate

amounts.[21] For years, the central administration ignored the South. Few national leaders traveled south of Rome. They had a preconceived idea of the people and the conditions in which those people were living. In fact, in the years immediately following unification, the people in the North believed the South to be very wealthy and richly endowed with natural resources. Later, when it became apparent that this assumption was wrong, the poverty of the southern peasants was blamed on their character.

It took a while after unification for the people of the South to realize that their real standard of living had not only failed to improve after they had been "liberated," but had actually deteriorated. There is much evidence to suggest that the lot of the southern peasantry had worsened since the time of unification. It is doubtful that the peasant ever enjoyed real prosperity in the past; however, there appear to have been happier times. Examinations of peasant dress—costumes and jewelry—indicate a relative degree of affluence existed in the South in the early years of the nineteenth century.

The stable equilibrium between population and food supply began to disintegrate as population numbers shot upward. The Italian population doubled from 1861 to 1901 (to 12 million) and increased to nearly half again as much (18 million) by 1916. During the crucial years following the unification, many of the economic gains were wiped out by an unchecked demographic increase.

The lot of the peasant entered a downward spiral as a result of overpopulation without a corresponding increase in agricultural productivity. One lesson could be learned from this period of history. The economic conditions of the *Mezzogiorno* were not irreversible. Neither geography nor climate determined southern agriculture. Rather, social, political, and economic factors were responsible for the civilization in the South.

In the decades following unification, the peasant sunk deeper into his misery. Caring little for the distant government in Rome or its foreign representatives on the local scene, the peasant erected psychological barriers of suspicion, indifference, and political apathy. When he dared to become politically active, it was to support the monarchy. The peasant fought and bled for the monarchy and returned to his fields to be exploited by it.

The agricultural crisis in Italy began to deepen. Parliamentary inquiries revealed the shocking conditions of the landed and landless poor, but to no avail. From 1861 to 1901, the number of landowners declined and the power of the landed estates increased. Only the safety valve of immigration prevented the complete collapse of the system. Disease and famine wreaked havoc among the impoverished population. Malaria, cholera, pellagra, vitamin deficiencies, dysentery, and other health hazards reduced the will of the Southerner to survive.

Governmental policies of the last part of the nineteenth century further crippled the South. The grist tax and salt tax hit hardest at the poor. Protectionist tariffs for northern industry and monetary policies lowering the value of agricultural products further discriminated against the South. Italian agriculture, lacking risk capital and transportation facilities, was unable to compete in any sector against the inroads of the French (wine), North American (citrus), and Greek and Spanish (olive oil) production.

The long history of exploitation laid a basis for the seething unrest which was to create difficulties for all subsequent governments of Italy. The alienation of the peasantry from an unfeeling bureaucracy could be likened to a social vacuum. Just as nature abhors a vacuum in the physical universe, the vacuum in the social universe was filled by forces which began to shape the peasant world. The peasant perceived the power of distant Rome and established a defensive network of social relations to protect himself. The intricate interlocking web of mutual obligation is evident in a variety of social forms. The system of patronage and *raccomandazione* (privilege-recommendation) worked to undermine an inefficient bureaucracy by rendering it even more inefficient.

Although the state attempted to tackle many of the problems of agriculture, too often it succumbed to halfway measures. Mindful of the pressures, the national regime began to create the infrastructure of modernization: railroads, highways, and water supplies. Yet, nature seemed to conspire against the South. Disasters—volcanic eruptions, earthquakes, landslides, droughts—wiped out many of the gains. Usurious rates of interest dried up sources of capital for the extension of agriculture and industry, leaving the South as impoverished as before. Repressive taxation further destroyed the initiative of the *Mezzogiorno*. Perhaps unintentionally, taxes on farm buildings favored the North, where structures were located in the sparse countryside, and worked against the South, where the peasants lived in village clusters.

Still another dimension to the South's lack of development was the failure to develop a modern educational system. Before unification, the governments of most Italian states had done little to promote public education. The very idea that the state should provide elementary education to people of all classes seemed subversive to Italy's reactionary rulers, particularly since the plan's most zealous advocates were nationalists and liberals. Only in Piedmont, beginning in 1848, were there any significant advances in the field of public education. Based on Cavour's doctrine of "a free Church in a free State," advances there had a marked anticlerical character: the privileges of the religious orders in education were abolished, and the influence of the ecclesiastical authorities in the state schools was ended. This change, plus the reorganization and expansion of the state schools, paved the way for the Casati Law in 1859.

This law, named after Count Gabrio Casati (1789–1873), provided the basis for liberal Italy's educational system. Promulgated shortly after the annexation of Lombardy to the Kingdom of Piedmont-Sardinia, is incorporated the most modern ideas of the first half of the nineteenth century concerning pedagogic principles, church/state relations, and the role of education in a developing society. Indeed, the Casati Law may be considered Cavour's most enduring legacy aside from political unification itself. The educational system set up by this law extended to all the annexed territories, from 1877 until the Fascists came to power in October 1922.

Until the end of the nineteenth century, very little was done for elementary education, especially in the South. There were several reasons for this: inadequate finances; resistance in rural areas; and relative indifference among the nation's liberal leaders. The problem of inadequate finances was aggravated by the determination of Italy's political leaders, whether of the *Destra* (Right) or the *Sinistra* (Left), to make their nation a great power. Given Italy's relatively backward economy, they had to spend a much larger proportion of the national revenue than the more advanced nations on the army, navy, and merchant marine.

In the late 1880s, the Italian government spent over 25 percent of its income on these three services, while only 2.4 percent was spent on education. This would have been a small amount in an advanced society; it was woefully inadequate for a country that had to cope with widespread illiteracy and had to enforce compulsory education at the most elementary level. Of course, the communities were supposed to provide the bulk of the financial support for their local schools, so that the low national figure is somewhat misleading. But it was difficult for the national government to force the communities to fulfill their obligations, especially in the South, where poverty and peasant hostility to any kind of forced instruction retarded progress.

The statistics of high illiteracy rates and erratic school attendance in liberal Italy are instructive. In 1861, 78 percent of the total population was illiterate; ten years later the percentage was 72 percent for the kingdom as a whole and 90 percent for the South. By 1881, the national figure had declined to 62 percent; by 1901, to 48.5 percent. But in 1901, the regional figures varied considerably: 17.7 percent were illiterate in Piedmont; 78.7 percent, in Calabria. Thus, in education as in almost everything else, North and South were two different worlds. The differences were increasing as the North moved forward while the South virtually stood still, despite all the reports and lamentations of liberal leaders about the "Southern Question."[22]

Figures for school attendance during the liberal period also misrepresent the poorer parts of the kingdom. In 1871, 51.3 percent of all children between six and ten years were supposedly in school, but those who completed the first two grades satisfactorily were usually not required to continue any further. (With only two grades of schooling behind them, the majority of these children soon relapsed into illiteracy.) By 1879, the national figure rose to 59.5 percent and reached 75 percent in the mid-1890s. Few percentages are available thereafter until the mid-1920s (81 percent in 1926), but we may presume that the average was under 80 percent. Again, however, school attendance varied and had different meanings in different parts of the country. Of the 3 million children enrolled in elementary school in 1910, 2.75 million were in the first three grades alone.

Before the First World War, Italy's inadequate effort to raise the level of literacy and elementary education had political as well as cultural and social consequences. First, it limited the number of voters, since literacy was a requirement for the franchise until 1912. Many illiterate Italian workers supported the socialists mainly because they championed their right to vote. Second, self-distrust, inexperience, and a sense of inferiority among these workers forced them to turn to middle-class ideologues to help them organize a labor movement (in contrast to Great Britain, France, the United States, and even Germany, where educated workers provided such leadership from their own ranks). On the other hand, like many developing countries, Italy produced an intellectual proletariat (laboring-class intellectuals).

To this day, Italy represents two distinct cultures—the industrial North and the underdeveloped South. This difference is not merely one of degree. It is a structural cleavage extending into the economic, social, and political systems. It presents concrete obstacles to political unity. Economically, Italy has a dual economy with a dual labor market. The South is predominantly agricultural, while the North is industrial. In the South, only four provinces out of thirty-five have more than 50 percent of the active population employed in areas other than agriculture.

Socially, there is a highly mobile and organized society in the North and a fragmented, developing society in the South. In the political realm, southern Italian politics are highly fragmented, while in the North, they have long been organized.

This cultural dualism was evident in the mass immigration period. The dualism, to northern Italians, was translated into feelings of superiority. The southern Italians initially blamed their lack of progress on northern neglect. Northerners charged that the South's lack of cooperation with the central government was at the root of southern backwardness.

The result of this controversy, which was articulated by politicians and intellectuals, was not only a feeling of superiority among northern Italians but a hostility toward those of the *Mezzogiorno*. The intellectual debate only crystallized the notion that the South was to be considered inferior to the North.

With immigration, northern opinion now affirmed that southern cultural backwardness was evidence of treasonable behavior of a people who were now deserting Italy.

The Italian government set up two sets of emigration statistics, one for the North and the other for the South. This practice was perpetuated by the United States government. In fact, the Italians were the only immigrant group on record for whom this regional distinction was made.

To this day, there is antagonism between the North and the South. With Italy's entrance into the Common Market, the Italian labor force attained new geographic mobility in the search for work. Because the North is the more heavily industrialized area, southern Italians traveled to northern cities in search of work. There they have encountered prejudice and discrimination which is exemplified in the northern reference to southern Italians as *terroni* (lowly southerners). Films and other materials which are disseminated in the United States continually refer to the North as "the" cultural and intellectual center. Americans have continued to make a distinction between the northern and the southern Italians. Very often, Italian-Americans who have identity conflicts, when asked if they are Italian, will either deny it or claim that they are northern Italian. The "Southern Question" continues to embroil every Italian political party. The southern peasant remains "an African" (racially different) in the eye of the northern urbanite. Although much of the old social order is changing, many of the stereotypes remain.

The Church and the great material power of the Holy Roman Empire made a durable alliance which lasted from the sack of Rome until September 1870.[23] This alliance preserved a splendid but corrupt and humiliating peace.[24] The Holy Roman Church opposed the creation of a united Italy, a stand which led to the papal prohibition against Catholic participation in the affairs of the new nation. For fifty years, the Church kept its adherents isolated from participation. When the Church lifted the ban, it was due to its fear of the growing forces of socialism.

Catholicism, since the end of World War II, has been the dominant force in Italian politics.[25] The Church was viewed as weighted down and tied inextricably to the past, rather than as a dynamic force seeking to meet the needs of the Italian people. The Church became so imbedded in politics that the Christian Democrats and the Church were almost synonymous. The Catholic party (Christian Democrats) is a league of different and often conflicting interests, local political machines, farm organizations, business groups, Catholic trade unions, Catholic intellectual associations, old notables, and Catholic Action committees. Except in its anticommunism and in its ultimate obedience to the Pope, the Christian Democratic party is an amorphous party. It seeks spiritual guidance from the Roman Catholic Church and its hierarchy.

The Christian Democratic party has recognized its dependence on the Church for a popular base, yet it also recognized it would somehow have to cut its bonds with traditionalism and clericalism if it was to compete in a relevant way on social issues. In the years since 1945, the party's political intervention was justified on the basis of the threat to it represented by Marxism.

The advent of Marxism in Italy, given the conditions that existed in the country, gave a more extreme shape to left-wing thought and attitudes toward existing institutions. The Italian state of affairs was filled by a variety of Marxisms that molded a basically antagonistic and alienative attitude toward politics and the state.[26]

Class, Status, and Power

At the end of the fifteenth century, the discoveries of Columbus and other explorers permanently shifted the center of world trade and civilization from the Mediterranean, where it had been for centuries, and left it commercially disadvantaged.

> The South was therefore locked into a pattern that would change only barely with the passing of the centuries. While in

northern Europe the accumulation of capital, the discovery of technology, and the breakdown of feudal class barriers would create a large, forward looking middle class, in southern Europe as a whole, and in the south of Italy and Sicily in particular, the overwhelming majority of the inhabitants—as high as ninety-six or ninety-seven percent—remained peasants, people without any power in their remote villages, repeating the same cycle of life as the generations that had preceded them. If anything they were poorer, more cruelly and inefficiently administered.[27]

As a young boy I often heard my father describe his *paese* (town or village) as "the place that God forgot." I never fully understood what he meant until some years later. In 1969, I read Carlo Levi's *Christ Stopped at Eboli*. I was struck by a passage which repeated and captured what my father had said so many times before.

> Christ never came this far, nor did time, nor the individual soul, nor hope, nor the relation of cause to effect, nor reason nor history.... No one has come to this land except as an enemy, a conqueror, or visitor devoid of understanding. The seasons pass today over the toil of the peasants just as they did three thousand years before Christ; no message, human or divine, has reached this stubborn poverty.[28]

What my father and Carlo Levi were describing was the poverty of the land itself. In the South, rain falls in the winter, not the best time for agricultural purposes. When the rains come, they take the form of torrents which run off swiftly, eroding the land. During the Roman Empire, the South was dotted with lush, verdant forests. Successive conquerors cut them down for their own use. The soil is generally poor and has been exhausted by centuries of exploitation.

Italy is quite limited in mineral resources and raw materials. It especially lacks the raw materials necessary for a modern industrial system. Nearly the entire length of the Italian peninsula is traversed by the Apennine range, which cuts the east coast off from the west coast and isolates many inland areas from closely neighboring ones. Poor communication and rural isolation characterized southern Italy for centuries.[29]

The South is also drier and hotter; dry winds blowing from the direction of the African deserts have been a great scourge to the farmers. There is no protection against these winds. Moreover, the lack of an adequate water supply for irrigation was a major problem for hundreds of years. The high level of soil impermeability, soil made mostly of clay, renders the southern

plains highly susceptible to erosion. In essence, the South lacks
arable land, since 75 percent of the land area of Italy is mountains and hills. The South has only 28 percent of all the arable
land in Italy, and it is marginal.

The typical southern Italian immigrant came from a rural city
with a population of thousands. Seeking refuge from brigands
and malaria, the *contadini* (landed peasants) huddled together
in these hill towns, living in stone dwellings under the most
primitive conditions. Leonard Covello describes the physical setting in this way:

> The typical southern Italian rural town usually consisted of
> a large compound of stone structures situated for the most part
> on the mountain slopes or even high on the mountain tops.
> The architecture, rugged uniformity of style, identical color of
> the buildings clustered together, scarcity of trees and a con-
> spicuous absence of high, protruding chimneys, gave such towns
> the appearance of castle fortifications rather than residential
> centers. Narrow, unpaved roads, leading from the valleys up-
> wards, were frequently hidden amid rocky formations and the
> many crevasses of the mountains.[30]

The hilltop location of the Italian town has provided a breath-
taking and picturesque view for many tourists. The reasons for
these locations are rooted in the early history of Italy: The location of the town in the higher elevations served as protection
against invaders such as the Saracens, Byzantines, and Normans.
"Deforestation, followed by water scarcity, or excess of water,
floods, landslides, deterioration of the soil's fertility—all of these
were sufficient reasons for migrating upward."[31] The most important reason was the widespread fear of malaria which festered
in the lowlands. With residence higher up, the distance between
the fertile lowland and the peasant increased.

The rural town in southern Italy was influenced greatly by
feudalism. The best land formed a ring around the town, which
belonged to the feudal baron. When feudalism was abolished,
little change occurred, since the land remained in the hands of
the wealthy and influential. Thus, a daily scene was one in
which streams of human beings descended the slopes each
morning to travel considerable distances to their place of work.
They spent several hours each day just walking to and from their
homes loaded with a hoe, a water bucket, and their lunch.

These towns were not simple communities of farm workers,
since their social structure included the gentry and middle class
as well as the peasants. Though the peasants were members of a
rural society, they were also town dwellers, village urbanists.
Even the smallest population centers in the South had the physi-

cal structure of a town. They were residential compounds which had an urban character to them. The peasants were agricultural laborers who lived in villages which sometimes numbered tens of thousands of people. The nonindustrial *Mezzogiorno* had the highest percentage of town dwellers in all of Italy around the turn of the century.

At the time of the *Risorgimento,* nearly 70 percent of the total labor force of Italy was employed in agriculture. It was not until after the turn of the century that this statistic dipped below sixty percent. Only after World War II was the agricultural labor force reduced to less than 50 percent of the working population. By 1961, Italy joined the rest of western Europe, with fewer than 30 percent of its workers employed in agriculture.

Prior to the mass immigration there was no social ladder to climb. Moreover, there were wide gaps between the upper and lower classes with divisions in the latter as well. At the bottom of the economic ladder were the *giornalieri,* the propertyless agricultural day laborers who comprised about 40 percent of the population. They lived as outcasts, in abject poverty on the outskirts of the town. The long distances from work to home led to frequent separation from the family. Their poverty excluded them from sharing in political power or in possessing political rights. Their principal aspiration was to save enough money to rent land and step up the social ladder.

These people were also known as *braccianti,* from the Italian *braccia,* meaning "arm"; a pair of arms for the day. They were hired on a daily basis for a specific job. Most were lucky if they could find work a hundred days a year. In every town in southern Italy, hundreds of the *braccianti* could be found at dawn squatting against a wall waiting to be hired for the day.

The remainder of the lower class consisted of about 15 percent *giornlieri,* people who owned small parcels of land, and 45 percent *contadini,* those who leased land. For the latter group, the future was always uncertain. They never knew what would happen with the termination of the lease. There were social and cultural distinctions between the *giornlieri* and the *contadini,* but both groups dressed and talked alike. Both held similar standards. The main difference was that the *contadini* had title to land either directly or by lease. They lived in towns and owned farm implements and animals. They also could borrow, which later proved to be a mixed blessing. Through constant exploitation they became indebted to the wealthy which led to further discontent. As is often the case, the meaning of earlier conversations and experiences becomes clearer with the passage of time. I recall my father often employed in his Neopolitan

dialect the word *fatiga* (fatigue) for work. The origins of this
word summon forth generations of peasant toil. Under peasant
conditions, work was fatiguing, not self-satisfying enjoyable
labor. The Italian peasant had an average of 2 to 3.5 acres of
land at the time of the mass migration. This was too small to
provide for a family. Productivity was low. Taxes were high. As
a result, the peasant was forced to work the land without pause,
which led to his exhausting the soil. Often the peasant had to
give up his land, which only caused further resentment. It should
be no surprise to learn that southern Italian immigrants held the
ownership of a home as a primary value. Their hand-to-mouth
existence led them to put a premium on security and survival.

The Italian writer Ignazio Silone depicts the status of these
poor peasants through one of his characters:

> At the head of everything is God, Lord of Heaven. After him
> comes Prince Torlonia, Lord of the earth. Then come Prince
> Torlonia's armed guards. Then come Prince Torlonia's armed
> guards' dogs. Then, nothing at all. Then nothing at all. Then
> came the peasants. And that's all.[32]

So for the millions of *contadini* and *braccianti,* hunger and
inner turmoil increased with every year. While the upper and
middle classes in the North sat down to sumptuous meals, the
southern poor ate a few slices of bread dipped in olive oil or a
plate of beans. Even spaghetti, that most Italian of all dishes, was
a rare treat for the poverty-stricken masses.[33]

The middle classes were formed by the *artigini* (artisans) such
as masons, craftsmen, blacksmiths, small businessmen, minor
government officials, and shopkeepers. The *artigini* were a little
better off economically than the farmers, and they were socially
removed from them. They were dependent for their living on the
farmers and the upper class. Often the *artigini* learned their
trade as boys serving as apprentices and worked their way up
step-by-step to economic independence.

The main ambition of the middle class artisans was to obtain
the title and prestige of being a *mastro*—master workman. Often
they were addressed as *Mastro* as a prefix to their names. Not
only did they have more status, but they had more opportunity
to do more meaningful work. They were separated from the
lower classes by education and land. They lived closer to the
town and dwelled in much better homes.

It was the southern middle class that Carlo Levi had primarily
in mind in *The Watch,* where he wrote of his countrymen as
being divided into two great groups: the *contadini,* who actually
worked and produced, and the *luigini* (after Don Luigi Maga-

lone, a southern local official), the appallingly numerous class of parasites who lived off the labor of the others.

At the top of the social ladder was the *Signori* or *galantumo—* doctors, landed gentry, lawyers, some priests, druggists, teachers —who composed about 1 or 2 percent of the town population. Their wealth, status, education, and lifestyle set them apart from the other classes.

The Italian aristocracy has a burdensome and useless heritage. The House of Savoy looked with distrust on that assorted antipasto of nobles of all shapes and descriptions which they had inherited with the unification. The Savoys had easily granted titles to Italians and foreigners without rigid criteria; they entitled anyone with sufficient persistence who was supported by political recommendations.

After the *Statuto* of 1848, which brought the beginnings of constitutional reform to Italy, and particularly after unification of the country between 1860 and 1870, the aristocracy were forced to exercise power with increasing subtlety. The coming to power of the democratic and nationalistic left on March 18, 1876, marked the end of the aristocratic hegemony. Until 1876, the ruling class, which had helped the revolution and fought in the wars of independence, was largely composed of nobles. If the aristocracy was not liberal, many liberals were aristocrats. Generals, prefects, magistrates, financiers, businessmen, and industrialists came from the aristocracy. Inevitably, their influence was felt in many fields. From 1876 on, only one of the prime ministers was a nobleman; all the others were of bourgeois origin.

Italian immigrants were not drawn entirely from the impoverished classes, but from a wider spectrum of the Italian population than is usually assumed. Poverty, it appears, was only one personal circumstance among the many factors that precipitated the great migration. The sense of adventure and individual family conditions were the significant personal factors influencing the decision to leave Italy.

To summarize, the factors inducing Italians to leave their homeland are rooted in the conditions of the land, their history, and the social-economic system. They include such factors as the following: pressures of population on the available land; the infertility of the soil; primitive agricultural methods; a heavy taxation system; a lingering feudalism; a stratified social system based on exploitation by the upper classes; the concentration of national wealth in the North and in the hands of a few; low wages; industrial backwardness; an inept national government; and a delayed and imperfect national integration.

These were the underlying factors in Italy which led to the

great exodus. Why was the period from 1880–1890 the decade which set in motion the floodtide of immigration? In the late 1880s, the Italian economy felt the impact of three crippling shocks which were to trigger the Italian immigration. The United States cut its imports of Italian citrus fruits due to improved production in California and Florida. Unable to compete, thousands of citrus farmers were stuck with surplus crops which they could not sell. They now were faced with a ruined export economy. At the same time, plant lice invaded Italian vineyards leaving thousands of acres destroyed. Moreover, France set up a high tariff which cut off a major market for the grape growers of Apulia, Calabria, and Sicily.[34]

Between 1884 and 1887, cholera epidemics killed thousands. In 1897, a poor harvest deepened the sense of frustration among the peasants. These developments stimulated riots from Sicily to the northern provinces.

All of these factors coincided with a surge of rising expectations among Italians. What they now sought to achieve—if not for themselves, then for their children—was an opportunity for a better life. Their journey to America occurred at the same time as the movement from the farm to the city in both Italy and America. In other words, their coming to America was part of the same process in which many Americans left the farms for industrial-urban America.

Needless to say, these conditions shaped the Italian-American character. The Italians who came to America expected improvement and searched for opportunity. They were achievement oriented. Having endured back-breaking toil, they fully expected and wanted to work hard. In America, they expected their hard work to result in an improved economic and social position. They had no difficulty in adapting to the work ethic in America.

The history of foreign domination in Italy led to a deep suspicion of governmental authority and helped to hold back the development of entrepreneurial skills. However, that deficiency was overcome with remarkable rapidity in the new environments of North and South America. Almost immediately, thousands entered the small business class in America. My father is a good illustration. When he arrived in America, he was befriended by a Jewish couple who owned a construction business. Papa went to work for them. Childless, they took care of Papa like their own son. They even suggested that he take over the business when they retired. My father, proud and independent, declined. He had to make his own way. One day, the proprietor of a tiny fifteen by twenty foot grocery store, situated below the apartment in which my father was living, spoke to Papa. Quite unexpectedly, he exclaimed, "Frank, how would you like to buy my store?" Without prior thought or hesitation, Papa replied yes! Papa went into business for himself and remained so until his retirement.

Italian history shaped the Italian-American character in another way. When Italians came to America, large numbers of them avoided going into farming. Being propertyless and exploited in Italy, their reverence for the soil was eventually destroyed. Moreover, when they first came to America they arrived with little financial resources. It has been estimated that the average Italian immigrant who arrived in New York in 1910 had a total of $17 in his possession, hardly enough to afford the trip to rural areas, much less enough to purchase the required land and equipment. Economic opportunities were seen as most promising in the commercial and industrial centers of the Northeast. Farmland symbolized a type of existence from which the *contadini* wanted to escape. Even if they traveled to small urban centers surrounded by small farms, Italians showed no overwhelming inclination to settle there. However, for the *contadini*, the initial experience of being without land instilled in future generations the desire and value of owning one's own home. One estimate indicates that, in 1900, two out of every three Italian immigrants in Philadelphia owned their own home. The uncertainty of life for the *contadini*, coupled with grinding poverty, was to make their children security-conscious. As Barzini observes:

> Italians learned long ago . . . to be sober and clear-eyed realists in all circumstances. . . .[35]

"*Il Destino!*" (Destiny!) was and is an expression commonly used by southern Italians. It reveals the fatalism and destiny which the Southerner perceives as the underpinnings of life itself. Papa would often express it in terms of luck, frequently muttering, "You've got to have luck in this world."

Italy and the Italians have a remarkable staying power. The Italians have had their lands occupied by foreign conquerors, but they—as individuals—have never been conquered. With an innate flexibility, they literally surrounded and absorbed their enemies. As was mentioned before, Italians developed a sign language out of necessity that was understood by other Italians but not by their conquerors. That sign language, with many regional variations, is still in existence today.

Italians brought these things with them to America. The account of Italian history given above centers around the problems encountered by Italians, which then impelled them to leave their homeland. But, when we consider what the Italians brought with them, we must consider the glory and achievement of an outstanding culture, which produced cultural and intellectual geniuses.

The attitude and policy of the Italian government and the attitudes of leading Italian thinkers toward mass migration during the period from national unification in 1861 to 1914 went through various distinct, overlapping phases. The initial regulations relating to the movement of Italians were written within the context of a law on public safety, part of a general law, approved on March 20, 1865. Article 65, Section VIII required that all citizens outside the district to which they belonged were to produce identification upon request to the police. Those failing to comply could be sent back to their home district. In another article, the same law could be applied by emigration agencies. It forbade immigration persons to enroll people without a license from the government. Despite this regulation, the recruitment activities of the emigration agents increased, often at the expense of the emigrants.

The role of emigration agencies and immigrant recruiters or agents had stirred a great deal of controversy. These agents often worked for foreign interests. As Grazia Dore observes:

> They performed the tasks necessary to obtain passports, negotiated for the sale of the peasant's meagre house or small fields, and directed the emigrant to small hotels in the port while awaiting embarkation. Scarcely then had a small group of fellow villagers formed a nucleus of compatriots across the ocean than the peasants reconstituted their old customs, the old mediations appeared again, the frightening rural usury followed them, providing labor contracts and assuring the first terrifying relations with the ensnaring bankers, bosses, or padroni.[36]

These agents used a variety of dishonest means and made hard-to-keep promises in order to induce the peasants to emigrate. Despite this, the peasants continued to do business with thousands of such agents whom they viewed as a necessary evil in the emigration process.

In an effort to please the property owners who opposed peasant emigration for economic reasons and to curb the activities of the emigration agents, the government issued a series of circulars condemning emigration. None of the circulars was effective in slowing down emigration nor in changing the practices of the recruiting agents.

Parliament first raised the issue of emigration on January 30, 1868, when Ercole Lualdi called for an investigation into the causes of emigration to see if its proportions could not be diminished. Prime Minister L. Menabrea replied that it was the responsibility of all citizens, especially the industrialists and the landowners, to provide work for potential emigrants. Otherwise, he added, they would have no other alternative but to emigrate.

The topic was raised in Parliament again on May 20, 1872, by Guglielmo Tocci and followed the same lines as that of 1868. Prime Minister Giovanni Lanza attempted to minimize the impact of emigration.

The idea that emigration was a natural phenomenon that should be protected rather than hindered began to gain more supporters both inside and outside Parliament during the 1870s and 1880s. A number of bills to regulate emigration were introduced in Parliament, but all failed to pass.[37]

During the American Civil War and the decades immediately following, a series of great economic changes occurred in the United States that revolutionized the life of the nation. Between 1860 and 1890, the railroads, already expanding rapidly before the Civil War, were extended across the continent to produce a national system of transportation. In this same period, small factories that had previously produced only for a local market grew into large corporate industries that produced goods and services for the entire nation. America's expanding economy, which depended on a cheap and abundant labor supply, became a great force in attracting the great tide of emigration.

Not only the phenomenal expansion of American industry, but also its changing character accounted for the huge volume of the Italian immigration. The introduction of additional mechanical devices and processes eliminated much of the need for industrial skill and experience and made it possible, even essential, for manufacturers to employ cheap, unskilled labor.

The Italian government eventually came to see the advantages of emigration. They later encouraged it. Emigration not only helped the individuals involved, but also helped to relieve the economic pressure on Italy by reducing the population to be supported. Emigrants also helped by sending money back to their families. These remittances gave the Italian government badly needed cash and became important in Italy's effort to balance her economy. The remittances were also proof that others would find jobs and money in America. Italian emigrants, by purchasing Italian products abroad, helped to create a demand for Italy's goods. By World War I, nearly three-quarters of a billion dollars had been sent to Italy by Italian emigrants in the United States. In short, the infusion of fresh capital bolstered the Italian economy in many ways.

The Journey to America

Letters written to Italy from relatives in tenement flats, sweatshops, and construction gangs in America spread the incentive. These letters awakened desires for a better life in the recipients living in tiny hamlets and large cities in Italy.

Thousands trekked to Italian ports. Long days and nights were first spent on the emigrant train to Naples. Men and women sat and stood shoulder to shoulder on wooden benches along the wall of the train cars. Small meals of bread and cheese sustained them during the trip. Arriving in Naples, they viewed the ship's great size with amazement. Hundreds of men, women, and children scrambled up the steep gangplank and disappeared into the steerage quarters of ships like the *Rex*. In some cases, whole villages filled the steerage quarters, their home for the next few weeks. Above them in first- and second-cabin classes were the more fortunate—the rich.

Fear, excitement, adventure, and nostalgia intermingled as the ship glided out of the Bay of Naples and as the native land receded in the distance. Behind lay memories good and bad. Ahead? Who knows? Hope! Opportunity! Many left owning only the clothes on their backs. Some converted everything they had owned to cover the $12 charge for steerage. How these brave people had the courage to embark on such a voyage we may never fully be able to comprehend.

My father was to be deathly afraid of boats all his life. This became apparent to me years later, when my brother and I bought an outboard boat; he never came to see it at its moorings nor did he ever step foot on it. Such was his fear of the ocean and boats. Years later, he and my uncle would recount that journey in more romantic terms. As one immigrant revealed, "I would have made that trip a hundred times. It was for the children. It was for them."

There were few diversions on board for the *contadini*. Even on the sunny days, when they all crowded onto the small deck, time passed slowly. Some read the few guidebooks on America available to them, but most of the information these contained was useless and inaccurate. Others played Neopolitan tunes on an accordian or mandolin. Women sewed, while older men smoked pipes and played cards or *mora* (a finger game). Mostly, they talked of the future, remembered the recent past, and stared at the waves, until bad weather drove them below the decks.

Italians tried to come to the aid of each other during the hard voyage. They brought supplies of cheese and salami which supplemented the miserable rations doled out to the emigrants. Lice, scurvy, and seasickness added to their misery. Men and women suffered together the humiliation of public fumigation.

Then one day, they detected a sudden change in the ship's motion and a different sound from the engine. The harbor pilot from Ambrose Lightship had just boarded. Cautious optimism exploded into a joyous explosion. "America!" they cried. Many peered at the American coast and broke into tears. In steerage, there was a frenzy of excitement as the *contadini* scurried about, arranging their bundles for the last time. Others washed their hands and faces in basins of cold, salty water and combed their unwashed hair. Money was counted for the hundredth time and hidden in some safe pocket or secret place. The deck became more and more crowded.

Everyone was on deck by the time the ship entered the Narrows, the harbor entrance between Brooklyn and Staten Island. They were surrounded on all sides by other ships from a variety of countries, including France, Greece, and Germany. The harbor was often choked with ships, each crammed with as many as twenty thousand passengers waiting to be ferried to Ellis Island, the next destination.

Many immigrants had to spend an extra night in steerage because there was no room for them on the island. Soon, a small cutter came alongside the ship. "A ladder was raised against the ship's rail, and two men and a woman in uniforms climbed aboard and pushed their way through the crowd of immigrants toward the second-cabin class area."[38] In the salon, the immigration inspectors asked two or three brief questions of each waiting second-cabin class passenger, while a doctor looked quickly at their eyes as they filed past. Full information about these travelers was listed on the ship's official passenger list. Those who showed signs of sickness were to be stopped at Ellis. When the last second-cabin passenger had been passed, the inspector ran his eyes down the first-cabin list of Americans and foreign "visitors" and simply muttered, "Okay, that'll do."[39]

While the inspectors departed, the immigrant ship moved slowly into the upper bay. As the harbor came into view, expressions of wonder and awe could be heard on the steerage deck, and people pushed to get a better look. Children were lifted into the air to see. "There! Over there!" came the excited shouts in a hundred Italian dialects joined by the chorus of other tongues. On the left stood the Statue of Liberty, lifting her torch of freedom to the sky. There were few dry eyes watching her from the deck. To the left of their view, just beyond the Statue of Liberty, were the red brick buildings of Ellis Island. That was the famous *Isola delle Lagrime*—the Island of Tears. There, dream and reality converged. Dreams were now edged with doubt.

"Before the immigrants were taken to Ellis Island, the immigrant liner docked at one of the row of piers, and the immigrants were pushed back from the rail, while the privileged travelers went down the gangway and vanished into the sheds."[40] Then it was the immigrants' turn. Guards shouted in many languages, "Hurry up there! Move along, stupid! Don't just stand there! Move!" as they pushed the immigrants along a roped enclosure at the end of the dock. Most of the immigrants carried all of their luggage with them. Some minutes later, their baggage was loaded onto the lower deck of a small ferryboat, and as many of the immigrants as possible were herded, with more shouting and pushing from behind, onto the upper deck. When the boat was full, the rest of them were loaded on two barges waiting behind. For one hour on the pier, they had been standing on American soil; now at Ellis Island they would be told whether they could stay for life. One mile of water separated them from America. As many as fifteen thousand Italians passed through Ellis Island each day.

Debarking from the ship, the immigrants were put into groups of thirty. Amid more shouts and shoving, they moved forward through the big doors into dark tiled corridors, then up a steep flight of stairs leading to the giant Registry Hall. Whole villages, which had filled the steerage compartments, now filled the great hall. But along with the Italians, there was a strange and great variety of people. The scene was like a roll call at the Tower of Babel. Some people were crying. The whole place was humming like a giant beehive, and, over the occasional baby's wail, names of people from all corners of the Old World were shouted: "Lepore! Bruno! Basile! Russo! Pellegrino! Gallo! Romano!" People were pushed along one of the dozens of metal railings which divided the floor into a maze of open passageways. They didn't realize it at the time, but they now had to run the gantlet from one inspector to another. The fate of these human beings rode on this conveyor belt of inspectors. America was the prize at the end of the journey.

Although they did not realize it, they passed their first test as they hastened down the row in single file. Twenty-five feet away, a doctor in the blue uniform of the U.S. Public Health Service was watching them carefully as they approached him. "All children who looked over two years old were taken from their mothers' arms and made to walk."[41] Physical exams were administered, designed to detect glaucoma and communicable diseases. A 3,000-mile journey could end here with the detection of a small rash or a cough.

The few moments before one saw the doctor seemed an eternity. Some breathed too heavily. Some tried to hide their limps behind big bundles. As each immigrant paused in front of him, the doctor looked hard at his face, hair, neck, and hands; at the same time, with an interpreter at his side, he asked short questions about the immigrant's age or work history to test his alertness. "In the doctor's hand was a piece of chalk; on the coats of about two out of every ten or eleven immigrants who passed him he scrawled a large white letter "H" for possible heart trouble, "L" for lameness, a circled "X" for suspected mental defects, or "F" for a bad rash on the face."[42]

Then the immigrants filed on to a second doctor, who was looking for diseases specifically mentioned in deportation papers: tuberculosis, leprosy, or a contagious skin disease of the scalp called favus.

Again the line moved on. Ahead, waiting in front of a window, were two more doctors, with basins of disinfectant and towels at their sides. They were the dreaded "eye men." The doctors peered down, tilting the immigrants' heads back slightly, and swiftly snapped back the upper eyelids over a small instrument. They were looking for a blinding disease called trachoma. Those whom they thought had the disease had their coats chalked with an "E" for eyes.

Those whose coats bore chalk letters were pushed into a pen for a more detailed medical exam. The rejected might be one member of a family—the mother, the father, or a child. Daily, weeping families gathered together in the hall trying to make a terrible decision: "Shall we go back together? Who will stay?"

Most of the Ellis Island inspectors were underpaid and overworked. Many tried to do a good job. But a large number, influenced by the nativism of the day, made subjective and arbitrary judgments. For example, the inspectors used as guidelines such documents as *Mental Examination of Immigrants, Administration and Line Inspection at Ellis*; to determine mental stability and fitness, the inspectors were guided by the following:

The alien's manner of entering the line, his conversation, style of dress, any peculiarity or unusual incident in regard to him are observed. Knowledge of racial characteristics, in physique, costume and behavior are important in this primary sifting process. . . . Experience enables the inspecting officer to tell at a glance the race of the alien. There are, however, exceptions to this rule. It occasionally happens that the inspecting officer thinking that an approaching alien is of a certain race, brings him to a standstill and questions him. The alien's facial expression and manner are peculiar and just as this officer is about to decide that this alien is mentally unbalanced, he finds out that the alien in question belongs to an entirely different race. The peculiar attitude of the alien in question is no longer peculiar; it is readily accounted for by racial considerations. . . . Those who have inspected immigrants know that almost every race has its own type of reaction during the line inspection. . . . If the Italian responded to questions as the Russian Finn responds, the former would in all probability be suffering with a depressive psychosis. . . .[43]

The guidelines were influenced by the nativism of the day and were based on stereotyped concepts of the physical types supposedly characteristic of each "race." These concepts were invalid. Anyone who tried to categorize the variety of people that crowded Ellis Island on the basis of physical type faced an impossible task. Moreover, to assume that those people exhibited either similar or dissimilar patterns of behavior because they belonged to a certain "race" was fallacious thinking. It would have required a skilled anthropologist to make these judgments, and a psychoanalyst to relate the data to mental fitness. The task was especially impossible in the two or three minutes allowed for the test.

The guidelines above allowed too much room for subjective judgment. At worst, they permitted a bigoted inspector to exclude perfectly desirable people on the most capricious grounds. If a prospective immigrant did not act the way he was supposed to, he was denied entrance to America. If he then exhibited such signs as "slow speech, low voice, trembling articulation, sad faces, tearful eyes, perplexity, difficulty in thinking," he was suspected of "psychoses of a depressive nature."[44]

At the end of the aisle, interpreters waved immigrants whose coats were unmarked back toward the main part of the Registry Hall. Now on to the final test. Immigrants waiting on benches talked anxiously and rehearsed for the last time their answers to probable questions about jobs, cash, or relatives. The waiting time, often an hour or two on busy days, seemed endless to the nervous immigrants.

At last, an interpreter moved them into the adjoining row. "He made sure they all had the same big number pinned on their coats. At the end of the aisle sat an inspector, on whose desk lay the manifest headed by that number."[45] Immigrants had two minutes to answer thirty-eight questions shouted in rapid-fire order: What work do you do? Do you have a job? Who paid for your passage? Is anyone meeting you? Where are you going? How much money do you have? Where did you get it? About 25 percent of all rejections came within these two or three minutes. Then, inspectors tried to change Italian names into acceptable Anglo-Saxon ones, but most immigrants successfully resisted these attempts to cut them off from their past and their family. Finally, the inspector's curt nod meant that they had won the prize—they could stay in America.

The next stop on the way out was the Money Exchange, where money from all over Europe was exchanged for American dollars. Two out of every three immigrants then traveled beyond New York City, and railroad tickets to places across the country were sold by a dozen agents in the railroad room. Agents struggled to find out where the confused immigrants wanted to go. One Italian insisted that his destination was "Pringvilliamas"—that was it was finally determined to be "Springfield, Mass." One group of fifteen Italian immigrants who wanted to go to Amsterdam Avenue, New York City, found themselves in the city of Amsterdam in upstate New York.

With their tickets and big, cheap box lunches in hand, immigrants sat in the large "Waiting Room Areas," which were marked for each independent railroad line. (Immigrants who preferred to buy single items of food could choose apples at two cents apiece, kosher bologna at thirteen cents a pound, sandwiches and pies for four cents each.) When the departure time for their trains drew near, they would be ferried on barges to the terminal stations in Jersey City or Hoboken.

Those who were going to stay in New York City were lucky in some ways. They walked down a corridor marked "To New York." A screen separated them from sight during the walk to the ferry, where often dozens of friends and relatives who had gotten passes to Ellis Island waited anxiously. They were met with tears and hugs and shrieks of recognition. Waiting in Battery Park was another crowd of welcomers. More tears of joy and relief flowed down almost every face.

The lone traveler faced the prospect of swindles and robbery. One reformer interested in the plights of these immigrants described the situation:

> The immigrant arrives at Battery Park. He is immediately and violently beseiged on all sides by tricksters and thieves in the persons of porters, hackmen, "runners" for employment agencies, many of whom speak his language. They profess friendliness and advise him about his lodgings, employment, transportation to his destination and the many things in which he needs help. Licensed city porters wear badges and pretend thereby to be city officials and get large fees for taking the mute stranger and his bundles to a lodging or agency. A case is known of an immigrant to whom five dollars was charged for a five cent elevated ticket, which was represented to be a "railroad ticket."[46]

While these experiences may not have been the best introduction, the real America lay before them.

3 We Have Arrived

Ellis Island, closed in 1954, was reopened in 1976 as a tourist attraction. As Joseph Marchesi, an immigrant from Italy in 1919, was preparing to land at the Battery after his visit to the site, he said, "Only an immigrant can appreciate America."

Mr. Marchesi spoke a basic truth. To the newly arrived, America was a ferment of possibilities. America was not discovered only once. It was discovered countless times by millions of people, each in their own way. The immigrant explorers discovered America anew for themselves. At the beginning of the great migration, the Italian usually came alone or with a brother, son, or friend. The newcomers were usually between the ages of fourteen and forty-five. As soon as the immigrant was able to save enough money, he sent for his family who had remained in Italy.

By 1903, there were 1.2 million Italians in the United States. About twelve percent of that number lived in New York City. Increasing numbers of immigrants simply stayed in the port in which they disembarked. New York City's population grew from 1 million in 1875 to 3.5 million in 1900. Thirty-seven percent of New York City's population in 1900 were foreign-born. Indeed, Italians could say with justification, *"Siamo arrivati!"* (We have arrived!)

Italians were also attracted to small urban environments like Mechanicville, New York, located about twenty miles north of Albany. Italian immigrants first came to Mechanicville in 1882, when railroad construction crews linked the village with the Hoosac Tunnel in western Massachusetts. Their number swelled to twenty-six hundred by 1925 (25 percent of the residents of Mechanicville) when paving, construction, and railway projects were expanded.

The search for employment was a major factor determining where Italians would settle. Large numbers of Italians were attracted to Chicago initially, and the suburbs of Blue Island, Cicero, Chicago Heights, and Berwyn received a steady flow who sought employment. Those who left for these suburbs did not experience an immediate, significant improvement in their occupational level. The families moved from the East in order to provide themselves with a better living environment. Italian men may have believed that life in a small town environment with work and pay equal to what they would receive in a large city would be a better way of life. Some moves may have also resulted from the desire to bring together people from the same *paese* (village or hometown).[1]

When an Italian came to America in the post-1880 era of immigration he had two urgent problems to solve: where to sleep, and how to find a job as quickly as possible. If a relative or *paesano* (townsman or fellow villager) was on hand to meet him, the solutions were a little easier. The newcomer would be taken home, bedded down in some corner of a small tenement room and introduced to a sympathetic boss or construction foreman. If he had no friends or relatives, then he was on his own.

Ghettoes now dotted the urban landscape, serving as the catch basin for an endless tide of humanity. The Lower East Side in New York City was crammed with 600,000 people in a one-mile-square area.

An Italian immigrant is said to have observed, "Before I came to America, I thought that the streets were paved with gold. When I arrived, I learned three things. First, the streets were not paved with gold. Second, the streets were not paved at all. Finally, I was expected to pave them." The vast majority of Italian immigrants had no such vision of streets being paved with gold. The decision to immigrate was based on an assessment or calculation of costs and opportunities. The crowds pouring into America's cities created a need for the unskilled labor they could provide. Cities struggled to pave streets and construct more housing for their residents. America's cities could not cope with the new demands placed upon them.

Italians, along with other immigrants, found work in the city's construction crews, laboring as ditch diggers, hod carriers, and stone cutters. As long as they had strong arms, it did not matter if they could not speak English or operate a complex machine.

Before getting a job with a private contractor, my father worked for the City of New York. He, like his fellow Italians, graded roadbeds, laid paving blocks, buried gas pipes, laid cables, and dug subways. Often, these workers faced the taunts of a bigoted foreman. Despite all of this construction activity, building of new housing lagged far behind the need. Whether they worked in construction, quarrying, railroading, or manufacturing, these workers were always given America's dirtiest and most dangerous jobs. Elsewhere, Italians cut timber and harvested fruits, vegetables, and grain throughout the countryside. They also worked in copper, iron, and coal mines and in factories manufacturing shoes, glass, and steel.

Every city and village touched by a railroad line had its complement of Italian day laborers. The first Italians to appear in Blue Island, a suburb of Chicago, were those who were part of a Rock Island track-laying crew. The same was true of Italians who initially went to Mechanicville, New York. It is thought that the epithet "dago" is derived from the fact that Italians were hired as day laborers (as the "day goes"). It is also thought that "dago" comes from the Spanish *diego* (devil). The first Italian communities often originated near the rail yards. Grocers and boardinghouse operators set up business on the fringes. These establishments served as immigrant centers for the large, mobile labor force making its way back and forth across the country. Often these establishments were a source of local employment.

In *The Uprooted,* Oscar Handlin writes of immigration as alienation complete with broken homes, isolation, and loneliness. Handlin's assertion does not apply to the Italian-American experience. The southern Italian clung tenaciously to his traditional social norms and values. He was not isolated as an individual, for he successfully reassembled his group life in America and developed a new set of institutions to deal with a new environment.

Italians brought two things that sustained them in the brutal ghettoes of strange cities: tightly knit family ties, and loyalty to their *paese,* or home village. Contrary to Handlin, the Italian family did not disintegrate but remained a bastion of warmth and security for its members. The family chain pattern to Italian immigration tended to reinforce the formation of "Little Italys." In New York, Boston, Chicago, San Francisco, New Haven, and elsewhere, Italians congregated in neighborhoods with their *paesani,* re-creating urban villages or Italian country towns in an urban environment. Hence, *campanilismo,* the Italian attachment to the town, their village-mindedness, drew Italians together.

These Little Italys took on a style of life which reflected the force of *campanilismo,* of the Italians' need to live near their jobs, and of the discrimination they encountered in their daily lives. Each Little Italy was in reality a conglomeration of small colonies with fellow townspeople occupying the same tenements and settling along the same streets. Within these transplanted miniature Italian villages and provinces which made up each Little Italy, Italians sought to maintain their traditional folkways. Since they could not draw upon a complete cultural base of their own in the New World, they lost the battle to maintain their indigenous ways. Through their relationships with other Italians, they became Italian-Americans with the speech, values, and behavior of a unique subculture.[2]

Large settlements in the cities often were divided into almost as many groups as there were sections of Italy represented. Few were exclusively Italian in makeup, and all were in a state of flux. Edward Corsi numbered twenty-seven different nationalities in the Lower East Side.

In the Little Italys, there was a block by block separation of Sicilians, Neapolitans, Calabrians, and Italians from other provinces as well. As one Italian described it:

> The old colony is composed of persons coming from nearly every nook and corner of the old peninsula. It is by no means strange, then, that they should bring with them local prejudices and narrow sympathies; it is not to be wondered that they feel that the highest duty is in being loyal to the handful who come from their immediate section and in manifesting opposition toward those who come from other localities.[3]

Gradually, the local mistrust led to a growing bond among the southern Italian immigrants and a common identification with one another.

This pattern in the development of Italian colonies prevailed in small urban centers as well. In Blue Island, Illinois, the Italian colony lived in five small half-block sections. Ninety-one percent of the Italians who lived on the east side resided adjacent to each other. By 1925, 88 percent of the Italian immigrants were crowded into the north end of Mechanicville, New York, and there they remained.

Philadelphia's Little Italy was one of the most picturesque sections of the city. The Italians were compressed in a thirty-five block area. One could walk the streets for some time and not hear a word of English. Black-eyed children tumbling in play together, the gaily colored dresses of the women, and the crowds of street vendors gave the section a vibrant color.

The Mulberry Bend portion of Little Italy in New York City

swung in a curve from Park Row, winding and changing direction, finally running parallel with Broadway. It contained tumbled-down houses which were converted into tenements. Ancient, one-story stables were converted into shops and drinking places, and everywhere steps led down from the sidewalk to cafes and other shops.

> One of the special features of the quarter is the sale of stale bread, which as a retail trade, is altogether in the hands of women. It is a systematized industry. The bread that used to be thrown away is now taken back by the big bakeries from the retail houses, and is collected by men, who sell it to the women; they later retail it at from one to three cents a loaf from the curbstone. Happily, stale bread is not chemically deteriorated, even when the mold has to be scraped from it; an all white bread is a luxury among these poor people, though it is a luxury now pretty generally indulged in. The economical, however, still purchase the black bread of their youth...at three cents a pound. This, too, is not injurious, as is most such very cheap food.[4]

The fact that Little Italys grew in number was proof to some native Americans that Italians were clannish. With their great emphasis on rapid and forced assimilation, native Americans did not understand the important role the immigrant colony played in the lives of Italian immigrants.

It was logical for people who could not speak English to want to be near relatives or those whose tongue and customs they understood. These neighbors gave them a sense of psychological security. In a Little Italy, the immigrant could be protected from the demands of an alien and restless society; it served as a kind of shock absorber. Relatives or *paesani* could help the newcomer with a job or a place to live. They could help in emergencies. Those without friends and relatives soon acquired "adopted" ones.

Little Italys served as a kind of staging area, a beachhead where the Italian immigrants could remain until they absorbed new ideas and habits that would make possible their adjustment to an alien environment.[5] When the Italian arrived in America, he came into the most advanced industrial system in the world. It was an industrial society that demanded a form of behavior totally foreign to the society whose culture was rooted in the soil. Serving as a buffer, Little Italys helped the newcomer to bridge the gap, fulfilling a vitally important function for both the immigrant and the society.

One Italian noted that "the reader of popular articles describing Italian life and customs, ... the enthusiastic and romantic slum visitor, who walks through Mulberry Street, and possibly peeps into the dark and dismal hallway of some dilapidated tenement ..., the theoretical sociologist" all misunderstood how Italians lived and what they thought.[6] While some Italians prospered, most were poor. Most landed in America with little or no money.

Whether in Chicago, Boston, or New York, housing conditions were extremely poor. Density of population was usually greater in the Little Italys than in other parts of the cities, and slum living was the general condition. The Italian district in Philadelphia contained one-sixteenth of the population in less than one one-hundred-and-fiftieth of the area.

Overcrowding prevailed. In one tenement in Philadelphia, thirty Italian families, 123 persons, lived in thirty-four rooms. Often, a family with four or five children managed to live in one small room. It was not unusual for a youngster to wake up in the morning to find a *paesano* who had just arrived sleeping in one corner. Hospitality was taken for granted and given freely.[7] *Paesani* would sit around the supper table with the new arrivals who would relay the bad and good news from Italy. In turn, they asked an endless array of questions about America.

The New York City Tenement Commission in 1900 reported that over a third of Manhattan's residents were crowded into forty-three thousand tenement houses which were dark, stuffy, dirty, and hopeless places in which to raise a normal family. The tenements were often vertical towns and villages for Italians from the same *paese*. Each floor in one of these buildings might have fourteen rooms, many of which received their only light and ventilation from dark air shafts. These rooms, in which the plaster was always falling down, were stifling in summer. The summers were painful. Babies whimpered and died. People poured onto the roofs at night to sleep. Mothers, young girls, fathers, the sick, old, and young—all sought an escape on the roof. In winter, the rooms were heated only by the tenant's coal stove. Many sent their children to scavenge for lumps of fuel in the freight yards. Stairs were broken and dirty. Water pipes often froze and floods spurted from the plumbing and dripped from the ceilings. Pools of stagnant water filled the unlit cellars. A row of privies stood in the yard behind some buildings. The alleys between the tenements were littered with filth and garbage. The separation was so narrow that neighbors in adjoining buildings

could reach out and shake hands. Bed clothes hung on fire es-
capes dotting the tenement canyons. There were people everywhere. They were looking out the windows. They were on the
streets. There was noise. Peddlers howled. Women screamed.
Dogs barked. Babies cried. Excitement! Dirt! Chaos! Hope! Disappointment! Heartbreak! Opportunity! "So this is America?"
some moaned. But many more exclaimed, "Tomorrow will be
better for the children."

Amid such conditions, the health of the immigrants was im-
periled. At the time of arrival, fewer Italian immigrants were
turned away for health reasons than any other immigrant group.
The Italian government, assisted by the Italian-American reformer Dr. Antonio Stella, conducted an extensive investigation
into the health problems of Italians in New York City. The findings seemed to corroborate those from other parts of the United
States. In the urban ghettoes, the Italian immigrant's health deteriorated. This led to the establishment of a health clinic in
New York City in 1910. Earlier, the Italian government had
founded the Italian Benevolent Institute on West Houston
Street, which provided refuge for the needy.

Tuberculosis was a prevalent illness. Forty percent of the slum
dwellers suffered from tuberculosis, and, in one district of tenements, six out of every ten babies died before their first birthday.[8] Consumption took a heavy toll of adult lives also. It was
not uncommon to have thirty or forty cases from each tenement
yearly. It is not hard to account for these health problems. The
once hardy *contadini* were herded together in overcrowded and
filthy buildings. Their working conditions were just as un-
healthy.

The strong bond of local loyalties produced one major disadvantage for the Italian immigrant. It hampered the development
of the Italian settlements into a cohesive ethnic group capable of
exerting social and political pressure to the advantage of all.

A sense of community emerged slowly. Differences in dialect
and written communication kept Italians apart. To communicate with Americans and fellow Italians, the immigrants used
their dialects as well as their limited Italian and English vocabu-
laries to improvise a shared jargon. The Italian-American equiv-
alents of street, camp, ranch, and car were *stritto, campo, rancio,*
and *carro.*

In time, out of the common experiences of living in the United
States, the Italian immigrants discovered a larger ethnic bond.
They were Italians, not just *paesani,* with a common heritage,

common interests, and common needs. One first-generation
Italian-American recalled how the immigrants helped each
other:

> Most of our immigrant parents were of the Italian peasant
> class. Many of the men found work as laborers in construction,
> although my father was a tailor who worked seasonally in a gar-
> ment factory in Manhattan. Since paid vacations and unem-
> ployment insurance were nonexistent in the 1920s and early
> 1930s, workers laid off during the winter months went without
> pay. Some local people, such as Beniamino Blanda, an under-
> taker who owned a twelve-family tenement and a grocery store,
> extended credit during the winter for food purchases. His wife,
> who had a reputation for being good-hearted and charitable,
> even gave their tenants rent credit without interest. With the
> coming of spring, the laborers returned to work, and debts were
> slowly repaid.[9]

The continued growth of the ethnic colony was accompanied by
the strong continuity in immigrant social life.

Slowly the immigrants created a set of new institutions. Their
banks, though lending at higher interest rates, were the only ones
willing to provide the immigrant with the capital to make a
start for himself. Travel agencies, boardinghouses, legal agencies,
mutual aid societies, parish churches, newspapers, and other
agencies served as the institutional network which bound the
community together and helped it to grow. In San Francisco,
there was such a proliferation of organizations among the Italian-
American community that a coordinating agency, The Italian
Federation, was formed in 1919.

The Italian newspapers, magazines, and other publications
that appeared in the communities by the first decade of the
twentieth century contributed to the growth of this ethnic identity. They often provided immigrants with a means of communication with themselves and with the larger American society.
When the establishment wanted to reach Italian groups, it did so
through the Italian language press. Italian newspapers gave advice, assistance, and comfort. They covered events in Italy's
towns. They listed jobs and instructed their readers where to
look for them. The general newspaper or specialized magazine
dealing with music and art reflected the intellectual growth of
the community.

Most important of all of the institutions with which the immi-
grant poor tried to help themselves were the mutual aid societies.
As one Italian told me, "While we second-generation Italian-
Americans had our street corners, our parents had their Mutual

Aid—*Mutuo Succorso di San Giuseppe Gesuriano*—Clubhouse for relaxation and the recreational pastime of conversation and discussion." These aid societies provided their members with sickness and death benefits and also offered activities of a purely social nature. The Italians of Chicago had over one hundred mutual aid societies representing a population of about 150,000. Members often came from the same Italian province and frequently from the same village. The most popular, the *Unione Sicilina*, had twenty-eight lodges. Sick benefits in this society ranged from $8 to $12 per week and a death benefit of $1,000. The monthly fees ranged from thirty to sixty cents. There was also a death assessment, making the average cost of membership from $12 to $15 a year. Funeral expenses which ranged from $50 to $90 were paid. Every member made a contribution of $2 to the family of the dead member. By 1912, there were 258 Italian mutual aid societies in New York. Most of them were supported by nickel and dime contributions. Had American officials and social workers cooperated more closely with the societies and with Italian authorities, immigrants might have been encouraged to scatter instead of settling primarily in congested areas. By 1910, there were 35 mutual aid societies in San Francisco. Unfortunately, Italians were not successful in using these groups or the social strength of their neighborhoods to build an effective national pressure group.

In 1883, the Italians represented in the Associations of New York, Brooklyn, Hoboken, and Newark formed a confederation to collect money for the victims of the earthquake that shook the Island of Ischia. In 1884, the confederation focused on the celebration of September 20 and collected funds for the Italian poor in New York. The Italian Community of New York Metropolitan Area looked with satisfaction and pride at its evolution over the past thirty years and advocated a permanent confederation. As Louis V. Fugazy wrote in 1884: "In such a confederation, the Italian Colony would acquire that power that today divided it doesn't have or it has only latent."[10]

In 1880, the foreign-born Italian population of the United States reached the figure of 182,880. New York City alone was to have almost the same number of Italians in 1890. The eighteen associations of Italians in New York City in 1884 numbered a little over two thousand members. The Italian colonies, as the settlements of the migrants were called, reflected the sociopolitical world of the Old Country. Each organization was organized along regional lines.

At the end of 1910, a survey was conducted to study the geographical distribution of Italians in America. Thirty-five states had Italian-American communities and each community was crisscrossed by dozens of societies. Of the 1,116 societies registered in the thirty-five states, 453 were in New York State, 113 in New Jersey, 147 in Pennsylvania, 72 in Massachusetts, 31 in Illinois, 35 in Michigan, 33 in California, 33 in Connecticut, 27 in Ohio, 20 in Texas, 13 in Washington State, to list a few. But, there were too many societies. Although their functions were useful, their small membership—very few had more than one hundred members—and their *companilismo* undermined their efficiency. These societies were formed and dissolved following the rise and fall of the jealousies and private interests of the presidents and secretaries. The Italian-Americans were fragmented, without leadership, and satisfied with little tokens at election time.

Banks were a source of community development. The first Italian bank in San Francisco opened its doors in 1893. Located on Mulberry Street, the Italian Savings Bank of New York was established in 1896. It was founded when small Italian banks were failing. Its depositers were mainly Italian, each with an average account of $170. Around Mulberry Bend, Baxter Bend, and Five Points, names which were synonymous in the public mind with poverty and squalor, there were sixteen Italian banking establishments.

The Italian Chamber of Commerce of New York, founded in 1887, was composed of two hundred Italian businessmen. Seeking to promote tighter commercial bonds between the United States and Italy, they also sought to lend their good offices in settling any differences which might arise among Italians or between Italians and other nationalities. Similarly, the Italian Chamber of Commerce of the Pacific Coast was established in 1885.

Italians also established a number of hospitals across the country. Columbus Hospital in New York City was founded in 1892 and helped not only Italians but all people in need. The hospital was supervised by the missionary Sisters of the Sacred Heart, an order of Italian nuns founded by Sister Francis Xavier Cabrini, America's first saint.

By far the most important organization to help the Italian poor was the Society for Italian Immigrants, which was incorporated in 1901. Its first secretary was Gino C. Speranza. It helped to bring together American reformers, the Italian government, Italian-Americans, and Italian-American leaders in an effort to uplift the Italian urban poor. While income remained low, Italians were never high on the pauper lists compiled by social workers. In 1904, records show that Italians did not become public charges or members of charitable institutions such as orphanages or old age homes. Cultural values viewed such institutionalization as disgraceful.

In small urban centers, the separation from the larger population also forced the Italian community to develop its own institutions. Professor Harry Jebsen, Jr., describes the situation in Blue Island, Illinois:

> The Martino Sample Room and Grocery became the first gathering place. This tavern and grocery store on Burr Oak Avenue became the place for Italian adult males to drink, gamble, and converse. And it quickly became the place for women to exchange gossip. Martino's served the drinks desired by Italian men. It also stocked the proper types of ingredients needed to make the pastas and sauces which the Italian cook needed.... The Martino family provided the initial matrix upon which much of the early community centered.[11]

In Mechanicville, New York, a variety of organizations arose to help meet the peculiar needs of the Italian immigrants and their children. Paul Loatman describes them:

> In 1918, the second chapter in the United States of the Young Men's Italian Association was organized.... The primary goal of the organization was to promote citizenship among Italian immigrants ... [and it also] provided many recreational and social outlets for the Italians. In 1916, a local chapter of the Sons of Italy had been chartered, providing financial benefits for its members, while advocating citizenship. ... The latter ... because of the poverty of many of their fellow ethnics, [sponsored] local housecalls by an Italian doctor to visit the sick in the community.[12]

Life for the children of Italian immigrants was filled with hard work and hope. One second-generation Italian-American recalled that boys' chores included buying ice for the icebox in the summer and fetching wood and coal for the stove in the winter. Other errands included procuring food from the small neighborhood stores, which individually sold bread, meat, vegetables, and canned goods. They worked also at jobs.

Boys were required to contribute their share to the family. Certainly no southern Italian family would have tolerated a boy of the age of twelve or so who failed to do his share. The nature of this contribution depended upon the type of employment available to the boys. It was almost always manual labor and usually related to the family interest, which, in the South, was generally in agriculture. Boys did not work as hard as girls and

could usually manage to obtain some free time, but the contributions of children, both boys and girls, to the family earnings must
have been significant indeed.

> Even in 1911, after considerable intervention by the national
> government... Italy had, out of a total of two and one-half
> million children between the ages of ten and fifteen, more than
> one and one-half who were gainfully employed.... Thus [more
> than] half of Italy's children were definitely contributing to
> the immediate or future gain of their families.[13]

Italian mothers desired to see the girls in the family married; to
see all her daughters *sistemate* (settled in marriage) was the con-
summation of her mission, before her death.

The role of children in the financial affairs of the family had
great importance when the southern Italian *contadino* moved to
America. The development of a tradition in which children must
provide for their own support was contrary to the traditions
which had developed in the United States, and it would cause
difficulties later.

To Italian immigrants, children were their greatest sources of
hope, pride, and anxiety. For many children and their parents,
education was the basis of their hope for the future. This they
perceived was the key to economic advancement. In addition,
their children's achievements would silence their American de-
tractors. As one observer noted, "They are rarely content to remain at their father's level [and are] roused in America by the
all-pervasive and generally effective idea of getting ahead." The
immigrant father of Leonard Covello told him, "Go to school.
Even if it kills you. With an education you have a chance to live
like a man and not like a beast of burden."[14] I recall that, when
I was nine or ten years old, I happily announced I intended to
fight in a local boxing league. My request was promptly rejected
by my father, who instructed me. "No son of mine is going into
a ring to have his brains knocked out. He's going to use them!"

So the children of the *contadini* went to school. They learned
to read and write. Seated at the lamplit table at home in the
evening, an Italian immigrant might also learn his ABC's as well
as his first words of English. The immigrant wanted his sons to
learn more than he knew and to be better than he could be. Education was not always stressed for the girls of the family. They
were often trained for marriage. The daughter's duties and responsibilities involved those tasks which would prepare her to be
a future wife and mother. One woman recalled her experience
for me, "As a second-generation Italian-American, I too was

raised under the benevolent dictatorship of the family. But these same cultural roots gave me a feel for the quality of life that now seems to be missing among other Americans. My father did not have a formal education, but he provided all of his five girls with as much as he could. Education was very important in our household, and schoolwork was more important than housework. Each of us graduated from high school, and my older sister went on to college. Daddy believed that as girls it wasn't too important to go to college, but if we wanted to we could. The opportunity was there—but only the stronger one could take it. . . ."

Children sensing their advantage questioned their parents' authority in all matters, often injecting into the conversation, "But the teacher told us!" Daughters came home with strange ideas about work and play outside of the home. Understandably, anxious parents were often deeply suspicious of the place where children might learn alien ways. In the parks and settlement houses, the children learned American games, songs, and customs. In school, they saluted the flag and learned American history. When schools closed, they went directly to the local branch of the public library where they did their homework. Many went to evening classes.

In cities such as New York, the number of students eligible to attend school was increased by the influx of immigrants and the passage of compulsory education laws. There were grave deficiencies in school facilities in New York. The problems there were compounded by the absence of exact records of how many children should be in school but were not. Thus, the Italian child was victimized by an educational situation which needed attention and help.

Italian children were present in all grades but were most heavily concentrated in grades one to four. Since there was no attempt to determine precisely how many Italian children lived in New York, there was no way of comparing the total school population with the total number of Italian children. One fact does become clear. A disproportionate number of older children were placed in the lower grades. There was an unusually high proportion of Italians in the primary grades due to the fact that they had only recently arrived in America. It was the practice at the time to place a child who could not speak English in the primary grades until he acquired some familiarity with the language. It was assumed that in the lower grades more time was spent on reading and the language arts, which would result in the immigrant child's learning English more rapidly. Rarely did the schools take into account the possibility that the child might already have had some education in his native country or that his or her ability might be far beyond the average for placement in the lower grades. Thus, there were many over-age children placed in the lower grades, which caused many problems for the students and the school.[15]

The public school system of New York City had no official attitude towards the Italian-American students. Schools were influenced by those who called for rapid assimilation and Americanization and were agents of the Americanization process. The school tried to accomplish this in a variety of ways. I recall an elementary school assembly in Hoboken, New Jersey, in which I and five other immigrant children lined up alongside one another, each holding cardboard letters which together spelled out "Yankee." Then came our little poems. I was the letter "Y." " 'Y' is for Yankee, like you and me, the home of the brave and the land of the free." How incongruous this all seems to me now. We were not "Yankees," and, instinctively, we didn't want to be.

There were relatively few Italians in New York City when the curriculum was originally developed. In the 1890s, the New York population was largely German–American and Irish–American, and the schools reflected this composition. The Italian was a silent partner in the schools. According to Leonard Covello, the Italian did not exist: "During this period, the Italian language was completely ignored in the American schools. In fact ... I do not recall one mention of Italy or of the Italian language or what famous Italians had done in the world ... (except Columbus) ...."[16]

Only when the Italian-American community of the city became so large and powerful that it could not be overlooked did the school system begin to make changes. One of the most significant of these was the introduction, in 1922, of the Italian language on a par with the other languages as part of the high school curriculum.[17]

The system lacked an understanding of the problems and background of the Italian immigrant, indeed of any immigrants, for that matter, and this caused considerable confusion and hardship. Teachers thought in terms of making the immigrant child into an "American" and ignored the peculiar problems the child faced and what education he may already have received in Italy.

> Many teachers fancy that they may change an Italian into an American by instructing him in the principles of American government. They think that, no matter how much a child may revere Garibaldi in his home, he can become a one hundred percent American by having reverence for George Washington drilled into him. A little knowledge of Italian human geogra-

phy, literature, and a few words of the language would help to
adapt these pupils more readily.[18]

Later, the school system came to realize the importance of this
need, but no official program was ever undertaken to assist teachers in understanding the Italian–American children in their
classes.

The ethnic composition of the administrative and teaching
staffs during the post-1880 period also presented a problem.
There were few Italian teachers in the earlier part of this century. Indeed, their numbers never were particularly large. The
vast majority of the teaching staff were of northwestern European origin. "The Irish furnished more than twice as many
teachers ... as any other race," noted one observer.[19] The Irish
were, of course, "old" Americans insofar as the Italian-Americans
were concerned, and the Irish were so far removed from their
own immigrant ancestors, they had little understanding of the
problems of the Italian immigrant or any other immigrant.

The need for teachers from among the members of the Italian-
American community was a serious one. Only they were able to
enter the homes of the Italian-Americans and communicate with
them in their own language. In addition, they were capable of
understanding more fully and effectively the problems of individual students.[20] Certainly it would appear that students
were impressed by and responded to teachers who were of Italian
origin. An incident from Leonard Covello's *The Heart Is the
Teacher*, illustrates this point very well:

Invited to teach Italian immigrant youths English at the
YMCA, Covello proceeded to use the standard textbook approach.
The students, all about his own age, were obviously uninterested,
and their response was poor. After some time at this, Covello,
by then thoroughly annoyed, made several excited remarks in
Italian. In the silence which followed, one student said to another, "*Pasquale, il professore è italiano!*" With that, the entire
atmosphere changed and, "After that it was easy. They lost their
fear of opening their mouths and making mistakes."[21]

There were three major problem areas confronting the Italian-
American, which were an integral part of the school system and
over which the system had, initially, but little control. First,
there was the weight of tradition in shaping the curriculum.
Second, there was a lack of understanding on the part of the
staff of the problems of immigrants. Finally, there was a serious
shortage of teachers who were themselves Italian-American.

These problems were largely the result of indifference rather than intent. There were other problems which were caused by malicious intent, and, of course, these created greater damage. The school system seems to have been remarkably free from bigotry. Unfortunately, one "noted educator" suggested that, if immigrants did not like "our" school system, they "should go back."[22] Another truant officer "aroused the ire of a parent by addressing her truant offspring as a 'Guinea bastard!' "[23] These people, though rare, did more harm than the vast majority of persons who, however misguided, were sincerely trying to help.[24]

The mission of American education that was conveyed by school administrators may be summarized as: *You are vicious, immoral, shortsighted, and thoroughly wrong about most things. We are right; we shall show you the truth.* Italian immigrants rejected that ideology. Their Old World cultural traditions, largely familial in nature, remained too cherished to be surrendered.

A number of myths and stereotypes arose with regard to the Italian and the desire for education. Italians were pictured as anti-intellectual. Thus, they were stereotyped as poor students. Moreover, they were portrayed as having very low aspirations for achievement. These views persist even in the serious literature of the late nineteenth and the early twentieth centuries. Part of the misunderstanding lies in some of the early test data upon which scholars still rely.

Many of the tests which were administered to Italian youngsters and those of other nationalities were ethnocentric. During this period, the intelligence tests in use were designed primarily with a white Anglo-Saxon Protestant, upper-middle-class ideal in mind. "Americans," whatever their class, were at least somewhat aware of this ideal and were, to a limited extent, able to cope with these tests adequately. Similarly, city dwellers from Europe had a slightly better chance, because city life did not differ too greatly on either side of the Atlantic. Peasant farmers, however, were unable to relate readily to the tests and, as a result, tended to do poorly. Much of the material contained in the intelligence tests was simply outside the frame of reference of both the southern Italian immigrant and his children, even if they were born in America. Children born in America of foreign-born parents would be exposed to more of the "old" culture than to the "new" and, in a sense, would be more at home in southern Italy than in an "American" community.

An intelligence test administered by the Immigration and Naturalization Service during World War I illustrates this point. One question asks the subject to interpret a picture. The picture shows neatly dressed children standing in an extremely clean farmyard. There are sheep grazing not far off and a barn nearby. One of the children has a shovel and is digging a small hole. Another child has an armful of flowers. At their feet lies an obviously dead rabbit. The picture is captioned "Last Honors for Bunny."[25] Now if we consider this a moment, it soon becomes evident that this is an absurd picture to give to an immigrant peasant, any immigrant peasant, not merely an Italian-American one, to ask him to interpret it. In southern Italy, a rabbit is not kept as a pet. If a person is fortunate enough to have one, it is fattened for the table. Obviously, persons who, in terms of their values, properly interpret this picture as representing a successful hunt of some sort will receive a low score on this test. Yet such tests were used to determine the mental ability of numerous individuals and, ultimately, the mental ability of entire nations during the debate over exclusion in the 1920s. In the twenties American psychologists fell in line with the nativist thinking of the era. The intelligence test was used to measure the psychic differences between races. Allegedly, IQ scores did not reflect education. Moreover, many psychologists contended the tests were independent of all environmental influences. Many segments of the intellectual community accepted the tenets of racial nativism as proved truths of science.

Prominent Italian-Americans founded the Verdi Ladies Auxiliary in New York in 1910 in order to raise funds for the establishment of a school in East Harlem. The need to enhance the civic, educational, and political life of the Italian led to the formation of the Italian Lawyers Association in 1905. Seven years later, the Italian Teacher's Association came into being and succeeded in introducing the study of the Italian language to the high school curriculum of New York.

Italian parents, particularly those in skilled and unionized trades, were most eager to cooperate with the schools. This presents a somewhat different picture of the Italian immigrant parent than is found in much of the literature. In 1904, a social worker questioned 143 children from four Italian schools in New York. These represented the poorest part of the Italian population, those with the least advantages. Over 75 percent of the children aspired to earn a higher living than that of their parents, and a number of the children chose the professions.

More recent studies continue to perpetuate the myth of the low achievement aspirations of Italian-Americans. Bernard Rosen holds that upward mobility rates are dissimilar for many racial and ethnic groups.[26] Those people with small-town or

urban origins were more likely to possess the cultural values
appropriate to achievement in American society than those
people whose culture was formed in rural, peasant surroundings.
Rosen tries to show that some persons have a higher need for
achievement, while others have a low need for achievement.[27]
According to him, there are three aspects of "achievement orientation": (1.) "achievement orientation"; (2.) "value orientation"; and (3.) "culturally influenced educational aspiration
level."[28] Rosen concludes, "As a consequence, achievement
motivation is more characteristic of Greeks, Jews, and white
Protestants than of Italians, French-Canadians, and Negroes.[29]
Italians have, in Rosen's terms, a "low need for achievement."
He also found that a great number of black Americans would be
satisfied with even the lowest jobs. This indicated to Rosen low
vocational aspiration.

Joseph Lopreato correctly exposes the false assumptions that
underlie Rosen's conceptual scheme and measures of motivation:

> It is hard to understand the "inconsistency" in the behavior
> of Black Americans was not sufficient to sensitize Mr. Rosen
> to the deficiencies of his methods. Can you imagine the Black
> American mother, endlessly accused of not raising her children
> to honor the American Dream, not telling interviewer "Joe
> College" that she "intended" to send her son to school as long
> as everyone did? ... But judiciousness is in short supply in our
> science; or as far as Italian-Americans are concerned Rosen
> might have wondered whether, according to such things as
> census materials, his reasearch tool had much predictive power
> at all.[30]

Lopreato proposes that what hard-working, deprived people
actually achieve is somehow a better measure of their potential
for achievement than the methodology of some social scientists,
which often says more about "the personality and the ideology of
the inquirers than about the achievement potential of the
interviewed."[31]

Italians were found by Fred Strodtbeck to be less mobile than
Jews in New Haven. Strodtbeck found that both Italian and
Jewish boys generally guessed that their parents would be satisfied if they chose high-status positions, but it was predominantly
the Italian boys who also thought that their parents would be
pleased with less. In his study, the Italians were found to be
more accepting of lower-status occupations.[32] Strodtbeck supports Rosen's findings of low achievement among Italians of
New Haven, which is due to "culturally influenced educational-
vocational aspiration levels," and concludes, "To the typical

southern Italian peasant, school was an upper-class institution and potentially a threat to his desire to retain his family life about him...."[33] Rosen's and Strodtbeck's explanations of apparent low achievement imply a certain antagonism toward school or "intellectualism," which was regarded with distrust. This explanation is not only inaccurate, but misleading. As Lopreato notes, "The peasants distrusted—and they still distrust —intellectuals for their constant abuses, not intellectualism or learning *per se.*"[34]

Early southern Italian immigrants did have certain attitudes about the formal American educational institutions which need clarification. They perceived correctly that the school and teachers in the era of the mass migration (1880–1924) were hostile to the family. Many southern Italian immigrants did not see the value of the education provided by the American high school of that period. In school, Italian children were advised to train for manual, working-class occupations. Many educators judged they lacked the mental endowments necessary for other occupations.[35] The Italian families, sensing this, felt the trades could be learned more readily and more expertly on the job, while the youngster was being paid at the same time.

The American schools held the immigrants and their culture in contempt. This middle-class institution effectively produced a rebellious reaction against itself and against parental authority, especially as the child became more successful. The southern Italian immigrant sensed quite perceptively that the school, with its Americanizationist and absorptionist thrust, would soon strip him and his family of their identity.[36] Lopreato observes, "The tendency to compare Italian-Americans to especially successful groups, to suggest, however unintentionally, that Italians are poor achievers, is patently unwarranted by the facts."[37] The success of some groups cannot be explained in terms of greater achievement motivation or a greater reverence for learning. Regardless of ethnic background, individuals "will set those goals that are highly valued in their society and appear to be attainable given their past experience with success and the means presently at their disposal."[38] Lopreato suggests that what may be more to the point is not that Italians are "under-achievers" but rather that some of these other groups may be "over-achievers."[39]

It is wrong or inaccurate to assume that cultural achievement results solely from mental powers and, therefore, that some people or groups want to get ahead more than others. "Rather, it seems obvious that, in addition to the questions of differential access to existing avenues to success, different people have different strategies and time schedules for the attainment of the same goals." Hence, the overemphasis on motivation and need for achievement does not take into consideration the unequal distribution of opportunities or what is achievable, but reflects "a preoccupation with 'the rat race' that, if what certain sections of our youth today believe is true, empties man too much of his human content."[40]

At first, most Italian immigrants had little interest or time for even the most meager cultural pursuits. There was strong pressure merely to survive. But gradually, they went to night school. Education came directly to those with jobs. The Society for Italian Immigrants conducted night classes among the non-English speaking at their place of work. The society established schools in several labor camps in New York and Pennsylvania, where Italian workers were taught English, arithmetic, geography, history, and civics. In one school, there were as many as two hundred Italians. At Ashokan Dam in New York, there was a nightly attendance of fifty Italian workers, who "cheerfully" contributed six cents for each lesson. Education was very difficult under these conditions, since many of them had a twelve to fourteen hour workday.[41]

The average Italian was sober, frugal, and hard-working. He usually drank less alcohol and worked longer and harder than other immigrants. When he drank, it was usually wine in the home and not hard liquor in the saloon. Italian housewives provided abundant meals on a limited food budget. They worked and sacrificed for a future for their children and themselves.

After supper, the Italians found pleasure in taking a *passeggiata* (stroll) or joining with *paesani* for a game of cards. As one second-generation Italian-American man noted, "The immigrant had little social life. For several reasons, socializing amongst themselves was more compatible with their interests. Language limitations, customs, food, work, and partly a fear of the unfamiliar hindered the establishment of friendships with men of other ethnic groups. The Italian men played their own bowling game, *boccie* (a game of bowls), and their own card games, *scopa* and *brisca*."

For the most part, mental attitudes and cultural practices, not residential location, determined ghetto reality. Individuals might live next door to each other but, owing to differences in culture, might remain socially invisible to each other.

In many ways, Jews and Italians were closer to each other in a social, political, and economic sense during the 1890s and early

1900s. In cities such as New York and Boston, they had common
political, social, and economic enemies. A great gap divided Irish
and Italian Catholics, and more hostility existed between the
Jews and the Irish than between the Jews and the Italians, who
resembled each other more than did either the Irish- or German-
Americans.[42]

During the day, pushcarts piled with merchandise lined the
streets. There were piles of fish, meats, chickens, ripe cheeses,
fruit, pickles, and huge loaves of dark bread. Interspersed between the food stalls were other carts laden with merchandise
ranging from lace to tinware. The poor bought groceries a pinch
at a time: three cents worth of sugar; five cents worth of butter.
Everything was sold in penny fractions.

In the evening, the Italian ghettoes came alive with playing
children, baby carriages, strolling lovers. The streets resembled
one continuous front stoop, as men and women chatted about
weddings, funerals, births, and the latest neighborhood gossip.

Italians had a cultural life of their own. Hutchins Hapgood, a
reporter, made the following observation in 1900:

> On Spring Street, within a few blocks of the Bowery, the
> heart of the Italian quarter is laid open to the stranger. In this
> little section are concentrated the Italian theater, properly
> speaking an Italian puppet show, and a characteristic Italian
> restaurant. The poor Neapolitan in New York frequents these
> resorts, and on the stage of the theater and the puppet show
> he sees what he is accustomed to in the little theaters of Naples.
> ...After his spaghetti, chianti... the suave and polite man
> with dark eyes and ragged clothes lights his cigarette, and with
> his black derby hat fixed permanently on his head he goes to
> see the continued fight between the armoured puppets, repre-
> senting Christian knights and Saracen warriours, at Spring
> Street, or to see Othello, some melodrama, or farce, at No. 24
> of the same street.[43]

As early as 1850, there was an attempt to establish an Italian
theater in San Francisco. Italian opera companies came peri-
odically and were well received by fashionable audiences. In
addition, informal amateur groups of Italian artists sprang up in
San Francisco and other centers of Italian population where
simple people got together to play the mandolin or guitar, sing,
perform pantomime, and, in general, to enjoy themselves and
entertain one another. These activities were to form the base of
the popular theater introduced by Antonietta Pisanelli.[44]

Born in Naples, Pisanelli first went to New York City and then
in 1905 traveled to San Francisco. There she established the *Cir-*

colo Famigliare Pisanelli—a cafe with tables grouped around a stage. There was no admission charge, but the enthusiastic public bought many drinks between the acts. Here Pisanelli continued her successful career as performer, manager, and impressario, supplementing her local talent with professional Italian companies from the East.

The *Circolo* became the main institution of the North Beach Italian community—a combination opera, theater, cafe, and club. The *Circolo* offered entertainment in the language of the southern *contadini*. It offered family entertainment which could be shared by all. The community made it a habit to spend Sunday evenings at the *Circolo*. The theater was a unifying force in the life of the community and its members. It united the Italian population by providing a common meeting place and a common set of experiences. It helped the younger generation to appreciate the language and tradition of their parents. Moreover, it helped the non-Italian population, many of whom were *Circolo* patrons, to see the Italian immigrants in a favorable light. The rich musical and theatrical tradition of the Italian community was reflected in the variety of programs offered at the *Circolo*. A different opera was presented nightly. Many of the poor immigrants knew opera and followed their favorite arias. The *Circolo* also presented comedy sketches in the tradition of the *Commedia Dell'Arte,* where the actors relied on improvisation.

Pisanelli expanded her operations and opened a series of establishments called nickelodeons. For a nickel or dime, the public could enjoy a vaudevillian Italian variety show of farce, song, and one-act comedies. In 1909, she opened the Washington Square Theater, with a capacity for a thousand people. It was the only theater to change its program every day. Programs varied from Shakespeare to opera.[45]

Another part of the cultural life of Italians was the *festa* (festival) either sponsored by the Church or a group society. It usually occurred "in midsummer, when prodigal decoration, street illuminations—such as one sees so frequently in Italy, fireworks, processions, etc.—are indulged in...."[46]

The literary attention of the immigrants seems to have been devoted almost entirely to poetry. Hundreds of poets wrote thousands of volumes of poetry. Many of the poets were self-taught men and women with an interest in history and literature. In their verse, the Italian poets focused their attention on political and philosophical questions, as well as religious and amorous themes. One immigrant poet, Arturo Giovannitti, gained the most critical acclaim. A labor journalist and IWW organizer, he won widespread public recognition for such poems as *The Walker*.

The Italian-American novel also served as a literary vehicle. The pattern of Italian-American fiction seems to have gone through five distinct stages. The first stage deals with the early impact, the problems encountered in America during the mass immigration; such novels as Luigi Donato Ventura's *Peppino* and Giuseppe Cautela's *Moon Harvest* are examples of fiction during this period. The second phase in the development reflects the attempt of the immigrants to root themselves in their new American environment; typical of this group of novelists are Louis Forginne's *Men of Silence* and *The River Between*. The third phase is the period of revulsion in which the writers rejected their heritage; this group of writers includes Bernard DeVoto, Paul William Gallico, Hamilton Basso, and Frances Winwar (Vinciguerra). The fourth stage is a return to the Italian-Americans' heritage and the treatment of themes in a more artistic, more symbolic, and more universal manner; there are many representative works in this phase, such as Guido D'Agostino's *Olives in the Apple Tree;* Jerre Mangione's *Mount Allegro*; Pietro DiDonato's *Christ in Concrete*; and John Fante's *Dago Red*. Finally, in the fifth phase the Italian-American became a part of the national complex in such works as Michael DeCapite's *No Bright Banner* and Rocco Fumento's *Tree of Dark Reflection*.[47]

One of the great scholars of the Italian-American novel, Rose Basile Green, concludes:

> The development of Italian-American fiction reveals a pattern—a pattern which parallels the growth of the national culture. But there was something unique in this side-by-side development. Italian-American writers constantly showed a constructive attitude towards their literary materials, a positive animus which galvanized the directions and solutions of their stories. In the long run, perhaps in innocence, perhaps in an inherited faith in humanism of the individual, these writers did not reflect the generally negative and self-despising treatment of the "official" national literature.... The heroes of Italian-American novels have struggles, they overcome these struggles, but their will power is stronger than an evasive fate.[48]

The millions of Italian immigrants who came to America wove some of the brightest strands in the American tapestry. Americans of Italian origin may be justly proud of their heritage, both in the United States and in world history. But they have more reason to take pride in their parents and grandparents—giants and culture heroes in their own right—who pioneered the United States with as much valor as the trailbreakers who are celebrated in our history books. In *Choosing a Dream*, Mario Puzo observes, "The thing that amazed me was their courage. . . . How did they ever have the balls to get married, have kids, go out to earn a living in a strange land, with few skills, not even knowing the language? They made it without tranquillizers, without sleeping pills, without psychiatrists."[49] Perhaps the answer lies in the ancient Italian phrase *sapire vivere*, knowing how to live—or, put in the modern vernacular, knowing how to cope.

In 1963, Dr. Stewart Wolf reported in the *Journal of the American Medical Association* that the people of Roseto, Pennsylvania, almost all of them Italian-born or of Italian descent, showed a remarkable resistance to heart attacks. The death rate from myocardial infarction in Roseto was only about half the national rate. There were few cases of ulcers or suicide. The study covered the period from 1955 through 1961 and showed that not one Roseto male under forty-seven had died of a heart attack during those six years.

The researchers found that the Rosetans were hard-working, most were employed at tough steel-mill and foundry jobs, but they were relaxed, easygoing, and secure in their off-hours. Dr. Joseph Farace, himself the son of an Italian immigrant and physician to many of Roseto's population, notes a change. "A lot of the old folks are still going strong, but that sure as the devil doesn't apply to the young people. There's just so much tension around these days. . . . These old people, they played hard, they drank hard, and they ate big. Then they went out and worked hard enough to knock it all off the next day." Dr. Wolf's associate, Dr. John Bruhn, talked recently about the lesson of Roseto. "It's about the importance of support groups, whether friends or family. In our society we've become too individualistic, and we pay a real price for economic success."

> The past lingers in Roseto, where rootedness and continuity are almost mythic qualities. Life was invariably simpler, more rewarding, less troublesome, even if it was harder. The present, for all its rewards—and Roseto is a prosperous town—never fully satisfies. People talk of an easier, less complicated life, where hard work was the only concern, and large families and many friends the major joys.[50]

A couple of years ago, I came across an item in a Rochester, New York, newspaper. It seems that Dr. Joseph Crupi of Memphis, Tennessee, played host to a reunion of the Crupi family. Some members came from as far as Florida and Georgia, all at the doctor's expense, which came to about $15,000. Crupi's father Giovanni, now dead, left Sicily during the mass migration period. Giovanni Crupi first went to Boston, where he was enlisted by a labor recruiting force to work in the Mississippi cotton fields. Conditions at the camp were so deplorable that Giovanni and another Italian laborer eluded the guards and escaped, hopping a northbound train. When the train reached Memphis, the first big city on its route, he bailed out and stayed there. When asked the purpose of the family reunion, Dr. Crupi explained it this way:

> I made a pledge some years ago to honor my father's memory in some way, and I decided he'd prefer me to do something like this, in which the whole family could take part, rather than build him a monument or something like that.[51]

It is the essence of the true Italian culture that one does not have to be great to be good. Exceptional talent has its place, but exceptional goodness is also to be venerated. The temptation is to dismiss the Italian immigrants as ordinary people. But the millions who came exhibited a universal gift. They shared a dedication and capacity for love and humility which was not shaken by hardship and discrimination. Mario Cuomo, the Lieutenant Governor of New York, himself a son of a Neopolitan immigrant, recalls his parents:

> [My father] never sermonized or lectured—he never gave a speech. But he taught us, and my mother taught us, every single day—just by being what they were. They taught us the simple values; respect above all things. Respect for your family, especially your wife. Respect for your children and to the parents who made you and raised you. Respect for yourself. They taught us all we needed to know about the things politicians talk about: the importance of family to society, about the need to care for our senior citizens, about instruction of the young. And they did this just by being what they are.... [They taught us] respect for the flag, respect for the nation, the need to fight when reason fails, law and order and holy strength.[52]

Yes, these earlier immigrants are the culture heroes of Italian-Americans. We grew up with heroes all around us. How many of the first and second generations appreciate this fact? I hope many do. The early immigrants set the tone for future generations through their values of independence, self-help, and a basic trust in the material attachments of home, church, and town. This faith in the concrete, this distrust of abstract, impersonal, and ultimately suspect forces, runs throughout the culture of the *Mezzogiorno* and flows in the veins of the second and third generations of Italian-Americans.

4 The Rich Have It All But Accomplish Little

Frank Capra, one of Hollywood's great film directors, recalls an incident in his autobiography, *The Name Above the Title*. After serving his country in World War I, the young Capra was in need of a job. He responded to an advertisement for a tutor. He discovered that his prospective employer was one of the wealthiest families in California. The job would require a person to tutor the spoiled son, Baldwin, whom they feared would not pass his entrance exams to the University of California. Having passed a rigorous interview with the parents, Capra would now have to pass muster with the young Baldwin himself. When he entered the young boy's room, he could not help but notice that Baldwin had every musical instrument imaginable. He looked at Capra with a distinct air of disdain. Capra recalls their encounter this way:

> "You play any of these?" I asked.
> "I play all of them," he said with that tired insolence of the rich that sandpapers nerve endings.
> "... Look, rich boy. You want me around here as your tutor, you better start calling me 'Sir!' Understand?"[1]

Capra put down the guitar, turned on his heels, and started for the door. Baldwin ran after him and implored Capra to stay on. Capra concludes:

> I was to live with Baldwin twenty-four hours a day, teach him enough math and chemistry to pass the exams at Berkeley —keep him out of trouble.... Two months later Baldwin passed the Berkeley exams ... and [I] left for the copper mines in Arizona—with two lingering conclusions: the rich have it all, but accomplish little; and, had Baldwin been born a poor boy in New Orleans or Memphis, he might have become one of our great jazz musicians.[2]

Capra wrote of a basic truth. More famous Italian writers have
come from impoverished Sicily than from any other Italian region of comparable size. Those who are best known include
Verga, Pirandello, Vittorini, and Tomasi di Lampedusa. Others
lesser known include Brancati, Patti, Capuana, and Di Roberto
di San Secondo. Like other famous novelists from the South, they
had the luck to be born in a defeated, impoverished, tragic, and
misunderstood land where injustice prevailed. There is a significant moral in Capra's story. Out of the poor Italian ghettos arose
scientists, educators, doctors, lawyers, businessmen, politicians,
musicians, artists, writers, and poets who enriched the spirit and
quality of American life.

Some Italians reached out for greatness but were denied their
place in American history. Such was the case with Antonio
Meucci.

Antonio Meucci was born in San Frediano, near Florence, on
April 13, 1808. Later Meucci majored in drawing and mechanical engineering at the Florentine Academy of Fine Arts, from
which he later was graduated. Until 1835, he was employed by
the *Teatro Della Pergola* in Florence and by various other
theatres in Italy.

In 1835, he went to Cuba to fill the positions of Superintendent of Mechanism and Scenic Designer of the Tacon Theater
in Havana. His wife, the former Ester Mocci, whom he had met
at the *Pergola,* was in charge of the costume department.

Meucci's scientific mind led him to study the wonders of
electricity. He used his spare time to read all he could in scientific research literature, especially concerning the work of Mesmer and Galvani.

While in Cuba, he established a profitable business in electro-
plating, a system he invented. He continued experiments on Galvani's work with electricity and Mesmer's work on animal mag-
netism. He developed an electric shock therapy for treatment of
the ill, and, while working on the project, he conceived of the
idea of the telephone, or as he called it, "the speaking telegraph." Through the electric wire, he heard an exclamation by
his friend, who was in another room.

For his experiments, Meucci needed a continuous supply of
batteries, magnets, and electrical components. It was necessary to
be near an industrial center where these supplies were easily
available. Thus, on April 7, 1850, Meucci left Cuba, arrived in
New York, and settled on Staten Island.

Meucci remained a poor businessman all his life, despite his
brilliant scientific mind. He had done well financially in Cuba,

because he had managed his own business directly and had easily learned the language. In the United States, he was handicapped primarily by his difficulty with English. He had to depend on various other individuals to convey his ideas, including the numerous political refugees who surrounded him. Most of them could only give poor and often confused translations to those Americans interested in Meucci's inventions.

With the desire to help his fellow countrymen and the hope of financing his experiments, he started a number of diverse businesses, including the manufacture of candles, pianos, and beer. The brewery business thrived for a while, but its management had been entrusted to a deceitful partner, and Meucci lost all of his money in the venture.

He continued electrical experiments throughout this time, becoming more and more enthusiastic about his *teletrofono,* a machine able to convey voices over considerable distances. Each time he worked on it, he obtained better results. In 1855, Mrs. Meucci became partially paralyzed. Her husband improvised a telephone system linking various rooms and the laboratory at the back of the house so that she could easily communicate with him.

In 1860, Meucci felt confident that his invention was ready to be launched into the market. He gave a public demonstration in which he had a young man sing "La Marseillaise" at one end of the apparatus while people listened one by one to his voice, clearly transmitted from a considerable distance. But the few people who had promised financial backing withdrew their support. They lacked Meucci's vision.

Shortly afterward, in 1861, a description of the "speaking telegraph" or *teletrofono* was published in an Italian language newspaper (*L'Eco d'Italia*). Copies of this article and a model of the instrument were taken to Italy by a Mr. Bendelari, who had hope of promoting some interest there. But on his return, Bendelari claimed that he had been too busy with his personal affairs to look for Italian investors.

Meucci struggled against dire poverty and misfortune. His financial resources depleted, he lived on bare necessities. Because of his poverty and difficulty with the language he was continually defrauded. In order to finance his experiments and to obtain money for survival, he was often compelled to sell patent rights for a few dollars or to go into partnership with people who would contribute the least in investment and demand the most in profit.

A fire in a plant adjacent to his house destroyed some of his equipment and notebooks. In 1871, the explosion of the boiler in the ferry boat *Westfield* almost caused his death. He was severely scalded. Following weeks of intensive care, Meucci was taken home, where he remained in bed for three months.

When he was ready to resume his activities, Meucci found that his wife had sold many of his models, batteries, and tools to a junk dealer for six dollars in order to pay bills. Immediately, he sought to recover his cherished property, but they had been sold to an unidentified young man.

Downcast but undaunted, Meucci worked feverishly to recon-struct the lost models, convinced that others were going to copy his invention. He hastened to make preparations for a patent. However, he was unable to raise the two hundred fifty dollars needed by the attorney to prepare for one. He had to settle for a caveat, which was granted on December 28, 1871.

In the summer of the following year, Meucci, accompanied by Angelo Bertolino as interpreter, went to see Edward B. Grant, Vice President of New York District Telegraph (a branch of Western Union) and asked him to try his *teletrofono* over the wires of the company. Grant promised to do so, but each time Meucci returned to inquire about the outcome of the experi-ment, Grant would say that he was too busy to try the invention. Foolishly, he left his models and papers with Grant. After two years of waiting, Meucci was informed that they were lost.

Two people enter the story and figure prominently in Meucci's tragedy. First, there was the American scientist and successful inventor, Elisha Gray. During the spring of 1875, he conducted experiments in the laboratory of the Western Union Company in New York City. In the same lab, young Alexander Graham Bell conducted some experiments of his own. Both men had contact with two electricians who had handled the "speaking telegraph" and the explanatory papers, which Meucci had left with the New York District Telegraph company three years earlier. Gray had a fair grasp of Meucci's idea and worked on some modifications that allowed him to present it as a new invention when on Feb-ruary 14, 1876, he applied for a caveat.

Bell, who had never worked with electricity before, found out about Gray's plan and in the rush to secure a stake for himself, picked up a drawing of a telegraphic gadget, attached it to an application, and succeeded in applying for a patent less than two hours before Gray applied for a telephone caveat. Although Bell's claim was falsely based (on patent 174,465) he applied for a patent on February 14, 1876, and received it within twenty-one days. Two months later, after he had examined Gray's caveat, he applied for another patent covering a telephonic receiver. Except for their titles, none of the papers received had anything to do with telephony.

In the spring of 1876, Alexander Graham Bell announced himself as the inventor of the telephone. Startled by the news, Meucci sent an inquiry to the patent office in Washington to vindicate his claim. Mysteriously, all of his papers relating to the "speaking telegraph" had disappeared from the office's files.

By 1888, the American Bell Company reached an out-of-court settlement with the American Speaking Telephone Company (organized by Western Union). Both companies were dealing with the same stolen goods, namely, Meucci's "speaking telegraph." Bell probably chose an out-of-court settlement to avoid a public trial in which the Meucci story would surface.

On September 22, 1883, Meucci assigned his claim to the Globe Telephone Company of New York. Shortly before this, the American Bell Company sent E.B. Welch as its emissary to purchase Meucci's caveat. When this failed, the Globe company petitioned the United States government to bring suit against the American Bell Telephone Company and Alexander Graham Bell to vacate the patent assigned to Bell by "fraud, misrepresentations, mistakes, and irregularities in procuring of said fringement of its patents." At a public hearing in January, 1886, Secretary of State Lamar stated that there was sufficient evidence to establish Meucci's priority in the invention of the telephone.

The day before this hearing, Lamar had written to the United States Attorney General to say that he favored a lawsuit in the name of the people of the United States contesting the validity of Bell's patent and the consequent monopoly of the Bell company. Bell had assets worth over 100 million dollars at that time.

The suit by the United States government began in Boston on January 13, 1887. The suit claimed that Bell had obtained his patent by fraud. Those documents Meucci was able to salvage were presented. Meucci's personal testimony was dramatic and compelling. Despite his seventy-eight years of age, he answered all questions directed to him accurately. Moreover, he explained precisely the various steps he followed in his experiments, the principles upon which they were based, and the results he had obtained. Bell could not match this performance, proving that he knew little of the technique involved and that the drawing which he later presented was not of his making.[3]

On July 9, 1887, Judge Wallace rendered his decision in favor of Bell. The case was appealed, but the hearing was postponed from one year to another, until finally it was abandoned. Meanwhile, a number of publications came to Meucci's defense, including *Scientific American, Electrical World,* the *New York World,* and the *Chicago Tribune.* The *New York Times* of September 27, 1884, noted:

> The decision of Judges Colt and Nelson in the United States Circuit Court in Boston, sustaining the demurrer of the Bell Telephone Company and dismissing the suit brought by the Government to annul the Bell patent was not unexpected. The judges of the First Judicial Circuit are of course learned and impartial; but up that way they have a habit of deciding everything in favor of the Bell monopoly and no exception to that custom was looked for in this case.[4]

The *New York World* of October 8, 1885, added its voice of protest: "We cannot help noting . . . Bell's reticence as to how he came to invent the telephone. At this point, it is interesting to find out what sort of a man Bell is. Is he a man capable of appropriating someone else's invention?"[5]

Meucci died in relative obscurity on October 18, 1889, in Staten Island, New York. No monuments have been erected to this great man. Only a tiny street in an Italian section of Brooklyn is named after him. His name does not appear in the standard history books. However, if Meucci's story ended in disappointment and obscurity, that of Amadeo Giannini substantiated Frank Capra's "adversity breeds success" theory.

> I am not a millionaire, and never expect or hope to be one. I have no ambition to become exceedingly rich. I have seen too many ultra-rich persons who were constantly afraid that someone would put poison in their food. . . . There is no fun in working merely for money. I like to do things, to create things, to be a builder. To build is a very fascinating thing. The idea of leaving millions for other people to spend is the height of foolishness. I believe in using money to help worthy causes while one is still living and thus get some satisfaction out of it. . . . God meant us to work. Those who don't work never amount to anything. To take from one the incentive to work is a bad service.[6]

This was part of the working philosophy of Amadeo P. Giannini, the son of a Ligurian immigrant, who rose from financial obscurity to become a giant among giants in the business world. By 1948, a year before his death, Giannini's bank, now known as the Bank of America, had become the largest such institution in the United States, and it has since become the largest bank in the world.

Amadeo Giannini was born in San Jose, California, in 1870.

He showed his great passion for work at an early age. Each night, shortly after midnight, he would tiptoe downstairs in his stockings, to avoid his mother's objections, and put on his shoes at the sidewalk. He worked until the early morning on the docks before he left for school. Young Giannini did very well in school. Immediately after classes he went back to his job on the docks until late afternoon, when he returned home for supper and study and early to bed. He repeated this disciplined cycle of work and study night after night.

Acquiring a share of a shipping firm, he worked and lived among growers and shippers. At the age of thirty-one, he felt there were few remaining challenges in the firm. All he did was sit back and count the profits. Soon, he sold his shares of the firm to his associates.

Shortly thereafter, he accepted a position as a bank director, but he soon resigned when his policies were not followed or accepted. Giannini believed in helping the small Italian merchant and farmer. Newly arrived Italian immigrants usually needed to borrow money to buy land and farming equipment. They needed capital to make a new start in their lives. Yet many Italians were suspicious of banks, which charged high rates of interest.

Giannini opened his first bank, the Italian Bank of California, in October 1904. He then changed its name to the Bank of Italy. Giannini had a very definite vision: no speculative exploits were to be undertaken with the bank's money. No officer of any of his banks was allowed to speculate or become interested in any other business. Giannini brought branch banking to California. This diversified his system since one district would pay off loans at the same time another section needed funds.

When local banks were taken over, their best officers were kept in their positions. Usually, small established banks were converted into branches.

Giannini gave the Italian community Italian-speaking tellers. His banks performed a variety of services free of charge, such as filling out employment, business, and naturalization papers, and the translation of letters. Giannini did not restrict his services to *paesani*; he sought out all Italians, regardless of their provincial ties and wanted them to feel a sense of pride in the growth of an Italian bank. He preached to them the advantages of interest-bearing accounts. He offered loans up to $25 on the basis of "no better security than the callouses on the borrower's hands."[7]

His institution was only a year and a half old when the 1906 earthquake and fire struck San Francisco. Paradoxically, this provided Giannini with his greatest opportunity. All the banks were closed. Before the fire, which resulted from the earthquake, Giannini removed the gold and securities from the bank. He hid them under a wagon load of oranges. Then the fire spread. Struggling through the maze of desolation, he reached his bank about noon. The flames were just a few yards away. Two horse-drawn rigs, commandeered from his old firm, were quickly loaded, one with money and securities, the other with a supply of stationery and furniture.

Giannini's Bank of Italy was housed temporarily in a waterfront shed. His was the only bank in San Francisco open for business before the flames engulfing the city had died out. Giannini flung a large plank across two barrels and opened his bank for business. The North Beach immigrants desperately needed cash. Giannini won their trust by allowing small withdrawals.

While the fire was still smoldering, Giannini sent a circular letter to all depositers announcing that their money was safe and available in cash. He offered also to lend money to those who intended to rebuild their houses destroyed by the fire and the quake. Thousands of people took advantage of this offer, with the result that the Italian quarter was rebuilt before any other. Records show that not one of all those people to whom money was lent failed to pay back the full amount. Giannini's name spread throughout San Francisco like the very flames that destroyed the great city.

Hardly a year later, Giannini won new prestige by anticipating the panic of 1907. Upon return from a trip to New York, he concluded with amazing foresight that serious financial trouble was on the way. He quickly ordered that the bank obtain the largest possible stock of gold. Soon the vaults of the bank were filled with gold and the overflow had to be stored in the vaults of another bank.

When the panic struck, all of the other banks were obliged to limit or stop gold payments. Only the Bank of Italy, solid as a rock, could meet every demand of its customers. The success of this maneuver attracted thousands of additional depositors.

Competitors unsuccessfully petitioned the state to eliminate branch banking. Although alarmed financiers fought him at every turn, the Giannini empire still grew. He furnished vast sums to motion picture producers at a time when other banks refused to finance film making.

In 1918, Giannini accepted an invitation of The Italian Chamber of Commerce and opened a bank in New York. The East River National Bank was acquired through a subscription of $1.55 million by one thousand stockholders.

Giannini had a fear of failure and its implications for the small depositor. He once stopped a run on Sacramento banks by stuffing mail sacks with $5 million in small bills and hiring an airplane to deliver them to the Bank of America, the Sacramento branch. To independent bankers, he seemed unstoppable. The harder they fought to contain him, the bigger he grew. He bid top prices for small banks, sometimes offering owners a free trip around the world to clinch a purchase. In the end, his offers were usually accepted.

By 1930, the empire had outgrown its old name; it became the Bank of America. Giannini lent money on security of farmers' crops as branch banks began to spread to agricultural regions. He saved many a grower when frost wrecked orange groves or when some other disaster threatened the wine vineyards.

Giannini survived the bitter downward thrust of the economy in 1931. He continued to lend money during the depression and continued to expand. He made one major error. Confident of his secure empire, he retired and turned over his control to Elisha Walker. By the next year, Walker had sold the New York banks and was preparing to dispose of the southern California branches *and* Giannini. Giannini secretly returned from Europe and barnstormed California, recapturing control. He returned in triumph to the Bank of America's big building on San Francisco's Powell Street.

Giannini, although technically retired at the age of seventy-five in 1945, was still in control of his sprawling financial empire. He remained "available" to the bank "in an advisory capacity." In 1947, a leading magazine named Giannini as one of the fifty foremost leaders of American industry.

After Giannini's visit to Italy in 1945, leftist Premier Ferruccio Parri resigned. It was believed that Parri's resignation was sparked by Giannini's visit and his comment that Italy needed a strong government if it wished the backing of foreign capital.

The quality of his greatness is not easily defined. A. P. Giannini was the greatest banker since J. P. Morgan. His bank vaults had contained billions of dollars. He left an estate of nearly five hundred million dollars to provide educational scholarships for employees of the Bank of America and to finance medical research, particularly into the disease that tormented his son throughout life, hemophilia.

Giannini's success stemmed from his obvious interests in all aspects of his community's life. He once said that anything which concerned people should also interest banks. Giannini was faithful to his philosophy of life and to the people he served.[8] For

Italian-Americans, Giannini became a symbol of success and humanity. Many a poor Italian-American voiced his support of America's future by scraping his nickels and dimes together and purchasing stock in the Bank of America. As a young boy, I was in awe when my father proudly announced one day that he had bought stock in Giannini's Bank of America.

Meucci was denied his just rewards by those who used the "system" to their own advantage. It is ironic that, had he been able to scrape up the necessary $250 for a patent, he might have been famous and rich rather than poor and obscure. Giannini understood the "system" and helped to mold it according to his terms.

There were to be many successes and failures among the masses of immigrants who came to America. There was a long road ahead for them, filled with hardships and brutality, as Italians sought bread, work, and justice.

5 Bread! Work! Justice!—From Salem to Paterson

Pane e lavoro! Bread and work! These were two of the principal goals of the Italian in America. But soon, an additional goal arose, one that took the form of a demand: Justice!

If you were to read the standard American histories, you would hardly be aware that the Italian immigrants were a major segment of the American labor force. Moreover, little recognition was given to their role and their significant leadership in some of the most important labor struggles of the nineteenth and twentieth centuries. When Italians are noted, they are often portrayed as strikebreakers and wage cutters who represented a threat to the native American workers. As a result of such portrayals, historians have perpetuated stereotypes of the Italian worker which were invented by his enemies almost a hundred years ago. Historians have merely constructed their stories on earlier distorted and biased accounts.[1] In 1914, Edward A. Ross, one of the leading ideologues of the Progressive movement, in *The Old World in New,* portrayed the immigrant as a strikebreaker and a scab who lowered wage levels and reduced living standards in his "pigsty mode of life."

Robert F. Foerster has contributed to this misunderstanding of the Italian worker by observing:

> Work that demands training, responsibility, discretion, is not for the great majority of Italians. But work that is simple and monotonous, that exhausts through duration rather than from concentrated application, that can be performed by men disposed in a gang, under the more or less military supervision of a foreman, so the worker becomes himself like a part of a machine, set in motion only when other parts are active, such work the Italians, helot-like, have performed satisfactorily.[2]

Foerster assumed the Italians lacked skills, yet the self-sufficiency of the southern Italian peasant household required its members to do their own sewing, cobbling, baking, and residential construction. Italians were the second largest ethnic group in the needle trades and were well-represented in the service trades as barbers, bakers, and waiters. Moreover, how much skill was actually required by industries such as the garment trade, where innovations in production so subdivided the manufacturing process that new employees could be taught their tasks quickly and easily?

During the Civil War and the decades immediately following, the United States experienced a series of great economic changes that revolutionized the life of the nation. The great era of industrialization unfolded in those years. The Civil War pointed the way to mass markets and mass production, and it taught the government habits of openhanded and reckless generosity toward private enterprises, which sought control of public funds and resources.

Throughout the last third of the nineteenth century, the federal government was controlled by men who were responsive to the wishes of the business community and eager to further its interests. The prevailing philosophy of *laissez faire* was used to justify the lack of a public policy on a variety of social and economic issues and the virtual absence of restraints on and regulation of business to protect the public welfare. Though debated in public, issues were often settled around the council tables of industrialists and financiers rather than in the halls of legislatures. The industrial entrepreneur was the lord of all he surveyed. What was before him was a potential empire, rich in coal, iron, oil, lumber—in short, wealth.

As the corporations grew in size and strength, the bargaining power of the individual laborer correspondingly decreased. Concentration of ownership in fewer hands and the creation of monopolies gave employers greater power to oppress. A small number of employers was produced by the concentration of economic power in fewer hands with a proportionately larger number of employees. By acting together and bargaining collectively, laborers might hope to protect themselves against industrial exploitation. Thus, the stage was set for a clash between labor and capital in the years following the Civil War.

The government was not a neutral party to this conflict. Reflecting big business interests, all the branches of government participated in the process of regulating labor. The courts regularly issued injunctions, which held various types of union action in contempt of court. Injunctions were enforced by dispatching state troops which had been federalized by the national government. State legislatures were at least officially more concerned with the issue of radicalism.

But the suppression by the employers themselves was even more persuasive. In company towns, the corporation made the laws and enforced them. Freedom of expression and association was allowed solely at their discretion. There were the economic weapons of blacklisting and of purposely flooding the labor market by recruiting immigrant labor. Private armies of strike-breakers who were really "goon" squads were employed to physically break strikes. Henry Ford hired a permanent force for "special services and projects." The rationale and legitimacy for all of these actions was enhanced by characterizing labor leaders and their unions as one giant conspiracy to subvert the American way of life.

The vast majority of Italian immigrants were tillers of the soil, shepherds, tenant farmers, small land owners, and day laborers. The peasantry of the *mezzogiorno* from the hilltowns of southern Italy were propelled from a culturally isolated society into the most dynamic industrial country in the world. The absorption of the *contadini* into the American labor force was one of their major adaptations to American conditions. But even this absorption must be understood in terms of the cultural heritage of the immigrants. Unlike the Irish fleeing famine, the Italians were less driven by such misery than drawn by rising expectations. Emigration was a means to an end.

Italians were to make up a relatively small proportion of America's farmers. Very few chose to do general farming. Those who were found homesteading and sheep herding in the plains of the Midwest were the exception, not the rule. Oscar Handlin in *The Uprooted* describes the peasant immigrant's reverence for the soil. His description is not an accurate one for the Italians. No sentimental ties deterred them from becoming artisans and shopkeepers. Unlike Handlin's peasants who meekly accepted their lowly status, the *contadini* were ambitious to advance the material and social position of their families. Emigration was one way of doing this.

The Italian immigrants were deterred from farming for other reasons. When they arrived, they lacked sufficient capital to buy land. Most of the cheap land was gone. Moreover, the land was a symbol of their oppression. The city represented opportunity. What else but urban concentration was to be expected from them when even the children of native Americans were leaving the farms in droves for the cities? The shift in the economy from agriculture to industry, the advent of hard times, and the emergence of big business in agriculture, all contributed to this flight to the cities.

Nonetheless, at the end of the nineteenth century, Italians were beginning to make their mark in agriculture, especially in California, where they specialized in the raising of grapes, fruits, and vegetables. The establishment of the Italian Swiss Colony at Asti in Sonoma County in 1881 sparked the development of the modern grape and wine industry and set the precedent for the widespread Italian participation that helped California gain importance in that industry. Italians also promoted the raising of green vegetables, tomatoes, and fruits, especially in the San Francisco area, where they literally dominated the field. By 1889, Marco Fontana was well on his way to making Del Monte a household word. Joseph Di Giorgio became the most important man in the history of California's deciduous fruit industry.[3]

Not merely the great expansion of American industry, but also its changing character accounted for the great numbers of Italians who came to America. The introduction of additional mechanical devices and processes eliminated much of the need for industrial skill and experience and made it possible, even essential, for manufacturers and mine operators to employ cheap, unskilled labor.

In a number of industries, the late nineteenth century brought a remarkable change of personnel. After 1890, most of the miners in the Pennsylvania coalfields were Italians, Slovaks, and Poles. In the garment trades of New York, Chicago, and Baltimore, there were increasing numbers of Italians and Jews.

A single assumption ran through the forty-one volume report of the Dillingham Commission set up by Congress in 1907 to investigate the question of immigration. They concluded that the early 1880s had seen a fundamental change in the character of American immigration. Up to that time, immigration had come almost exclusively from the countries of northern and western Europe and, according to the Commission, had been largely a movement of families seeking a permanent home. Those who were part of the old immigration, the Commission claimed, "entered practically every line of activity in nearly every part of the country." Many of them became farmers. And despite the fact that a large proportion had been non-English speaking, they had "mingled freely with ... native Americans" and had therefore been quickly assimilated.[4]

Far different, however, was the Commission's view of the movement which had begun about 1883 from the countries of southern and eastern Europe. This new immigration had consisted, it declared, largely of unskilled male laborers, a large proportion of whom had come to the United States not as permanent settlers but simply as transients. Almost entirely avoiding agriculture, they flocked to the industrial centers of the East and Middle West, where they "congregated together in sections apart from native Americans and the older immigrants to such an extent that assimilation [had] been slow."

The Commission drew attention to the fact that, in the period 1899-1909, the percentage of skilled laborers among immigrants from northern and western Europe was twice as great as among those from southern and eastern Europe. This was a misleading comparison. In the period named, the proportion of unskilled laborers from northern and western Europe was low only because of the extent of competition from southern and eastern Europeans. A more accurate comparison would have been between the era of 1899–1909 and the period of 1871–1882 in which the old type of immigrants predominated. This would have shown that the older immigration had only a slightly higher proportion of skilled laborers than the new—22.9 percent as compared to 18.1 percent.[5]

Initially, a large number of Italians did intend to stay in America temporarily. These immigrants' motive was to earn and save money with which they could buy land upon their return. What must be taken into account is the number who actually did return to Italy only to make the trip back and establish a permanent residence. By the early 1900s, the number of returnees to Italy dropped significantly.[6] The overwhelming number of Italian immigrants decided to stay in America.

In either event, it is important to recognize that it was the steamship, not the shift in the source or character of immigration, that was responsible for the number of returnees among the immigrants in the post-1880 era. The Atlantic crossing was made regular, fast, and somewhat more comfortable than earlier modes of travel. British and German skilled workers began in the 1870s to shuttle back and forth across the Atlantic in response to wage movements in America and the homeland. Great numbers began to go out to the United States each spring with the intention of returning in the fall. It was the availability of a better mode of travel instead of the character of the people that accounts for the transient migration. During the pre-Civil War era of sailing ships, the trip was too hazardous and uncomfortable. Out of necessity, the trip was in one direction, since there was really no practical means to return. Since they came from isolated hilltop villages, the *contadini* had not been affected by the great economic, political, and ideological revolutions of the nineteenth century. They had not developed a consciousness of belonging to a proletariat nor even to an Italian nation. Their identification was with their own *paese* better known as *campanilismo* (sound of the village bell).

In the late nineteenth century, peasant leagues of resistance were established in various sections of Italy. Such leagues were relatively absent in the areas of the heaviest emigration. John McDonald has contended that, for the peasantry, emigration was an alternative to collective action. In those parts of Italy where there was active organization of the workers of the land to improve their conditions through unions and cooperatives, the rate of emigration was much lower than in those regions where such class solidarity was lacking.

In most of southern Italy and Sicily individualism rather than collectivism prevailed among the peasantry. But it was a family-centered individualism rather than the American version. Loyalty to the family was so strong that it excluded loyalty to a larger community or class. Both socialism, which was based on class consciousness and solidarity, and trade unionism, based on job consciousness, were foreign to this peasant mentality.

Often the Italians emigrated as a group from a particular village, clinging together in the Little Italys. Often they worked together. Once here, they recruited other *paesani* through the process of chain migration. For a variety of reasons, they became dependent upon a *paesano* who could serve as intermediary between them and America. Hence, they developed the *padrone* system. The *padrone*, or boss, served the immigrants as employment agent, banker, saloon and boarding-house keeper, and political leader.

The *padrone* system was not imported from Italy, nor was it uniquely Italian. Other national groups, such as the Greeks and Chinese, had their own versions of the *padrone*. Moreover, it was the general economic structure of the United States that was responsible for the growth of the American version of the *padrone*. The precedents for the *padrone* can be found in the colonial practice of apprenticeship and indentured service and in the practice of peonage in the South after the Civil War.

With the expansion of American industry and commerce, employers in every state of the union sought a large supply of unskilled labor. The *padrone* served as a labor agent for employers, since he could locate large numbers of laborers, first in Italy and then later here in America. Soon the *padrone* commissioned other Italians to act as his agents. When an employer needed workers, the *padrone* would contact his banker or labor agent in New York City or Philadelphia. He then would round up, organize, and ship the men to the proper destination. This was a satisfactory arrangement for both the *padrone* and the employer. For the latter, it insured the availability of a labor supply and relieved him of the responsibility of hiring an interpreter. In addition, he obtained control of the workers through the supervisory power of the *padrone*.

Through the contracts, the *padrone* charged the laborers handsome fees; a *bossatura* for the job, inflated prices for transportation and for food and supplies at the commissary, a fee for sending remittances to Italy or for writing letters, or arbitrarily lowered wages. The helplessness of the workers created many opportunities for graft and exploitation.

The *padrone* system was a common institution among the immigrants from southern and eastern Europe. What made the Italian version unique was the commissary system. As Professor Luciano Iorizzo notes, other immigrants were willing to use the boarding trains of contractors and railroads, but the Italians soon demanded their own kitchen. They clearly asserted their preference to cook and eat food suited to their Italian tastes and traditions. Moreover, they could eat cheaper this way. Italians *per capita* were able to save more money under the same conditions than any other nationality group of the time. "From a monthly salary of $35, the Italian could save $25 or more. Other immigrant groups were reported as saving $20."[7]

The Italians who worked under the *padroni* could start from New York City without any money and go to almost any destination in the United States. The Italians did not ignore the advantages present in many regions of the country. Hence, *padroni* were also active in the Midwest and West. Yet the *padrone* was an essential middleman between the immigrants and the American employers. The *padroni* played a vital role in stimulating and directing Italians to America. Travel with the *padroni* opened up new vistas. The *padroni* definitely influenced the distribution and residence patterns of the Italian immigrants.

The Italian laborer suffered extreme hardships and exploitation, often working in isolated locations on railroads and public works. At best, they labored from sunup to sundown in all kinds of weather. They were driven by slave-driving foremen who were often Irish. Foremen turned into petty tyrants, as my father can readily attest. He often recalled how the foreman would verbally abuse and taunt the workers with shouts of "dumb wops" and "dagoes." Nor was the foreman's abuse just verbal. On many occasions, the foreman would use a nearby shovel on one of the workers with whom he was displeased. The Italian worker was housed in ramshackle huts or ancient railroad cars. These were overcrowded, poorly ventilated, and unsanitary. The workers were served meager meals of pasta and stale bread. The men often found themselves owing money in order to buy supplies. All this they endured for $1.00 to $1.50 a day.[8]

Many who were shipped from New York or Chicago to God-forsaken sites in West Virginia or Wyoming never returned. An agent of the New York Society for the Protection of Italian Immigrants was sent to investigate the conditions in West Virginia. There, in isolated camps, he found Italian workers shut off from the outside world by high mountains. Many workers unfit for the work to which they had been sent under false pretenses showed visible signs of suffering. One boy of sixteen admitted to the agent that he had been beaten frequently. Fifteen dollars in carfare was invested in every laborer taken from New York, to be deducted from his wages. If the laborer attempted to leave when he found out the nature of the working conditions, he was forced to remain. Armed guards were a frequent sight. A gatling gun on a hill overlooked the labor camp. The contractors and their men carried revolvers; some rode with rifles in their hands.[9]

Italian workers might be taken to a desolate swamp or desert in Texas or Kansas and left there without work, forced to walk hundreds of miles back to the city. Or they would arrive at a job location only to find a strike in progress and be confronted by a hostile mob who denounced them as dago scabs and showered them with rocks and bullets.

Italians figured high in the toll of casualties of industrial America, of those killed or maimed by explosions, cave-ins, train accidents, and thousands of other industrial accidents. No one knows how many thousands had their American adventure end in a lonely grave.

When accidents occurred, and they were common because of the general fatigue and the lack of safety precautions, there was no compensation, and fellow workers, all underpaid and with their own obligations, would have to take up a collection for the injured worker and hope that it would last until he got well. If it did not, he often returned to work before recovery, aggravating minor illnesses into serious chronic conditions.

The laborers had few ways to resist. They had neither the capacity nor the opportunity to organize. Some Italian journalists exposed the *padrone* system, such as Secchi di Casali in

L'Echo d'Italiano and Oscar Durante in *L'Italia* published in Chicago. More often, the Italian colonies were dominated by the *prominenti* (the influentially prominent) who were many times *padrone* bankers, such as Carlo Barsotti.

The Italians found it difficult to reform themselves. Various attempts were made to destroy the *padrone* system and the general exploitation, including the efforts of the Italian government's employment bureau, the Scalabrini Fathers' *Societa San Rafaele,* and the Society for the Protection of the Italian Immigrants.

At the turn of the century, workers in mass-production industries and the garment industries were unorganized, with the exception of the small unions of the highly skilled workers. The United Garment Workers and United Textile Workers were craft unions which represented the elite of the labor force. However, they neglected the vast numbers of semiskilled and unskilled workers. The snobbery of the skilled workers, combined with ethnic differences, explains this state of affairs. The skilled workers were "native" Americans or old time immigrants (British, Irish, German). The unskilled machine workers were Italians, East European Jews, and Slavs. Both of these ethnic factors nearly created a caste system in the industrial labor force. Employers played off the various groups against each other and relied upon ethnic differences to prevent the emergence of a unified working class.

When the *contadini* were employed in the factories, a class-conscious industrial proletariat did not suddenly emerge. Rather, deeply implanted peasant values were brought by them to their work, but there was an ancient hatred of the *signori* based on their grievances and bitter experiences in Italy. Thus, an embryonic class-consciousness existed in the peasant psychology. On occasions, these emotions found an outlet in periodic uprisings of the *contadini* followed by a lapse back into apathy and indifference.

When pushed too far, the *contadini* took matters into their own hands. Although they lacked formal organization, the *paesani* in the labor gangs had a sense of solidarity based on *companilismo.* Spontaneous strikes occurred which resembled peasants' revolts. Such uprisings usually ended badly for the workers. The Italians would rise up, attacking and sometimes killing the foreman. Or they might march into the nearest town with a red flag at their head, fighting off strikebreakers, only to be beaten into submission by a sheriff's posse or the state militia. These labor revolts had little lasting effect. Sometimes they moderated the behavior of the *padroni*, but more importantly for us, they disprove the stereotype perpetuated by some historians of the Italian as a passive, docile worker willing to submit to exploitation without protest.

When an employer in Boston arbitrarily reduced by 10 percent the wages of his Italian workers, the workers, though indignant, said nothing. The same night, the workers concocted a plan of their own. The next morning, the Italian laborers reported for work as usual, with one change. The end of each worker's shovel had been cut by an inch. Their wordless declaration had been accomplished. Less money, less dirt.

More than four thousand Italian subway workers helped to dig the New York underground system. One of them, an intelligent youth named Salvatore Ninfo, organized a union among them. After he won better working conditions and higher pay for his men, construction workers elsewhere demanded the same benefits.[10] It was to be these Italians who were to participate in some of the fiercest and most important labor struggles in American history. From these struggles emerged a mature Italian-American labor movement.

American labor leaders were not sympathetic to the plight of the Italian immigrants.[11] They denounced them as *padrone* slaves, often comparing them to the Chinese coolies. By the 1890s, the American labor organizations began to agitate for restrictions upon Italian immigration, which ended in success in the 1920s.

Terrance V. Powderly of the Knights of Labor and Samuel Gompers of the A.F.L. agreed that the Italians were undercutting the American workers' standard of living, that they were unorganizable, and that their immigration should be halted. Gompers openly declared that the wrong kind of immigrants were to blame for America's labor problems. He harshly condemned the immigrant as "the type of immigrant who undermined the wage scale, who could not be organized, and who made possible the introduction of machinery that displaced workers." The A.F.L. kept out Italians and other immigrants by claiming that only the skilled worker could become a member. Other unions followed suit, like the Building and Trades, Stone Cutters, Marble Workers, and Painters Unions.[12] Curiously enough, labor leaders also said the Italians were violent and anarchistic and could not be controlled by union officials. The rank and file of the American labor movement shared these prejudices against the Italians. Especially the Irish, with whom the Italians often came in conflict over jobs, developed an intense hatred and prejudice for the "dagoes." Open physical clashes were frequent occurrences.

Labor's opposition to Italians was an expression of racial prejudice as well as economic competition. Employers and labor officials, influenced by the nativist denunciations, regarded the Italians as "black labor." Hence, they regarded Italians as non-whites. Rather than being welcomed as fellow workers, the Italians were regarded with contempt. This prejudice was to become a major obstacle to the incorporation of the Italians in the American labor movement.

To what extent the entry of southern and eastern European immigrants into industry displaced native Americans is a question which aroused considerable controversy. The Dillingham Commission's position was that, in certain industries, such as coal mining and iron and steel manufacturing, the immigrants had ousted both native Americans and older immigrant employees. It is unlikely that this occurred to any considerable extent. One reason why there were fewer native Americans and northwestern Europeans in the Pennsylvania coalfields after 1890 is that many of them were attracted to the newer mines in the Middle West. Those workers who remained had been able to move into executive and technical positions. It was unskilled labor which provided this opportunity for "native Americans" to go into skilled, white collar, and professional work.[13]

According to the Commission, the immigrant coming from the eastern and southern portions of Europe came from economically depressed countries. His original working conditions were so bad, the immigrant would be happy to accept lower wages than his counterpart—the native American.

If the immigrant was so successful in underbidding and then displacing the native competition, then a high percentage of unemployment should be found among the native workers. Statistics, however, show that unemployment was the same for both groups. If the Commission's premises were valid, where there were greater numbers of immigrants in certain parts of the country, we should also find heavier unemployment. This was not the case. The ratio of unemployed was the same in the North Atlantic States with a large immigrant population as it was in the South Atlantic States, where there was a small immigrant population. Pennsylvania, which had the highest percentage of immigrants, had the second lowest percentage of the unemployed. The highest ratio of unemployed was found in West Virginia, where the percentage of immigrants was next to the lowest.

The effect of immigration upon labor in the United States had been a readjustment of the population on the scale of occupations. The majority of native workers were engaged in farming, business, professions, and clerical work. The majority of immigrants were in the industrial sector of employment. In the course of the industrial revolution, some trades declined because of the new methods of production. In the few industries where the immigrants may have replaced the native, this was due to the younger generation declining to follow their fathers' occupations. There were many new openings for the native worker—openings that never were available to the immigrant.

The objection to the unskilled immigrant was based on the assumption that, because of his lower standard of living, he was satisfied with lower wages than the native. The factor that determined wage scales was the introduction of labor-saving machinery. It is this machinery that displaced the skilled worker for the unskilled immigrant. There was no "immigrant problem;" there was a general labor problem.

Italian immigrants could rarely find jobs for which they were trained if they did not know English. Artisans sometimes dug coal or carried bricks. Since there was a surplus of doctors, lawyers, musicians, and classical scholars in Italy, they too accompanied the *contadini* to America. Often they found their talents were unrecognized, and they were reduced to manual labor.

In time, the *prominenti* (prominent, influential) formed an elite group who published the newspapers and organized and directed the affairs of the Little Italys. To a great extent, these *prominenti* had a vested interest in the maintenance of the subordinate position of the Italian worker. Among those who resisted were socialists and anarchists who took up the cause of the embattled *braccianti*. Many of these radicals were to emerge as leaders of the Italian-American labor movement.

In the Italian immigration, one can see the so-called migration of skills. The transoceanic movement of craftsmen who came to practice their crafts and trades included marble cutters from Carrara who went to Barre, Vermont, to work in the quarries and textile workers from Piedmont who went to the silk mills of Paterson, New Jersey. From southern Italy came a significant number of tailors, shoemakers, barbers, bricklayers, stone cutters, and masons.

Because of their skills, they were able to establish themselves in more permanent employment than the *braccianti*. In addition, they came into contact with socialist and union ideas more than the *contadini*.

In many trades, there were efforts to exclude Italian workers. Unions employed high initiation fees, licensing, or other such restrictions. Reluctantly and out of necessity, unions eventually did put their prejudices aside and absorbed the Italians. If not, they were impressed with many of the Italian labor leaders and those who showed potential. Mutual aid societies evolved into labor organizations. Thus, those Italians who had skills in the American economy were incorporated into the American trade unions.

Edwin Fenton, in his study of the Italians in the skilled trades, concluded they were as willing to join unions and to support collective action as any other ethnic group.[14] By the 1880s Italians could be found in the Knights of Labor, and subsequently in increasing numbers in the AFL building trades, stone cutters', tailors', and barbers' unions. These trades accounted for only a small percentage of the Italian workers, as they did of the American labor force as a whole.

Especially after 1900, an increasing number of *braccianti* began to establish themselves in the cities and to enter urban employment. When a man's family joined him in this country, or, if he was single, when he married, he often gave up the type of job which forced him to move around the country continuously. He then looked for a job which would give his family a steadier sort of existence. Gradually a few gained entry into the factories and opened the way for others to follow. Much of this employment was still seasonal and casual. It depended upon the patronage of the *padrone*-politician, but it spared the laborers the dangers of work in the country. Moreover, it permitted them to establish a family life.

Labor extended into family life, as was the tradition in Italy. As long as the law permitted it, thousands of women and children entered the garment trade and other factory employment under sweatshop conditions. Women often took piece work in their homes.

The children of all impoverished immigrants, not only those of the Italians, were expected to help with the family's income, even when both parents went out to work. To free the mother for her job or sewing tasks, one of the daughters would mind the baby. Young sons acted as assistant lamplighters, going out at four in the morning to extinguish the gas streetlights before breakfast and school. Older boys found dozens of odd jobs to do late into the evening—running errands, delivering telegrams, shining shoes, selling newspapers.

In the clothing industry, where the sweatshop system based on subcontracting flourished, Italian women soon come to dominate the finishing of garments. The "sweating system" is the process by which ready-made clothing was manufactured in tenement houses. The materials were cut and bunched for each garment by the manufacturer. They were then distributed in large lots to contractors, each a specialist in his line. One half of the goods were made up in the contractors' factories. As to the other half, the contractor sublet his work to a "sweater," whose shop was generally one of the two larger rooms of a tenement flat, accommodating from six to fifteen employees—men, women, and children. In the other large room of the flat were living, sleeping, and cooking quarters. There were also tenement homeworkers. These immigrant men and women would receive work from a sweater to be completed at home.

Since the garment manufacturers strained to undercut one another's prices, the clothing workers fared worse than the laborers in factories and mines. Paid at piecework rates, they rarely earned more than two hundred dollars a year, and they worked extraordinarily long hours. Some girls were reported working a 108-hour week.

In many of New York's clothing factories, females outnumbered males. Both had to put in a minimum of thirteen hours a day to earn a maximum of six dollars, sometimes as little as three dollars. By the first decade of the twentieth century, Italian tailors and especially Italian girls had become an important source of labor in both the men's and women's garment industries. The Women's Trade Union League of New York tried to convince Italian women of the benefits they could get from joining the League. The Women's Mutual Benefit Society got their support by providing them with inexpensive medical insurance.

My mother did not escape this brutalizing experience. She was recruited to work in a garment factory in Newark, N.J. As a boy, I recall having to probe insistently in order to piece together the full picture of the horrible experience of immigrant labor. Mom seemed to want to put that memory behind her. Under the watchful eye of her boss, she often worked twelve- and fourteen-hour days. Paid by piece work, the workers had no time for coffee breaks or lengthy lunch periods, not that the employers would have permitted it. Mom, like thousands of others, could be replaced. In the summer, the factory, lacking proper ventilation, was oppressively hot, and in the winter, it was unbearably cold.

During the national depression of 1907, the influx of Italian shirtwaist makers coincided with a growing fad for more casual women's wear. These workers were nonunionized and willing to work part time on a piece work basis, but by the early 1900s, Italians were so active in the Journeymen Tailors' Union that they aroused the hostility of Jews and Bohemians, who were afraid that their leadership in the union was being threatened. These early Italian labor leaders set the stage for the key role that Italians would later play in the formation of the Amalgamated Clothing Workers of America.[15]

The Italian-American labor movement must be viewed in terms of the labor movement in Italy. As a result of the mass emigration, the Italian worker constituted an international proletariat working in the mines and factories in Europe, South America, and North America. The Italian labor movement was in every sense international. Ideas and leaders moved across national boundaries and oceans. Trade unions and cooperatives emerged in Italy in the second half of the nineteenth century. Much of this activity centered on the factory workers, particularly in the industrial centers of the North. But there was also a rising class consciousness among agricultural workers who organized leagues of resistance and formed cooperatives among the peasants in central and southern Italy. Since labor organizations in Italy fought for the reconstruction of society rather than just bread and butter issues, the Italian labor movement is intimately related to the history of Italian socialism.[16]

The *Risorgimento* which led to national unification was not a social but a political revolution. Since it was a movement of the upper and middle classes, the conditions of the masses remained the same. The major thrust of the Italian labor movement was to correct the major inequities of Italian society, but bitter factionalism divided the Italian revolutionaries. Their feuding absorbed as much of their energies as their fight with the monarchy or the capitalists. Mazzini, Marx, and Bakunin furnished the principal ideological notions fighting for supremacy in the Italian labor movement. These intense doctrinal disputes were transplanted to American soil, constituting a disruptive influence on American socialism. The first militants to reach America were refugees from the suppression by the Italian government that destroyed the First International in Italy at the end of the 1870s.[17]

A series of strikes swept the United States on May Day of 1886. The purpose of these strikes, in which 340,000 men participated, was to promote the cause of the eight-hour day. On the afternoon of May 3, 1886, August Spies, an anarchist editor, was addressing a meeting of strikers and strike sympathizers on a vacant lot not far from the McCormick Harvester Works in Chicago, when the police attempted to disperse the meeting. Several strikers were killed, and about twenty were wounded. The next day, many meetings of protest occurred, the most important being the one set for the evening at Haymarket Square. An orderly crowd heard the speeches of three leading anarchists. The police appeared again to disperse the meeting. This time a bomb was thrown, police were killed, and fighting broke out.

A feeling of blind rage was accompanied by a demand for victims. Efforts to find the guilty were unsuccessful. Police stations for days were filled with suspects, most of whom had no knowledge of nor any part in the bomb-throwing incident. For the lack of better scapegoats, eight anarchists, including August Spies, were arrested, tried, and convicted. Though no evidence was produced that any of the men had anything to do with the bomb, seven of the men were given death sentences, and the eighth, imprisonment for fifteen years. It was clear the men were convicted because of the opinions they held.

The trial of the Haymarket Eight was to be representative of a pattern of reaction to strikes and unions by the business establishment. The motive of the trials was to deal with actual and potential threats to their power. The standards of impartiality left much to be desired. In the Haymarket trial, no concrete evidence was produced, yet the eight were convicted.

The capture and use of the government to reinforce the business establishment's position can be seen in the Pullman strike and the passage of criminal anarchy laws. In 1894, a strike originated among the factory workers and then spread to the railway workers of George M. Pullman's model company town just south of Chicago. Railroad lawyers found it easy to persuade President Cleveland and Attorney General Richard Olney to intervene. Olney secured an injunction against the union; Cleveland followed by sending two thousand troops. Violence broke out. The effect of the government's action was to break the strike —by Olney's own admission, the goal it sought to accomplish.

Eugene Debs, head of the American Railway Union, and other union officials were tried and sentenced to jail for contempt of court in disobeying the injunction. By suggesting that a strike might be viewed as a conspiracy in restraint of trade, the government placed a powerful weapon in the hands of management for use against unions.

During such labor unrest, anarchist and socialistic ideas were making their most determined challenge to the conventional values and opinions of the day. New York State passed the first state anti-sedition law, under the heading of criminal anarchy laws. The law stated it was a criminal offense to advocate, either by speech or writing, the doctrine that organized government should be overthrown by force or violence or by assassination or any unlawful means. It was also unlawful to join any organization or attend the meeting of any organization that advocated the overthrow of the government. In 1903, Congress passed a law excluding even peaceable anarchists from entry into the country.[18]

During the 1890s, Italy was the scene of violent labor upheavals and in that respect resembled the United States. This widespread discontent created the opportunity for socialists to spread propaganda. Large numbers of both urban laborers and farm workers were enrolled in the *Fasci dei lavoratori* in Sicily. Deep resentment among the lower classes led to strikes and violence. A policy of stern suppression was advocated in 1893 by Francesco Crispi, the new Italian prime minister. This policy was applied first against the *Fasci* and then against the socialists in all of Italy. Newspapers were closed, socialist leaders were arrested, and protests were cruelly suppressed.

The increasing number of protests and demonstrations culminated in the "Four days of Milan" in May 1898. This was a bloody clash between workers and the military, resulting in the deaths of eighty to four hundred people. To avenge the "Four days of Milan," Gaetano Bresci, a silk weaver and anarchist, returned from Paterson, New Jersey, to Italy and assassinated Umberto I at Monza on July 29, 1900. Following the Milan incident, the suppression of socialists and anarchists gained momentum, with the arrest and conviction of thousands. During these years, many socialists and anarchists went into exile to France, Switzerland, Argentina, and the United States. This political emigration continued until the outbreak of World War I.[19]

By the 1890s, an Italian anarchist colony was well established in America, particularly in the industrial centers such as Paterson, New Jersey, and New York City. There were ties between the American colony and the parent movement in Italy. Every important leader visited America. These included Francesco Saverio Merlino in 1892, Pietro Gori in 1895, Enrico Malatesta in 1899, and Luigi Galleani in 1901. The latter was so important to the development of anarchism in America that "the mainstream of Italian anarchism in America might well be described as 'Galleanista.' Other leaders who visited America included men like Carlo Tresca, Giacinto Menotti Serrati, Arturo Caroti, Nicola Barbato, and Giuseppe Ciancabila."[20]

There were hundreds of other individuals whose names are unknown in Italian history but who played important roles in the Italian labor movement in the United States. These were leaders, inspired orators, effective polemicists, and dedicated idealists who aroused the Italian working class and imbued it with revolutionary spirit. It was these radical emigrès who undertook the great job of politicizing and organizing the masses of Italian workers in America.

The radical emigrès founded scores of newspapers and journals to propagandize their doctrines. These included: *L'Anarchio* (New York) in 1888; *La Questione Sociale* (Paterson) in 1895; *L'Aurora* (West Hoboken) in 1899; *Il Grido degli Oppressi* (New York) in 1892; and the socialist journals—*La Cronaca Sovversiva, Il Proletario,* and *La Parola dei Socialisti.*[21]

The Italian radicals formed discussion groups, cooperatives, libraries, and schools. They lectured widely within the Italian-American colonies. They founded the Italian Anarchist Federation and the Italian Socialist Federation of North America.

All of the ideological controversies which fragmented the Italian left were brought to America. Not only were there disputes between anarchists and socialists, but the disputes also involved anarchists and the anarcho-syndicalists, and parliamentary and revolutionary socialists.

As a result of these disputes, the radical movement in America splintered. Time, energy, and money were spent on these doctrinal issues. The radicals also brought with them an intense anticlericalism which was rooted in Italian history. In America, they waged a campaign against the churches and the capitalist system. This only resulted in increasing the conservatism of the Catholic church. Even those Italian priests imbued with the ideas of Christian democracy of Bishops Bonomelli and Scalabrini were unable to collaborate with the labor radicals whose anticlericalism was such that they were called *mangia preti* (priest eaters). In order to solve the variety of problems of American capitalist society, the anarchists advocated its complete transformation through social revolution. Italian anarchism, however, was not simply an import from Italy. Over the course of a century, the movement developed a character and thrust all of its own.

The emergence of a radical movement among the Italians inspired new fears among native Americans and added to the already existing stereotype of the bomb-throwing anarchist. American labor leaders who were tied to business unionism viewed the Italian emigrés with disdain. To their charge that the Italian was

a docile servant of the capitalists, they now added the indictment that he was a violent and uncontrollable worker.

When we compare the experiences of Italians in the United
States with those in Argentina, a country which had witnessed a
large influx of immigrants, we see that about two out of every
five organized workers in Argentina were Italians. The Italian in
Argentina was the most important single leadership element
within the labor movement. They were more active in labor
organizations and in strikes than were the Argentines.[22]

As still larger numbers of Italian immigrants came to America
after 1900, the anarchist movement continued to expand numeri-
cally and geographically. There were thousands of anarchists
from coast to coast. The largest concentrations of anarchists were
in the large cities like New York, Paterson, Boston, Chicago, San
Francisco, but there were sizable colonies in New England in
such places as Barre, Lynn, Providence, and Nedham. They were
also to be found among the cigar makers of Tampa, Florida, and
in the coal fields of western Pennsylvania, West Virginia, and
Ohio.

The growth of the movement must be attributed to the social
and economic conditions which the immigrant experienced. It is
certain that the majority of Italians who became anarchists did
so after their arrival in America.[23]

The Italian radicals exerted a significant influence upon
Italian workers. They distributed propaganda tracts, the writings
of Marx, Bakunin, and Kropotkin, as well as works of literature
and science. They organized Italian workers into dramatic clubs,
discussion groups, reading societies, and labor unions. With the
outbreak of strikes, the radicals organized the workers, published
strike bulletins, and inspired the strikers with their oratory.
Whatever class consciousness developed among the Italians was
due to the dedicated work of the radicals. Their most notable
gains were among those immigrants who had been exposed to
socialist ideas in Italy.

Most of the Italian radical leaders were from South Italy, from
Abruzzi, Campania, Calabria, and Sicily. They tended to be of
middle-class families of artisan and tradesmen origins. They had
more education than the average immigrant. Some of the radicals
received their education in seminaries before they lost their
priesthood vocation. Others were medical doctors. Among the
southerners, it was the literate craftsmen rather than the peasants
who adhered to the socialist teachings.

The radicals found considerable difficulty in breaking through
the mass of illiterate, family-centered, and provincial loyalties of

the *braccianti*. Although they might follow the radicals, they resisted conversion to Marx or Bakunin. No doubt this lack of responsiveness to socialist teachings was a source of frustration and disappointment to the radicals.

Although some of the moderate socialists worked as organizers for the craft unions among Italian shoemakers and tailors, most of the radicals regarded the AFL, with its emphasis on bread-and-butter issues, as anathema. However, the Italian socialists did contribute to the organization of the coal miners in the United Mine Workers, an industrial rather than a craft union. Recognizing the necessity of enlisting the Italian miners if the union were to be victorious, the President of the UMW used Italian organizers and Italian literature. The Italian coal miners proved themselves to be militant strikers and loyal union men; in the successful strike of 1897 in the bituminous fields, the Italians and Slavs were reported even more tenacious than the old immigrants.

The Paterson silk mills were the scene of recurring strikes in which the Italians were actively involved under the leadership of the anarchists. In 1901, Luigi Galleani led the strikers in a seizure of the mills, perhaps the first sit-down strike in American labor history. But it was with the establishment of the Industrial Workers of the World that many Italian radicals found a suitable vehicle for their labor agitation. They were attracted to the IWW because of its doctrines of the class struggle, the general strike, and One Big Union; these ideas were more compatible with their Italian experience than was the business unionism of the AFL.

Unlike the International Ladies Garment Workers Union (ILGWU), the Amalgamated Clothing Workers of America (ACWA) emerged from its beginnings as an equal partnership of Italians and Jews, and other groups as well. The Chicago clothing strike of 1910 was the first step toward the formation of the ACWA and produced such future leaders of the Amalgamated as Sidney Hillman and A.D. Marimpietri. On this occasion, where ten thousand Italian immigrants stood solidly behind thirty thousand other strikers, they were led by A. D. Marimpietri, one of the founders of the ACWA, and by Emilio Grandinetti and Giuseppe Bertelli. Grandinetti and Bertelli were editors of newspapers and used their papers to expose the exploitation of the immigrants by their bosses. Although this strike ended in failure, it led to the founding of the ACWA, which, by the end of the decade, had succeeded in completing the organization of Chicago's garment workers and established standards for wages, hours, and shop conditions in the entire industry.

On January 11, 1912, the cry "Short pay! Short pay!" echoed throughout the mills in Lawrence, Massachusetts. The employers had decided to cut wages by thirty-two cents a week—and that bought ten loaves of bread. Prior to the pay cut, the workers had already received starvation wages. Now, thousands of workers swarmed into the streets in protest. Within twenty-four hours, Lawrence was in the midst of a general strike.[24]

Within a day, Giuseppe Ettor arrived from New York City with his twenty-seven-year-old Italian-born friend, Arturo Giovannitti, a poet and labor organizer, who was described as a young Byron, with velvet jacket and ascot. Ettor was described as "a short, stocky Italian . . . with a thick shock of hair upon which a small hat sits rather jauntily. He wears a flannel shirt and a large bow for a tie. . . . He has a kindly, boyish face . . . an apparently unlimited supply of physical vitality, and a voice that is strong and resonant."[25] At twenty-four years of age, Ettor was rapidly becoming one of the most prominent labor leaders in America. Ettor was a fine orator in English, Italian, and Polish and could speak a little Yiddish and Hungarian. The Brooklyn-born fighter for the rights of working men now found himself in the middle of one of the most crucial battles in the history of labor.

To the left of the American Federation of Labor (AFL) was the militantly anticapitalist International Workers of the World (IWW). They preached the abolition of the wage-earning system and sought ownership of the means of production by the workers themselves. Though some of its members were Marxists and some were anarchists, the IWW was a native labor movement that had grown up in reaction to the often brutal labor conditions in the late 1800s and the early 1900s. That the foreign workers at Lawrence should have rallied so solidly behind the IWW was symbolic of their desperate economic plight and of their sense of being outcasts from the American promise.

In January 1912, the total union membership among the thirty thousand mill workers was less than twenty-five hundred. The AFL's local union, the United Textile Workers, had given no thought to organizing the vast majority of workers in the mill. The officers of the union had said it would be a waste of effort and money to attempt to organize Lawrence: "The settlement in Lawrence of some fifteen thousand immigrants during the period of 1905 to 1910 added to the population of that city an unassimilated and un-American element so large and so varied in its racial compositions as to make it well nigh impossible to disseminate among these people the advantages of unionism."[26] Be-

fore the Lawrence strike was to end, ten thousand Lawrence textile workers had become members of the IWW.

The Lawrence strikers were soon to see themselves fighting not
only the employers, local and state authorities, police, militia,
citizen groups, religious leaders, and the press, but also the AFL.
Here, in one of the most important strikes in labor's history, the
righteous members of the AFL were the strikebreakers. They did
not approve of this strike and actually tried to break the Lawrence strike, to no avail.

By January 15, morale was wearing thin; however, that day
was to be the most crucial in the strike. About fifteen thousand
workers, demonstrating outside of a mill, were confronted by
militiamen with fire hoses which sprayed water in the subzero
temperatures upon the workers. Now they were more united
than before.

With nearly fifteen hundred militiamen in addition to the
police and state troopers in town, Lawrence was rapidly becoming an armed camp. Ettor sought to organize the strike and
called mass meetings among the many nationalities to try to elect
strike committees from the many mills. The really interesting
thing about the Lawrence strike was the manner in which the
workers responded on an ethnic basis. When the Lawrence workers struck, it seemed as if the American "melting pot" had suddenly boiled over, for they represented twenty-five different
nationalities. The largest of the groups was the Italians. For the
most part, old stock immigrants, such as the Irish, disapproved of
the strike. The pre-Civil War immigrants were apathetic.

The Italians became the backbone of the strike and provided
an important part of the local leadership. In one of the clashes
with the police, Anna LoPezzi, a woman striker, was killed.
Tension mounted as the funeral which had been planned for
LoPezzi was banned by Colonel Sweetzer, the commander of the
militia. He issued orders to his men to shoot to kill, and not to
salute the Stars and Stripes when carried by the IWW. He was
not averse to having his men ride into picket lines on horseback, swinging clubs, or having those on foot lunge with their
bayonets into the crowds—which often included women and children. These workers, like so many others in this era of labor and
capital conflicts, were being forced back to intolerable conditions
by guns, bayonets, and clubs. The militia baited the strikers and
sought confrontation.

Businessmen and commercial interests in Lawrence made efforts to discredit the workers by blaming them for the violence
and also by deliberately framing them. This was an all too-

familiar pattern. Twenty-eight sticks of dynamite were found in three different locations in Lawrence, but it was not the work of the strikers but the businessman, John Breen. Arrested and convicted, he received a mere fine of $500. Middle-class Americans needed no convincing. The violence was the work of the strikers.

On January 30, the police charged a striker, Joseph Caruso, with the murder of Anna LoPezzi and held Ettor and Giovannitti as accessories because they had advocated picketing.

The Italian laborers organized defense committees in every large city of the United States to collect funds and to obtain publicity for the release of Ettor and Giovannitti, who were awaiting trial on the trumped-up murder charge. The strikers made this issue into a world-wide *cause célèbre.* Led by the Italians, another strike was called, and 10,000 textile workers walked out of the mills to voice their protest against the imprisonment of their former leaders. If the cause was right, the Italians could be superb in their defense of justice.

After being postponed from May, the trial finally opened on September 30. The trial itself covered the same ground as that of the inquest. Ettor and Giovannitti, who as IWW leaders had come from New York to throw themselves into the strike, were charged with inflaming men to the actual murder by a propaganda of violence.

The state of Massachusetts had to prove two things: first, that the strikers, or their sympathizers, fired the shot; and second, that a convincing connection existed between their acts and those of the strike leaders, a point involving far-reaching issues of strike leadership and responsibility. The evidence on both points proved insufficient. The man who fired the shot was not identified, although the defense produced witnesses who saw a policeman fire several shots at Mrs. LoPezzi.

The state introduced testimony concerning speeches made by Ettor and Giovannitti. This charge and the resultant line of court questioning turned the trial into a political one. The natural and intended purpose of the speeches, the district attorney argued, was an organized attack on the peace and well being of Lawrence.

Partly because Ettor's speeches were delivered in English, the brunt of the evidence was directed against him. The beliefs held by leading exponents of the Industrial Workers of the World were read into the record, and Ettor's views as an anarchist were also emphasized by the court. The defense produced witnesses who testified as to the peaceful intent of his speeches.

The strength of the defense's case rested on the testimony of the defendants themselves. Ettor revealed an amazing grasp of facts. He not only recalled day by day the events that had taken place, but even recited the words of his speeches.

"Do you remember," the prosecutor asked, "that in the police court I asked you so and so, and you replied so and so?"

"I do not," Ettor would counter. "I did say in substance what you have just read, but it was in answer to another and a subsequent question, not the one with which you seek to connect it."[27]

When the trial was all but over, Ettor and Giovannitti disregarded the advice of their counsel and made a dramatic plea for freedom. In an impassioned speech of mingled defense, persuasion, and appeal, Ettor protested against being tried for his social ideas. He said:

> If you believe that we should not go out with our views, I only ask that you will place the responsibility full on us, and say to the world that Joseph J. Ettor and Arthur Giovannitti, because of their social ideals, became murderers and murdered one of their own sister strikers, and you will by your verdict say plainly, that we should die for it.... I neither offer apology nor excuse; I ask no favors; I ask for nothing but justice in this matter.[28]

"Joseph J. Ettor, look upon the foreman, Mr. Foreman, look upon the prisoner." The two men gazed at each other.

"What say you, Mr. Foreman, upon your oath—is the prisoner guilty as charged?"

"Not guilty."[29]

This was the verdict of the jury. The jury had been made up of four carpenters, a hairdresser, a sail maker, a leather dealer, a stock fitter, a grocer, a driver, and a lamp worker. Aften ten months in jail and fifty-eight days of trial, Joseph Ettor, Arturo Giovannitti, and Joseph Caruso left the courthouse as free men.

While the trial was in progress, events of the strike were moving toward a conclusion. The strikers remained in good spirits. Ray Stannard Baker, a progressive journalist, reported that "It was the first strike I ever saw which sang...."[30] Often these songs were in the strikers' native tongue, mostly Italian.

One of the most potent strike weapons occurred out of necessity. Lawrence was in the grip of a severe winter. This made the burdens of the workers even harder to bear. With only about thirty-three cents per striker per day from relief funds, families could hardly survive. The strike committee decided to evacuate all children from Lawrence in order to save them from starvation. For the first time, outsiders could now really see the conditions which confronted the strikers. The obvious signs of poverty and suffering could not escape notice. Moreover, the repressive actions of the militia were in evidence even against these children. The children of forty strikers bound for foster homes in Philadelphia were separated from their parents at the Lawrence railway station by two hundred policemen armed with clubs. Their mothers were arrested.

As public indignation mounted, the employers capitulated on March 1, 1912. The textile companies announced wage increases. This victory was to be disturbed by another strike less than one year later. Again, Italians were to play a leading role.

With the acquittal of Ettor and Giovannitti, close to a year of titanic class struggle ended in Lawrence. In the face of all possible obstacles, an aggregation of over twenty thousand workers who spoke forty-five different tongues had given the labor movement an amazing demonstration of solidarity and fortitude. The idea so widely spread by the AFL that the foreign-born worker was unorganizable and could not be welded into an effective fighting machine was completely disproved by the miracle of Lawrence. The Lawrence strikers were the forgotten refuse of a labor movement interested only in organizing the skilled craft minority. Ignored and disdained by the AFL, these neglected, downtrodden masses, foreign-born and unskilled, had proved to the entire labor movement that they were capable of maintaining the discipline, spirit and unity of and faithfulness to unionism.[31]

During the New York strike of 1913, the Bellanca brothers, Augusto and Frank, who had recently arrived from Sicily, emerged as the most effective Italian leaders, beginning long careers in the Amalgamated Clothing Workers of America and in the Italian labor movement. They were aided by a young lawyer, Fiorello la Guardia, who exhorted the strikers with his equally broken Italian and Yiddish. Since the United Garment Workers' leadership was opposed to the dominant role of the Jews and Italians in the big cities, these groups seceded in 1914 to form the Amalgamated Clothing Workers of America.

With the emergence of the garment workers unions, the Italian labor movement had achieved maturity. Its leaders were drawn from the ranks of the socialists and radicals, but they had put aside the objective of social revolution for the more immediate goals of improving wages and working conditions. Yet they did not become simple trade unionists; they retained their idealistic vision of the cooperative society. Sharing this vision with their Jewish brethren, the garment unions became agencies of cultural and political education among the workers. In 1919,

an Italian Chamber of Labor was established in New York by the
Italian labor unions to carry out a broad program of education
and cooperation among the Italians. Unfortunately, it did not
survive the economic recession and political conflicts of the postwar years.

Paterson, New Jersey, was a cosmopolitan textile town whose
workers were Italian, German, and Irish. Men made $10.59 a
week, women made $7.17, and girls under sixteen earned $1.85.
The silk workers were the lowest paid employees of the top
twenty-five industries in the United States. Many worked fifty-
five hours a week. The dyehouses were unbearable:

> The steam is so thick you cannot see the worker opposite
> you. The atmosphere is unbearable, filled with fumes from
> bleaches, acids, and other chemicals. Floors are running with
> water. Workers in rubber boots or wooden shoes work ten,
> fourteen hours a day.[32]

On pay day, the workers came to the realization that they didn't
have enough to pay their bills.

On January 27, 1913, some eight hundred workers at the Doherty Silk Mill walked out in protest against the firings of fellow
workers. Within a month, the strike had hit the whole town. Before long, all three hundred mills were closed with twenty-five
thousand workers out on strike. Many of the strikers were
Italians. The demands included the eight-hour day, increased
wages, and better sanitary conditions. The manufacturers viewed
the strike as a virtual take-over of the industry. The strike spread
to sympathy walkouts by all the ten thousand silk workers in
New York City and Connecticut and New Jersey. The employers
refused to deal with any of the representatives of the strikers.
Moreover, they refused all efforts of conciliation.

As on other occasions, the strikers were to gain the reputation
of being violent anarchists. This became the justification for
their suppression. The strikers were being starved into submission. As the strikers grew hungrier, the police became tougher
and more arbitrary. Where there was picketing, the police would
seal off the block and sweep in on horseback from both sides.
Anybody in their way was arrested. By the end of the strike, from
fifteen hundred to three thousand strikers had been arrested and
Italians were among the five who had been killed. The city
issued an order completely suppressing freedom of speech and
assembly. Strikers were even arrested for walking toward a strike
meeting. A local newspaper critical of the tactics of the police
was raided and wrecked, and all copies of that issue were con-

fiscated and thrown on the streets. Four dealers and the editor were arrested and sentenced to one to fifteen years in prison. Paterson had its martyr in Modestino Valentino: he was killed by a detective's bullet. Twenty thousand strikers marched in his funeral procession.

The end came after twenty weeks of striking. The Paterson strike had failed. Funds had run out and the workers were hurting badly economically. During the strike, the city verged on economic ruin. In the end, it was an empty victory for the mill owners. After the strike was crushed, 10 percent of Paterson's twenty-five thousand silk workers left and never returned.

Randolph Doherty's grandfather owned the silk mill where the strike began. The company is now located in Lakeview, New Jersey. Randolph Doherty as a boy lived in the better part of Paterson. A man of means, he now lives in an exclusive section of Englewood, New Jersey, and is a member of the Arcola Country Club. He married an heiress of another textile company of which he is chairman.

Enrico Guabello's father was a mill hand and shop delegate of the IWW in Doherty & Co. As a boy, he lived in the poorer section of Paterson. From grade school, he joined his mother and father who were weavers in a mill. He now hangs around a senior citizens group in a veterans' hall. There is something disturbingly poignant about the contrast between Doherty and Guabello.

In the Paterson strike, Carlo Tresca emerged as one of the most dynamic of the Italian labor leaders, an orator of great power, and a fearless combatant. Tresca continued his career until he was assassinated in New York City on January 11, 1943. His murder has never been solved.

The First World War furthered the integration of Italians into the American economy. Labor shortages opened areas of employment that previously were closed to them. Greater numbers of Italians were working in the automobile plants of Detroit, the steel mills of Pittsburgh, and other industries as well. Wages increased with the cost of living. With the end of World War I, rising prices exceeded wage increases resulting in a series of strikes among steel workers, textile workers, and garment workers. Most of the strikes ended in failure. The Bolshevik Revolution produced a reactionary counter-tide. During the Red Scares, Italian radicals were a special target. Many were imprisoned and deported.[33] This repression dealt a major blow to the IWW and to Italian radicalism. Two victims of this repression were Nicolo Sacco and Bartolomeo Vanzetti.[34]

The Italian radical movement was dealt a series of set-backs due to internal divisions. The war and the rise of fascism in Italy attracted some of the old radicals into becoming fol-lowers of Il Duce. Edmondo Rossoni, IWW leader and editor of *Il Proletario,* for example, returned to Italy where he became Minister of Fascist Corporations. But most of the radicals took up the anti-Fascist cause which was reinforced by exiles like Vincenzo Vacirca. During the twenties and thirties, when Musso-lini was still highly regarded by the American government and the American public, they were waging a fierce warfare against the Fascist movement. This is beyond the scope of this book, but it is a story worth reading.

Communism was also a disruptive force on Italian-American radicalism, causing a cleavage in the ranks. The most idealistic and clear-eyed of the radicals, such as Carlo Tresca, fought both Fascists and Communists with impartiality.

During the 1930s Luigi Antonini was to play a key role in organizing the Italian garment workers.[35] Before World War II, he opposed the appeasement of the Fascist regime in Italy. Be-cause of his opposition to radicalism as well, he broke with the American Labor party and helped establish the Liberal party of New York. In addition to Antonini, E. Howard Molisani was to become a major labor leader in the ILGWU.

Today, American workers of Italian-American background are active in the labor unions of the country, and many of them are leaders at the local, regional, or national level. In New York City, there are at least seventy-five Italian-Americans in key leadership positions in unions.

Lawrence and Paterson were epic struggles. They rank beside Haymarket, Homestead, and the Pullman strikes in the struggle for the rights of the working man. Italians played a significant role in those two epic struggles and in the labor movement as they searched for bread, work, and justice.

6 "The Dagoes Shot Me"

One of my most vivid recollections of encountering prejudice because I was an Italian-American occurred when I was eleven years old. At that time, I attended a parochial school in Hoboken, New Jersey. The school used the town's recreation center since it did not have gym facilities of its own. Following a basketball game one afternoon, I returned to the gym, having forgotten something in my locker. As I entered the now darkened building, a light shone from the second floor. As I climbed half-way up the stairs, I overheard voices. The director contemptuously exclaimed, "Why did they bring that little dago bastard here?" I stopped in my tracks, realizing that they were talking about me. They proceeded to discuss the "dago problem" in Hoboken. As I fought to hold back the tears, I turned around and went home. "Why? What had I done?" I was to ask those questions over and over again. I was an Italian, and those men were bigots.

In the eighteenth century, it was customary for wealthy Englishmen to take the "grand tour." Accompanied by servants and tutors, they wandered about Europe, starting in France and ending up in Italy. Italy in those days was the main attraction, since the whole point of the trip was to add to a gentleman's "education."

This practice was naturally extended to the wealthy in the Colonies. It greatly increased in the nineteenth century. The notables are too many to list, but they included representatives from all fields. Dr. John Morgan, father of American medicine; John Singleton Copley, artist; Charles Bulfinch, architect; Washington Irving and Nathaniel Hawthorne, writers; George Bancroft, historian; Samuel F. B. Morse, inventor—all went to admire the Italian culture and learn more of the latest scientific and cultural advances. And there were hundreds of others.

Most of these travelers moved in exclusive, wealthy circles.

107

Many learned a great deal. But their perception of Italy and the Italians was contradictory and ambivalent. Oblivious to Italy's economic and social problems, they saw only a distorted image of the country. Many went to Italy with prejudices already formed. Some saw the moral and intellectual gradeur of Italy as exhausted and decrepit. They perceived Italy as a land of widespread poverty that had tumbled into degeneracy from the heights of Roman antiquity and Renaissance brilliance. Yet, they came to Italy to learn from such Italians as Giovanni Battista Beccaria, Gaetano Filangieri, Cesare Beccari, Giovanni Morgagni, and Giovanni Piranesi.

Some Americans based their estimates of the Italian character on preconceived notions. Few spoke Italian, and they were unable to make direct contact with the Italians as individuals. The vast majority of American visitors made no effort to meet with Italian intellectuals. They did not make friends in Italy and remained outside of Italian social life. Few probed beneath the surface of their own negative perceptions of the Italians.

Some felt that all Italians were liars and cheats. To them, dishonesty was bred in the Italian character. On one hand, they praised the work, genius, and industry of Italian civilization, and on the other, they saw Italians as lazy and indolent. Some viewed Italians as intellectually deficient, yet they acknowledged Italy's great achievements and were in Italy to learn of the latest advances in science and medicine. To others, Italians were clannish, yet they were struck by their friendly, hospitable and gregarious manner. If some Americans saw the Italian as devious, he was also open and courteous. Protestant Americans blamed the "backwardness" of Italians on Catholicism. Needless to say, Italians quickly penetrated the hypocrisy inherent in these attitudes.

Some of the most influential and important people in America visited Italy and translated their images into the mass consciousness, but before the millions of Italians began to arrive those images were to remain latent and dormant.[1]

Nativism, as John Higham notes, "is distinctively American, a product of a specific chain of events in eastern American cities in the late 1830s and early 1840s."[2] Nativism may be defined as an intense opposition to an internal minority on the grounds of its foreign origins. It has usually risen and fallen in relation to other intense kinds of national feeling. In each of the periods in which nativism was at its peak, confidence in the homogeneity of American culture broke down. In desperate efforts to rebuild national unity, men rallied against the symbols of foreignness.

Three themes dominated American nativism. The first was anti-Catholicism. Catholics were looked upon as dangerously un-American by certain elements of Protestant America. Catholic immigrants were pictured as sent here to subvert American institutions. A second theme of foreign radicalism became prominent after the 1850s. Immigrants were viewed as being prone to political revolution. To nativists, they imported subversive political doctrines. Antiradical nativism crystallized at the end of the eighteenth century.

These two nativist themes were to merge with a third. Racial nativism stated that in some special sense the United States belonged to the Anglo-Saxon race. Here was the intersection of racial attitudes with nationalistic ones, the extension to southern and eastern European nationalities of that sense of absolute difference which already divided white Americans from people of other colors.[3]

Prior to the mass immigration, Italians had formed no distinctive place either separately or collectively in the American "mind." They existed in the form of a few vague stereotypes. After 1880, they became a significant factor in the growth of American nativism.

In the 1880s and the 1890s, Italians were increasingly visible. Either urbanites or industrial workers, and usually both, the Italians played a role in American life that lent itself to nativist interpretation. They were to symbolize the social and economic ills with which the nativists generally identified the immigrants. At the turn of the century, more than 50 percent of them lived in the cities and 72 percent in New York, New Jersey, Pennsylvania, and New England.

The pattern of nativist thought changed fundamentally after 1880. Gradually and progressively, it veered toward racism. The immigrants in the post-1880 period had the distinction of having all three nativist impulses directed against them: antiradicalism, anti-Catholicism, and racial nativism.

The wave of Italian immigration came during an era of intense social and economic upheavals which "native" Americans did not understand. The development of slums and a variety of social problems coincided with an increasingly urbanized America. Increasingly, industrialization led to millions of skilled and unskilled workers crowding into the cities. Monopolies hit the farmer first and hardest. Rural America no longer promised a living. America had long supported the belief in upward mobility. With increasing change, middle-class reformers saw the influx of immigrants as polarizing American society. In their minds, the immigrants were linked in some way with every conceivable problem.[4]

Richard Hofstadter has observed:

> Up to 1870, the United States was a nation with a rather broad diffusion of wealth, status, and power, in which the man of moderate means, especially in the small communities, could command much deference and exert influence—the small merchant or manufacturer, the distinguished lawyer, editor, or preacher of local eminence in an age in which local eminence mattered a great deal.[5]

All this was to change with rapid industrialization and urbanization and the emergence of the corporation as the dominant form of enterprise. The old society in America was transformed. The distribution of power and prestige was revolutionized. The newly rich, the masters of the great enterprises, were by-passing the men of the Mugwump type—the old gentry, the merchants, small manufacturers, the professional men, the leaders of an earlier period. In an economic sense, they did not become poorer; they were being surpassed in status and influence by the newly rich. This was the basis of their reformism. They and their sons were to form the backbone of reformism in the late 1890s and early 1900s.[6]

Richard Hofstadter notes:

> In a score of cities and hundreds of towns ... the old-family college-educated class that had deep ancestral roots in local communities and often owned family businesses, that had traditions of political leadership, belonged to patriotic societies and the best clubs ... were being overshadowed and edged aside in the making of basic political and economic decisions. In their personal careers, as in their community activities, they found themselves checked, hampered, and overridden by the agents of the new corporations, the corrupters of legislatures, the buyers of franchises, the allies of the political bosses.[7]

As a result, they sought to rewrite the rules of the game in order to put themselves back in the economic and social race. But their reformism for the most part was not going to include the disadvantaged in society—the immigrants. The typical Progressive and the typical immigrant were immensely different, and the gulf between them was not usually bridged. The immigrant could not respond to the Progressive's call for rapid Americanization. Moreover, the immigrant looked to politics not for the realization of high ideals, but for concrete and personal goals. He sought these gains through personal relationships of which the political boss was to become master. The immigrant was driven from the ranks of the Progressives by the strident racism that all too frequently characterized their thought and actions.

These reformers fixed upon the immigrants in general, and the Italians in particular, as the major source of social disorders. In discovering the immigrant problem, the social critics in their traditional assault on immigrants as a foreign enemy linked the issue of assimilation with the broad issues of the day. Consequently, they laid the basis for a more ugly form of nativism. Nativism emerged in the mid-1880s when the movement to redeem the cities became an organized crusade.

To nativist reformers, the Italian immigrants were the source of the squalor and corruption of the cities. To workmen, they were a threat to their livelihood. Militant Protestants saw them as tools of Rome. Thomas Nixon Carver, a conservative economist, blamed them for causing the widening gulf between capital and labor. *The Nation* attributed the deep agrarian unrest to the "peasants fresh from Europe." The major strikes of the period evoked references to dangerous foreign radicals who menaced orderly freedom.[8]

"Native" workingmen were increasingly convinced that immigration was hurting their trade. While economic stresses in the mid-1880s encouraged a fear of immigrant competition, the questions remain: Why did the issue arise during and after so short-lived a depression? Were workers responding to attitudes that went beyond their job consciousness?

To the workers, the immigrants seemed both symbols and agents of the widening gulf between capital and labor. The hatred of them was a hatred of the corporation. They perceived the corporate magnates as trying "to degrade native labor by the introduction" of a class of subhumans.[9]

In the coalfields of western Pennsylvania, the Italian immigrants ran a gamut of indignities and ostracisms. They were, as John Higham observes, "abused in public and isolated in private, cuffed in the works and pelted on the streets, fined and imprisoned on the smallest pretext, cheated of their wages, and crowded by the score into converted barns and tumble down shanties that served as boarding houses."[10]

One group of one hundred fifty Italian laborers was hired by the Armstrong Coal Works in 1874. They were met by riots and armed attacks in which several were killed and the rest were driven from the mines.

In 1884, the Knights of Labor brought the case of the union to

Congress. There, sympathetic legislators repeated the charge that monopolists were shipping from Italy, "as so many cattle, large numbers of degraded, ignorant, brutal . . . foreign serfs"[11] to replace American citizens.

Attacks against Italian-Americans were particularly evident in the writings of Irish-Americans of the 1880s. "The Italian," the Irish-American critic noted, "was all too ready to ask for public assistance." The absence of the "manly qualities," separated Italian immigrants from others in America.[12]

The Haymarket riot in 1886 was to convince Americans that immigration, radicalism, and lawlessness were parts of the same whole. One month after the Haymarket incident, Federico Villarosa of Vicksburg, Mississippi, was lynched on suspicion of having violated a ten-year-old girl.

During the 1880s, the American press often associated the south Italians with criminality and a lowering of the standard of living. In the *North American Review* of 1888, Terrence V. Powderly, president of the Knights of Labor, argued that the immigrants were semibarbarous. "Anti-foreign sentiment filtered through a specific ethnic stereotype when Italians were involved; for in American eyes they bore the mark of Cain. They suggested the stiletto, the Mafia, the deed of impassioned violence."[13] The *Baltimore News* noted, "The disposition to assassinate in revenge for a fancied wrong is a marked trait in the character of this impulsive and inexorable race." The press was quick to point out the nationality of every incident involving an Italian. The most trivial fracas caused a headline on the "Italian Vendetta."[14]

On March 5, 1888, the *Buffalo Courier* reported: "Captain Kilroy of the first precinct sent consternation into the Italian colony last night in the persons of forty-two stalwart bluecoats who were ordered to bring in all the male Dago [sic] that looked as if they carried knives." The paper went on to report that 325 swarthy foreigners were taken. The end result was that two knives were confiscated by the police. To many, this was proof that the Italians were devious.

As the decade of the 1880s closed, an initial distrust born out of contact with different cultures swelled into a pressing sense of menace, into hatred and into violence. Italians in the 1890s and beyond were viewed as a dangerous class. They were a class hostile to the nation's institutions or to its best interests. The rapid increase in their numbers called forth the most dismal forecasts from Americans. Individually and collectively, Italians were perceived by many as a dangerous people. The press accounts and descriptions added that Italians were lazy, filthy, cruel, ferocious, and bloodthirsty.[15] As one daily noted, "No epithet is too insulting to apply to the 'dago.' " Iorizzo and Mondello conclude:

It remained for Francis A. Walker, the president of Massachusetts Institute of Technology and a prominent economist, to give academic weight to these fears and to translate them into a comprehensive sociological treatise which seemed to point irrefutably to the demise of the American race should the immigration from southern and eastern Europe go unchecked. Reversing the older Darwinian assumption of emigration as the selective process through which only the most industrious Europeans crossed the Atlantic, Walker argued in 1891 that only the unfit were now moving to America. The native-American population, he warned, was declining, for Americans preferred to have smaller families rather than accept the immigrants' lower living standards. The "indiscriminate hospitality" which the generous Republic had extended to Europeans through its liberal immigration policies had to be brought to an end for the bulwark of democracy was under siege from "an invasion in comparison with which the invasions under which Rome fell were no more than a series of excursion parties."[16]

On June 16, 1892, four Italians were lynched near Seattle, Kings County, in Washington. Six months later, a group of Indians lynched an Italian on December 21, 1892, near Guthrie, Oklahoma. The negative image of Italians was not confined to "old stock" white Americans. The images of Italians held by blacks from 1880 to 1900 were also negative ones. During this era blacks were hostile to the Italian immigrants, viewing them as criminals and economic competitors both in northern urban areas and southern farms. Typical was the black newspaper, *The Detroit Plaindealer,* which, in its May 29, 1891, issue was certain that "the Italian . . . does not make a good American."[17] On June 26, 1891, the same paper noted, "Give the Afro-American a quarter of a century more to grow in, and the question will not be what shall we do with him, but what shall we do with the Italian and other undesirable foreigners, who are pouring into this country in such large numbers."[18] Similar views were expressed in the *Washington Colored American,* which dismissed the Italian as a "Dago" and a "periputetic [sic] organ grinder."[19]

An ominous article was to appear in the *Popular Science Monthly* of December 1890. The article, entitled, "What Shall We Do with the Dago?" cited a grave threat to all Americans by the stiletto-carrying Dagoes who delighted in using their knives "to lop off another Dago's finger or ear, or to slash another's cheek." What was to be done with the "Dagoes" was to be answered in New Orleans, Louisiana.

The negative stereotypes of Italian immigrants conveyed by the American press and created by them were also in evidence in the New Orleans press. A study of this subject by Anthony Margavio indicates that "in the 1880–1882 period, 78 percent of the articles reported crime and misconduct"[20] of Italians.

On October 15, 1890, the New Orleans superintendent of police, David C. Hennessey, a detective since the early 1870s, was ambushed and killed by five men. In a dying declaration, the chief proclaimed: "The Dagoes shot me ... the Dagoes did it." But when asked specifically who had done it, "he shook his head from side to side in a negative way." None of the witnesses could identify any of the assassins.

Armed with Hennessey's statement, Mayor Shakespeare called out the entire police force "to arrest every Italian you come across." Forty were arrested that day. One hundred Italians were arrested in the next few days. People were convinced the murderers came from the Sicilian ghetto. Describing the jailed suspects, the *Times-Democrat* reported:

> The little jail was crowded with Sicilians, whose low, repulsive countenances, and slavery attire, proclaimed their brutal features. Many of those captured had large sums of money in their possession, but to all inquiries relative to themselves or where they had got the money came the invariable answer that they could not speak English.[21]

All but nineteen were subsequently released. Ten were accused of plotting Hennessey's murder and nine of committing it. Mayor Joseph Shakespeare announced that "the evidence collected by the police department shows beyond a doubt that he [Hennessey] was the victim of Sicilian vengeance...." Meanwhile, the jail guards beat the prisoners while the prosecution requested a severance and never attempted to prove the State's case against the remaining ten.

It is interesting to note that many of the names of the accused were typically Albanian (Matranga, Barbato, Schiro, etc.). They can be traced to the village of Piana dei Greci (Piana degli Albanesi) a suburb of Palermo founded at the end of the fifteenth century by a number of Albanians fleeing the Turks. To this day, the population retains its Albanian customs, language, and Uniate Catholicism.

The trial seemed to offer to Americans a clear-cut confrontation between a society based on law and a society rooted in evil.

It lasted from February 27 to March 13. The defense attorney tried to prove that none of the accused was in the vicinity of the shooting. The prosecution produced a total of sixty-seven witnesses. The trial resulted in the State abandoning its case against Bastino Incardona, the trial judge instructing the jury to acquit Charles Matranga for lack of evidence, and the jury bringing a verdict of "not guilty" with respect to Antonio Bagnetto, J. P. Macheca, Antonio Marchese, and Aspero Marchese.[22]

Of the eleven victims, three had been tried and acquitted, three had their trial end in a hung jury, and five had not yet had their day in court (James Caruso, Loretto Comitez, Rocco Geracci, Frank Romero, and Carlo Traina). While the Italian colony celebrated, people in another part of town denounced the verdict and grew angrier by the minute.

On the day after the jury gave its verdict, the *Times-Democrat* announced: "All good citizens are invited to attend a mass meeting on Saturday, March 14, at 10 o'clock A.M., at Clay's Statue, to take steps to remedy the failure of justice in the Hennessey case. Come prepared for action." The paper listed the names of prominent citizens who endorsed the meeting.

On the next morning, March 14, 1891, a mob of 6,000 to 8,000 people, led by prominent citizens, descended on the parish jail to get the "Dagoes." While state and local law officers, as well as the governor, who was in the city at the time, stood by and did nothing, the mob hanged two of the suspects from lampposts, and lined nine of them up in front of the prison wall and blasted their bodies with rifles, pistols and shotguns, taking less than twenty minutes for their grim work. Of those murdered, three were Italian subjects and the others were immigrants who had become naturalized Americans or had declared their intentions of becoming citizens.[23] The eleventh Italian, whom the mob shot and then hanged while he was still alive, was in jail for some petty crime. The largest mass lynching in American history was completed. Within four hours of the lynching, the *New Orleans Daily States* noted:

> Citizens of New Orleans, you have in one righteous upheaval, in one fateful gust of mighty wrath, vindicated your laws, heretofore, desecrated and trampled under foot by oath-bound aliens who had thought to substitute Murder for Justice and the suborner's gold for the freeman's honest verdict. Your vengance is consecrated in the forfeited blood of the assassins.

News of the violence reverberated around the country and beyond. Newspapers in Louisiana and throughout the South sanctioned and justified the murders. Theodore Roosevelt considered the mob's action "rather a good thing" and said so at a dinner party with "various Dago diplomats . . . all much wrought up by the lynching."

The *New York Times,* in editorials of March 16 and 17, 1891, seemed to justify the activities in New Orleans, noting, "Those sneaking and cowardly Sicilians, the descendants of bandits and assassins, who have transported to this country the lawless passions, the cut throat practices, and the oath bound societies of their native country, are to us a pest without mitigation." The following day they asserted that "the Lynch Law was the only course open to the people of New Orleans. . . ."

The reaction of the Afro-American press to the incident in New Orleans is summarized by Arnold Shankman:

> In the South, lynching was a form of punishment usually reserved for blacks. Thus, Afro-Americans paid attention when eleven white men were hanged. . . . As might be expected, news of the violence engendered some sympathy for the Sicilian newcomers and modified somewhat their image as law-breakers. The Richmond Planet, unable to shake the view that Sicilians were the "scum of Italy," claimed that, if the Mafia really existed, "it should really be stamped out, but it can and should be done according to the forms of law." What was surprising was that the lynching did so little to rehabilitate Sicilians in the eyes of black editors.[24]

In the ensuing weeks, the national press circulated reports of Italian immigrants riddling an American flag with bullets. A rumor arose that armed uniformed Italians were drilling in New York. One "patriotic" society demanded war if Italy continued shipping criminals to the United States. Outraged Italians gathered in angry demonstrations in Pittsburgh, Philadelphia, New York, and Kansas City. These fears were heightened when jingoism intruded upon an internal episode, transforming it into a nationwide commotion and a diplomatic episode. Italy sought redress for the victims' families and punishment of the mob that murdered the men. Secretary of State James G. Blaine treated the plea cavalierly, whereupon Italy abruptly recalled her minister in Washington.

Despite the threats of war, cooler minds prevailed. President Benjamin Harrison could find no constitutional means empowering the federal courts to take jurisdiction and prosecute the leaders of the mob. In his annual message in 1891, Harrison called the slaughter "a most deplorable and discreditable incident, an offense against law and humanity" and apologized to the Italian government. This was followed by an indemnity of $25,000 which was to be divided among the families of the eighteen victims. In the final analysis, public sentiment across the nation leaned to the view that justice had triumphed—in the streets, if not the courts. The questions remain: Why did this massacre occur? Was there something more than these known events? Who were the Italians of Louisiana?

There was a small Italian colony in Louisiana between 1800 and 1850. The evidence seems to indicate that they met with little discrimination. It is certain that at least the New Orleans Creoles had no qualms about allowing Italians to be buried alongside persons of French and Spanish blood in the city's oldest cemetery, for more than one hundred of the tombstones in the "Old Saint Louis" cemetery have Italian names on them.

As early as 1850, thirty years before the start of mass immigration, Louisiana led all other states in attracting Italian settlers. Census totals show an increase in foreign born from 2,527 in 1880 to 20,233 in 1910. Ninety-three percent of the Italians in New Orleans were Sicilian. By 1910, New Orleans had a larger proportion of Italian inhabitants than any other American city. The majority of these Italians were Sicilians. Of the 13,090 immigrants admitted through the Port of New Orleans in 1891 and 1892, 43.1 percent were Italians.

There is a connection between Italian trade routes and Italian immigration to Louisiana. Mediterranean ports were destinations of Louisiana shipping. New Orleans was a center for distribution for the Midwest.

> The citrus fruit trade centered in Sicily, hence there was a long tradition of commercial transactions between the island and New Orleans. In addition to this history of trade with Mediterranean ports, the ethnic make-up of the New Orleans business community began to reflect this contact.... The substantial Italian colony which grew in this city before the Civil War centered around the fruit trade. Italians not only imported and distributed the citrus fruit, but they also unloaded the ships and peddled the fruit through the city and surrounding suburbs.[25]

Italians were sought by Louisiana planters as substitutes for black laborers, and as "docile" whites, whose presence and, most importantly, whose votes could be used to keep the Negro Radical Reconstructionists in place. Roger Shugg has shown that in Louisiana the proportion of land controlled by plantations doubled (from 31.29 percent to 68.21 percent) between 1860 and 1880.[26] Undoubtedly, the hardships of the reconstruction era

brought some changes in land ownership, but they did not dis-
rupt the traditional Southern pattern of large plantations. The
result was that the rural parishes, where blacks composed as
much as 90 percent of the population, were literally battle-
grounds.

If the gentry expected the Italian to be a panacea for their
racist quagmire, they were quickly disappointed. Cunningham
has described the situation:

> In Louisiana lived some foreigners, however, whose character,
> language, and heritage set them apart, and to whom Demo-
> cratic demogogy did not have the same appeal as it did to
> native white Louisianans.... In the sugar cane fields, Italians
> performed tasks which native whites considered as suitable only
> for Negroes. Apparently the newcomers were not so sensitive
> about color that they could not begin at the bottom and work
> up. Their comparative lack of prejudice and their economic
> status fitted them for Populism.... Thus many of the Italians
> were in a predicament. They could find sustenance and success
> only by disregarding the southern mores which made so much
> of racial background. Native whites generally classed them with
> Negroes, because they did what the whites looked upon as
> Negroes' work.[27]

In addition, the Italian immigrant was unsuitable in the
gentry's scheme of perceptions. Being adapted to a more modest
standard of living, he neglected to patronize the "company store"
or accept credit on the scale which characterized other laboring
groups. And, unlike their *compari* in other sections of America,
the immigrants in rural Louisiana preferred investments in land
to remittances. The profits to be made were enormous, and his
previous economic incorporation provided him with the specialized knowledge necessary to succeed in the garden produce
and, particularly, fruit culture. Iorizzo and Mondello report
profits of $500 to $1,000 per acre in the strawberry fields of
Tangipohoa parish.[28]

The profits from the agricultural sector made the Italian
presence felt in New Orleans by the 1880s. Starting as street
peddlers of their garden produce, Italo-American entrepreneurs
developed the fruit business to the point where the importation
of fruits took on prime economic significance for the port. Native whites were, in the words of the *Picayune,* "amazed" and
"suspicious" at the "phenomenal growth" in the industry after
the arrival of the Italians.[29] The existence of an "Italian" industry within the city provided the opportunity for later immigrants to obtain jobs as longshoremen (within America, a his-

torically "ethnic" industry; and within New Orleans, a traditionally Negro occupation) and traders.

New Orleans was a city which functioned more than any other
in America in a manner the Italian could understand, being an
administrative and cultural center rather than an industrial one.
This economic opening in New Orleans allowed immigrants to
opt for their already expressed preference for urban environments. This concentration in agriculture, stevedoring, and, for
the lucky few, commerce brought the immigrant into conflict
with the powerful and entrenched forces of the Crescent City. It
also produced an employment distribution (for males ten years
and older) totally unlike that of Italians in other states. This may
be seen in the following statistics:[30]

Occupation	Percent		
	California	New York	Louisiana
Agriculture	33.8	1.0	43.1
Professions	1.4	1.7	.6
Domestics (laborers)	25.6	48.5	20.0
Transport and trade	16.5	19.4	24.9
Manufacturing and mining	22.7	29.4	11.4

There was a concentration of the Italian-American working
force within highly organized activities (plantation agriculture,
stevedoring, etc.) that required the *padrone* middle man. Conflicts between groups over whose clients would be employed are
inevitable in such situations. One such on-going confrontation
during the 1880s was between the Matranga group (representing
Sicilians) and the faction led by the Provenzano brothers (representing Neopolitans), which was the direct cause of Hennessey's
murder—in the official opinion.[31]

However, before attempting to discuss the events surrounding
the shooting and the subsequent lynching, it is necessary to return to 1877 and explore the crystallization of the local political
situation in ethnic and class terms. The watershed year in post-
bellum Louisiana politics was 1877, the date when Louisiana
was relieved of military occupation and returned to the Bourbon
Democrats as a result of the "compromise" of the preceding year.

The Radical Republican machine was smashed; it had relied
upon military force in the countryside and the "dreaded" Metropolitan Police in New Orleans to maintain order. Just as significantly, the Republican defeat doomed the aspirations of two
ethnic groups, German-Americans and Irish-Americans, which
had come to power with the Union victory and to riches during
the corrupt occupation. Former Radical Governor Henry War-

moth recognized this ethnic element in his biography; so did the Bourbon Democrats, the white Southerners.[32]

With "Republicanism" dead, Irish-Americans, who were hardly secure in their American identity, joined the old Whig faction of liberal Democrats. These were willing to foreswear a measure of racial bigotry directed against the black in the interests of business, in holding on to power in the city through the Choctaw Club, the urban machine *par excellence*.[33] The Choctaw Club exercised power through its police and, typically for the day, a series of private detective agencies capable of raising *ad hoc* strong-arm squads. Equally typical of the period was a rampant corruption, with the police in the forefront controlling prostitution and gambling "as scientifically as a biologist does a bacteria culture."[34]

The Bourbon Democrats, uneasy allies of the Choctaw Club, controlled the plantation parishes and represented the rural elite and middle class. The support of the Choctaw Club was vital to the rural Democrats. Whereas their own constituencies were predominately black, the city with its white majority provided the swing vote, particularly on the vital issue of the day, the disenfranchisement of the negro voter.

The coming of the Italian immigrant and the rise of the Populists, who appealed to the rural poor and the immigrant population, further muddied the waters. At least one scholar has viewed "the Italian issue" as the lynchpin of contemporary Louisiana politics.[35] The Bourbon Democrats feared the Italian-American block would support the Populists or the Choctaw Club. This would further reinforce that club's tendency to dominate state affairs and to favor urban/industrial issues at the expense of agrarian conservatism. The Choctaw Club membership was at odds on how to prevent the immigrant from joining the Populists, thus weakening their urban hegemony.

Events reached a climax in 1890. In that year, Senator Henry Cabot Lodge had introduced the "force bill," which was to place federal supervision over registration and voting into law, "arousing the ire of white Southerners and making them conscious of their minority status in the Union." The Populists were threatening to gain control over the state legislature and making overtures for a fusion ticket with the Republicans. The Bourbon Democrats and the Choctaw Club were locked in a bitter battle over the abolition of the state lottery (which the club controlled and utilized as a patronage and fund-raising facility).

Violence was in the air. The White League and the Knights of the White Camellia were again attempting to suppress opposition to the Democrats and to force the Choctaw Club to endorse "white supremacy." (The last time the League and the Knights fought the Metropolitan Police of the club in 1874 there were at least 27 dead and 105 hospitalized in New Orleans alone.) [36] The Italian-American community was in the middle:

> In the midst of the "force bill" crisis, the lottery problem, and the Populist onslaught, the Italians were not behaving in a manner pleasing to white supremacists. By 1890, a large number of the Italians of New Orleans, illiterate and unable to speak the English language, had not been assimilated into Southern culture nor, for that matter, into American culture. Senator Henry Cabot Lodge, the sponsor of the "force bill," pointed this out in a speech supporting a restrictive immigration bill he introduced in 1896. Lodge said that Italians had not begun to be absorbed in the "melting pot." White Democrats of Louisiana, no doubt, could have said the same thing: Italians were not assimilating themselves into the culture of white Southerners.[37]

In the way of the unification of southern whites under the banner of "white supremacy," stood the Italian immigrant. They were a white group that gladly performed Negro jobs, a community that built the fruit industry and dominated the waterfront, a bloc of voters who tended to side with the Populists and Negroes, and, most galling of all, a people who preferred their own customs, language, and traditions and who paid no lipservice to southern "honor" and "tradition."

Traditionally, the suppression of immigrant populations within American cities has fallen to the police. It is impossible to determine if Chief Hennessey was given such instructions from the bosses at the Choctaw Club. What is known is that the club wanted the Sicilian quarter brought into "neat and clean and well-advised" subserviency.[38] Hennessey would have been the logical choice, since he had served the interests of the Irish-American politicos and bosses of the Choctaw all his adult life.

Hennessey was the only son of a member of the Union Army that occupied Louisiana, who stayed on as a member of the hated Metropolitan Police and who was the personal guard for Mayor Godfrey Weitzel. When his father was killed in a saloon in 1867 (his father's killer was shot down two years later in "vendetta" fashion on the steps of the District Court), young Hennessey, although only nine at the time, was accepted as a "messenger" for the head of the Metropolitans. His cousin, Mike, joined the force at the same time. "Dave was the typical policeman of the old regime, a man of iron nerves, implacable, unscrupulous, who would have been what we nowadays call a 'gangster,' if he had not happened to line up on the side of law and order."[39]

Was Hennessey on the side of "law and order"? The same evidence that is marshalled against the entire Sicilian community to prove the existence of the Mafia is present in the life of one Irish-American stalwart. He was so closely associated with the Irish-American leadership of Choctaw that when, in 1875, the entire police force was dismissed to allow the new chief to pick his own men, he was one of two exceptions, the other being the former head of the department. And, in 1876, when the radical police were disbanded, he was again one of the chosen survivors. In 1878, having killed a man in a barroom brawl, he was forced to retire temporarily. (His cousin Mike, who was also tried and acquitted in the crime, left the city for Houston, where he "fell victim to an assassin's bullet.")

In the same year, he joined the Farrell police, a private police force for the Farrell political machine. (As late as 1896 Bourbon Democrats would exclaim, "There are two too many Farrells" in the party.[40]) In 1885, he went into partnership with still another former Chief of Police, T. N. Boylan, in still another private police force. Three years later he was picked to head the city's police. From what is known of city police and private police establishments of the era (not to mention Irish-American political machines), from the rumors concerning Hennessey himself, and from the history of New Orleans, it is difficult to view this man as a guardian of "law and order."[41] He must be likened to Becker in New York, Ames in Minneapolis, or McClane in San Francisco, all his contemporaries, who used the police to organize criminal activity for personal profit and political power.[42]

Perhaps the clearest indication that exists of the dynamics of the situation in New Orleans in 1890 is the chief's involvement with Joe and Pete Provenzano. Hennessey had practically invented the Mafia in New Orleans. There was a good deal of competition for handling ships' cargoes between the Matranga and Provenzano groups. Hennessey had allied himself with the Provenzano faction, which had lost out to the Matrangas.[43] In fact, on May 1, 1890, the Provenzano group attempted to murder the Matranga brothers. While six of the Neopolitans were tried and found guilty, an interesting feature of the trial was the large number of police officers appearing for the defense (including attesting to the convicted men's alibis). This was interesting enough for a grand jury to investigate the police involvement. The conviction, nevertheless, was overturned, and a new trial was to be convened beginning on October 22. Moreover, Hennessey was reportedly ready to testify on behalf of the defense, "to go on the stand himself...."

If the Matrangas were Mafia, what, then, were the Matrangas' competitors, the Provenzanos? If both were Mafia, what was a "law and order" man doing associating with the Provenzanos? How could *his* Mafia help the defense of alleged members of that organization? Presumably, those without official protection are Mafia, those with it are police, the legal guardians of society.

When Hennessey was murdered just one week before he was to testify on behalf of the Provenzanos, it was clear proof that the Mafia did it. The Provenzanos provided the final evidence, lest any doubts remained, that their dear friend was a Mafia victim. They produced a blackmail letter, supposedly from the Matrangas, that they had received several years before, which demanded payment, "if you don't want to be done up by the Mafia." (Actually, the payees described the Matrangas as "a branch of the Mafia, known as the Stoppaghiera"; and, of course, the alleged blackmailers maintained that they too had received a threat from the Mafia, and the Mafia resided with the Provenzanos.)

Numerous historians have taken this *Pirates of Penzance* farce at face value, Coxe pronouncing the consensus thusly: "The significance of the letter lay in the fact that it revealed the presence of the Mafia in New Orleans and demonstrated some of the methods of the oath-bound organization. The letter showed that the society was engaged in blackmailing, in murdering, and in other infamies."[44]

The view of the incident held by the official "historians," Coxe, Kendall, and Karlin ("official" insofar as their works have been accepted at face value by government committees) is enlightening as an example of the intellectuals' defense of societal beliefs. Even ignoring the derogatory adjectives prefixed to describe the Italians in these histories, which cannot but be interpreted as an indication of that piquant southern custom, racism, the genteel sensibilities of these scholars preclude their mentioning, let alone commenting upon, significant facts. While every possible crime of the Italo-American community is recalled and placed within that special history which is Mafia mythology, only one mentions Hennessey's connection with the Red-light Club, "an organization of rather doubtful reputation," which was, in fact, a whorehouse in which Hennessey had held an interest ever since his days with the Boylan agency. The Boylan "detectives" were guards at this establishment, and the agent on duty the night of the killing was the second person on the scene. Nor do any of the other historians mention the proximity of the club to Hennessey's home, "in a disreputable part of town," for, as the chief explained it, his reason for remaining in this quarter was his aged mother's preferences for the old neighborhood and old friends. (Hennessey's defense for his involvement with Provanzanos was that they too were members of the club.) [45]

Nor do any of the official historians elaborate upon the membership of the two committees formed to deal with the "Italian problem." The first committee was formed immediately after the shooting to "devise ways and means of effecting the arrest of the assassins." This "Committee of Fifty" (in fact, there were eighty-three members), in Kendall's opinion,

> ... seems somehow to have identified itself with that extra-ordinary "special police" which bobs up in the history of New Orleans whenever there is any serious situation to handle, whether political or criminal, about which so little is known definitely, but which seems to have been a continuer of the White League of the Reconstruction era. . . . [46]

Kendall is correct in identifying the connection between the Committee and the "special police," though the link need hardly be supposed, for no fewer than three heads of private police forces were among its members (including Thomas N. Boylan, Hennessey's former partner; General A. S. Badger; and Walter Flower) . The Committee's activities ranged from sitting in upon grand jury deliberations to the hiring of Pinkerton men to terrorize the defendants.

What remains inexplicable is Kendall's contention that the Committee and the "special police" were part of the "White League." First, the 83 members were a cross section of the establishment, including Jews from the Harmony Club, a "Hebrew crew (S. Hernsheim, B. F. Eshleman, etc.) , Hispanics, Irish-Americans, southern whites, and Franco-American members of the planter aristocracy." Second, the "special police" and the "White League" were opposite sides of the same coin; if one had the "White League," there was no need for "special police."

Kendall's rationale is made somewhat clearer when he maintains that the Committee of Fifty "was as much responsible as anything" for the subsequent lynching. The *ad hoc posse* of 61 men who signed the advertisement inviting the populace to "come prepared for action" bears little in common with the committee.[47] This latter band of justice seekers shared only five members in common with the committee: Edgar Farrar, J. L. McLean, S. P. Walmsley, H. D. Bruns, and George Denegre. Eth-

nically, some Jewish businessmen, Irish-American politicians
and leaders of the "private police," and the Hispanics have disappeared, for this was in essence the list of patrons who supported
the "White League," the aristocracy of Bourbon Democracy.
(Farrar, "foremost among outspoken white supremacists and
leaders of the disfranchisement movement in Louisiana," was
the titular head of the Bourbon wing of the party).[48]

Those who composed the jury of Judge Lynch were led by
William S. Parkerson, acknowledged leader of the "White
League" in Orleans Parish. The organization of this quasi-group
is clear due to Parkerson's pride in his achievement in killing
the eleven "reptiles." Returning home after the verdict, he found
a large crowd awaiting him. This delegation was composed of
citizens far beyond Parkerson's station, including some "old
enough to be my grandfather," who "told me they had come to
ask me to take some measure to right it."

During an organizational meeting the same night, he was continually "appealed to," until he finally consented to lead the
mob. These sober men of position appealed to a man who had
made himself respected for his defense of Southern tradition,
fully conforming to the honor that would have been expected of
a Southern gentleman.

Parkerson's clients were the aristocracy, his followers bound by
an instrumental friendship. To read his statements is to be impressed with the formalized relationships that existed between
his clients (who composed the first meeting) and friends (who
attended the evening session) and himself—it could very well be
a Hollywood stereotype of the Mafia. And the same evidence
which the official historians present to prove the existence of the
Mafia is presented by Parkerson. The secret meetings, the signals,
the "typical weapons" (in this case 150 Winchester repeaters,
kept at a friend's rooms, without which one could not be admitted to the "core's" private execution within the prison
grounds), the appeals to honor and friendship, and, foremost,
the ever present consciousness of their acts as a defense of their
world and its relations.

Time and time again, violence struck at Italians in the 1890s.
Two major incidents preceded the mass lynching in New Orleans. In 1891, a wild rumor that drunken Italian laborers had
cut the throats of an entire family in West Virginia set off
further rumors of a pitched battle between a sheriff's posse and
the assassins. In 1894, several hundred Italians were driven from
the city by an armed mob. Many were wounded and their homes
burned.

Five months after the New Orleans lynching, on August 9, 1896, three Italians were lynched in the town of Hahnville, Louisiana. Again, the Italians were accused of murdering white citizens. Though no sufficient evidence existed to establish the guilt of any of the accused, they were summarily lynched.

When the southern Colorado coal fields were gripped by violent labor strife in 1895, a group of miners and other residents took the law into their own hands and systematically massacred six Italian workers implicated in the death of an American saloon-keeper. Two years later, three Italians were jailed on suspicion of homicide and lynched in Hahnville, Louisiana. In 1899, five more Italians were dragged from a jail to be lynched by a crazed mob in Tallulah, Mississippi.

What happened to the Italians after the New Orleans massacre? Objections to Italians continued, as seen in a photographic study of the Italian Quarter in the 1907 edition of the *Times-Democrat*.[49] The scenes shown were squalid. They depicted crowded rooms, large families, and groups of ragged children playing in the streets. Any citizen of the time who saw this pictorial coverage might well be expected to have felt some twinge of hatred for these foreigners who were invading his city. But most of these causes of prejudice can be considered either direct results of or offshoots from the economic threat that they posed. The man on the street found it would be easier to ostracize the Italian than to compete with him, hence the new immigrant was an outsider from the very start. He was forced to band together with his fellows out of social and economic necessity. The Italian colony in New Orleans was not formed for the sake of either isolationism or convenience; it was formed for survival.

As the colony began to unite itself, it grew even more powerful and prosperous. Italian fruit vendors and wholesale grocers began to cooperate with Italian farmers in outlying parishes, and soon a larger portion of the fruit and vegetable market was in Italian hands.[50] Other immigrants became wealthy by catering to the needs and wants of the growing colony. Cusimano and Sona Importers got exclusive rights from the Italian government to import tobacco and olive oil from Italy to New Orleans.[51] After the substantial success this firm had, a number of other Italian importing companies were founded. Other popular Italian businesses were ice factories and laundries. A majority of the people in both of these services were Italian.[52]

In the grocery business, the Italians were so active that they controlled more than half of the retail outlets in New Orleans by 1920. Out of 1,357 retail grocers listed in the City Directory in 1920, 689 were either of Italian birth or ancestry.

The Italians felt they had earned a place in American society and were disappointed and even embittered by the fact that acceptance was long in coming. These sentiments often found their way into print in the Italian newspaper of the city. In an article which appeared in *L'Italo-Americano* on October 5, 1912, the citizens of the colony were urged to celebrate Columbus Day on October twelfth in order to honor the memory of a great Italian *and* to "remind the Americans at least once a year that the descendants of Columbus, more than any other populace, have the right to expect the warmth and sympathy of this great nation."[53]

The desire for acceptance spurred the Italians to improve their educational position. A large number of Italian immigrants in Louisiana were illiterate. The United States Census of 1920 bears out this fact in stating that 24 percent of all foreign-born whites in the state were illiterate, as compared to only 15 percent for whites of native parentage. But if we look at the figures for whites of foreign or mixed parentage, we find that the illiteracy rate is an amazingly low 3.6 percent.[54] It is clear the immigrant learned the value of an education in the space of one generation and he learned his lesson well. The same pattern hold for school attendance. Native whites of foreign or mixed parentage had an attendance rate of 69.7 percent, higher than any other group listed.[55] Certainly, these immigrants' children sought an education for more reasons than community acceptance and recognition, but, if they had not been spurred on by this goal, their attendance records would not have been so markedly above the norm.

Only a small number of these immigrants received a higher education, and the Italian community took great pride in those of its members who did attend college. The Virgilian Society, founded in 1921, opened its membership only to persons having a college degree. Organizations such as this one increased the prestige and honor attached to a higher education, thereby encouraging members of the colony to seek admission to colleges and universities. Those who were admitted often found that they were discriminated against on campus. Those who finished their education in spite of the prejudice manifested against them often became spokesmen for the cause of assimilation.

Some forms of education were directed specifically toward assimilation as an end. Schools such as the one established by the

Italian Methodist Mission aimed at bringing the Italian's "home life up to the modern ideals" and at "quickening his social amalgamation."[56] In this particular school, mothers were banded together and taught to be American housewives. For the men, there was a literary discussion club which included American members.

Clubs and social organizations were very popular in the Italian colony, and practically all of them supported better relations and closer understanding between the Italian community and the city's populace. The *Giovanni Bersaglieri,* the Virgilian Society, and the Italian Union all supported programs aimed at these goals. The Italian Union, for example, sponsored a speech given by Edwin J. Jackson, the superintendent of the U.S. Naturalization Office, on the duty of all immigrants to become citizens.[57] The superintendent mentioned in his talk that a large number of Italian immigrants were now becoming naturalized, and he expressed his hopes that the trend would continue.

Mr. Jackson need not have worried. The Italians had no sooner naturalized enough people to form a voting bloc than they founded a political organization. The *Associazione Politica Italiana* held its first meeting at the Italian Union Hall on September 24, 1922, and it drew delegates from all over the state. This organization sought to unite all of Louisiana's Italians into a political pressure group which could effectively defend the rights of the Italian minority. To this end, each member of the colony was urged to become naturalized so that he could use his vote to protect what he valued. Though the group did not nominate any candidates for office, it expressed the hope that an Italian could be elected to a prominent position in the not-too-distant future.[58]

Similarly optimistic views began to crop up in the Italian press, which became unusually active during this period. There were two Italian newspapers in the colony: *L'Italo-Americano* and *La Voce Coloniale. L'Italo-Americano* was the oldest Italian-language newspaper in the South, having begun printing in 1885. For decades, it simply reported news that was of interest to Italians, with special reprints of articles from Italian newspapers. But around 1915, it took on a crusading spirit which it had not displayed previously. Its articles began to ring with appeals for better understanding between New Orleanians and Italians, and local news took up much more space than it ever had before.

At least part of the reason for the change in the *Italo-Americano* can be attributed to the introduction of *La Voce Coloniale* in 1914. This publication was openly political and dubbed itself the "official organ of expression for the Italian colony." Its articles all aimed at exposing discrimination against Italians, applauding accomplishments of Italians, or encouraging Italians to take a more active role in community life. The editors felt, quite rightly, that the colony could not achieve social equality without achieving effective assimilation. With this in mind, they made sure that all their articles had a strong assimilationist flavor.

While the newspapers urged the Italian colony to blend itself into the American culture, the Italo-American Publishing Company was making sure the colony would not forget the contributions Italians had made to the city's growth and development. This small publishing house put out a booklet containing biographies of rich and influential New Orleans citizens who had come out of the Italian community.

The story of Luigi Tortorici is typical of those which appear in the collection.[59] Born in Contessa Entellina, Sicily, he came to New Orleans when he was fourteen. He began his business career as a fruit vendor in the French Market, but, within twenty years, he had become a very prosperous real estate man. Almost all of the biographies show this same rise from abject poverty to commercial success. The value of material gains was strongly emphasized, and the stories were designed to illustrate that the road to prosperity in New Orleans was open to the Italians of the colony. Between the influence of such booklets and the influence of the newspapers, it was hoped the Italian would become a part of American culture while still retaining pride in the Italian tradition.

This same end was being accomplished through much less noticeable, though probably more effective, means by intermarriage between Italians and other national groups. They had no qualms about marrying into English, French, or Spanish families. In fact, the frequency of such marriages was so high that it would seem Italians encouraged it. During the years 1914 to 1920, fully 20 percent of all the marriages which took place in St. Mary's Italian Church were mixed. Considering that the Italian colony, with its different language and customs, was considered a closed society, and that it was often the object of discrimination and hatred, this is a remarkably high percentage.

The most important factor in the assimilative process, however, proved to be the very thing which had generated so much ill feeling against the Italians in the early years of immigration. Now that these former peasants were becoming affluent, economic pressure began to work for them instead of against them.

In the 1920s, Italians were practically in control of the fruit-vending and wholesale grocery businesses in New Orleans. They owned three of the largest hotels in the city. Many of the famous restaurants and entertainment spots were in the hands of Italians. The Standard Fruit Company, which owned a fleet of thirty-nine freight and passenger steamers and had interests in four Latin American countries, was controlled by Italians.[60] The Vaccaros, descendants of a poor immigrant from Contessa Entellina, were the richest people in Louisiana. Bruno Roselli asserts that during this period Italians "owned outright one-third of the total real estate in the parish of Orleans."[61]

The Italian colony knew how to use this new wealth to its best advantage. It encouraged its members to give economic support only to those businesses which were sympathetic to Italians. The Italian press often made a point of stressing the necessity of such action. The September 30, 1922, edition of *La Voce Coloniale* contained an article on the recent appointment of Andreo Schiro, a prominent member of the Italian community, to the position of manager of one of the Hibernia Banks' new branches.[62] The article applauded Mr. Schiro's achievements and then went on to say that it was now the *duty* of every member of the colony to patronize this bank and no other, until all the city's banks became aware of the "advantages" of employing Italians. The article ended by noting that the colony still has a long struggle ahead of it, but that Mr. Schiro's achievement "is a great step forward."[63]

Pressure of this nature on business establishments no doubt had a telling effect, for it is clear that at this time the Italian community had a large amount of capital at its disposal. This fact is illustrated by the history of the Italian Homestead Association, which began operations in March of 1922. Its offices at 213 Camp Street were said to be "the handsomest homestead quarters in the city."[64] The heads of the largest banking establishments in the city were present at its opening on March 22, and the day's business exceeded all previous records for a homestead association in New Orleans. In the space of just four years, the association built up over two million dollars in assets. Though Italians achieved economic successes in New Orleans by the early 1920s, prejudice and discrimination were still widespread. The earlier events in New Orleans were a portent of things to come.

7 That Agony Is Our Triumph

The nativism of the 1880s and 1890s had great significance for Italian-Americans. In the long run, nativist thought was incorporated in the immigration legislation of the twentieth century. In addition, it set the stage for a new and violent surge of nativism which continued from the turn of the century through most of the 1920s.

The conception that the peoples of southern and eastern Europe were inferior to those of northern and western Europe is rooted in the openly expressed and widely accepted racist beliefs of the 1880s and 1890s. At the heart of such beliefs was the notion that the peoples of the Mediterranean region were biologically different from those of northern and western Europe and that the difference sprang from an inferiority of "blood" and could be observed in certain social characteristics. This belief was given forceful expression by the noted anthropologist Madison Grant in *The Passing of the Great Race,* published in 1916. According to Grant, the "new" immigrants were not "members of the Nordic race as were the earlier ones":

> The new immigration contained a large and increasing number of the weak, the broken, and the mentally crippled of all races drawn from the lowest stratum of the Mediterranean basin and the Balkans, together with hordes of the wretched, submerged populations of the Polish ghettos. Our jails, insane asylums, and almhouses are filled with this human flotsam and the whole tone of American life, social, moral, and political, has been lowered and vulgarized by them.[1]

Intellectually, the resurgent racism of the early 1920s would receive its impetus mainly from Grant's book. The emotional presentation of a racial philosophy captured the imagination of many literate people and influenced many of the writers of the early 1920s.

Edward A. Ross, one of the leading ideologues of progressivism, wrote a tract on immigration, *The Old World in the New,* that expressed the anti-immigrant case from the Anglo-Saxon progressive standpoint. Attacking on every conceivable level, Ross noted that Italians bred in such numbers that they were increasingly dominant over the native stock and thus threatened to overwhelm "American blood" and bastardize American civilization.

The violence against Italian-Americans continued with little interruption in the era from 1900 to 1929. On July 15, 1901, in Erwin, Mississippi, one Italian-American was killed by an armed mob and another was lynched. Four months later, four Italian-Americans who had been doing very well in the dry goods business were driven from Marksville, Louisiana. In June of 1906, sixty Italian-Americans tried to quit their jobs with the Spruce Pine Carolina Company, a railroad construction company located in Marian, North Carolina. The workers protested the working conditions. When the Italians attempted to set up a meeting time to discuss these conditions, they were greeted by a company posse. Two were killed, five wounded, and nine were jailed for "assault, battery, and conspiracy."

How were Italians perceived by the Afro-American press after 1900? In the early twentieth century, thousands of blacks made their way to the industrial centers of the North. As a result, the image of the Italians among blacks was somewhat modified. "Though [the Italian-American] remained a feared competitor for jobs and housing, he was increasingly perceived as shrewd, hard working, and thrifty. Therefore, those black editors, seeking to persuade their readers to emulate these qualities, downplayed the image of the Italian as gangster."[2]

But what of the "liberal" progressive reformers? The fact of the matter is that the nativist reaction in the twentieth century with regard to Italians was spearheaded by liberal reformers and the mass media. The latter were often liberal journals and newspapers. Progressivism combined a reactionary with a reform impulse. Progressives came to believe that crime in America was an imported disease that could be reduced by limiting the influx of southern Italian immigration in particular and by the forced Americanization of all immigrants. Iorizzo and Mondello have concluded: "Progressive views on the question of crime among Italo-Americans reflected the nuances of liberal thought and served to establish the emotional foundations for the Black Hand myth, which followed the Mafia myth of the 1880s and 1890s and preceded the Cosa Nostra scare of the 1950s and 1960s."[3]

While the progressives acknowledged the existence of social

problems, they still supported the restriction of immigration in order to prevent "racial suicide or degeneration of the superior American race."

The liberal press played up incidents in the Italian ghettoes which Americans could only interpret as a vast criminal conspiracy. By 1909, the widespread acceptance of the Black Hand myth reinforced the older stereotype of the Italians as an inferior, morally degenerate, and criminally inclined race.

Increasingly, the press demanded a special police force to combat what it viewed as organized crime dominated by the lower classes of Italians in New York. This led Police Commissioner Theodore Bingham of New York to declare a war on the criminal conspiracy.[4] In December of 1906, a special squad was established to investigate crime among Italian-Americans. The squad was placed under the direction of Joseph Petrosino. They soon discovered that, while Italian crimes were essentially against their own people, the individuals involved either acted alone or in small independent groups.[5]

Commissioner Bingham concluded that if the Italian criminal records of such suspects could be discovered, it could lead to quick deportation without a trial. This accounts for Petrosino's selection as the head of the squad. He was to seek the cooperation of the Italian government in a special mission.

Bingham had asserted that foreigners, especially Russian Jews and Italians, accounted for 85 percent of New York's criminals. The facts about crime in the Italian-American and Jewish neighborhoods did not support this bigoted assertion. Crime in the ghettoes was almost exclusively against other Italians and most often involved small thefts, robberies, and assaults. Italian victims did not go to the police, whom they regarded with suspicion.[6] There were all too many instances of police brutality. Often the community imposed its own justice on criminal behavior. The police, the press, the progessives, and the larger public misunderstood this silence. It was interpreted as further proof of a secret, powerful, organized criminal conspiracy.

Joseph Petrosino was now sent to Italy. While in Italy, on March 12, 1909, he was shot and killed by an unknown assassin. The news of Petrosino's murder caused an immediate and angry reaction. It was decisive in the minds of the American public who saw this as evidence that the dreaded society did exist, that it was responsible for most, if not all, unsolved crimes, and that all Italian-Americans were to blame.

Several theories were advanced to explain Petrosino's mission. Some thought he was dispatched to Sicily to find out about those

Italian criminals who were about to come to the United States. Still others thought he sought to prove the direct connection between an Italian and an American criminal network. Petrosino privately had not believed in any of these theories and his squad had found no evidence of a transatlantic connection. It is not likely that anyone in Italy would be afraid of one lone policeman. His mission was to obtain information on Italian criminal "suspects" so that they could be deported without trial.[7]

Why then was Petrosino killed? Petrosino may have represented a symbol of power. If so, his death would serve to enhance the hold on the local people that certain criminals might have. Perhaps he was regarded as an intruder. Here was a naturalized American who came from Calabria representing a remote and distant government. To the assassin, he may have been someone who took the side of strangers against one's own people.

In either event, the *New York Times* was to argue for years that the South Italians had brought a monolithic criminal organization to America. They were frequently to identify all crime with all Italian-Americans. Mass arrests of innocent Italian-Americans followed the death of Petrosino. In Chicago, in one sweep alone, 194 Italians were jailed, all of whom had no link with any crime at all. All 194 were subsequently released.[8]

The stereotypes followed Italians into the suburbs as well. In Blue Island, Illinois, the local newspaper, the *Sun,* in October of 1914, reported: "The area of State and Union (in the heart of the Italian section) is fast gaining the reputation as a bad corner; several shootings and stabbings have occurred there." A new editor stretched reality completely beyond its bounds when he convinced the community that organized Black Hand activities existed within the Italian community. He implied that the local priest and other citizens had been threatened and intimidated by organized crime. The entire conspiracy had been fabricated by the editor for the purpose of selling newspapers and building his reputation with the publisher.

On September 20, 1910, two Italians in Tampa, Florida, were taken from custody and lynched. That same year, the nativist attacks against Italians and other southern and eastern European immigrants were to be "validated" by the American government from two governmental investigations. The first was a detailed study by the Immigration Commission under the chairmanship of Senator Dillingham. The second was a report by Dr. Harry H. Laghlin of the Carnegie Institution for the House Committee on Immigration and Naturalization.

The reports were to influence directly the passage of restrictive immigration legislation. Moreover, they supported both theoretical and concrete bigoted opinions with what appeared to be official and supposedly scientific proof. The Immigration Commission presented its conclusions in 1910 in a forty-two-volume report.

Many expected that out of the deliberations of the commission a body of verified and indisputable facts would supply the groundwork for future action. Though a million dollars was spent by the commission, which employed a staff of three hundred, its report was neither impartial nor scientific.

No public hearings were held, and no witnesses were cross-examined by the members of the commission. It was a study largely conducted by "experts." Each compiled reports which were not printed until after the commission had reached its conclusions. It is unlikely that the commission members had the time or interest to examine the reports in manuscript. They most likely based their judgment on a two-volume summary prepared for them by a group of experts on the staff. The final report was adopted within a half hour of the time when, under the law, it was supposed to be filed.[9] Most of the key experts already had preconceived ideas on the "new" immigration and the necessity for its restriction.

The commission took for granted the conclusions it intended to prove—that the new immigration was essentially different from the old and less capable of being Americanized. This assumption is set forth in the beginning of the report:

> The old and the new immigration differ in many essentials. The former . . . was largely a movement of settlers . . . from the most progressive sections of Europe. . . . They entered practically every line of activity. . . . Many of them . . . became landowners. . . . They mingled freely with the native Americans and were quickly assimilated. On the other hand, the new immigration has been largely a movement of unskilled laboring men who have come . . . from the less progressive countries of Europe. . . . They have . . . congregated together in sections apart from native Americans and the older immigrants to such an extent that assimilation has been slow.[10]

The assumption with which the commission started conditioned the preparation of the whole report and made it certain that the conclusions would confirm the prejudgment. To quote their own words: "Consequently the Commission paid little attention to the foreign-born element of the old immigrant class and directed its efforts almost entirely to . . . the newer immigrants."[11]

All this conditioned the techniques the commission was to employ. There was no effort to give a time dimension to its data. It used no information except that gathered by its own staff. The data in state and federal censuses was hardly used. State bureaus of labor statistics were also ignored. Information gathered by other government and private agencies was also omitted from consideration.

The commission, time and time again, neglected to consider the question of duration of settlement. It assumed that a group which had lived in the United States for five years could be treated on the same footing as one that had lived here for thirty-five.

In most cases the individual reports—on industry, crime, nationality, education, and literacy—did not contain materials for proper conclusions; the committee's conclusions for the most part sprang from its own prior assumptions. "Through it ran a persistent, though not a consistent, tendency to determine race by physical types, to differentiate the old from the new immigrants racially, and to indicate the superiority of the former to the latter."[12]

The intensity of nativist attacks on Italians and their fellow immigrants increased between 1910 and the outbreak of World War I, this particularly so in the case of the progressive reformers based on the existence of urban problems which they could not solve. The election year of 1912 brought Woodrow Wilson to the presidency. Wilson, whom Richard Hofstadter has described as the conservative as liberal, sought the Democratic nomination. In 1902, Wilson, as a historian, had had harsh things to say about the immigrants from southern Europe in *A History of the American People*:

> But now there came multitudes of men of the lowest class from the south of Italy and men of the meaner sort of Hungary and Poland, men out of the ranks where there was neither skill nor energy nor any initiative of quick intelligence; and they came in numbers which increased in numbers which increased from year to year, as if the countries of the south of Europe were disburdening themselves of the sordid and hapless elements of their population...."[13]

In the preconvention months of 1912, Wilson's political opponents discovered these uncomplimentary remarks. Pressure from the affected ethnic groups increased. Fearing that the hostility of these ethnic groups might hurt his chances for the nomination, Wilson sought to explain his earlier statements. He now claimed that he had the highest admiration and respect for the new immigrants. Wilson also promised that he would insert an erratum slip in his book retracting his earlier aspersions, that he would rewrite the passage in the next edition. Wilson then informed his publisher that he wished to remove the passages. After his election, the supreme moralist allowed the new edition to be published without making any of the promised changes.

The need for scapegoats was heightened by the recession of 1913 and the outbreak of war in 1914. On October 10, 1914, in Willisville, Illinois, and later on June 12, 1915, in Johnson City, Illinois, two additional Italians were added to the growing list of victims of mob violence. With the outbreak of World War I, nationalism was to be added to racial nativism, and a new and potent form of nationalism sprang on the scene in 1919.

In 1917, stirred by the national crisis, Congress succeeded in overriding a second veto by Woodrow Wilson and passed a law requiring an immigration literacy test. The law stated that no alien over sixteen would be admitted to the country unless he could read some language. Congress was influenced by an alarmist press and a public that was quick to believe that the foreign-born radical and the educated Black Hander were leading ignorant southern and eastern European immigrants into subverting American institutions. To President Wilson, the purpose of the law was restriction, not selection. The literacy tests, he said, "are not tests of quality, or of character or of personal fitness, but tests of opportunity. Those who come seeking an opportunity are not to be admitted unless they have already had one of the chief of the opportunities they seek, the opportunity of education."[14]

When the literacy test failed to limit the tide of newcomers, Congress adopted laws which limited immigration still more drastically. Immigration laws established national quotas. The laws rested on the racist assumption that some people were more desirable than others, and thus the laws discriminated against those people who came from southern and eastern Europe, as well as against all orientals.

Newspapers throughout the country continued to fan the fires of prejudice by grave warnings about the Italian inclination to violence and crime. In Mechanicville, New York, the local editor, Farrington Mead, asserted that all Italians were heavily armed and ready to strike. In 1919, Mead happily announced that the reputed leader of the Black Hand had been arrested. Though no evidence or convictions were forthcoming, the continual assaults by the editor created a negative image of Italians in Mechanic-ville. Similar reporting in other communities and cities around the country continued.

In 1919, World War I came to an end. The great crusade was over. The general public was caught in the middle of the twin problems of postwar reconversion of industry and the demobilization of the armed forces. In addition, a surging postwar inflation was an immediate cause of instability and unrest. In the interest of unity, labor reached a truce with management. Labor unrest after the war involved the issue of unionism and collective bargaining. Businessmen saw both of these factors as the "ultimate capitulation of organized capital." American businessmen looked to regain lost ground suffered during the progressive reform era.

In the postwar years, people still worried about internal subversion as they had during the war. As labor unrest increased, the nation appeared to many people to be under serious attack. Each social and industrial disturbance was viewed as proof that radicals were all about. The nation was overcome with fear. The public received dire warnings from the press, business, and patriotic organizations. A sampling of press headlines will illustrate the mood of the times:

THE SEATTLE STRIKE IS MARXIAN
THE STEPPING STONE TO A BOLSHEVIZED AMERICA
REDS DIRECTING SEATTLE STRIKE—
    TO TEST CHANCE FOR REVOLUTION

In 1919, a series of events took place in rapid order which were to set in motion another wave of political trials. These events were the Seattle general strike, the Boston Police strike, and the steel and coal strikes. Each of these served to exaggerate people's fears of an existing radical menace. As a result, all unions, labor leaders, and radicals were lumped together by businessmen, government officials, and the press.

A pattern of response and reaction was set in motion which would be standard for the rest of the Red Scare period. Labor was placed in the position of making some disastrous mistakes which constantly subjected it to public suspicion. Employers, in turn, were brought to the realization that the issue of radicalism could be helpful in their fight against unionism. To certain politicians it became clear that radicalism would make an excellent political issue by which free publicity as well as votes could be obtained. The general press, meanwhile, found in the issue of radicalism an immediate substitute for waning wartime sensationalism and eagerly busied itself with reporting exaggerations instead of facts.[15]

During the war, state and federal governments sought to enforce loyalty by passing a mass of sedition and espionage legislation. These remained in effect after the war and became the basis for criminal prosecutions of radicals. The Sedition Act of 1918 gave the federal government power to punish any expression of opinion that, regardless of whether or not it led to actions, was "disloyal, profane, scurrilous, or abusive" of the American form of government, flag, or military uniform. Passed during the war and intended for wartime use, the act was now to be applied in peacetime.

It was Attorney General A. Mitchell Palmer who was to lead the federal government's efforts to curb radicalism. The fear that Communists and leftist radicals would topple the Constitution—the so-called Red Scare—swept the nation. It soon reached hysterical proportions. Palmer had his eye on the White House and played up the Red Scare for all it was worth. He thought his aggressive stand against the Reds would be the primary means of projecting himself into the presidency. Palmer began his attack on radicalism partially to do something to satisfy the mounting pressure from businessmen, the press, and the frightened public. He was also motivated by a deep fear that the Communists were about to take over the nation.

In November 1919 and January 1920, Palmer, with help of the Labor Department, unleashed a series of raids on suspected radicals. This became the signal for local and state authorities to follow his example. Along with the Secretary of Labor, Palmer decided that alien members of the Communist and Communist Labor parties were subject to deportation. Aliens were singled out in particular for a variety of reasons. The Red Scare coincided with a growing prejudice against all immigrants. Immigrants were seen as the cause of many of the social and economic problems of the day. Moreover, many Americans believed that the immigrants were the ones who brought with them the radical doctrines which were threatening the very fabric of America. Aliens were also vulnerable to governmental action. The Secretary of Labor signed three thousand warrants for the deportation of "alien radicals."

Deportation did not involve criminal proceedings. It was not regarded as a legal punishment. There was neither a judge nor a jury. The cases were handled administratively by immigration officials through the Secretary of Labor. Palmer thereby circumvented the judicial process through an administrative agency. Had he gone to the courts, he would have been required to present an indictment and evidence that would be subject to the evaluation of trial by jury. Palmer also circumvented the Sixth Amendment—the right of a speedy public trial by an impartial jury. By using the administrative agency, the same result of a trial was achieved without having to follow trial procedures.

Interestingly enough, the Commissioner of Immigration who assisted Palmer was Anthony Caminetti. Caminetti was a Californian who was destined to be the first Italian-American to be elected to Congress. His appointment by President Wilson as Commissioner of Immigration in 1913 was intended to placate the immigrants. However, even Caminetti succumbed to the instincts of the "pure" American nativists.[16]

With few exceptions, public opinion supported the Palmer raids. Palmer was looked upon in most quarters of the American public as the savior of the republic. Palmer emerged as the strong man of Washington. He seemed to be converting one-hundred-percent Americanism into a system of government.

During the Red Scare era, the conspiracy theory was upheld by the major power interest groups. These included business, the press, federal and state governmental agencies, and the super-patriotic societies. Each cooperated with the others. The Department of Justice cooperated with privately employed detectives, labor spies, and corporations.

Some big businessmen and public officials supported the Red Scare and endorsed super-patriotism because they sincerely felt that America was in danger. Others exploited the hysteria by stereotyping their opponents as radicals, even though they knew full well that they were not.

A major reason for supporting the Red Scare for many was that of self interest. For a member of a super-patriotic society, it could mean a salary increase if he identified his or her quota of "radicals." By expanding its antiradical efforts, the Justice Department could obtain an increase in its budget. For the military, conspiracy could justify an undeclared war in Siberia whose object was to bring down the Bolshevik regime. To businessmen, the Red Scare could be used to break strikes and unions.

As the Palmer raids subsided, the antiradical theme was picked up by private patriotic organizations such as the One Hundred Percenters, The American Defense Society, The National Security League, and hundreds of others.[17]

By 1920, the image of the Italian immigrants as radicals was added to the stereotype of the Italian-Americans as criminals.

This marks the full flowering of the composite stereotype of the Italians in the nativist literature of the 1890s.

Thousands of workers were idle and restless due to a strike in the coal mines where a large number of Italians were employed. A series of bank robberies occurred, and the townspeople were quick to blame it on a criminal conspiracy of the Italian residents. This was followed by the kidnapping of two boys. A city-wide explosion erupted following the discovery of their bodies. During the night of August 5, 1920, and through the following day, hundreds of people laden with clothing and household goods filled the roads leading out of West Frankfort, Illinois. In town, their homes were burning. Mobs had driven every foreigner out of town. The chief objective was the Italian population. Crowds burst through the Italian neighborhood, dragged residents from their homes, and clubbed and stoned them. This turmoil lasted for three days. Five months earlier, another event occurred which in many respects was to be the epitome of blind nativist prejudice.

On the morning of April 15, 1920, in South Braintree, Massachusetts, the payroll for Slater and Morrill, a shoe factory, arrived from Boston. At about three o'clock in the afternoon, Parmenter, a paymaster, and Bernardelli, his guard, were killed by two men as they were carrying the payroll from the company's main office to the factory. A dark, curtained touring car containing several other men drove up to the spot. The murderers picked up the money boxes, threw them into the car, and jumped in themselves. The car sped away across the railroad tracks. On April 17, the car was found abandoned in woods in West Bridgewater. Leading away from this spot were the tracks of a smaller car. At the time of the holdup, the police were investigating a similar crime in the town of Bridgewater. To the police, both cases bore some general similarities. Michael E. Stewart, chief of police in Bridgewater, was looking for that car at the time of the Braintree holdup. He thought he had found his man in Mike Boda, whose car bore a general resemblance to the one used in the robbery and was being repaired in a nearby garage. Stewart instructed the proprietor of Boda's boarding house to call when anyone came to get the car. Stewart learned that Boda had been living with Feruccio Coacci, an Italian anarchist.

One day, after the Braintree murders, Stewart, under the direction of the Department of Justice, was in the process of rounding up Reds. To most Americans at this time, all radicals, Communists, and Socialists were viewed as "Reds." He had gone to Coacci's house to see why he did not appear at a hearing about his impending deportation. The police chief found Coacci packing a trunk. Later, when the tracks of a smaller car were uncovered, Stewart made the connection between Boda, Coacci, and the trunk. Thinking the trunk contained the money, he decided to investigate. His theory fell to pieces when he found nothing related to the crime in the trunk. Stewart still clung to his theory that Boda was involved. Whoever called for Boda's car would be a suspect.

On the night of May 5, 1920, Boda and three Italians came for the car. What brought them there was their fear of the Palmer Raids which were now in high gear. Earlier, they learned that a close friend had been caught in one of these raids. He was held in custody in the offices of the Department of Justice. On May 4, they found out their friend had mysteriously "fallen" fourteen floors and had been found dead. Frightened by the raids and this latest event, they decided to hide anarchist literature and warn friends. For this purpose, they needed a car, and they appealed to Boda. Two of the four were Sacco and Vanzetti. The police were called but did not find the men. Since the car was not available, they left the house. Sacco and Vanzetti boarded a street car for Brockton where they were arrested. A third man named Orciani was arrested, but the fourth man and Boda disappeared.

Police chief Stewart applied his theory of one gang for the two jobs, but the theory didn't fit. Stewart was convinced that he had the right men. To him, Godless men, atheists like Sacco and Vanzetti, were capable of any crime. However, Orciani had been at work on the days of both robberies.[18]

When the two men were arrested, they asked why they were seized. "Oh, you know, you know why," the officer replied. During the long night of questioning, no explanation for their arrest was forthcoming. With the memory of their friends in their minds, they believed that their turn had come. They were anarchists, and Italian aliens. Their fears were reinforced when Stewart opened up his questioning by asking them about their political beliefs. Were they Anarchists? Were they Communists? Did they support the United States government?

Frightened, they lied to Stewart about their associations and movements. When District Attorney Frederick G. Katzmann questioned the two men, they still were not told why they were being held.

> Later in the day several dozen witnesses were brought from
> South Braintree and Bridgewater to see if they could identify
> the prisoners as participants in either holdup. In the small

Brockton police station there was no attempt to have the two
Italians mixed with other suspects in a lineup. They were
merely led into the emergency room by themselves where they
stood docilely until ordered to kneel, put on and take off
their hats, raise their arms, and assume the crouching position
of a man firing a pistol. The various witnesses walked around
them slowly observing them from every angle.[19]

Later in the trial, defense counsel Fred Moore was to cast doubt
on this procedure. Both Sacco and Vanzetti carried guns which
were seized immediately as evidence against them. This evidence
was not marked, so that there was no way of knowing whether
they really were the guns that had been taken from the suspects.
Since the evidence was passed around so casually, there was no
way of determining if those weapons and bullets had indeed
been the ones taken from the defendants.

The frightened defendants spent the night in jail.

> Neither Sacco nor Vanzetti had been behind bars before.
> Now, in adjoining cells under the shadowless glare of the over-
> head light, with a wooden shelf to sleep on and a seatless toilet
> in the corner, they sensed the isolating fear of arbitrary imper-
> sonal force. To the policemen going on and off duty they
> were curiosities and as such subject to a certain amount of
> crude horseplay. When the two men requested blankets the
> reply was that they would find it warm enough when they were
> lined up in the hall for a little live target practice, and one
> patrolman showed Vanzetti a cartridge which he then slipped
> into the barrel of his revolver, cocking it and pointing between
> the bars. When Vanzetti did not move, the other spat on the
> floor contemptuously and turned away.[20]

Vanzetti, a fish peddler at Plymouth, self-employed, was
charged with both crimes. The head of the state police did not
share Stewart's beliefs and consistently claimed the robberies to
be the work of professionals.

Sacco and Vanzetti were indicted on September 14, 1920, and
put on trial May 31, 1921, at Dedham, Norfolk County. The presiding judge was Webster Thayer of Worcester. The chief defense counsel was Fred H. Moore, himself a radical and professional defender of radicals.

> Moore, then in his late forties, was the barrister-bohemian in
> looks, dress, and manner. His long hair seemed to flow back
> from his forehead, he often wore sandals, and the broad-
> brimmed Western hat he brought with him from California
> became almost his trademark in Boston.[21]

It became obvious that Thayer took a dim view of Moore and consistently overruled his objections in court. Frederick Katzmann served as the prosecuting attorney. The Sacco-Vanzetti trial was no ordinary case of robbery. Other issues were involved, namely, the defendants' political views and their ethnicity.

The matter of identification became an early focus of the trial. Fifty-nine witnesses testified for the prosecution and ninety-five for the defendants on this point. It amounted to a mass of conflicting testimony. The prosecution's witnesses' identifications were full of ambiguities. One witness testified that she ran to a window after the shot had been fired. She was placed before Sacco at the time of the arrest. Three weeks later at the hearing, she was unable to identify Sacco as one of the murderers. Yet one year later she proceeded to identify a man with amazing detail who was from sixty to eighty feet from her at the time of the crime, in a car traveling from fifteen to eighteen miles per hour, all within a space of three seconds.

Testimony for the defense placed both Sacco and Vanzetti elsewhere at the time of the murder. Sacco was identified by the Italian Consul in Boston as being in his office on April 15 seeking a passport to Italy. Vanzetti's claim to be at work on both days was corroborated by thirty-one witnesses. Beltrando Brini, a thirteen-year-old boy, testified that he had worked all morning helping Vanzetti. He proved to be the most important defense witness. His testimony and that of the other witnesses contained details that would have been hard to falsify.

The court dwelt on evidence which attempted to show that Sacco and Vanzetti, by their behavior and conduct after April 15, had acted like murderers. Yet, their behavior contradicted this assertion. They had not gone into hiding. Neither of them had been accused of a crime before their arrest. The money from the robberies never came into their possession. In fact, it was never found.

Both Sacco and Vanzetti took the witness stand and accounted for their movements on April 15 and May 5. They testified as to their activities, their pacifism and their flight to Mexico to escape the draft. With Katzmann's cross-examination of Sacco and Vanzetti, the trial took a decided turn. The defendants' political views, their radicalism, and their patriotism became the dominant issues. The Red hysteria now took over the courtroom. The prosecutor systematically played on the feelings of the jury by exploring the "unpatriotic" political beliefs of the men:

> KATZMANN: So you left Plymouth, Mr. Vanzetti, in May, 1917
> to dodge the draft, did you?

VANZETTI: Yes, sir.

KATZMANN: When this country was at war, you ran away, so you would not have to fight as a soldier?

VANZETTI: Yes.

KATZMANN: You were going to advise in a public meeting men who had gone to war? Are you that man?

VANZETTI: Yes, sir, I am that man, not the man you want me, but I am that man.

Katzmann hammered at their political beliefs, as illustrated in the following exchange with Sacco on the stand:

KATZMANN: Did you love this country in the last week of May, 1917?

SACCO: That is pretty hard for me to say in one word, Mr. Katzmann.

KATZMANN: There are two words you can use, Mr. Sacco, yes or no. Which one is it?

SACCO: Yes.

KATZMANN: Don't you think going away from your country is a vulgar thing to do when she needs you?

SACCO: I don't believe in war.[22]

The temper of the times made it the special duty of the prosecutor and the presiding judge to keep the court free from prejudice and passion. These restraints were not adhered to in this trial. During the trial, Thayer spoke outside the courtroom in terms that were bigoted, sneering, and extremely vindictive. Judge Thayer seemed to be obsessed in his hatred of "Reds." Thayer allowed a line of cross-examination which explored political beliefs and would only inflame the passions of the jury.

The collusion between the District Attorney and the Department of Justice was later revealed. Even before Sacco and Vanzetti were arrested, their names were in the files of the Department of Justice, which was eager for their deportation but did not have sufficient evidence. Their arrest provided the Department with an opportunity to eliminate two more "undesirables." The Justice Department planted spies next to Sacco's cell and on the defendants' defense committee.

Katzmann had not undermined the defendants' explanation of their conduct but had exploited their political beliefs. His last words to the jury were, "Gentlemen of the jury, do your duty. Do it like men. Stand together, you men of Norfolk."

Judge Thayer, in charging the jury, began to rehearse the testimony though he was not expected to do so. In doing so, he made several factual mistakes in stating the testimony, which were corrected when the defense called them to his attention. He persisted in referring to the defendants as slackers—a loaded word in Massachusetts at the time.

> The Commonwealth of Massachusetts called upon you to render a most important service. Although you knew that such service would be arduous, painful, and tiresome, yet you, like the true soldier, responded to that call in the spirit of supreme American loyalty. There is no better word in the English language than "loyalty."[23]

Thayer reminded the jury that the men they were judging had shown no such loyalty.

On April 9, 1927, Vanzetti addressed the court before his sentencing:

> This is what I say: I would not wish to a dog or to a snake, to the most low and misfortunate creature of the earth—I would not wish to any of them what I have had to suffer for the things that I am not guilty of. But my conviction is that I have suffered for things I am guilty of. I am suffering because I am a radical, and indeed I am a radical; I have suffered because I was an Italian, and indeed I am an Italian.... I am so convinced to be right that if I could be reborn two other times, I would live again to do what I have done already.[24]

On July 14, 1921, at 2:30 P.M., the members of the jury retired to consider their verdict. By 7:30 they had reached their decision: Guilty of murder in the first degree. Sacco broke the stillness, "They kill an innocent man. They kill two innocent men."

As the weeks passed, a mass of new and significant evidence was uncovered and became the basis for motions for a new trial. Judge Thayer's duty was one of determining whether there was material fit for a new trial. This he did not do. He was not supposed to determine the defendants' guilt or innocence nor was he supposed to determine the truth or falsity of the new evidence. He did both of these things in rejecting the motions for a new trial. The final sentence—death in the electric chair during the week beginning on July 10, 1927.

Public pressure mounted. Defense counsel pressed for a thorough review of the case. Governor Alvin Fuller of Massachusetts received more than seventeen thousand letters and telegrams of protest and petitions for further investigation signed by more than 600,000 persons.

On July 24, 1927, Mussolini's government in Italy cautiously protested the fate dealt Sacco and Vanzetti by the state of Massachusetts. That day, Il Duce sent a letter to Ambassador Fletcher which he labeled a personal letter. In it, he gave Fletcher the liberty to do with it as he saw best. He also indicated he would approve of its transmission to Governor Fuller. Mussolini claimed to be addressing Fletcher as "a man who is sincerely your friend and none the less sincerely the friend of the people of the United States." Mussolini argued for the commutation of the sentences on the grounds that it played into the hands of the Communists, by martyring the two anarchists. On August 9, 1927, Mussolini informed Sacco's father that he had exhausted all avenues through which he might save his son.

Clearly the Mussolini government did not seriously attempt to aid the doomed men. The government made a conscious effort to suppress indigenous reactions within Italy. This was born out of a fear of economic reprisal, particularly on further restrictions of Italian emigration. With the passage of the restrictive legislation of 1921 and 1924 there was an even greater need to cultivate friendlier relations with the United States. Only when emigration became a liability rather than an asset did the Italian government protest.[25]

Governor Fuller appointed a committee with authority to review the case. On the first of June, 1927, the so-called Lowell Committee came into existence. There were three committee members: Samuel Stratton, president of the Massachusetts Institute of Technology; Robert A. Grant, a former judge of the probate court; and A. Lawrence Lowell, president of Harvard University. Fuller allowed no defense lawyers to appear and no record of the court proceedings was made available to the committee. The Lowell Committee concluded the trial had been fair.

Amid a storm of protest and controversy, time ran out on August 23, 1927. Sacco and Vanzetti were dead. As Charles Russell observed:

> Sacco and Vanzetti were figures of Greek tragedy.... Sacco scarcely missed a day at his factory except the day of the murders. If he had missed another day, the factory records would have been his alibi. Without him it is agreed that Vanzetti could not have been convicted. Fate engineered the almost accidental arrest of the two men as they were riding on the Brockton streetcar. But for fate, Sacco would have been off to his native country in three days.... That is the basis of high tragedy, a tragedy such as theirs that they played out to the end with bravery and dignity.[26]

Many would read and remember the words of Vanzetti. In a final speech, Vanzetti made his last statement to the court:

If it had not been for these things I might have live out my life talking at street corners to scorning men. I might have die, unmarked, unknown, a failure. Now we are not a failure. This is our career and our triumph. Never in our full life could we hope to do such work for tolerance, for justice, for man's understanding of man, as now we do by accident. Our words, our lives, our pains—nothing! The taking of our lives—lives of a good shoemaker and a poor fish peddler—all! The last moment belongs to us—that agony is our triumph.[27]

Nicola Sacco and Bartolomeo Vanzetti were the victims of a society in which prejudice, chauvinism, hysteria, and malice were endemic. Theirs was not merely a trial in court nor even a sociological phenomenon in the history of the United States. It was a spiritual experience and setback which only a fundamentally healthy America could have endured.[28] The tragedy of Sacco and Vanzetti was summed up by Vanzetti: "I have suffered because I was an Italian, and indeed I am an Italian. . . ."

Through violence, the nativist hysteria was to traumatize Italian immigrants and the first and second generations of Italian-Americans and impel them in a conservative direction. It was to end the Italian-American radical movement, which sought the correction of deeply imbedded social wrongs, and to damage the progressive forces in the Italian-American community. For some time many Italian-Americans would depend upon the political *padroni* and the *prominenti* in politics.

Fifty years after the Sacco-Vanzetti trial, Massachusetts officials moved to vindicate the two men. A proclamation declaring August 23, 1978, a memorial day for Sacco and Vanzetti was signed by Governor Michael S. Dukakis. At his side stood Spencer Sacco, grandson of Nicola Sacco and Italy's Consul General Francodi Bruno. The proclamation stated that the famous murder trial was unfair. The proclamation was based on a report by Governor Dukakis's legal counsel, Daniel Taylor, who reviewed the Sacco-Vanzetti case and said, "[There is a] very real possibility that a grievous miscarriage of justice occurred with their deaths. . . . There are substantial, indeed compelling, grounds for believing that the Sacco and Vanzetti legal proceedings were permeated with unfairness."[29]

Governor Dukakis then decided against issuing a pardon, because it would imply Sacco and Vanzetti were guilty. The proclamation declares, "Any stigma and disgrace should be forever removed from the names of Nicola Sacco and Bartolomeo Vanzetti, from the names of their families and descendants, and so from the name of the Commonwealth of Massachusetts." The proclamation calls for vigilance "against our susceptibility to prejudice, our intolerance of unorthodox ideas, and our failure to defend the rights of persons who are looked upon as strangers in our midst."[30] Alvin T. Fuller, Jr., son of the Massachusetts governor who denied clemency to the doomed pair in 1927, maintained that Dukakis had disgraced "himself, his office, and his state," and should resign.[31] "Sacco and Vanzetti paid for what they were, as well as for their alleged crime, and so we still have them on our conscience."[32]

8 La Famiglia

To speak of Italian-American life is also to speak of the family. Luigi Barzini has said of the Italian family:

> Scholars have always recognized the Italian family as the only fundamental institution in the country [Italy], a spontaneous creation of the national genius, adapted throughout the centuries to changing conditions, the real foundation of whichever social order prevails. In fact, the law, the state, and society function only if they do not directly interfere with the family's supreme interests.[1]

For a variety of historical reasons, societal organization in Italy has been relegated to a position secondary to the family. As another scholar of the Italian family has written: "It appears through default of an incomplete feudal order or tradition and the many historical upsets that the rural social structure was atomized and the kinship systems came to prevail over other forms of organization as the central referent."[2]

The first step in understanding any culture is to investigate its language and the special meanings that are attached to certain words. So it is with the Italian family. Let us examine four words: *nipote, salutare, rimbambito,* and *visitare.*

Nipote means grandson. But if a member of an Italian family introduces a child to you as his nipote, he or she might very well mean that the child is his nephew. The same word is used for both. Confusing? Not to the Italians. The word has been extended to cover all young cousins. Moreover, it is used frequently, and fondly, to describe the younger sisters and brothers of the fiancée of one of the sons. If the marriage results, *nipote* is warmly extended to the children of the in-laws. Thus la famiglia (the family) heart has very wide bounds. Everyone is treated alike, and no distinctions are made.

Nipote then leads to the heart of the matter of *la famiglia.* To the southern Italian, family still means not only husband and wife and children, but also grandparents, uncles, cousins, and godparents, in short all blood and in-law relatives. In any southern Italian community, one can observe several or more family units. However, while the strongest bonds are within the nuclear family, the links with the extended family are firm indeed.[3] Family solidarity gives the family its essential unity and cohesiveness. The behavior of one member of the family is often an item which concerns all family members. Covello says: "The family solidarity was manifested by uniformity of behavior, adherence to family tradition, and also a community of economic interests."[4] Jerre Mangione recalls this aspect of the family in Mount Allegro:

> All I know is that my relatives seemed happiest when they were crowded in a stuffy room noisy with chatter and children. Their passion for human company probably accounted for their relentless urge to produce children . . . and the deep pity they expressed for parents who only had one or two. . . .
> When their children were infants, they could hardly wait for them to grow into adults who would drink and eat with them, and in their impatience to see them would feed them bits of spaghetti and sometimes sips of wine. . . .[5]

Important to our understanding of *la famiglia* is "familism." Familism as a descriptive construct refers to a pervasive psychic interest and cultural value which arises from the family system. As a cultural characteristic of the South Italian social structure, it is internalized in the individual personality. What develops is a cultural disposition of southern Italian society and the personal predisposition of southern Italians.

Barzini has noted the role of the family in Italian society:

> The Italian family is a stronghold in a hostile land; within its walls and among its members, the individual finds consolation, help, advice, provision, loans, weapons, allies, and accomplices to aid in his pursuits. No Italian who has a family is ever alone. He finds in it refuge in which to lick his wounds after a defeat, or an arsenal and a staff for his victorious drives.[6]

In the past, the lack of secondary group structures gave the family a "functional autonomy" which was in keeping with its position in the larger society.[7]

The southern Italian family is still father dominated but mother centered. Polizzi suggests the family might be better viewed as pyramidal:

> Despite rather clear sex role differentiation in the family, the potential power of the father as an absolute authority figure is often seriously lessened by the social emotional leadership of the mother. . . . The woman holds a rather central postion but not a pedestal image. . . .[8]

The role of the wife is primarily concerned with the private life of the family, with the public role being the father's province. While the separation has been maintained in the past, the changed status of women will have a significant impact on the southern Italian family. Many changes can be expected to produce areas of strained relationships. What will be the impact of the legalization of abortion or the reform of the divorce laws on the Italian family? How will the Italian family adapt?

La serietà was a requisite characteristic of Italian woman. *La serietà* as best translated means seriousness, reliability, and strength in independent action. It is through *la serietà* that Italian women were able to help maintain *virtù* (virtue) which to Italians means dignity and self-respect.

Leonard Moss in his studies of the southern Italian family concludes after interviewing residents of several small towns in the 1950s that women more willingly accepted new ideas than did their husbands or brothers. Women organized into groups more frequently and discussed their problems with greater freedom than did men in the same towns. Moss also describes Italian families as "mother centered" rather than patriarchial. Southern Italian mothers privately and within the family achieve a level of dominance by verbally disarming the father. Any observer of the Italian family will note the steady barrage of banter, criticism, and kidding that occurs between husbands and wives. At times it appears to be restrained verbal warfare.

While children are an integral part of the family, it is still adult-centered. Yet it would be misleading to think that a seen-and-not-heard philosophy dominates the South Italian family. Regarding the role of children in the family, Polizzi writes:

> The child in southern Italian peasant society is not conceived of as someone whose inherent make-up necessitates that he be sheltered and nurtured in a separate existence. The child participates in two worlds, that of children and that of adults. Only infrequently is he left out of adult gatherings . . . his early socialization is rather informally shared among several village "agents" both inside and outside the nuclear family unit—with nearby or visiting aunts, uncles, cousins, godparents, neighborhood adults, and playmates.[9]

Children are taught not to think of "I" or "me" but primarily of "we" and "us." The rural southern Italian family in contrast to the urban family is a "productive consumptive unit." Perceptions of the outside world are sifted through an "economic filter." "An economic interpretation of reality seems at least, to be pervasive and to be reflected in practically every sphere of southern Italian life."[10]

Covello has noted that the similarity of his respondents in all dimensions indicated a social structure in which communal norms were so powerful that individual reactions were part of the traditional reactions of the community: "There was little need for the individual to assert himself; all his activities, all his thoughts, were prescribed by a traditional set of folkways, mores, customs."[11] The family as the center of the individual member's loyalty made it difficult to develop a social outlook which went beyond that of the family.[12] The importance of this factor to the development of community interests is noted by Covello:

> The social training of the young people, therefore, was directed toward a sharp discrimination between the family to which one must pay all kinds of allegiance, and the other families of the community itself which consisted of strangers and, as such, were due no special consideration. . . . A demarcation line was always drawn between the home and the community, and allegiance to one's family was made to appear more significant, more imperative, than allegiance to groups larger than the family.[13]

A third word which tells us something about the Italian family is *salutare*. It means "to greet." Used in the family, it has a very special meaning. Every member of a family has a birthday. On this occasion, he or she must be greeted by every other member of the family. The primary gift is the warm embrace and kissing on both cheeks. Jerre Mangione observes in *Mount Allegro*: "There were so many relatives that it was physically impossible to make the gatherings complete, but they took place frequently, and there was always a careful account made of those not left out the next time."[14]

In addition, each member of the family has a name day, which is rarely the same as the birthday. He or she must be greeted equally warmly on this occasion. There are other events in each member of the family's life which are marked by a joyous family festivity. Another student of the Italian family concludes:

> The immigrant remembered and tried to live in a cyclical rhythm of the seasonal and church calendar. Individual partic-

ipation was actually family participation in those activities sanctioned by traditions of the village as well as the social and economic system. To the immigrant, repetition was not necessarily to be avoided as boring or unproductive; on the contrary, he lived for the celebrations of Christmas Eve dinner, Christmas, Carnevale, Easter, the annual feast in honor of the patron divinity, and the christenings and weddings of family and *paesani*.[15]

It is not hard to see why the Italian family is, in fact, united. The ceremonies are so arranged that they leave little time for it to be anything else. There are, of course, arguments between siblings as there are anywhere else. But they must be made up before any of the ceremonial occasions.

But what about the elderly members of the Italian family? A fourth word, *rimbamito,* helps one to understand why the elderly are an integral part of the family. The phrase *rimbamito* means you have become a baby again. It is accepted by the family that an old person will be quirkish and garrulous. As one elderly man described it:

> And one day, when you've done something silly like burning your coat with tobacco from your pipe, you'll hear it said in the next room: "Rimbamito." From then on your life is not your own. I like to read sometimes—the old books I used to read. But sure enough someone will say, "Don't read so much, *nonno*, you'll tire your eyes." I still read without glasses, but they're right. It does tire your eyes. They've taken away my pension that I saved all my life for in that damned school over there. Of course, I must pay my share. But they dole the rest out to me in little bits, like a boy's pocket money. . . . And once a day I'm pushed out of the house because I must get some sun and air; and I must be back at mealtime or there'll be somebody shouting out of the window: *Nonno, nonno*, where are you? But still you've got your family around you. You've got someone to talk to. You're never lonely.[16]

The Italians need their old people.

After a young couple marries, they will set up a house of their own. Here we must study another word. *Visitare* means "to visit." The young couple will be visited by *La famiglia* on both sides. With the birth of children, the whole string of relationships is kept alive and perpetuated.

Edward Banfield, in a study of the South Italian community Montegranno, described it as a social system which lacks moral sanctions outside of the immediate family. The Montegranesi are pictured as opposed to any meaningful association outside the nuclear family. They are unwilling to engage in any political problem or activity in the interest of the community. Moreover, they are unable to achieve and maintain formal organizations. He suggests that the Montegranesi behave always as if they were following the rule of amoral familism: "Maximize the material short run advantage of the nuclear family; assume that all others will do likewise."[17] This rule becomes the dominant ethos of Montegranno, and the nuclear family is the dominant social unit. What follows is the absence of corporate groups or informal stable group alliances between the nuclear family and the community. Community leaders are few in number, and political alignments remain temporary and contingent.

Leonard Moss has noted, "Perhaps, with a bit more thought and effort, some author might come up with a more fortunate title than *The Moral Basis of a Backward Society*. Edward Banfield's research of twenty years ago continues to be quoted and continues to generate controversy."[18]

Banfield's use of the term amoral familism has a number of weaknesses. Upon what standard of morality is the term based? He is not justified in qualifying familism as amoral because, in the psychological, cultural, and economic context in which South Italians live, it is the only possible morality.

For the Italian to invest trust, the functional basis of morality, in an individual or institution other than the family is to run the risk, in the event of forfeiture by the trustee, of losing all. To appeal outside the family is to engage mechanisms of recourse belonging to state and church; that is, to entangle oneself in a situation where the language is incomprehensible, the form alien, the access unequal, the rules unknown, and the justice pernicious.

Leonard Moss has observed:

> Though there is a morsel of truth in Banfield's concept, the logical extensions are not, in fact, borne out. From the literature and from personal experience, there is no evidence to support the view that anarchy reigns at the village level. I cannot explain Banfield's narrow picture, except to note that he missed a great deal in terms of comparaggio, patron-client relations, trade networks, peer groups, and circles of intimacy.... In any event, most researchers report the family to be very moral and village life as something less than chaotic...."[19]

Amoral familism, or, as I prefer, just "familism," is a highly developed avoidance relationship that protects the individual in a stratified society. It protects the individual from entering into arrangements that may entail the interjection of state or church or of enmeshing one in a web that could destroy the individual and the family. Moreover, it protects the village society from rupture. All people recognize that to accept interaction is, in essence, to enter into a bond; therefore, one limits relationships outside of the family to those that are carefully defined.

Thus, familism is the law of a different society, and this different law is not uncivilized. If civilization means above all "an unwillingness to inflict unnecessary pain," then one must view this avoidance relationship as a highly civilized manner of maintaining social cohesion.

While Banfield's ideas still retain a core of validity, they must be modified. According to Silverman:

> Extrafamilial ties are not lacking, but those that exist (friendships, patronage relationships, casual groupings, etc.) are shifting, informal, and dyadic. Moreover, political action (as reflected in voting behavior, political machines, and the like) is regular and explicable, though it is flexible and lends itself readily to realignment.[20]

Ethos is not an adequate explanation of behavior. There are the realistic conditions of overpopulation, underemployment, land hunger, and so on. There are the external constraints of the state which remove responsibility at the local level, impose restrictive regulations on voluntary organization, and leave power to officials and those with influence. The Italians then see politics and political action as hopeless. Community is a weak structural unit.[21] Banfield's basic insight was essentially correct, but it is not an ethos which is the cause of the nuclear family as the dominant social unit. It other words, his explanation is backwards. According to Silverman, "It is not the ethos of 'amoral familism' that is the cause of these characteristics of the social system, but they are the basis of the ethos."[22]

The ethos of familism then may be seen as emerging out of southern Italian social patterns. To the extent that sanctions are lacking in relation to persons outside the nuclear family, it is a reflection of the scarcity of lasting extra-familial ties. Other aspects of this ethos are also expressions of southern social organization: the mistrust of persons outside the immediate family, the skeptical attitude toward cooperation, etc. Also closely related is a general apprehensiveness toward the world and the future and a feeling of helplessness about one's ability to control the environment.

There are a number of myths surrounding the Italian-Ameri-

can family. This is due to the assumption made by some observers that the family unit has not changed with time or with
the movement to an urban environment. Such views do not take
into consideration the changes which occur through the generations. Thus, the Italian-American family of the third generation
is falsely treated as if it were the same as that of the immigrant
generation. To see what happens to the southern Italian family
when it moves from an essentially rural environment to a new
and urban one, let us look at what happens to the Italian-
American families of the immigrants and trace them through the
third generation.

Consider first the matter of decision-making in the Italian-
American family. In my earlier study, *Ethnic Alienation: The
Italian-Americans,* thirteen immigrant respondents indicated
their fathers were the principal decision-makers. That same
number indicated their fathers were the chief disciplinarians
when decisions were made. Only three of the fifteen immigrants
maintained there was ever any extended discussion. Fourteen out
of fifteen of the respondents showed little dissatisfaction or disagreement with the decision-making and discipline arrangement.
This would seem to indicate the family patterns remain relatively stable during the initial years of living in urban America.
However, the southern Italian family gradually becomes less
patriarchial as loyalties outside the home start to impinge upon
its traditional role.[23] As Ianni notes:

> The adolescent children of the immigrant families in conflict
> in the past became the teenagers in conflict popularly identi-
> fied with the Little Italies of the Twenties and Thirties. The
> street corner gangs made famous by William Foote Whyte
> emerged as teenagers, no longer encompassed by an integrated
> and need satisfying family, took to the street corners and peer
> group associations. The family had neither the means nor the
> living space to provide recreation to replace the labor previ-
> ously expected of the adolescent. New conflicts also appeared in
> the parent child relationship as the teenager attempted to trans-
> mit his newly acquired American expectations of life into the
> weakened family structure.[24]

Four of the five first-generation respondents held that their
fathers were the principal decision-makers in their family. This
same number indicated their mothers were increasingly consulted on a variety of matters, but there was little discussion with
the other members of the family. Four of the five first-generation respondents expressed no strong disagreement with this
arrangement. The female members of the first-generation family

are increasingly provided with formal education as well as family education for marriage. The son is expected to work hard and to contribute to the family income. The rights of the individual member of the family are increasingly recognized, however not as much as desired in some cases. These are indications that the father is starting to lose his primary status in the family; while the mother is still the center of domestic life, work outside the family gives her more importance and independence.[25]

The first-generation family is in transition, in conflict, and disorganized, and the family culture is in question. Children in the first-generation Italian family become increasingly independent of the family as a result of outside employment.[26] The position of the family is further aggravated by the loss of that strong family culture which had been an indispensable part of its unity in Italy. While Italian culture is transmitted only by the family, American culture is transmitted by American institutions other than the family.[27] A first-generation college student described her family situation this way:

> Since I am a first generation Italian, I find the situation of dealing with my parents unbearable at times. Not growing up here they do not know the ways and customs and will go by what they believe and how they were brought up ... my freedom to do certain things results in many arguments. But at times I give in because they are too good to fight with. Because of the family ties, and from the Italian-American people with whom I have spoken, I feel that the Italian parents are among the most helpful and ready to do anything they can for their children. I cannot think of one incident where I would ask my father for something and he would not do it if he could.

Four of the five second-generation respondents asserted that there was shared decision-making with the other members of the family. Discipline was shared between mother and father. Individual members of the family often shape their own goals in life as a result of their increased independence. There are many signs of the subordination of the family to the individual. Female members of the family are educated with reference to personality development rather than to future marriage.[28] The son is expected to acquire an education. The mother's role is also altered in that her independence from the family is not only in the form of work, but in an increased social life, apart from it. The second-generation family moves further from the traditional Italian pattern but does not abandon it entirely.[29]

Four of the five third-generation respondents indicated that their fathers and mothers shared decision-making and disciplinary roles. There was more room for disagreement, and children were regularly consulted. There was also greater evidence of satisfaction with this arrangement than with the other generational groupings. The third-generation family tends to be urban, democratic, and modern. In-group solidarity decreases compared to the first- and second-generation families. The functions of the third-generation family are limited primarily to affectional.

Many an Italian-American, regardless of generation, will remember the discipline at home. Many will recall fathers or mothers biting their hands or knuckles inflicting pain on themselves as a show of self-restraint. My father rarely hit my brothers and sisters, but when he did—look out! There is a very personal and tender side to Italian men. Just one side of this tenderness is the capacity for Italian men to cry, sometimes unabashedly. Italian men and women are sentimentalists and romantics at heart. Jokingly, I would tell my father and others that he would cry over Hallmark Card commercials. I did not mean this as a criticism but, in fact, as a matter of admiration. When I received my master's degree, my father openly wept out of happiness and pride from the start to the very end of the commencement. I cannot conceive of an Italian-American writing a *Portnoy's Complaint* about his or her family. Mama and Papa are loved and respected.

We may also obtain an understanding of the impact of the urban environment on the Italian family by looking at family size and immediate and extra-familial participation.

The immediate family of the Italian immigrant respondents tended to be larger than that of the first, second, and third generations: 6 for the immigrant respondents; 5.4 for the first generation; 3.3 for the second generation; and 4.4 for the third generation. In addition, immediate family participation is higher for the first generation than for the second generation.[30]

It is interesting to note that five of the seven Italian immigrant respondents who had parents living in the United States also were living in the same neighborhood as their parents. Twelve of the fifteen immigrant respondents had a member of the extended family either in the neighborhood or the same city. Four of five of the first-generation respondents had their parents living in the same neighborhood. All of those of the first generation had a member of the extended family either in the same town or neighborhood. Three of the five second-generation respondents lived in the same neighborhood as their parents. All five had a member of the extended family in the same town or neighborhood. The relative stability of this pattern is seen in the third generation where four of the five respondents had their parents and a member of the extended family living in the same neighborhood or, at minimum, living in the same town.

Members of the first generation lived in closer physical proximity than either the second or third generation. If we consider visiting patterns on a per week basis, the second- and third-generation respondents visited relatives and were in turn visited more frequently than the first-generation or the immigrant respondents. These findings suggest that the second- and third-generation respondents became increasingly active outside the family as they acculturated urban values, but at the same time, they retained family contacts. The extended family plays a greater role for the second- and third-generation respondents than for those of the first. However, through all generations, the Italian family remains an extended family in a psychological sense.

One final note must be made about the Italian-American family in America in the 1970s and beyond. Some Americans are individualists. Essentially, they seek their own welfare first. Others are "family people." For them, the first unit of concern is the family. What helps it? What causes injury to it? To Italian-Americans, the family is of primary concern.

> The Italian immigrant came [to the United States] with an extraordinary sense of independence because he had experienced many dimensions of history: He had not the preoccupation with bureaucracy of other nationalities, but he understood the interworking of organizational structure and its personal dimension in the family, the village, and the church; he had won national status but he was even worse off; he came to America at the zenith of its industrial need for manual labor which he offered in exchange for a relative degree of family integrity; given his historical position, he realized the shallow alternatives offered by bureaucratization, and, in a persistent way, he found to maintain the familiar and essential familial.[31]

In our society, the corporation, the government, and the media have been devastating to family people. Almost everything about jobs, work conditions, government programs, and the images flooding out from the media ignores the needs of families and injures families.

For Italian-Americans, the family is the chief source of nourishment and joy, of conflict and struggle. It is in the family that moral values are quietly and silently inculcated—honesty, questioning, obedience, respect for others, manners, courage, cynicism, civic responsibility.

Sociologists, educators, social workers, and many others have all traced a number of social problems to the breakdown of the family in America and, strangely, have extolled the nuclear family model as truly modern. To Italian-Americans of the third generation, the extended family exists in a psychological sense. To Italian-Americans, the family is primary. The Italian-American family is an important model for a society reeling under the impact of broken marriages, disaffected young, and discarded old.[32] One of the most reliable indicators of family stability is the divorce rate, where it is found that the Italian-Americans along with the Irish have the lowest incidence of divorce. There is a low percentage of Italian female-headed households. The net effects of this stability can also be linked to the low rates of mental illness among Italians.[33]

What the Italian-American example serves to teach is that, when families break down, the molecular structure of society disintegrates. What families leave undone, social institutions can repair only at great expense. To many Italian-Americans, the hallmark of modern man is knowing when to be traditional.

9 Cabrini and Covello

Cabrini! Cabrini! In reverent tones the name of this remarkable woman spread like wildfire in the Italian ghettoes. She elicited hope, devotion, and pride, not only to the embattled *contadini* and their children, but to all people.

I recall, as a young boy, the reverence with which she was mentioned—not only in our home, but in those of our friends and relatives as well. I also remember the frequent visits to the old chapel of the Mother Cabrini High School where she rested. "Glory of America" and "Mother of Immigrants" are two of the more powerful phrases used to describe the life of Mother Frances Xavier Cabrini. The titles tell something of the life of this spiritual woman of God who walked among the streets helping the needy, not only of New York, but of hundreds of other cities in the United States and Latin America.

On July 15, 1850, Agostino Cabrini was swinging his flail, threshing wheat, while his wife Stella was giving birth two months prematurely to their thirteenth child. They were no longer young; Stella was fifty-two. Tragedy had followed upon tragedy; nine of their children had died, leaving only Rosa, Maddalena (hopelessly crippled by polio), and Giovanni.

Francesca Cabrini was born in the small city of Sant'Angelo in Lombardy in northern Italy. Her mother was a Christian, a sweet and tender woman. Her father, Agostino Cabrini, was a sensible man of great integrity and also a fervent Christian. He was a farmer, honest and sober. Francesca was the youngest child. Physically sick most of the time, she never showed any great physical strength, but the spiritual strength of this child was the strength of a giant. Her parents were examples to her of Christian love, especially her father. She recalled that, at the age of nine, when the Austrian Army was invading the western part of northern Italy, her father, although Italian, had Christian love and understanding for the soldiers. He did not hesitate to let them in his home, feed them, give them something to drink, and show love without malice or prejudice. A couple of months later, the same army was marching back to Austria defeated by the Italian Army. At this particular time, Agostino Cabrini did not hesitate to make a field hospital out of his own house. He let the wounded men, Austrian and Italian, come into his home. There was no partiality shown, only concern for his fellowman. Although a first cousin of Agostino Cabrini was a fervent politician who later went to Rome as a representative of that area of the country, Agostino never took part in politics. His aim was to be a good Christian and a man of God. Mutual respect and kindness abounded in the Cabrini home. The reward of a day's work well done was an evening of prayer after supper. The Scriptures, the stories of martyred saints, and the Annals of the Propagation of the Faith were read aloud in their home in the evenings. These spiritual readings made a deep impression upon the child Francesca and had a far-reaching effect in the shaping of her future.

The child was a dreamer and would often go to a small river which flowed near her home. There, she would daydream, make paper boats, load them with flowers, and then send them off to strange lands. She used to dream of the day when she could go away to strange lands in search of souls.

She remembered on her eighth birthday that, when she received the Sacrament of Confirmation, she felt enveloped with a supernatural power; it was a feeling she could not describe. According to her, it was the time when she was annointed with the Holy Ghost and she received the blessing of God. It was the event that changed her whole life. At eleven years of age, she made a vow of virginity. She decided to become a missionary, a spouse of Jesus Christ. She felt sure that God was calling her, and she was determined to consecrate her life entirely and completely to the Master's call, the love of Jesus Christ, and his wonderful work for the redemption of lost souls throughout the world. In this beautiful atmosphere of Christianity and a happy family, she grew up to be a young lady.[1]

At the age of thirteen, she was admitted to the Daughters of the Sacred Heart school. During the following five years, she mastered Latin, Italian, French, history, mathematics, geography, and natural science.

Classic literature, geography, and history were of particular interest to her. She acquired extensive knowledge of ancient civilizations, races, and social systems, of myth-shrouded Egypt, of Old Testament Hebrew titans, of Chaldean wisdom, of Grecian grace, and of the builders of imperial Rome.

Francesca was exposed to the works of Tintoretto, Mantegna, Bellini, and Raphael. They had worked at their art in her native Lombardy. Leonardo da Vinci's "Last Supper" is on the wall of the refectory in the church of Santa Maria delle Grazie.

On graduating from school, she became a school teacher. During the cold winter of 1869, she lost her father, and in 1870, her mother died. In 1872, there was an epidemic of small-pox throughout the country. Although she was afflicted, she recovered quickly. She started helping her Uncle Luigi, a priest, in aiding the smallpox victims. Her sister Rose also worked very hard in helping Francesca and their Uncle Luigi in tending the sick. In 1872, her beloved uncle, Father Don Luigi, and her sister Maddalena died.

After the epidemic was over, some local priests asked her, since she had teaching certification, to substitute for a couple of weeks in the little hamlet of Vidardo. She accepted and stayed not a couple of weeks, but years. Later Monsignor Serrati convinced her to go to Codogno and help in the House of Provi-dence. It was a home for orphans and abandoned children that some sisters were running. It was a rough experience for Frances. The place was not run like an institution but like a crazy house. There was no discipline whatsoever, and Frances had a hard time organizing things. The sisters running the home acted as if they were out of their minds. They were full of mistrust and jealousy. It was a difficult situation, but Frances acquired the experience and the toughness she would need for her future life. As a matter of fact, she repeatedly stated in her letters, "If you encounter difficulties it is a good sign, it is a sign of future blessings."

Not long after, she decided to join the order of the Sisters of the Sacred Heart, and she founded her own orphanage and school with the help of Monsignor Serrati. Her main ambition was not only to take care of Italian orphans and Italian people, but to go throughout the world, particularly East, perhaps China or India, and care for the unsaved ones. She wanted to bring these unsaved people to Christ.

Five months after Francesca took her vows, Cardinal Vincenzo Gioacchino Pecci was elected Pope and became Leo XIII. The new Pope was confronted by hostile governments. Capitalism, the Italian industrial revolution, revolutionary theories, all came together at this time. Leo XIII intended to forge a reconciliation between the church and the people. He believed theology had to be reconciled with science. He believed in education and encouraged the study of astronomy and natural science. Additionally, Leo XIII was destined to be the Pope and a friend of Francesca's life and mission. Frances decided to take a trip to Rome with the intention of opening another school and orphanage. She was discouraged by Monsignor Serrati from making this trip. In spite of this, she decided to go. No one could persuade her not to, and upon her arrival in Rome she met Cardinal Vicari Parocchi.

Cardinal Vicari was a hard man to convince. He told her it was impossible to have another school and orphanage in Rome. It was not needed. The old city was full of orphanages and schools. Above all, where was she going to get the money to start such an enterprise? He suggested she go back to Codogno and continue working in that area. On the way back home, Mother Cabrini told her weeping companion, "God will change people's hearts. We will pray, and you wait and see." She never gave up. She went back twice more to see the Cardinal. Finally, he told her that, instead of opening a house in Rome, she would start two—a free tuition school for the poor in Porta Pia and a nursery in Aspra.

By 1889, Francesca had opened seven houses and had the friendship of Cardinal Parocchi. Through him, her work became known at St. Peter's. On March 12, 1888, Francesca received from the Vatican the Decretum Laudis, the recognition and approval of her Institute of Missionary Sisters.

During this period of time, Bishop Scalabrini, who was aware of the tremendous spiritual need of the Italian immigrant in America, asked Pope Leo XIII for permission to gather together a group of zealous missionary priests to go to America to minister among the Italian immigrants. In 1889, Cabrini opened a college in Castelsangiovanni in Piacenza. Scalabrini was the bishop there. He and Cabrini became friends. Scalabrini visited America and was appalled at the conditions he found there. He made the emigrant cause his cause. He founded the Congregation of St. Charles Borremeo in New York and set about organizing aid for the immigrants.

Bishop Scalabrini was a great judge of human nature, and he realized from his first meeting with Mother Cabrini that beneath the fragile suffering frame there was a great worker for the Lord. Later, they were to become co-workers together in the vast unattended vineyard across the Atlantic.

After his second meeting with Mother Cabrini, the bishop

invited her to send some missionary sisters to New York. Frances Cabrini realized the great necessity of working among the Italian immigrants in the new world, but her dream had always been the Orient, and she always thought her destination would be China. When Bishop Scalabrini insisted, she said, "I am sorry, but the world is too small for me to be anchored to one spot. I want my work to encompass every field and reach every area." Bishop Scalabrini did not give up easily, and he insisted again.[2] He told Mother Cabrini the first Italian parish in the Archdiocese of New York, called the Mission of St. Charles Borromeo, was in desperate need of Italian sisters to open a school for Italian immigrant children. Before she made a final decision about America, she had an audience with Pope Leo XIII. The Pope listened carefully and attentively to her, but when the audience was over, he said, "Not to the East my daughter, but to the West, that is where you are needed the most." On March 23, 1889, Francesca, accompanied by six nuns, left Le Havre for America.

Italian priests and nuns, though unwelcome by the Catholic hierarchy in America, were needed badly. On a rainy night in 1889 she arrived in New York. To her surprise, nobody was there to welcome them. Promptly, Mother Cabrini took her six nuns and proceeded through New York City to their destination. The next day, she met with Archbishop Corrigan, who promptly informed her that the orphanage to which she had been assigned was nonexistent. He strongly urged the group to return to Italy. Mother Cabrini insisted she was here to stay. Archbishop Corrigan then arranged for her nuns to teach Italian children at St. Joachin's Church near Mulberry Street.[3]

The first few months the women worked very hard. They climbed narrow staircases, descended into filthy cellars, and entered dives where policemen were afraid to go alone. She and her daughters were some of the first nuns to visit jails and to bring comfort and word of hope to inmates. Many times, they spent hours and hours among people who were going to be executed to give them the spiritual comfort needed. An article in the *New York Times* said, "They are all slender, delicate women, and their mode of dress is a bit different from what we are accustomed to seeing. They only speak a few words of English. They belong to an institution that looks after the orphans and all of them are Italian."[4]

Mother Cabrini received some help from Count diCesnola who was then Director of the Metropolitan Museum of Art. The Count's wife was stirred by the plight of thousands and thousands of Italian children made orphans through industrial misfortunes. Not long after that, Mother Cabrini opened a house of her own on 59th Street and started taking in orphans. At this point, Bishop Corrigan informed Mother Cabrini she would have been better off to have an orphanage in Little Italy in the middle of the Italian section, because she could not count on much support from the American establishment. The facts were that most of the help she received came from the poor Italians living in Little Italy. People gave her whatever they could. When the orphans started coming in, they were not only orphans of Italian parents, but also of other nationalities and races and of many different religions. As long as there was room available, none of them was turned away.

During this time, Bishop Scalabrini, who was running the first Italian Catholic Parish in New York, had opened a hospital to help the Italian immigrant. This hospital was badly run, and Bishop Scalabrini asked Mother Cabrini to help out with some of her daughters. Mother Cabrini obliged, but the hospital was in such bad shape physically and financially that it had to be closed. She had had no intention of opening a hospital of her own, for her main concern was orphans and schools, but she finally decided to open a hospital where she could run it properly and see that her patients would receive proper care. The first thing she did was get a small house. There were no facilities and no doctors. The sisters even had to get soup from a nearby restaurant. While the patients were in beds, her daughters were sleeping on hard floors, but she knew that God would help. She prayed and prayed. Not long after, people started donating beds and supplies, and doctors, many of them non-Italians, started to volunteer their services free. Later, she had an opportunity to buy a former fire house on 163rd Street and Edgecomb Avenue in Manhattan. An addition was added, and this became the first good-sized hospital for Italian immigrants; it housed about 165 beds. From New York, she moved to Chicago, where another large and modern hospital was built, Columbus Hospital. Then she moved back to New York and went from there to New Orleans. Her arrival there coincided with the lynching of eleven Italian immigrants accused of having committed a crime of which they were innocent. The condition of the Italian immigrant in this city was the worst in the States. She managed to buy a house and start a Sunday School, a regular school, an orphanage, and a small hospital.

When everything was running smoothly, she went to Nicaragua, invited by a woman she had met during a trip from Europe.

By this time, she had made several trips to Italy and back. In Nicaragua, she established a small school for the elite class. With the help of this Nicaraguan lady, she bought a beautiful colonial style home in the city of Granada. First, she was shunned, because the people were skeptical about seeing Italian sisters starting a school. They had no idea of how capable the group of sisters would be in teaching their children. The school was soon filled to capacity.

While she was in Nicaragua, this frail nun of forty-two years decided to explore the San Juan River whose outlet was Lake Nicaragua. Her sole companion was a Nicaraguan girl who served as an interpreter. With the utmost simplicity, she began an expedition through the jungles, a 140 mile trip. There, she met some Indian people who were called Mesquiots. She started preaching the gospel to them. Mother Cabrini promised she would be back some day and build them a church. Unfortunately she never found the time to go back. She always said to herself, "I must go back; I must go back." After this exhausting journey, she contracted yellow fever and almost died.

She recuperated quickly and took another journey to visit the Italians in the United States. Besides Louisiana, she went to Virginia and the Carolinas, where the Italians, mostly Sicilians, were considered on the same social level as blacks. She stayed for a time to help her own people.

Returning to New York, Cabrini started a home on a big estate that she bought in West Park on the Banks of the Hudson River. Later, she bought some property near Fort Tryon Park on a street now named Cabrini Boulevard. The Mother Cabrini High School was built on this site, and it has become one of the finest high schools for girls in the city. Next to the high school, there is a chapel where her body still remains. A big hotel was for sale on 19th Street and 2nd Avenue. Cabrini took the opportunity to purchase it and opened a hospital. Today, an ultramodern hospital named Mother Cabrini Memorial Center is there. She was always on the move. Near Chicago, she bought a farm so that her hospital could have fresh milk and eggs for its patients. Another orphanage home in a beautiful villa at Dobbs Ferry was started.

From there, she moved back to Rome and went from Rome to Codogno, where she rested for a while. Then she went to Paris, Madrid, and London. Every place she went, she established schools, old age homes, orphanages, and homes for noviciation. It was back-breaking work, and she was not physically well. From England, she came back to New York. Mother Cabrini checked and inspected what she had already started. From there she went to South America.

She proceeded to Panama and Nicaragua, then traveled by boat to other countries and cities in South America. In Chile, she established another school. From there, she decided to cross the Andes to Argentina. Most of this trip was done on muleback. It was a miracle that she was able to complete the trip. While going through the Andes, an accident occurred while she was jumping over a crevice and only a last-moment rescue saved her life. After a long, hard, exhausting trip she reached Argentina and Buenos Aires, there establishing a hospital, an orphanage, and a school. Mother Cabrini went on to Brazil, where many Italians lived, to establish schools and hospitals. Just a few years earlier, a plague in Rio De Janeiro had killed nine thousand Italians.

From Brazil, she came back to New York to rest. She was aging, tired, and weary, but her rest did not last long. She was "back at the drawing boards," as she used to say many times. She went to Pennsylvania and established another school and a college. She was always in search of souls to be saved or people who needed help. I say "people," because, even though originally she started to work for the Italians, her work of love, hope, and mercy encompassed people of every race, nationality, and creed, who were all helped by the Cabrini institutions. Nobody who asked for help was ever turned away.

When in Madrid, Cabrini met a princess who was a member of the Spanish royal family. This princess was so impressed with Cabrini's work that she introduced her to the queen. The queen asked if she would send some of her nuns to teach Italian to the children of the court and to tutor them in other subjects. Mother Cabrini firmly declined this invitation to the amazement of the Spanish bluebloods. The queen could not understand how a group of sisters could go to the wild, vast country of Bilbao and open an orphanage while turning down the tremendous advantages and opportunities of teaching at court. But Mother Cabrini said to her daughters, "The court is no place for the King's Brides." She was always more concerned about spiritual well-being than physical. She felt that each ·person ought to shoulder his own cross and confront his own sacrifice with silent dignity and courage.[5]

By 1906, on the twenty-fifth anniversary of the founding of her order, Mother Cabrini had missions in eight countries, operated by a thousand sisters.

Death came to this holy and revered woman on December

22, 1917, in Chicago. After her death, miracles and cures were attributed to her. On July 7, 1946, Pope Pius XII conducted a solemn ceremony which made Frances Xavier Cabrini a canonized saint, the first American citizen to be elevated to sainthood.

Mrs. Josephine Canelosi recalled her audience with Mother Cabrini in 1907 at the Missionary Sisters of the Sacred Heart Chapel in New Orleans:

> The Sisters had told us before the interview to be careful, that in their estimation she was already a saint, that we should be sure to kneel in her presence.... Mother Cabrini, I remember, asked my name, my age, and what I was doing with my life. At that time, I wanted to be a nun, to join the Missionary Sisters of the Sacred Heart, and I told her this. Mother Cabrini told me to pray to the Virgin for guidance but to remember that my mother needed me since my father had died.... It was a strange feeling when she was canonized to realize that I had met and talked with a saint.[6]

At the time of her death, Mother Cabrini had left behind sixty-seven Catholic institutions, one for every year of her life. Her nuns were at work in eight countries in North and South America and in Europe.

There were once several landmarks in New York City connected with Mother Cabrini, but they have all virtually disappeared. All that remain are memories of the buildings which once stood there. For example, the Church of St. Joachim in lower Manhattan where Mother Cabrini and her group first actively began their ministry in New York was torn down two decades ago when the area underwent vast renewal changes.

However, today there does exist in New York the supreme shrine constructed in 1959–1960 to Mother Cabrini, the one which contains her remains. The Shrine chapel has been incorporated into the high school run by the Missionary Sisters of the Sacred Heart of Jesus. Under the altar, exposed to view in a crystal casket, the body of Mother Cabrini lies covered with a wax mask. The peace of death compares drastically with the dynamics of the woman when she was vibrantly alive and amazingly active.

To those who wish them, statistics abound as to the number of orphaned children cared for by Mother Cabrini and her congregation, the multitudes of sick to whom they administered, the thousands they taught in their schools, and the thousands they comforted in jails. No statistics will ever be available, however, on the comfort given by the saint—comfort to the unlearned immigrant in a strange land, to the despairing and the poor, to the thousands in the cities throughout the world.

I doubt if the name of Mother Cabrini will ever fade. She is a symbol of hope and inspiration for all people. Since my visits to the Cabrini chapel, I have remained devoted to this great lady, the "Saint of the Immigrants."

It was a number of years ago that I first met Leonard Covello at a small gathering in East Harlem. I came to receive advice and help with my doctoral dissertation. Following the meeting of the newly formed American Italian Historical Association, Dr. Covello came to me and greeted me so warmly that I felt I had known this man all my life. He radiated intelligence and a humanity that distinguish only those rare, great individuals. Since that first encounter, he remains a very dear and close friend.

Leonard Covello was born on November 26, 1887, in Avigliano (Potenza), Italy. He came to the United States with his parents in 1895. They settled in West Harlem.

To arrive at Ellis Island at the age of eight from a village of southern Italy was an overwhelming experience. It is difficult to capture accurately the impact made by the teeming metropolis of New York City with its buildings, elevated railroads, and tenements on a young boy uprooted from the insulated yet secure atmosphere of a poor town in the Basilicata region of Italy. Moving into a depressed section of a huge city, living in tenements, and going to a school where the language spoken was unfamiliar presented large problems and required serious adjustment. It is just this kind of experience and the resulting understanding that enabled Leonard Covello to recognize the many frustrations and problems facing immigrant and migrant groups when they move into new and totally different environments. The crucial importance of the schools in these areas, not only for the children, but also for their parents, was appreciated by Dr. Covello. Covello's life is closely bound to East Harlem, which was an immigrant enclave in the northeast section of Manhattan Island. There were eighty-nine thousand Italians living there by 1930.

Leonard Covello went through the schools very successfully. He went to P.S. No. 83 and Morris High School in East Harlem, received a scholarship to Columbia University in 1907, and graduated as a member of Phi Beta Kappa in 1911. He continued working at Columbia for his master's degree and began teaching French at DeWitt Clinton High School. World War I interrupted his teaching career; he served as a member of the Intelligence Service in France and Spain. Following his war service, he had a brief career in the competitive world of advertising, then returned to teaching at DeWitt Clinton High School in 1920. In 1934, he became principal of the newly created Benjamin Franklin High School in East Harlem and remained at that post until 1956.

Italian parents were often left untouched and outside the life of the school. Parents learned about America from their children, but their own contacts with the school were almost nonexistent.

> Not being able to speak English well if at all, ignorant of the mechanisms of the system, possessing little understanding of what transpired within the walls of the school, the parents stayed away. The school seemed to accept this state of affairs, and so it prevailed.[7]

One significant attempt was made to change all this. It came in the form of Leonard Covello.

In many respects, it was Dr. Covello who originated the community school concept. He dramatically demonstrated its application during his tenure as principal of Benjamin Franklin High School. At Franklin, he worked out an educational program which was community centered and which could have become a national "prototype for the reformation of urban education in a democratic society." His school did not concern itself solely with the academic subjects taught to students but attempted to develop for both the students and their parents, and for the people in the community, those programs which were designed to promote the well-being of the community and the development of the principles of a democratic society. In 1936, Dr. Covello stated:

> In New York City, the public-school system occupies not only an important strategic position, but also a unique position in the life of the community. It is the only social agency that has direct contact with practically every family within the community and the educational law makes this contact with the family compulsory from the early childhood to the late adolescence of every boy and girl. This is important when one realizes that the public-school system functions in a city which has a population of close to seven million people, of whom one million two hundred thousand go to school. . . . The school, and the cooperating agencies in the neighborhood, are centering attention and effort upon certain fundamental aspects of the educational problems of the community because of the conviction that to correct the causes of maladjustment is patently the

task of any school that wishes to aid in transforming these communities of foreign-born people into an integral part of the larger American community to which they should, for the good of all concerned, belong fully and happily. To accomplish this, it is necessary first to allay the distrust and the antagonism that have risen out of misunderstanding and indifference. Disruptive forces must be replaced with a spirit of friendliness and intelligent cooperation in the building of wholesome social and civic relationships. There must be a spirit of tolerance and of mutual give and take between the immigrant and his children and the native born and his children.[8]

To Covello, the crucial problem for the Italian-American youngster was that the schools in which he found himself were not designed with him in mind. In Covello's view, "the traditional American school was planned for an 'Hypothetical' American child whose contact with American civilization was assumed to be extensive, whose intelligence was supposed to be higher, and whose knowledge and use of the English language was assumed to be more perfect than that of the Italo-American child." In an article written in 1936 on "A High School and Its Immigrant Community," Covello posed a series of questions he felt needed answering: "What role has the public school played in immigrant or foreign communities in which it has been located? What role is it playing today? Has the school really felt the life of the community pulsating beyond its four walls? Has it made an attempt to realize the problems and the difficulties with which the immigrant community is faced?" His conclusion was that the "answer to all these questions, unfortunately, is very discouraging."[9]

Covello's own experience, as he recalled it in *The Heart Is the Teacher*, was one in which he and his friends were made to feel inferior and forced "to make a good impression on our teachers...at the expense of our family and what was Italian in us."[10] And he found that, during the period in which he was a teacher, Italian students felt the same way. From Italian college students came the following response to questions about their earlier schooling: "Our school...'solved' the problem of the Italian group which characterized our neighborhood by ignoring the subject. To be Italian was virtually a fauxpas and the genteel American ladies who were our teachers were tactful enough to overlook our error"[11] "The school... never suggested respect for my parents and for their culture," Covello wrote.[12]

Covello believed in becoming involved in the day-to-day life of the student:

> To function successfully, it [the school] must know not only
> the social and educational background of its boys and girls, but
> it must go one step further: it must strive to understand the
> individual child in his social relationships outside of school.
> More important still, it must play an active and aggressive part
> in the affairs of the community . . . it must be the leader and the
> coordinating agency in all educational enterprises affecting the
> life of the community and, to a certain extent, the pivot upon
> which much even of the social and civic life of the neighbor-
> hood shall turn. . . . The surging life of the community as a
> whole . . . will either promote or destroy the work of the
> school.[13]

As principal of Benjamin Franklin High, Covello was able
to put into practice these beliefs. Benjamin Franklin High
came into existence only after Covello and others in East Harlem began putting pressure on the Board of Education for
a high school to serve this area. Even then, the key was not,
as Covello has acknowledged, the sympathy of the Board of
Education, but the election of Fiorello LaGuardia, formerly
the Congressman of East Harlem, to the office of Mayor of
New York. "Mayor LaGuardia's approval was the deciding
factor in the establishment of Benjamin Franklin High,"
Covello notes in his autobiography. With the establishment
of Benjamin Franklin, Covello and his staff were able to begin
organizing a community-centered school without worrying about
intereference. In the summer of 1935, they brought together
a Community Advisory Council of Benjamin Franklin High,
whose membership consisted of representatives from various
community agencies and whose task was to help link the school
to the community. By the fall of 1935, an active community
program was underway. At the dedication ceremony in 1942,
Covello was able to speak of much more than educational
triumph!

> Believing that a school building should be available to all
> the members of the community, all the time, the Board of
> Education has conferred a signal honor on Benjamin Franklin
> High School. By a special vote, it has decreed that our building
> is to be open every hour of every day of the year. This means
> that we who live and work in East Harlem are free to use its
> magnificent resources at all times.[14]

In making the school part of the community, Covello had
reached new heights. But his innovations are also to be measured
in terms of how the programs he developed worked within
the school. These programs served a broad range of students

at Benjamin Franklin, not just Italian. They were, however, developed initially for Covello's Italian students at DeWitt Clinton, and it is with the needs of these Italian students in mind that they are best understood. The "within school" results of Covello's work are particularly visible in three areas: language learning, curriculum, and teacher performance.

For Covello, who as a child remembered the "Italian language was completely ignored" so that he got the idea that "Italian meant something inferior," it became crucial to organize a program in which Italian children should feel pride in their own language. When he began teaching, it was possible for a student to get credit for Italian by passing a Regents' Examination, but no high school had an Italian department. Covello's first step was to begin teaching Italian to Italian students who wanted to learn it under the informal auspices of an Italian club, *Il Circolo Italiano*. In short order, his teaching had progressed from a club to a formal class, and an Italian department was begun at DeWitt Clinton to accommodate the fact that in five years' time the number of students taking Italian rose from 30 to 528.

With the development of an Italian department, it was not just the Italian language Covello had made part of the school curriculum, however. He had also helped to rekindle a general sense of cultural pride in his students, and their interest in Italian began to go far beyond a concern with language. They began "to speak or write on Italian subjects in the English, social studies, art classes of the school." Like Covello's other educational innovations, this one, too, had its final measure in the student seeing that his adjustment to America need not come at the expense of his heritage.

As a result of his involvement in the Italian program within the school, Covello saw his relationship to his students and their parents strengthened. "The Italian teacher became the representative of the school to Italian-speaking parents, as an interpreter and as a sympathetic listener, and the instrument of adjustment of behavior problems and scholastic difficulties in the school and the adjustment of child-parent conflicts in the home." For Covello, this larger bond only strengthened his belief in the value of having a teacher and authority figure in the school with the same ethnic background as his pupils. Such a figure, he wrote in *The Social Background of the Italo-American Child*, was a "stimulus to the student toward broader education and continuation of schooling" plus an additional factor in mitigating "the sense of inferiority on the part of

the Italo-American student." For Covello, who as a child remembered "our teachers impressed us mainly because they did
not live in the neighborhood," only one further step remained
for the community-oriented teacher who wanted to be in touch
with the most important forces in his students' lives, and that
was to do as he did after he became principal of Benjamin
Franklin High—move to within walking distance of the school
where he taught.

In 1944, Covello completed his doctoral dissertation, the
monumental, *The Social Background of the Italo-American
School Child.* This study, which largely went unheralded, is
one of the finest and greatest studies of an ethnic group. It
was finally published in 1967. Dr. Covello's study leads one
to the basic conclusion that, to be successful in education, one
must certainly have a more than cursory knowledge of the whole
background and life style of the individuals or groups whom
the school serves. As one reviewer noted:

> If more teachers of the present day knew more of the things
> about their students that Dr. Covello pointed out as it con-
> cerned the southern Italian family structure, such as the atti-
> tudes of family tradition, the wife's attitude toward the tradi-
> tional roles of the husband in the family, the various ap-
> proaches to the early training of young girls in the home, the
> approach to adolescence, the standards of sex morality, the
> basic concerns of brothers over the marital status of their
> sisters, the father's attitude toward the daughter's marriage, the
> concept of dowry, the status of young wives, the economic worth
> of wives, the mistrust aspect of wives, a whole host of other cul-
> tural contextual ideas, values, and practices, things might be
> different in many schools.[15]

What Covello was to demonstrate is that an understanding
of the cultural background and the life-style of the child is
basic to the establishment of a worthwhile and meaningful
educational program.

Dr. Covello touched the life of the Italians in New York
City in ways that are beyond count. There was no activity organized by Italians in which he did not participate.

> Leonard Covello touched the life of the Italian community
> in New York City in a multiplicity of ways: There was virtually
> no activity organized by Italians in which Dr. Covello did not
> participate. As early as 1910, he (with John Shedd) organized
> the Lincoln Club of Little Italy in East Harlem. At De Witt
> Clinton High School, a Circolo Italiano was established as
> early as 1914 under Dr. Covello's sponsorship; and he partici-

pated in the work of the Italian League for Social Service
(organized in 1915), and the Young Men's Italian Educational
League (organized, 1916), energetically ambitious early efforts
to improve the lot of Italian-Americans. From its inception in
1912, Dr. Covello served as vice-president of the Italian Teachers Association (New York City), a major force in stimulating
Italian language study; and he was the guiding force behind
the Italian Parents Association (organized, 1927) which afforded a bridge between the schools and the Italian community.
It was Dr. Covello's strategic deployment of the influence of
the order Sons of Italy which helped lead in 1922 to the New
York City Board of Education granting parity to Italian with
other modern languages in the city schools. And there were
continuing involvements and participations: in the work of
the Italian Educational League, the Italy-American Society;
the Casa Italiana Educational Bureau; and the *Instituto di Cul-
tura Italiana* (later, the Casa Italiana of Columbia University);
and it was Dr. Covello who provided the major impetus for the
founding of the American Italian Historical Association in the
mid-1960's (whose operating expenses he assumed for several
years in a lonely vigil passed in an East Harlem brownstone,
as though awaiting the Italian community, long since gone,
to be reborn).[16]

On June 2, 1970, Columbia University belatedly conferred
its "Medal for Distinguished Service" on Dr. Covello. The com-
mendation was honoring a distinguished alumnus:

> Declared by generations of his professional peers to be one
> of New York City's greatest educators, having demonstrated a
> quarter of a century ago that a large urban high school can
> serve its whole community; a man who throughout his career
> as teacher, principal, and consultant has demonstrated the
> vitality of our great ideal of equal, excellent, integrated educa-
> tion for people of all races, creeds, and conditions....[17]

Professor Jerre Mangione stated this universal tribute: "He
personifies all the fine qualities that are ideally found in a
man: a strong sense of humanitarianism and social responsibility, which can only come from love of mankind, as well as
the ability and willingness to express that sense in concrete
terms."[18] At the age of ninety-three, Leonard Covello is now
in Sicily working to help the poor and the aged. Recently,
during a visit to the United States, he was again honored by
his friends and some of those whose lives he has touched. Just
as I was to leave my home with my wife, my son asked us where
we were going. "Well, we're going to see Dr. Covello. He's going
to be given an award and a party." Andrew's eyes lit up: "Wow!

Can I come? He's a great guy!" My son summed it up for us all.

A recent letter to me from Dr. Covello concluded: "Today a man raises his hands towards the skies in a yearning for peace; tomorrow another man will stretch out his hands; some day all men will stretch out their hands; that day we shall all be brothers."

10 The Saints Are Older Relatives and Friends

The religion of the Italians from the *Mezzogiorno* was woven into the fabric of everyday life, as an individual, as a member of a family group, and, more remotely, as a member of a community group. The village Church in Italy was the center of community life for the people. The Church was a religious as well as a social force. The people turned to the Church in times of sorrow or in times of celebration. The days of *festa* were the important points of the inhabitants' year. They came to church not only to pray but to socialize. This was important to them, since it meant the church was a part of their lives, rather than an institution with limited functions.

The southern Italian came to the village priest for advice on temporal matters on business, travel, and marriage. The priest did not serve as a binding moral force, since the villagers reserved the right to do what they wanted if they disagreed with the advice. The local priest was viewed as a friend, as one of their own, since he was a man who had been born a peasant. He was admired, because he was educated. He understood his people and made allowances for their shortcomings.

By virtue of a number of factors—historical, ethnic, geopolitical, and cultural—two interrelated religious systems developed and were fused together to form the religion of the *Mezzogiorno*. One was the official Roman Catholic Church and the other a parallel system which is peculiarly southern Italian. As Covello observed:

> The religious patterns of the southern Italians, that is primarily the peasants, were based upon a belief of a twofold order of reality; the one visible, subordinate to the laws of nature; the other invisible, intangible—the mystic sphere which encompassed the first.... Not even the literate classes clearly defined the distinction between the two worlds.[1]

Special powers were attributed to individual saints. Local saints and Madonnas were real personages whose power had been attested to by miracles. In the belief of southern Italians were occult powers that brought a person good or bad luck, but these powers operated through persons who possessed them. The *mal' occhio* (evil eye) represented a fundamental attitude of southern Italians who attributed many mishaps to the influence of an ever present menace, the power of human envy. Protection was found in amulets and lucky charms especially in the shape of horns (corne) which would ward off evil spirits.[2]

But there is a paradox in the southern Italian religion. While there was religious devotion, there was also a strong undercurrent of anticlericalism. The latter was extended to the Church's hierarchy, not to the local priest. In the *Mezzogiorno,* the Church for centuries was tied to the exploitive landowning classes. It regarded its interests as the same as those of the landowners. The Church was the largest landowner prior to the unification of Italy.

The *contadini* supported the move to take away Church lands during unification, because the Church was identified with the upper class. When the confiscated Church lands were then turned over to the landowners following unification, the *contadini* then became antigovernment. Following unification, the Church compromised with the *Mezzogorno* by allowing a parallel religious system to exist. Thereafter, the southern Italian regarded the Church as any other worldly power and separated as much as possible religious beliefs from attitudes toward the Church.

In the southern Italian family, the division of religious duties followed the overall family pattern. The women attended to daily belief and practice, while the men attended to political and economic relations with the institution. There were political and economic advantages for a family to have a son enter the priesthood. It provided an education and security. "Protection by the Church's power and other advantages could flow to the blood relatives of the parish priest, or even better of a man who managed to climb to the higher rank of the Church."[3]

The southern Italians transplanted their religious practices to America. The cults of the saints and Madonnas, the *feste,* the rituals and symbols survived the crossing.

But things also were different in America. In the large cities, the Church was just one of many social forces. Roman Catholicism was a minority religion rather than one which was officially supported by the state. The politician seemed to hold the real power. For a variety of reasons, the Italian immigrant tended to turn to the politician when in trouble rather than to the Church.

To the Italian, the American Catholic Church was predominantly an American-Irish Church. While the Church membership was Irish and German, the hierarchy was Irish-dominated. The Irish, who followed their own unique religious folkways, found the Italian practices pagan and sacrilegious. The Irish were proclerical and were loyal to the Church as an institution. They were shocked by the Italians' pragmatic attitude toward the Church and their strong sense of individualism.

Portions of the services were conducted in a language many of the Italian immigrants did not understand. The rituals were different. The Irish priest stood aloof from his parishioners, while the Italian was accustomed to a personal relationship with the local priest. To the *cantadini*, the American Catholic Church was austere, cold, and too puritanical. Theirs was a moral personalized and less formalized religion where one could talk directly to the saints and Madonnas. Creedal tenets were less important than the warm presence of the Madonna. Italians have always had a special and deep devotion to the Virgin Mary. In her sonnet "Religion," Rose Basile Green puts it beautifully: "The saints are older relatives and friends."

American Catholics following the Irish custom gave money to their church as they entered it for Mass. The Italians thought this was like paying at the movies. The Italians, who had been unaccustomed to contributing money for the support of the church, felt that the priests were preoccupied with fund raising and that they were not sympathetic to the plight of the poor by asking large contributions from those who were unable to afford them. In the Italian village, the support of the church and priest had been more informal and consisted frequently of services and food. One of the greatest shortcomings of the American Catholic Church was its failure to respond to the social-psychological needs of the Italian immigrant masses.[4]

As one can see, there were major clashes between American Catholicism and southern Italian Catholicism. The former regarded the religion of the latter as hardly Catholicism at all, and many said so openly.

Underneath lay a deep cultural antagonism between the Irish and the Italian immigrants which was carried into their religious encounter. The former regarded the immigrant masses as an economic and social threat to their own upward mobility. In

Mechanicville, New York, the refusal of Irish Catholics to permit Italian children to attend their parochial school heightened the sense of ethnic competition and hostility.

The newspaper headlines of February 24, 1908, rocked a nation worried about the menace of the giant immigrant wave and the Black Hand criminal conspiracy. On February 23rd in St. Elizabeth's Church in Denver, a Sicilian anarchist had shot and killed a German-born priest. A series of reports came out of Denver which inflamed public opinion. Catholic officials blamed elements of the Italian community for inciting the criminal act. To Catholic officials and laymen the Denver incident proved that Italians were extremists who swung from Catholicism to atheism and from conservatism to anarchy. This provided good reason for such people to discredit those progressive reformers and social workers who worked among the Italian poor.[5] As Richard Varbero concludes:

> A view of Italians through the Irish perspective confirms the threat to that culture.... Southern Italians commanded public attention. Often they supplanted the Irish on road gangs.... Crime and violence, however falsely attributed, advertised their presence. Disparate events, from the lynching of reputed mafiosi in New Orleans to Black Hand accounts in Eastern cities, linked the Italians to unsavory activities. While American academics theorized about Nordic supremacy and Brahmins agitated for the Immigration Restriction League, social reformers located the *contadini* in every unhappy element of American society: labor exploitation and *padroni*, squalid housing, farm tenancy, criminality were but a few. Would the Irish be bounded to this people by virtue of a shared religion? Would they, in the pursuit of Victorian respectability, be tainted by the Mediterranean?...
>
> The answer, and the solution, seemed clear from the Irish viewpoint. Laity and clergy were aware how painstakingly the edifice of Irish Catholicism and Americanism was being erected. The Irish had become American in order to preserve their Catholicism. Now the southern Italians must become Catholic in order to become American.[6]

In 1917, the Archbishop of New York was advised by the Irish pastor of Nativity Church that, "The Italians are not a sensitive people like our own.... The Italians are callous as regards religion."[7]

The *Catholic World* noted on a number of occasions that the Italians lacked some traits of the American character. As Bernard Lynch states, "especially what we call spirit.... They for the most part seem totally devoid of what may be termed the sense of respectability. . . . Italian clergy and immigrants were looked upon with suspicion and hostility." As an Irish pastor remarked, "Italian priests here must be servants."[8]

The Italians perceived the Church as pervaded with a super nationalistic spirit, identified with all things Irish. They saw the Church's schools as institutions operating to further the ethnic traditions of an alien group. Rather than send their children to a parochial school to become Irish they went instead to the public schools. Parochial schools in the United States refused to teach the Italian language. The experience in Boston, New York, and Chicago, all testify to the "heroic" Irish struggle to bring southern Italians into the Church proper and to Americanize them.

In 1890, the San Raffaele Society was founded by Pietro Bandini, a Scalabrinian priest. In that year, the society helped more than twenty thousand immigrants and opened an information office at Ellis Island in 1891. In 1891, the Society of Saint Charles established eleven missions to help the Italian poor. By 1918, twenty-six religious orders had founded schools, churches, hospitals, and other societies for the Italian immigrants. Important work was carried out by a number of religious orders like Missionary Sisters of the Sacred Heart and the Pallotine Sisters.

Italian nuns and priests were not welcomed by the American Catholic hierarchy who thought the spiritual needs of the Italian immigrants could be better served by Irish-American clerics. They felt they were better able to Americanize the Italian masses. Often Italian priests were not allowed to preach to Irish parishioners. American teaching orders vigorously opposed the introduction of Italian nuns. Behind all of this was the belief that the Italian clergy would somehow subvert Irish-American Catholicism.

One elderly woman recalled:

> We waited three years for your grandfather to send for us. He and your two uncles had gotten jobs in a dye factory, which was quite a come-down for one who had been a *padrone* in Italy. We came here because we had a large family to support and our farmlands kept producing less and less while our farmers demanded more and more pay for less labor. Your grandfather was so incensed at their lack of respect in requesting these larger wages that he sold most of our property and came to America. With grandpa gone, it was my duty to hold the remainder of the family together, and I was much comforted by the priest in our village. He ate with us on holidays, and I was proud to wash and iron the altar vestments. All of us went to mass daily.

When grandpa sent for us, we came expecting to perpetuate our religious life here, but we were sorely disappointed. The whole church was run by the Irish. Your grandfather was so against the "American Church" that we had to sneak out of the house to get there. Finally, we stopped going altogether. It was a terrible thing until Father Mazurka opened a church in the empty store next to a tailor shop. We were only too happy to support him. All the Italian ladies in the community cooked for him and cleaned his church and forced the children to his religion and Italian instruction classes. It was a good feeling. Almost like being home again.

Italians who, like their fellow immigrants, experienced Irish hegemony in church, neighborhood, police, and on the job, did not recognize the "sweet charitableness" of Irish clergymen nor the warmth of Irish parishioners. Immigrants of that generation can recall the intemperate outbursts of choleric priests who literally castigated Italians from the pulpit. A variety of churchgoers from immigrant working-class families retain vivid memories of the basements of Irish churches and of homes converted into places of worship, the insults and scowls. In short, little in the immigrant past of both Italian immigrant and Italian clergy elicits recollections of a spirit of generosity or Christian fellowship on behalf of the new urban villagers.

Italian immigrants were not unaware of the practical results issuing from such prejudices. They were relegated to basement quarters on numerous occasions and, once Italian parishes were established near existing ones, the immigrants were turned away from the latter. Some recalled the abrasive treatment accorded them in their childhood years by the sisters. The nuns stood guard, as it were, to the entrance of the church, driving off the Italian children with the cinctures to which their rosaries were attached with the admonition that "the dirty little greasers" should go to their own church now that one was built.[9]

Prejudice followed those who converted to Protestantism. In *The New Americans,* Constantine Panunzio writes of his experience in America, after he had been befriended by a Maine family who gave him his first taste of "the real America I came to love." They showed him a new path to follow which led through the Protestant religion (he had been a Catholic) to the Wesleyan seminary, subsequently to Wesleyan University at Middletown, Connecticut, and eventually to the Boston University School of Theology. He admits that it was not until he was well advanced in his school work that he began to acquire an "American Consciousness."

But even after his ordination as a minister, he did not escape the epithets "dago" (since he was dark-skinned) and "sheeny." American churchgoers objected to having a minister with such an "outlandish" name. In some churches, he was considered too much of an Italian, and in others, too little of an Italian. Eventually, he left the pulpit to turn to social service. In his work as superintendent of a settlement house in the North end of Boston, he found snobbery and disregard and contempt for immigrant traditions. During World War I, he served in the Italian theatre of war and could have remained in Italy, where all doors were open to him, but by this time he had made a commitment to America.

It is important to note that the church structure of an ethnic group with a threatened loss of identity organizes the group as a community system. Whether Italians attended Church regularly or not, religion, and the Church in particular, pervaded every level of their society. To the Italian, religion was more than a life-style. It was a great force that fashioned interpersonal relationships and self-image and provided support in the face of cultural shock. A distinction has to be made between religion and the Church. The former involves the belief system. One of the reasons for the relative absence of suicide among the Italian population is the function of the religious belief system, which contains sanctions against the taking of one's own life. In terms of the Church as a social structure, the principal development during these years was the emergence of the ethnic parish.

Enormous pressure was being generated in this country to create a homogenized and largely Irish-American Church. The Irish-American Church is not the same as the Irish Church. The Irish-American Church tended to be more pragmatic, more rationalistic, less colorful, and more "Protestant" than the Irish church. "Poles, Italians, and others learned to feel overpowered in face of the Irish hierarchs. In Polish and Italian neighborhoods, the phrase 'the Americans' meant the others: usually Irish."[10]

The major initial reactions of Italian-Americans to an established Irish-dominated Catholic Church was either internalization of Irish Catholic norms or a withdrawal by independence. In the first type, the internalized norms are not primarily ideological. Most Italian immigrants withdrew by independence.

The historical growth of Italian ethnic parishes first attempted to incorporate the Italian immigrants within the Irish parishes. This was followed by a clear separation between the two and ultimately a fusion of Italian and Irish into a new type of social group. The Italian parish emerged in response to increased demands of the Italian-American community led by a vocal and sympathetic Italian Catholic clergy. The ultimate formation of ethnic parishes resulted in the formation of an Italian national identity and a power base that allowed Italian-Americans to move into American life. The Italian national parish helped to generate the formation of an Italian-American community and was able to link the immigrants with the larger national society.[11]

The Irish Catholic Church was losing millions of Italian adherents. Yet to allow the Italians churches of their own would only increase the chances of being charged that the Catholic Church was a foreign institution that hampered Americanization. This resulted in the dual parish, separate but unequal accommodation, in which Italians held separate services with their Italian priests in church basements. The "better class" would worship upstairs and the Italians downstairs. The antagonism between the Italian priests and the Irish hierarchy was growing. The Italian immigrants had their own solutions—they stayed away from church in large numbers. They demanded Italian national parishes.

In time, they had their demands met. Italians did not accept decisions by the Irish hierarchy. Richard Varbero describes the Italian opposition in Philadelphia this way:

> Instead of capitulating, however, and accepting the official statement of necessary administrative changes, the Italians took to the streets when ordered to attend neighborhood churches ... eventually an angry mob besieged the church for three days; insurgents captured the belfry and tolled its bell incessantly until it cracked.[12]

In Mechanicville, it was decided that a separate national parish should be organized in 1919. Only then, with a separate national identity established, did the Italians begin to make their way back into the Church.

In Blue Island, Illinois, the Italians wanted their own church. By 1911, the first full-time priest arrived, and St. Donatus Parish became a reality. This church became the chief cultural institution for the Italians of Blue Island. Father Ottorino Papitto provided spiritual and secular counseling which promoted the acculturation of recent Italian immigrants and helped to hold the community together.[13] In other communities, Italian priests spearheaded community development. In Roseto, Pennsylvania, Father Pasquale DeNisco became the *de facto* mayor, building inspector, health department, arbiter of all questions relating to social conditions and business undertakings, chief of police, president of the union, and founder of clubs. He established Roseto's roots deeply and permanently, pleading and organizing and doing the sweaty, hard labor needed to clear fields for schools and cemeteries.

One of the focal points in the life of the southern Italian immigrant and thus the Italian national parish was the religious festivals on various saints' days. Most of the *feste* were local affairs in honor of the patron saint of a city. These feast days were not only an expression of devotion; they also reflected the nostalgia for the life they left behind. The procession, the street fair, the crowds of *paesani* created the illusion of being once more back home. One first generation young man recalls this event:

> The local Roman Catholic Church of St. Rita was established in 1913 as a national Italian parish to accommodate the immigrants in the neighborhood. When its pastor, Father Anthony Manno, opened a parochial grammer school in 1927, several of my friends and I transferred there from the local public school. The church had a greater influence on the women of the neighborhood than on the men. Its range of influence was limited to religious society meetings, religious services, and schooling. However, once a year, starting in 1918 until 1968, this church was the center of a *festa* honoring the twin Saints Cosmans and Damina. This feast was a replica of the one celebrated in Bari, Italy. The mutual aid society bearing the same name initiated this festival by underwriting the costs of special street lighting and fireworks. The Saints were carried from St. Rita's Church through the lighted streets in the neighborhood. The procession was preceded by all those who were devotees of the Saints and by others who sought their intercession for special help. There were also one or two musical bands in the procession. . . .

> The public would pin money on the Saints. They were carried by men who were the highest bidders for this honor. Also, there would be food stalls in the streets and vendors of hats, balloons, dolls, and games of chance to provide the needs of the people who would come to participate or out of curiosity. . . .

> There would also be a bandstand where musicians would play selections from the opera and also popular Italian and English songs for professional singers. . . .

All monies collected and donated were used to pay for the expenses of the *festa*. A donation was also made to St. Rita's. The Mutual Aid Society received the profits if any. These were used by the Society for its members and also for donations to several church related charities in Italy. . . .

The *festa* ended with a great fireworks display held in either the Long Island freight yard or in a large empty parcel of land across the street. This feast was a great opportunity to renew old acquaintances and customs of Italy. It attracted people who came by chartered buses from New Jersey and Connecticut.

Perhaps the most famous *festa* in this country is that of Our Lady of Mount Carmel, celebrated in July, in New York City. The church, planned, built, and paid for by the Italian immigrants in the area, was established in 1884. The celebration of the feast in this country was begun in 1881 by the Society of Our Lady of Mount Carmel, which was mainly composed of immigrants from Polla. Masses, novenas, and processions have taken place every July 16 since 1881. Of the festivals, Jacob Riis wrote, "The religious fervor of our Italians is not to be pent up within brick walls, and sunshine and flowers belong naturally to it."[14]

If we distinguish between "moral," or practicing, and being "religious," we can conclude that the ethnic parishes with their saints and festivals, novenas and processions, and their so-called "indifferent" congregations helped to hold the Italians together in America. . . . The network of ethnic parishes became the basis of religious success.[15]

By the 1960s, when the process of establishing natural parishes ended, there were seventy-four Italian Churches in New York City. Forty-four of them were established between 1900 to 1924, with an additional fifteen established outside the city limits but within the archdiocese. By 1918, 580 Italian parishes served an Italian population of 3,028,000 throughout the United States.[16]

What will happen to a system of national parishes when the Catholic population moves to the suburbs? Since the end of the second World War, there has been very little construction of national parishes. While some ethnic enclaves have appeared in the new suburbs, the demand for specifically national parishes has not been very strong. Attempts to maintain customs from the older neighborhood national parishes encounter resistance not only from the Americanized members of the ethnic group but also from the other ethnic groups who happen to be within the boundaries of the suburban "quasi-ethnic parish."

What has happened to the immigrants who are coming to the United States? Is the Church responding to their needs or are they following the path they took during the mass migration? Interestingly enough, the leadership in this area is being taken by the "ethnic" Catholic.

Immigration history is repeating itself in the New York area. Since the passage of the Immigration Reform Act of 1965, more than twenty thousand Italians arrive each year from southern Italy and Sicily, most of whom, not unlike the Italians at the turn of the century, settle in the tri-state New York metropolitan area.

The wholly urban Diocese of Brooklyn (comprising the two New York City counties of Kings and Queens) is host to the largest number of Italians—four thousand five hundred annually. In February 1972, Bishop Francis J. Mugavero established the Brooklyn Diocesan Migration Office. The 1970 census indicated that there were 151,076 Italian-born persons in the diocese, and if you include the second generation, the number totaled 511,425.

With the approval and encouragement of Bishop Mugavero, five offices were opened over a period of fourteen months, in precisely those five communities which, according to the census, had the highest concentration of Italian immigrants.

The storefront offices provide a variety of services. The late Father Nicholas Russo, the former coordinator of the Apostolate for the Italian Speaking, pointed out:

> Absolutely no charge is made for our services. The storefronts are open five days a week, and usually one evening or one Saturday morning. Any immigrant is welcome. The immigration counselors speak Italian, Spanish, and English; one also speaks Portuguese, and another speaks French. Once the word spread, we found ourselves assisting Spanish-speaking people from Central and South America, Haitians, Portuguese, Barbadians, English-speaking Indians, Irish, and one Ghanian.[17]

Each office keeps a supply of U.S. Immigration forms, citizenship applications, and Social Security, Medicare, and Medicaid literature. The immigration counselors often have to accompany immigrants to the Immigration Department, utility companies, social agencies, and schools.

They assist local schools at times of registration, acting as advocates and interpreters. Today, there is a grave need of bilingual classes for Italian immigrant children in New York City. Their number is estimated at fifteen thousand, and, to date, the city has done little to alleviate the problem. The New York City Health Council estimates that in one year (1970), 3,335 children were born to Italian immigrant mothers. Of these, 1,501 were born in Brooklyn and 925 in Queens. Italian is spoken almost exclusively in these households.

The storefront offices keep a list of all doctors, dentists, and lawyers who speak Italian, and the immigrant is referred to them. Through the cooperation of the business community and several charitable agencies, the storefront offices supply information about available jobs and housing and aid the immigrant in filling out the necessary application. With the help of Italian-American women who speak Italian, immigrant women are taught to comparison shop and are informed of the importance of inoculating their children.

Adapting to a different culture takes its toll in the form of neuroses and marginal individuals, especially the children, who must live in an Italian folk society at home and in a confused, violent urban atmosphere on the outside. Family counseling and assistance in problems of delinquency, truancy, and drug addiction are among the many services offered.

Elderly persons from the old and the new immigration often have problems with Social Security, Medicare, food stamps, and Italian pensions. Out of a sense of pride and dignity, they seldom ask for welfare, even that small supplement to which many are entitled, but to help them, all of the social workers speak Italian.[18] This effort in New York is surely a viable model for the Church in America.

What has happened to the sons and daughters of the Italian immigrants? What is the nature of their religious practices and beliefs? The antipathy between Italian-Americans and the American Catholic Church is far from resolved. While Italian-Americans are the largest single Catholic group in the country and regard themselves as true Catholics, they still retain the anticlerical views of their ancestors, a stubborn individualism concerning doctrinal interpretation, and a distrust of the Church as an institution.

For Italian-Americans in a lower socio-economic status (SES) 56 percent of the women and 41 percent of men attended mass once a week or more; 29 percent lower SES Italian-Americans and 29 percent of the second generation were supporters of

Catholic elementary schools. What accounts for this pattern? Harold Abramson argues that in places like southern Italy there was the absence of any societal competition with a foreign religio-cultural system. In these instances, the formal expression of religious involvement is lower than in other historical ethnic experiences because the competition is missing. Since relations between southern Italian peasants and the Church were often strained, the results was a lower association with formal religious requirements.[19]

What was the ultimate success of the American Catholic Church as the great Americanizer? It does not appear that the American Catholic Church melted down the Catholics of all nationalities into American Catholics. The American Catholic Church, as far as the Italian Catholics were concerned, did not serve as a primary agency for integrating the immigrants into American society.

Have Italian-American Catholics become Irish? This question was posed by Will Herberg, who answered it with no data but plenty of speculation. Herberg said that, because of intermarriage, Italians in the United States were assimilating within the larger Catholic subculture and were accepting the norms and practices of Irish Catholics as a model.[20] Glazer and Moynihan argued the same case, that, as the Italians experienced increasing social mobility and increasing assimilation, their religious patterns would become "Irish" in the sense of greater formal religiosity.

In my recent study of Italian-Americans the marriage patterns of my three-generation sample showed that all of the respondents had parents who were Italian. Of those who were married, all chose Italian mates. Most of the Italian immigrants interviewed were not inclined to marry non-Italians; however, the first generation respondents were even more resistant to the idea than the immigrant group. Despite some equivocation, most of the first generation respondents inclined towards Italian mates. Paul, for example, asserted, "I don't have a preference... but I'm more likely to marry an Italian girl because of our mutual background and understanding." Bob, on the other hand, assured me, "I thought a lot about it... but my view changes. I know one thing—I wouldn't want my children to be completely cut off from the Italian heritage." Among the second generation, most Italian-Americans were like Lou, "I married an Italian girl. As far as my sons are concerned, I'll go along with whatever makes them happy. If they ask me,

I'll tell them that living with someone like yourself makes it easier to get along ... but, it would be their choice."[21]

Among third-generation respondents there was a strong tendency to be more receptive to marrying a non-Italian. Thus, a predilection for out-group marriages is present in the second and third generations, but our findings are inconclusive on this point.

B. R. Bugleski found that the 1930 pattern of in-group marriages had been reversed in 1960, when two-thirds of the marriages studied involved partners from different ethnic groups.[22] He also found that Italians in Buffalo had a higher rate of out-group marriages than any other group studied, and he asserted confidently that by 1975 the Italian wedding would be a thing of the past.

Kennedy, in her study of intermarriage rates from 1870 to 1950 in New Haven, found an increasing trend toward the breaking down of national origin barriers in marriage. However, she found a "triple melting pot" effect in which inter-ethnic marriages tended to take place within the three major religions: Catholicism, Protestantism, and Judaism. While declining, the in-group marriage rates for certain ethnic groups was still high. While the rate for Italians in New Haven had fallen from 97.1 percent in 1900, it had only declined to 76.70 percent by 1950. Thus, as late as 1950, 75 percent of the Italians in New Haven selected mates who were also Italian.[23]

While our findings can neither support or refute the above in absolute terms, there is some inferential support. However, we do suggest that the more segregated the Italians, the more there was the tendency for in-group marriages; and the more recently arrived, the more segregated the people were.[24]

Another dimension to the acculturation of Italians is along religious lines. In his study, Professor Nicholas Russo hypothesized that in religious matters, increased Americanization would bring about an increasing resemblance to Irish norms. Italians reacted to Irish Catholicism in two different ways: either they first conformed and then internalized Irish-American religious norms, or they challenged those norms either from within or without the Catholic Church. Most followed the first course of action. The Catholic Church and its school system have contributed to the cultural assimilation of Italians in New York City. The intermingling of the Italian-American in the Irish Church and parochial schools fostered out-group marriages. Russo, to prove his point regarding the conformity to Irish norms, examines church attendance, reception of holy communion, family size, and parochial school education across a three-generational span, and then compares this data with that of the Irish. He concludes that, while there is some retention of identity, there is an absorption of the cultural patterns of American Irish society. In addition, social assimilation into the primary Catholic groups is well underway.[25] To Russo, generation alone or social class alone do not influence Italian ethnic traditions as much as others presumed.

In Harold Abramson's study, *Ethnic Diversity in Catholic America,* he found that Italian-Americans were not disappearing into the greater body of American Catholicism through intermarriage. In-group marriages among Italians were occurring at the rate of better than six out of every ten. Abramson concludes that, while a minority of Italian-American Catholics do intermarry, there are signs of changing religious behavior: of increased church attendance and of a greater inclination to send the children to the parochial school; but, "curiously, such religious change comes about only when intermarriage and generational experience happen together."[26] In other words, traditional religious patterns persist for Italians of two or more generations in America when the marriage is Italian on both sides and despite higher social-class background. Abramson notes, "it requires increased generation and interethnic marriage to foster a change in religious style." Since Italian-Americans are not intermarrying into other Catholic backgrounds at excessive rates, the Italian variety of religion is not becoming Irish in terms of high religious involvement.[27]

Another reason for the increased antipathy between the Italian-Americans and the American Catholic Church is the disproportionately low numbers of Italian-American clergy in the church hierarchy. It wasn't until 1968 that Francis J. Mugavero became the first bishop of Italian extraction in New York City. Neither the cardinal, archbishop, co-adjuctor archbishop, nor ten of the eleven auxiliary bishops is of Italian origin. The entire administrative machinery of the Catholic Church in New York appears devoid of Italian leadership. Of the nearly 58,000 American priests, only six or seven thousand or about 12 percent were Italian-Americans. Only about 7 percent of the nuns, 10,000 of 153,000 were Italian-Americans: Paul Asciolla makes this historical analysis and contemporary plea:

> But, as a matter of fact, the American hierarchy is heavily loaded with what have come to be known as "Irish bishops." ...
> This again is no mere coincidence, as the history of the Church in this country will demonstrate. But things don't have to remain that way. ...
> Historically, when the institutional church failed to be sen-

sitive to real needs, for different life-style and cultural preference within its ranks, drastic things have happened. The Old
Catholic Church, the Polish National Catholic Church, the
Armenian National Catholic Church, the transference of many
Ukranians to the Russian Orthodox Church, the attempted
establishment of an Italian-American "diocese" in New York,
New Jersey, and Pennsylvania in the late 1880's, and many
more instances of alienation and discouragement on the part
of many groups in the not too distant past....

There is no need for this because, since the days of the primitive church and through the centuries, the Church has been
conscious of the differences—not divisions—within the lifestyle
of its members and has not always been sensitive to their needs.
But lip-service is paid to the cultural pluralism within the
church, which should not be confused with divisiveness from
doctrine or tradition—which form the golden thread of unity
in the institutionalized church....

American Church History will likewise reveal a succession
of power plays which resulted in heavily dominated English,
French, German and now Irish hierarchies. Despite the huge
number of Mexicans in the southwest, only in 1970 was a
Mexican-American priest made Auxiliary Bishop of San Antonio, Texas.[28]

The highest post held by an Italian-American in the American
Catholic Church was the president of the National Conference
of Catholic Bishops. Joseph Louis Bernadin was elected to
a three-year term in 1974. Bernadin is the Archbishop of Cincinnati. The Archbishop, son of an immigrant stonecutter,
was born on April 2, 1928, in Columbia, South Carolina, where
his parents had settled after immigrating from Italy.

After studying for the priesthood in Kentucky and receiving
a master's degree from Catholic University, Washington, D.C.,
in 1952, he was ordained the same year. He served the diocese
of Charleston until 1966, rising from assistant pastor to administrator of the diocese.

Thereafter, he served two years as Auxiliary Bishop of the
Archdiocese of Atlanta, becoming the first general secretary
of the then newly organized National Conference of Catholic
Bishops in 1968. He was named Archbishop of Cincinnati,
a nineteen-county diocese covering southern Ohio, in 1972.

Catholicism is not a universalizing religion. It is incurably
particular, concrete, fitted to diversity, yet the qualities dear
to "other Catholics" seem slighted by American Catholicism
and are underrepresented, sometimes even mocked. Instead of

being nourished in their differences, "most ethnic Catholics feel as much coerced by the sameness within Catholicism as that within America as a whole."[29] The family and the Church remain two of the most important institutions in Italian-American life.

11 LaGuardia and Marcantonio

"Now we have a mayor of New York," Judge Samuel Seabury exclaimed when Fiorello H. LaGuardia was sworn in on January 1, 1934. Thus was inaugurated the greatest showman, the most accomplished political impresario, and the least inhibited chief executive ever to occupy City Hall.

Though born in New York City, he was western bred and, like many New Yorkers, he was an outsider. But he became the cosmopolite of the most cosmopolitan city in the world. Significantly, he once said he'd rather split an infinitive than an idea.

Fiorello LaGuardia was to be regarded as the consummate ethnic politician, building an unbeatable base of Italian and Jewish voters.[1] He spoke, according to the occasion, Yiddish, Hungarian, German, Italian, Serbian, Croatian, and Spanish. He was born in Greenwich Village, raised in Arizona, married first to a Roman Catholic, then, when his wife died, to a Lutheran. He was a Mason and an Episcopalian.

LaGuardia was many persons in one, and New Yorkers of every sort were able to identify themselves with him—but rarely for the same reason. The most obvious thing to say about him is that he combined many of the elements that made him an irresistible public figure. A mixed metropolitan and far western background, a military interlude in the past, contempt of red tape, a love for the effective gesture and grimace, and a talent for dramatic vigor were all characteristic of him.

Fiorello LaGuardia was born in a New York tenement in 1882. His father was Italian, but, in the Garibaldi tradition, anti-clerical and agnostic.

Shortly after his birth, LaGuardia's father enlisted in the U.S. Army as a bandmaster, and the family moved to Prescott, Arizona. His mother, Irene Coen, came from Trieste. She was Austrian in citizenship, Jewish in religion, but Italian in culture.

As a young boy in Prescott, Fiorello experienced the hurt that comes from prejudice. There, he was often taunted by the other children, "Hey Fiorello, you're a dago too. Where's your monkey?" As he recalled: "What I saw and heard in my boyhood days in Arizona made lasting impressions on me.... For instance, I loathe the professional politician.... This attitude had its origin in the badly dressed, slick and sly Indian agents, political appointees, I saw come into Arizona ... robbing the Indians of the food the government provided for them."[2] Later he was to do something about the needs of the poor.

At the age of eighteen Fiorello worked at the American consulate in Budapest doing health checks on departing immigrants. At twenty-three, he returned to New York City and held a variety of jobs. He finally received a civil service appointment as an interpreter at Ellis Island. Fiorello shuttled back and forth from Ellis Island to New York University where he received his law degree in June, 1910. He was twenty-eight years old when he was admitted to the New York State Bar and started his law practice. LaGuardia developed a practice in immigration law and handled the cases of new arrivals.

Fiorello lent his support to the striking immigrant workers of the United Garment Workers. "LaGuardia, racing from picket line to picket line, taunting the Tammany-controlled police to arrest him, flamboyantly dressed in a black ten-gallon hat and a string bow tie, was instantly recognized by those struggling Lower East Side immigrant workers as a new leader."[3] As Professor Mann, his biographer, noted, "It was not N.Y.U. but the East Side that grounded LaGuardia in the slashing, hot, gospel style of oratory for which he was known."[4]

Short, stocky, with rumpled black hair and glistening dark eyes, possessed with demonic energy, LaGuardia carried all his combat with operatic gusto. Wherever he went, there was noise and movement, explosive laughter, pounding on the desk, farce, and melodrama. His mind was sharp and quick. His disposition was mercurial. His loyalty went to principles rather than people.

LaGuardia's Republicanism was nominal, and his relation with the state organization tenuous. In 1914, LaGuardia made an unsuccessful bid for a Congressional seat in the Fourteenth District against great odds. Two years later, he came back and beat the Tammany-backed candidate by 350 votes. Fiorello became the third Italian-American in American history to be elected to Congress. He joined the army in 1917 and resumed his congressional career following the war. During his congressional career, LaGuardia represented two New York City districts: the 14th on the Lower East Side and the 20th in East Harlem. In all of his campaigns, LaGuardia appealed to the ethnic vote, which was predominantly Italian. While campaigning in 1916, he promised Italian-Americans that Italy would regain Trieste. Italian-Americans found in LaGuardia a champion of their cause. In Congress, he condemned the quota system and other restrictive laws as bigoted legislation. He often exposed the racist bases of that legislation.[5]

Fiorello LaGuardia's career was tied to the politics of East Harlem. Vito Marcantonio's life and career was also inextricably bound to that portion of New York City and to LaGuardia. How and why did Vito Marcantonio, an outspoken radical, born in East Harlem at First Avenue and 112 Street, win several terms in the United States House of Representatives?

He served in Congress as its representative from the Upper East Side of Manhattan for fourteen of the most critical years in American history, a time that spanned the period of the Depression, the Second World War, and the Cold War. He frequently was the sole spokesman in Congress for America's radical left.

The "Red" tag on Marcantonio did not deter those who worshipped "The Marc." What mattered to them was not whether Marcantonio was red, pink, blue, or black, but that he was their congressman, a tireless fighter for the man of the streets—in East Harlem. He was willing to live in their slums, rub elbows with the best and the worst. He never lived more than four blocks away from his place of birth.[6]

Born in December 1902, Marcantonio was a product of the ethnic ghetto and later its leading personality. Despite access to avenues of mobility familiar in the history of ethnic America, including professional school and a career in law, he lived out his life in East Harlem. East Harlem was home, and Marcantonio shaped his routine and schedule to be there as often as he was able. In Washington for fourteen eventful years, he held to a limited circle and commuted weekly to New York. He traveled minimally. He saw little of the United States and, except for a single trip to Puerto Rico, never left its continental boundaries. East Harlem was his America, and he clung patriotically to the predominantly Italian-American yet ethnically diverse and economically depressed area at the same time as he masterfully dominated its politics.[7]

Marcantonio's father was an American-born carpenter and the son of a skilled artisan from Picerno, Basilicata, in southern Italy. Marcantonio grew up in Jefferson Park among other

Italians. The Marcantonios raised their son a Catholic. Off-spring of the *artigano* class, a rung above the peasant *contadini*, they were of broader social and intellectual outlook and en-couraged young Vito's education. In addition, unlike many neighborhood families, the Marcantonios were never poor; young Vito was never forced to select between school and supple-menting the family income. He attended P.S. 85 and then, al-most alone among East Harlem Italian-American adolescents, enrolled in the prestigious academic and predominantly Jewish DeWitt Clinton High School on the West Side of Manhattan.[8]

Outside school, young Vito's education was enriched by ex-posure to the world of squalid East Harlem, roughly the area north of 97th Street between Central Park and the East River. A crowded residential district that bulged with the weight of the new immigration, East Harlem housed above a quarter-million persons and had an exotic mixture of nationality groups in 1910–1920. Italians predominated east of Third Avenue to the East River; Jews were in the majority west of Third Avenue; small concentrations of Germans, Irish, Spanish-speaking immigrants, and Negroes filled out the area. "A com-munity always in transition," as Leonard Covello called it, East Harlem would undergo a change by the 1930s.[9] The Jews de-parted in great numbers for more congenial settings in the Bronx and Brooklyn, their space to be filled by the beginnings of large-scale Puerto Rican migration. The Italians, considerably more stable, would continue their dominance in the area until after World War II. By 1933, there were more than 150,000 first- and second-generation Italians in East Harlem. For the moment, however, despite differences in background, culture, jobs, and politics, the ethnic elements in East Harlem shared a common deprivation. According to contemporary testimony, its inadequate and congested housing, poverty, disease, and crime, all qualified East Harlem as a classic American slum.

In this milieu, the young Italian-American boy quickly de-veloped as brash and "socialistic." Entering DeWitt Clinton in 1917, perhaps the influence of his history instructor, Abra-ham Lefkowitz, the socialist spirit there, or the general leftist antiwar sentiment in New York City was formative. Or perhaps the vibrant Socialist party politics of the war and postwar years, particularly in Lower East Harlem, where a Socialist (August Claessens) was elected to the state legislature for three terms and Morris Hillquit was defeated for Congress only by a coali-tion of the major parties, was important. Whatever the source, Marcantonio developed as a man of the left. He was active

in *Il Circolo Italiano* and *Circolo Mazzini* at DeWitt Clinton
High School and later, at NYU, he headed the East Harlem
Tenants League, and he labored in adult citizenship classes
at *La Casa del Popolo* and later as naturalization aid director
at Harlem House.

During his senior year at DeWitt Clinton High School, Marcantonio delivered an impassioned speech on the old-age problem and Social Security. On the platform on that day sat Fiorello LaGuardia, then president of the Board of Aldermen
of New York City. He congratulated Marcantonio on his zeal
and his progressive thoughts.[10] Undoubtedly, LaGuardia was
struck by their similarities in size, temperament, and outlook.
Undoubtedly as well, recent family losses by the two men played
a part. Later inducted into LaGuardia's legal firm, Marcantonio was offered nothing less than the opportunity to become
his mentor's professional heir. Three years later, based on this
chance meeting, Marcantonio became LaGuardia's campaign
manager for the congressional contest in 1924.

In 1922, Fiorello LaGuardia accepted the Republican nomination for Congress for the Twentieth Congressional District—
East Harlem. He won a close election. Fiorello was sure of the
Italian vote in the Twentieth, but the western section was still
Jewish, a fact which almost defeated him in 1922. In 1924,
he broke with the Republicans and endorsed Robert LaFollette's
Progressive party. However, the Progressive Party was not formally on the ballot in New York, so LaGuardia accepted the
endorsement of the Socialist party. The alliance with the Socialists strengthened his position in the Jewish area in 1924.[11]

In Washington, LaGuardia's Arizona background surfaced.
He discovered his natural allies among the western progressives.
He admired men like Robert M. LaFollette and George W.
Norris. While LaGuardia was in Congress, Marcantonio was
the New York window for him, keeping him informed about
new immigrants, family feuds, job losses, political in-fighting
in the Twentieth Congressional District. While LaGuardia
labored in Washington to press the perspective of urban immigrant slum life through the complacent political consensus of
the Republican New Era, Marcantonio handled his affairs
in the district. Here, he learned the curious blend of paternalism
and progressivism that made up the politics of the ethnic ghetto.
He ministered to constituent requests for aid in immigration
matters, worked on tenant cases, and provided legal aid. He
learned the art of political "wheeler-dealering." He proved
himself a masterful public speaker, whose speeches, building

to a frenzied crescendo, could command the attention of East Harlem. A successful political apprenticeship, this period laid the basis for Marcantonio's career.[12]

> Marcantonio was more than good at it. Politics in the ethnic ghetto, particularly LaGuardia's brand of insurgent populist politics, it seems, offered Marcantonio an opportunity to chan- nel his ambivalent feelings as a second-generation Italian- American. He had early experienced the stresses of socialization in contradictory cultures. A man set apart from his origins by virtue of his education and ambition for mobility, he nonethe- less was burdened by his inability or unwillingness to break the tie: he clung to East Harlem. Politics in East Harlem offered a resolution to his dilemma of ethnic identity and vocation. It also offered an outlet to his populist rebellion—a rebellion which might embrace formulas of revolt ready at hand but which was nurtured in instinct as well as mind, in personal ex- perience as well as social analysis. As master of politics in the ethnic ghetto, Marcantonio could channel and make construc- tive his sense of marginality. It would never relieve his sense of uprootedness which continued the rest of his days. Yet it came as close as anything to giving him a sense of identity, vocation, and place.[13]

Mainly, though, Marcantonio kept LaGuardia's personal ma- chine intact. This insured him against dependence upon the Re- publican party, even though Fiorello formally returned to the GOP in 1926. This personal machine took legal form when the F.H. LaGuardia Club was formed in 1929. LaGuardia began organizing the Italians during the early 1920s into Republican Clubs and eventually into his own political machine, the F.H. LaGuardia Political Club. Increasing ethnic awareness among Italian-Americans allowed LaGuardia to be elected and eventu- ally to convince the Democrats that they had to compete for the support of the Italian-American community. [14]

LaGuardia, who was childless, was drawn to Marcantonio as father to son, as mentor to protégé. With LaGuardia's subse- quent re-election to Congress in 1926, 1928, and 1930, Marcan- tonio was rewarded with the position of Assistant United States Attorney General for the New York City District.

In Congress, LaGuardia was a maverick with a flair for inde- pendence. As such, he came up against the establishment which froze him out of positions of power. LaGuardia soon made himself the most influential progressive in the House. He de- scribed his role in this manner: "One of the weaknesses of the Progressive group was that each was a prima donna. Teamwork was lacking. It was not until the Seventy-first and Seventy-second Congresses that I succeeded in providing a certain degree of leadership."[15] Oddly enough, a major break in the wall of established power came with the Depression.

The Depression began with the stock market crash in October, 1929. Business leaders talked optimistically to keep their courage up. American business, they recited almost in unison, was fundamentally sound and would carry on as usual. Political leaders, not to be outdone, joined in with the same refrain. But they were all wrong. Prices dropped sharply, foreign trade fell off, factories closed, business failures multiplied, banks went under, unemployment mushroomed.

During November and December of 1929, while President Hoover was still not convinced the economic situation was serious and was still relying on voluntary methods of solution, LaGuardia was already formulating his fight.

In a speech given in early 1930, he disagreed with the passive way in which Hoover was dealing with the crisis. He first disclosed many of his ideas which, with the advent of the New Deal, would ultimately be accepted. In this speech he said:

> We must face the situation: there is at present unemployment in every industrial center.... Uniform labor laws, unemployment insurance, old age pensions, a shorter work week, these must be pressed into reality to save this country from a real crisis. We have ... excess profits and unemployment. The two are inconsistent.[16]

Together with a small group of progressives, he worked for emergency and long-range legislation to aid the cities' unemployed and the poor farmers, to create jobs, and to protect savings accounts in case of bank failures. He also directed a steady attack against the President.

When farmers revolted against foreclosures, LaGuardia encouraged them further: "Fight, farmers, fight. Fight, for your homes and your children...." When bankers sought government aid, LaGuardia mused, "The bastards broke the people's back with their usury and now they want to unload on the government. No, No. Let them die; the people will survive."[17]

He joined forces with New York Senator Wagner to get antidepression laws passed. He worked feverishly in the early months of 1930 to get House action on Senate-approved bills authored by Wagner. These included the compilation of unemployment statistics, the long-range planning of construction projects as a preparatory measure against future unemployment, and a free national employment service to serve as a clearing-house for jobs and job seekers, to be managed locally. La-Guardia led the campaign for its adoption, fighting claims that it violated states' rights. However, this particular bill left committee with its most vital parts, including the call for public works planning in advance, eliminated.

The Congress obviously felt the country was not ready for proposals such as these. However, many of these things were eventually realized in the New Deal. His demands pertaining to public works and the National Employment Service were in some measure adopted with the formation of the PWA, the CCC, and the WPA in the New Deal. Old-age pensions were partially realized with the advent of Social Security and the Old Age Assistance programs.

He also urged, as a long-term solution, shorter working hours. While the labor leaders were striving for a forty-hour work week, LaGuardia urged for a thirty-hour standard. Anticipating the usual argument that it would lead to idleness, he argued that it would give workingmen educational opportunities, recreation, and travel, which would help create more job opportunities.

In the mid-thirties, mass unemployment and the resulting competition for jobs afforded employers the opportunity to lower wages. There was no federal minimum wage in those days. Hoping to prevent widespread salary cutting, LaGuardia introduced a resolution urging the President to call a conference of governors to agree on the passage of uniform labor laws throughout all the states of the union. Although President Hoover thought it unnecessary, and the resolution was defeated, Franklin Roosevelt later called such a conference, and appropriate laws were passed during the New Deal period. One example is the Fair Labor Standards Act which established a minimum wage and set a maximum upon the number of hours an employee could be asked to work without overtime pay.

In December of 1930, Hoover attributed the depression to outside forces, but he did express a willingness to expand public works appropriations for the next fiscal year by $130 million. LaGuardia, realizing the inadequacy of such an allotment, spoke against it in the House. He explained that it would be insufficient even for the employment of a thousand men for any significant period of time. LaGuardia's recommendation was about fifteen times the figure proposed by Hoover. Again, this showed evidence of New Deal thinking; this much money and more would be allocated to public works under the WPA and PWA in the New Deal.

Two weeks later, LaGuardia continued his fight against the depression by introducing "a bill to provide for an unemployment commission, the creation and maintenance of an unemployment insurance fund, and raising necessary revenue therefor." Based on the right of the House to tax, he wanted to tax every employee five cents a week, and every employer ten cents to create the fund from which the benefits would be paid. However, the House was unwilling to pass any legislation which appeared socialistic. It was allowed to die in committee. Here again, Congress was not ready to accept his New Deal thinking, but the FERA was formed during the New Deal to provide just such relief. This idea of unemployment insurance is still in use today.

His enthusiasm was so great that at one point he felt cheated when Congressman Steagall beat him to the punch in announcing a plan which would protect the savings accounts of small depositors. He said privately, "He swiped that idea; nobody ever thought of it before me." The concept of savings insurance again represented New Deal thinking. One of the first adopted measures of the New Deal was the establishment of the Glass-Steagall Act, which established the FDIC to protect the small savings accounts.

In March of 1931, Hoover vetoed the remaining two Wagner bills which LaGuardia had pushed through the House. "The issue of the welfare state philosophy versus the concept of rugged individualism had been squarely posed, and decisively answered."[18] Again his thinking was too far ahead of the Hoover administration. The Wagner bills were, however, ultimately incorporated into the New Deal.

During the fall of 1931, Roosevelt proposed, and battled through, a program of unemployment relief in New York called the Wicks Bill. It established a Temporary Emergency Relief Administration for direct aid and work relief. Roosevelt insisted that the twenty-million-dollar relief program be financed out of an income tax increase. Applauding this, LaGuardia told Roosevelt, "In the name of thousands of innocent victims of the present depression with whom I am in contact, thanks."

In 1932, LaGuardia and a group of fourteen other progressives formed an unofficial committee in the House, chaired by John Mead. They were finally able to push through a relief measure, sponsored by John Garner, appropriating over two billion dollars for relief to the unemployed. Wagner sponsored a similar bill in the Senate. Finally, just before adjournment, it was passed by both houses. However, it was vetoed by the

President, and Congress adjourned. Once again, LaGuardia was involved in New Deal ideas which the Hoover administration just was not ready to accept. They were later accepted, and put into effect, during the New Deal.

President Hoover was committed to the idea of running the government on a balanced budget. To accomplish this, he sent two bills to Congress: the Revenue Act of 1932 and an economy bill.

The Revenue Act called for the largest peacetime tax increase in history. It proposed to raise more than half of its one-billion-dollar goal with the imposition of a 2.25 percent sales tax on manufactured goods. This would have raised about $600 million. When the House Ways and Means Committee reported favorably on the bill, little opposition was expected because of the congressional leaders' agreement to support it. However, it was LaGuardia who led the opposition to this "bipartisan steamroller." His group of progressives took the floor of the House, denouncing what they called an attempt to soak the poor, at the same time when poor could barely keep alive. They picked up support from the American Federation of Labor, the Railroad Brotherhoods, and from correspondents throughout the country. As the days and weeks passed, unemployment mounted. While there were five million unemployed in 1930, there were now thirteen million people out of work in 1932.[19] Support within the House began to form behind LaGuardia, and continued to grow. Finally, on March 24, 1932, the House rejected the sales tax portion of the Revenue Bill. This climaxed LaGuardia's emergence as the leading spirit and organizer of the progressive block in the House. Depending upon the paper you read, LaGuardia was characterized either as a communist dictator or as a legislative hero.

To replace the sales tax in the Revenue Act, higher taxes on big estates, big incomes, stock transfers, bonds, expensive jewelry, pleasure boats, golf clubs, and other material accessories of high living were included. These changes, initiated by La-Guardia's fight against the sales tax, were accepted. The opposition of LaGuardia toward the sales tax in favor of the luxury taxes was again the type of thinking that led to the New Deal.

The economy bill hoped to lower the budget by $250 million. However, LaGuardia fought the proposed cuts in veterans' benefits, government workers' salaries, and appropriations for the Childrens' Bureau, Office of Education, and other government agencies which policed big business or social welfare. In the end, only $38 million of the proposed economies were passed. This also represented New Deal thinking, as during the New Deal, money would be allocated into these programs, rather than being economized out.

Finally, the passage of the Norris-LaGuardia Anti-Injunction Act was possibly his greatest Congressional achievement. This act barred the use of injunctions to prevent strikes or union organization, limited the application of any injunction to the charges specified in the complaint (thus barring "catch-all" injunctions), provided for jury trials to those charged with violating injunctions, and barred all yellow-dog contracts (where one was forced to agree that he would not join a union). It also allowed for the formation of unions by individual workers.

This was one of the strongest moves toward the New Deal made by LaGuardia while in Congress. This act led directly to similar ones made during the New Deal such as the National Labor Relations (Wagner) Act, which reiterated many of the principles of the Norris-LaGuardia Act. Plainly, it also went along with the government's prolabor feelings of the New Deal period.

In spite of LaGuardia's admonition to support Franklin Roosevelt, he exhibited a legislative position not only to the far left of his own party but also to the left of the most fervent New Dealers. He attacked the appropriations bill for the War Department, the Reserved Officers Training Corps section, and military training in general. He attacked the administration's Social Security bill and backed the Frazier-Lundeen Bill, supported also by the communist party which probably played an important part in its formulation.

This bill was considered the height of radicalism and would be still considered so in the 1980s. It provided for prevailing wages, regardless of occupation, for the full period of any unemployment, with escalating clauses for cost of living increases. These insurance features were to be administered by members of labor and farm organizations, thus keeping control in the hands of the working class.

The entire costs of this bill were to be funded by taxes on individuals and corporations whose income exceeded $5000 per year and by capital gains and taxes on all inheritances.

It was his intense preoccupation with economic issues which made LaGuardia a nascent New Dealer. It was this that led Howard Zinn to say:

> LaGuardia's specific legislative program was an astonishingly accurate preview of the New Deal. The battle for Muscle Shoals and Boulder Dam led to the T.V.A., the domestic allot-

ment plan to the A.A.A., and so on, in the areas of unemployment insurance wage-hour legislation, child labor, debtor relief, securities regulation, and other issues. The impressive
legislative structure of the famed first hundred days of the
New Deal owed much to the foundation dug earlier by La-
Guardia.... If the New Deal was born before Roosevelt took
his oath of office, a political paternity would probably attribute
parentage... to the little group of congressional progressives
(led by LaGuardia) who jabbed at the conscience of the
twenties.[20]

It is apparent that, while trying to solve one of the major
problems in the country's history, LaGuardia became the transi-
tional figure from progressivism to the New Deal and thus
had a major effect on the American character.

LaGuardia had now earned a national reputation. For him,
life was a perpetual combat in which he was forever fighting
the people's fight. He identified himself passionately with the
oppressed and the defenseless—with the poor, with the foreign-
born, with children.

Fiorello LaGuardia was defeated in the 1932 Roosevelt landslide victory which helped James Lanzetta unseat the "Little
Flower." Undaunted, in 1933 he ran for and was elected as mayor
of New York City. Many Italian-Americans had responded
to his appeal, particularly following the Depression. They saw
in him a possible solution to their political and economic problems. During the mayoralty campaign of 1933 the Italian-
American community was strongly in favor of his candidacy.
The election returns indicate the importance of ethnicity for
the Italian-Americans. LaGuardia received 90 percent of the vote
within Italian-American districts.[21]

LaGuardia was able to convince the Italian-American community that in electing him, they too would achieve recognition
and power. On the heels of the Great Depression many Italian-
Americans viewed LaGuardia as a possible solution to their
political and economic problems. The Democratic party was not
helping in terms of either political positions or politically connected jobs.

LaGuardia was able to secure the support among all income
groups among Italian-Americans, particularly the middle class.
His capturing of the Italian vote shows the impact of his personality and his ethnicity in areas where the Republican party was
not dominant. In the early 1930s, most Italian-Americans were
working class and were recruited into the Democratic party. With
a membership of 150,000, the Italian Federation of Democratic

Clubs publicized all Italian candidates, including LaGuardia.[22] Mayor LaGuardia became one of the best-known political leaders of his time. As Andrew Rolle observes:

> He ran an efficient government and personally participated in many aspects of the city's busy life. Fiorello ... sped to fires, went on rounds with policemen, and reported to the populace via a weekly radio program. During a newspaper strike, he kept restless youngsters and adults alike informed about the latest comic strips; he read his favorite Italian recipes, as well. Immigrants found him a champion of their interests. ... He won everyone's trust, standing against government by favor and connection.[23]

For LaGuardia the mayoralty was much more than just another job. He viewed government not in traditional American terms of economy and efficiency, but in the sense of a loving supervision of all aspects of the community. He said, "You know I am in a position of an artist or a sculptor. ... I can see New York as it should be and as it can be if we all work together. But now I am like the man who has a conception that he wishes to carve or to paint, who had the model before him, but hasn't a chisel or brush."[24] On another occasion LaGuardia said, "Too often life in New York is merely a squalid succession of days; whereas in fact it can be a great living, thrilling adventure."[25] LaGuardia made it an adventure for all New Yorkers. Unlike other reform mayors, LaGuardia was never a bore. LaGuardia's style was personal government, yet government dedicated to civic ideals.

LaGuardia was more than just a good mayor. He was an important political thinker. He aggressively fought for the rights and aspirations of the American people. His enemies considered him a radical. In truth, he was a fighter against his time.

LaGuardia's mayoral victory in 1933 paved the way for Marcantonio to emerge politically after having served his apprenticeship with skill for over ten years. Whatever his own tendencies, Marcantonio was a Republican throughout his years of association with Fiorello; however, this close association paradoxically proved to be a handicap.

Being a maverick's protégé, Marcantonio was denied the regular Republican nomination and became involved in a primary fight between Progressive Republicans and Old Guard Republicans. Marcantonio won this fight in 1933, thus paving the way for his congressional nomination in 1934. He was also the nominee of the LaGuardia influenced City Fusion party and the reformist Knickerbocker Democrats. And he was supported

by the Italian sections of the needle trades unions, particularly
the International Ladies Garment Workers (ILGWU) and Amalgamated Clothing Workers (ACWA). His opponent was the
incumbent Democrat, James Lanzetta.

It would have been difficult for any ordinary politician to
follow LaGuardia as East Harlem's representative in Washington. The "Little Flower" had a national reputation, an instinc-
tive rapport with his constituents, and a sense of the dramatic.
Lanzetta did not compile any legislative record of note. He had
comparatively little press coverage and had no flair for politics
or public relations. However, Lanzetta did show astuteness in
one area. He recognized the importance of the growing Puerto
Rican minority in East Harlem and took every opportunity to
remind the House of its responsibility to Puerto Rico.[26]

During the campaign, he favored more liberal immigration
laws and more home relief, another appealing point in a slum
neighborhood with large amounts of unemployment. But he
spent most of the time berating Tammany Hall.

A week before the election LaGuardia endorsed Marcantonio
with the statement, "I have confidence in you, and I know
you will join with the progressive forces of the House for good
government and progressive social welfare laws. I know that
you will support the President [Franklin D. Roosevelt]."[27]
LaGuardia's pronouncement went a long way toward confirming whatever doubts regular Republicans might have had about
Marcantonio's reliability.

Marcantonio won the election by the margin of 257 votes
out of 24,145 ballots cast. It is difficult to account for the
election of *any* Republican in 1934, a year when some Democrats increased their majorities in both houses of Congress.
Only seven Republican governors were left in an election which
was called by the *New York Times,* "the most overwhelming
victory in the history of American politics."

Marcantonio and LaGuardia seemed to be more New Dealist
than the Tammany people. Marcantonio generated excitement;
he was one of them. There was the Depression itself which
enabled many new political figures to enter Congress.

Once in Congress, Marcantonio developed into an avowed
radical, friendly to labor and the Roosevelt New Deal but to
the left of both on essential issues.[28] He supported the Wagner-
Connery National Labor Relations Act as a "great step toward
a Magna Carta for American labor" but pressed hard for the
inclusion of agricultual labor under its provisions. He opposed
the administration's social security bill and supported the more

radical Frazier-Lundeen measure which would place the burden of taxation on the shoulders of the wealthy. Consistently, he opposed expenditures for armaments and war. Persistently, he pressed for adequate appropriations for work relief for the unemployed. In diplomatic matters too, he stood to the left, and helped the majority in Congress erect a barrier of neutrality legislation against American involvement in another European conflict. He lashed out against "militarism," "imperialism," and continued American hegemony over Puerto Rico. What an unusual Republican East Harlem had selected to represent it on Capitol Hill. Fellow Congressman Maury Maverick dubbed him the "Pink Pachyderm." On many matters, especially his concern for America's underclass, Marcantonio stood apart from the main political drift.

With the growth of the welfare state, Marcantonio's East Harlem constituents were now dependent for aid and employment upon distant, impersonal bureaucracies. Marcantonio set up his congressional office which would become a very effective constituent service operation. No matter was too small or inconsequential for him. He helped in finding work, welfare, and housing. He provided free legal advice and helped on immigration and naturalization problems and countless other matters. His were ritualized attacks against the "Big shots" and "Wall Street"—symbols of those who stood apart from the poor and helpless in East Harlem.

In seeking a scapegoat, many Americans found it easy to place the responsibility on immigrants. Congressman Martin Dies is representative of the prevailing mood: "If we had refused admission to the sixteen and one-half million foreign born living in this country today, we would have no unemployment problem to distress and harass us."[29] Marcantonio realized that Italian-Americans would be prime targets of a new wave of discrimination. "On every issue regarding the welfare of immigrants, Marcantonio was on the liberal side. During the war Italian aliens became the objects of suspicion since they were classified as 'enemy aliens.' More than any other congressman, Marcantonio fought in their behalf both inside and outside the halls of Congress."[30]

Marcantonio's career was marked by controversy. His relations with LaGuardia became strained when he came out against LaGuardia over cutbacks in the WPA and the Emergency Relief Bureau. He called Fiorello "no friend of labor." In 1936, he wished to hold a demonstration parade in New York City, in protest of continued high unemployment. LaGuardia refused to grant a parade permit. Marcantonio then accused him of acting like Mussolini.

On the labor front, Luigi Antonini broke with Marcantonio over Marcantonio's insistence on aligning himself with the Communists. Antonini had had a long struggle with the Communists for control of his International Ladies Garment Workers Union and was deeply bothered by Marcantonio's association with them. The loss of Antonini's support was also politically harmful, since the former friend was a key figure in forming a third party in New York in 1936, The American Labor party.

Organized primarily to win support for Roosevelt, the party had wide labor and left-wing support. It could have been important to Marcantonio, who was closer to the ALP than to either of the major parties. But with the ILGWU, the strongest of the labor organizations backing the new party, Marcantonio received no help from that quarter.

In 1936, Marcantonio ran on the All Peoples party—a Communist-backed group. With only a token endorsement from LaGuardia (actually unexpected, considering the verbal abuse he had been receiving) he lost by some fifteen hundred votes to Lanzetta.

However, the loss of the seat was not really a repudiation of Marcantonio by the voters but a result of the Roosevelt landslide. Nonetheless, Marcantonio seemed to be politically dead. The Republicans divorced him, the American Labor party would have no part of him, and Tammany was out of the question. He had the personal machine but no place on the ballot; he had to keep in the public eye for the next two years. He did so by acting as labor counsel for numerous labor organizations. He gained national publicity by attacking the deportation of Harry Bridges and becoming violently involved on alleged violations of civil rights by the Hague machine in Jersey City.

Even though Marcantonio still had enemies in the leadership of the ALP, he announced himself, in July, 1938, as a candidate for the party's designation as a representative for the Twentieth Congressional District. This caused an uproar in the ranks. He was denounced by the East Harlem ALP Club, and someone else was endorsed.

Six days later, Marcantonio was suddenly designated as the official ALP nominee and was endorsed by Alex Rose, a member of the ALP State Executive Board and an anti-Communist. The designation of Marcantonio to be the nominee has always been shrouded in speculation. However, it is felt now that it was solely through the efforts of LaGuardia that he was selected. By cross-filing, he appeared on both the Democratic and Republican tickets in the primaries. In addition to the ALP, he kept the Republican and ALP nominations and defeated Lanzetta again in November, 1938. Marcantonio operated this way politically because he needed the Republican party to win in Italian East Harlem. He was not interested in building the East Harlem ALP into a strong independent organization. The ALP was a vehicle to be used to consolidate his own political power and to insure his election. He was to continue to serve in Congress until 1948.

During his first administration LaGuardia provided political recognition and some solutions to the problems confronting Italian-Americans. Italian-Americans were becoming more powerful politically, but the process was largely dependent upon the election of an Italian-American Republican mayor. The mayor swiftly used his Italian appointments as a means to retain the support of his Italian constituency. His Italian Re-election Committee noted in 1937 that Italians had begun to achieve their first genuine share of representation in the government of New York City. The vote in the Italian election districts was 62.6 percent in LaGuardia's favor with strong support coming from all income groups.[31]

By 1941, LaGuardia was facing political difficulties. During the previous year, many Italian voters had turned away from President Roosevelt because of his foreign policy toward Italy and his "stab in the back" speech. LaGuardia campaigned for FDR in 1940 and was closely identified with his policies. Despite this, large numbers of Italian voters still chose LaGuardia, although his percentage dropped to 46 percent. With anti-Italian discrimination increasing in the United States due to Italy's entry into the war, it was natural to perceive and complain about their lack of political power and advancement. This was a period of great insecurity for the Italian community. During the period of 1933 to 1945, Italians doubled their representation in the government of New York City.

There is a puzzling relationship between LaGuardia and Marcantonio. In 1940, LaGuardia had again endorsed Marcantonio, even though the latter was against lend lease and the former was a rabid interventionist. Any attempt to account for LaGuardia's action is a welter of contradictions. There was a deep affection between the two men, going back twenty years. Though LaGuardia disagreed on many subjects with Marcantonio, he had enough respect for Marcantonio's independence of mind and his abilities to respect his views on this important issue-lend lease.[32]

Marcantonio is most often explained away as a party liner, a demogogue, or a Russian agent. His elections are regarded as mysterious. Yet, in analyzing his career, there is nothing mysterious. He was an American radical. But what was a radical in the 1930s and 1940s would be considered a liberal today.[33]

Marcantonio was hardly a tool of the Communists. He was primarily a politician and as such used the party as a mechanism for attainment of political power. Marcantonio mobilized that power to sustain himself—the radical—in Congress. His was not radical activity. Marcantonio worked creatively within existing structures.

Vito Marcantonio's radicalism consisted of being against the poll tax, for desegregation in federal government, and for use of the Constitution to assure blacks their constitutional rights. These have come to pass. He was ahead of his time.

In the foreign policy area, Marcantonio was wrong and has been proved wrong in the Fascist Hitler-Mussolini era. He believed in co-existence with the Soviet Union in the post-World War II period. He could have been wrong for assuming that this could be attained easily, but he was not wrong in seeking peace.

Both LaGuardia and Marcantonio were important vehicles for the attainment of political power and political recognition by Italian-Americans. Both were political mavericks with independent and unique political styles. Both were considered radicals. The two men were aggressive champions of the rights and aspirations of the American people, especially the Italian-American masses. Both were "fighters against their time."

12 Neither Black nor Red

With the outbreak of World War I, Italy had three alternatives: to continue neutrality; to join the Central Powers; or to join the Anglo-Russian combination. The decision to abandon neutrality in 1915 appears to have been the most tragic error in the history of modern Italy. A small minority went against the will of the majority and pushed Italy into a struggle far beyond the resources of the country to sustain. The whole social, economic, political, and spiritual fabric of the nation was shaken. Mussolini and Fascism appear today as almost inevitable results of the error of 1915.[1]

World War I had brought Italy nothing but grief. The nation's families mourned their dead and wounded. Many thousands of returning soldiers could not find work. The government did not keep its promises of land reform to the peasants. Food shortages in large cities caused riots. The financial burdens led to drastic inflation and increases in prices. The nation's diplomatic and territorial hopes had been destroyed at the Versailles Peace Conference. It came to pass that Italy emerged from the war not with a feeling of victory, but with a deep sense of grievance and frustration, if not actual defeat, and there arose the myth of the lost victory. In a sense, the myth and the grievance corresponded to reality.[2]

With the end of World War I, the progressive faith in the United States yielded to a complex of anxieties, many of them irrational, that turned a majority of Americans away from reform. For a time, they found it more comfortable to subordinate mind to emotion. They succumbed to fatigue, fear, selfishness, and thoughtlessness. This retreat from responsibility began to grip the nation soon after the armistice of 1918. It played a part in America's rejection of the Treaty of Versailles, and it helped set the course in domestic affairs. America's attitude toward world politics was inevitably affected by her in-

217

volvement in the conflict in Europe. She had entered this war in a great crusade "to make the world safe for democracy." The harsh realities of that war and the dissillusion which accompanied the Paris Peace Conference, in which each power selfishly sought to advance its own national ends, made Wilson's idealism feel hollow and false. This reaction manifested itself in the spirit of isolationism. This was unfortunate, indeed, for the United States was needed in restoring the stability of Europe so necessary to the maintenance of world peace. The rejection of the Treaty signaled the desire to forget foreign problems and to enjoy the good rich life that American industry and technology seemed to promise. The new politics of the 1920s emphasized "normalcy," complacency, and prosperity. Events in Italy were met by smug indifference.

The history of fascism as a movement began officially in March, 1919, with a meeting of a handful of disgruntled Socialists and political extremists in Milan's Piazza San Sepolcro. Mussolini was expelled from the Socialist party for his support of Italy's intervention in World War I. He took with him a group of intellectuals and agitators who adhered to the syndicalist current of socialist ideology and extolled violent action as an end in itself.[3]

From the very start, the Fascists renounced any commitment to a specific political program, thus providing themselves with a maximum of flexibility. Sergio Panuzio, one of the apologists for the regime, described fascism as a synthesis of Italian nationalist and syndicalist thought. Not only was fascist thought often activist, pragmatic, and explicitly anti-ideological, but there was also a wide assortment of "fascisms" in Fascist Italy. Nationalism and, to a lesser degree, the cult of leadership were virtually the only ideological axioms shared by all these groups. No contemporary movement displays less homogeneity and more internal contradictions than Italian fascism.

Between 1919 and 1922, virtual civil war existed throughout Italy, as mass unrest spread. The Socialists gained in popular support and became the largest single party in the Italian parliament. Strikes and violence spread. The government seemed powerless to act.

Mussolini promised jobs and national greatness in world affairs. Fighting the Communists and Socialists in the unions, the factories, and the streets led to an escalation of violence and further inaction on the part of the government.

Fascism is often described as a middle-class phenomenon, and it is true that in Italy the movement drew a disproportionate share of its strength from the hard-pressed, economically and socially marginal elements of the lower-middle classes. Movements like fascism are not neatly explicable in class terms; their appeal is amorphous, and they draw adherence from those discontented and rootless individuals in the society who have lost their bearings in a period of rapid social change. For large numbers of such people, fascism represented a force of protest against the chaos of the times. To the more timid of the propertied classes, Mussolini could present himself as the savior of Italy from communism. Fascism was anti-Communist, antiliberal, and anti-Parliament; what it was in favor of, besides the greatness of the nation, no one was then able to determine.

Behind the bombast, showmanship, and false front which Mussolini presented to the world lurked a timid, uncertain, weak-willed, and badly informed man with an inferiority complex. There was an air of irritated impatience at generals who explained maneuvers to him, at maps that unfolded too slowly, at the officer who didn't come quickly enough when called, at the driver who didn't bring the car around fast enough, or at someone's slowness in thinking over a reply before giving it.

Luigi Barzini describes him this way: "He had a small cyst like a spring potato on his bald head; he had a dark oval mole under his chin (it must have bothered him when he was shaving), his teeth were the color of old ivory, and they were small and separated from one another, the kind of teeth that are supposed to be lucky."[4]

Mussolini was the logical leader of fascism precisely because he knew how to deal with and hold together the most disparate elements in Italian fascism. Far from being the iron-willed Duce, he was actually a most accomplished compromiser and temporizer. Largely as a result of the internal heterogeneity of Italian fascism and of the type of leadership provided by Mussolini, the history of the Fascist regime is essentially a history of compromise and flexibility. This accounts for Italian fascism not going to the extremes of German nazism.

Sensing that the moment was at hand, Mussolini staged the March on Rome in October 1922. At a mass rally of the Fascist party in Naples, Mussolini, now called *Il Duce* ("the leader"), and the other leaders decided to deal with the central government in Rome as they had done with local elected administrations. A quadrumvirate, formed by Italo Balbo, Michele Bianchi, General De Bono, and Dino Grandi, was entrusted with the execution of the plan. Fascist squads numbering about thirty thousand men were concentrated in localities around the capital. On October 28, they marched on Rome. The *marcia Di Roma,* patterned on D'Annunzio's *marci di Rochi,* aimed at replacing the parliamentary regime founded on free elections with a centralized all-powerful executive. Not trusting the loyalty of the armed forces, whose commanding officers were generally sympathetic to fascism, Facta's ministry resigned, leaving King Victor Emmanuel III with the responsibility of deciding whether to entrust the government to the hands of the Fascists or risk a civil war. The king chose the first alternative. On October 31, Mussolini formed a new government that included his own Fascists, several nationalists, and a few right-wing Catholics and liberals.[5]

What accounts for the collapse of democracy in Italy? The primary responsibility rests with the Italian Socialist party. The election of 1919 had made them the strongest party in the Chamber of Deputies. Together with the Popular party, they could command a majority. It seemed that all they needed to do was to establish an alliance with the Catholic Popular party to proceed to make democracy a reality through a program of social reform.

The Socialists thought revolution was at hand in Italy. The result was the phenomenon of *maximalism*—the fatal weakness of Italian socialism. Maximalism meant adherence to the maximum program of the party. The Maximalists mistook words for deeds. They labored under the illusion that the revolution was so inevitable that they needed to do nothing to bring it about. Had the Socialists, or some of them at least, been courageous enough, not so much to fight the Fascists in the streets, as to be willing to assume the responsibilities of government, the old system might have survived the crisis.

The Catholic responsibility in the failure of Italian democracy is connected with the errors of the Socialists. The leaders of the *Popolari* (Popular party) could not ally with those who preached violence and revolution. Though they advocated social reform, they became the defender of the interests of the Church before those of democracy. For them, the idea of a parliamentary alliance with the anticlerical Socialists was out of the question. The *Popolari* put their faith in legal methods and parliamentary activity. They expected their opponents to follow suit. To the end, they remained true to their doctrine of peaceful negotiation while Fascists and Communists were removing the foundation of democracy brick by brick.

The final responsibility for the collapse of democracy in the years 1919–1922 rests with the government itself. The four ministries that followed each other in these years were far different from the long-lived, solid governments over which Giolitti had presided in the years before the war. The postwar ministries were makeshift affairs living from day to day as best they might. No longer could they rely on a majority of loyal deputies who owed their election to the local prefects. The new system of proportional representation that had been inaugurated in 1919 ruined the traditional electoral contrivances. Under these circumstances, the government was at the mercy of the two large popular parties. And the Socialists and *Popolari*, while they criticized the conduct of the government freely, were not ready to take over that responsibility themselves. Hence no one really governed; the nation drifted, while the countryside sank into civil war.[6]

Mussolini assumed power in a technically constitutional fashion; the majority of the center party deputies—including the *Popolari*—decided at first upon the fatal policy of collaboration in the hope that the movement could be civilized. For his part, Mussolini began by respecting the outward forms of legality. While his armed action squads roamed the country at will, intimidating and even annihilating troublesome opposition elements, Mussolini governed with a coalition cabinet responsible to Parliament. Early in 1924, new elections were held in an atmosphere that can at best be described as one of semi-coercion. The Fascists won an overwhelming majority in Parliament.

However, there still existed in Italy an organized political opposition. This was to come to an end with the Matteotti crisis. Matteotti was a leading Socialist deputy who had been particularly outspoken in his denunciation of Mussolini's rule. In July 1924, he was captured upon leaving the Chamber of Deputies and beaten to death by Fascist thugs. This event brought about what was known as the "Aventine Secession" of a number of deputies, who boycotted Parliament in protest over the illegality of the Mussolini regime. Although he at first appears to have wavered in the face of the immense popular indignation over this political murder, Mussolini decided to resolve the crisis with a frank policy of repression and dictatorship. In his important speech of January 3, 1925, he declared the Aventine oppositionists permanently expelled from Parliament. This inaugurated an era during which all parties other than the Fascist were outlawed and all intermediary organizations such as trade unions, professional associations, and youth groups were replaced with a single national network of associations rigidly controlled by the Fascist party.

After many years of tension, the establishment of a strong government headed by a young man (Mussolini was thirty-nine) capable of enforcing order, putting an end to strikes, making public services efficient again, and dealing from strength in foreign affairs produced a genuine feeling of relief among millions of Italians. Then and later, the Fascists, who believed in violence as the foundation for a totalitarian state pursuing national greatness, were never more than a small minority of the nation. However, admirers and supporters of fascism were many. Fascism satisfied the nationalists' craving for aggrandizement and the young radicals' craving for a new social order. It satisfied the Catholics' desire to stamp out atheism and materialism and the property owners' desire to stamp out collectivism. It satisfied the general longing for order. Popular support for fascism was particularly strong between 1927 and 1936 when Ethiopia was conquered.

With the enactment and rigid enforcement of the Special Laws in Defense of the State of November 1926, the Fascist government put an end to all legal opposition to its power. From the mid-1920s to 1939, the spirit of active resistance to fascism was kept alive by workers, journalists, intellectuals, and political leaders who chose exile or who remained and engaged in various forms of conspiratorial activity. Among the most important of these activities were the printing and distributing of underground newspapers. With the exception of France, in no country with organized resistance movements was the underground press as large and various as in Italy. From 1943 to 1945, 650 secret underground newspapers were published by anti-Fascist organizations in Italy.[7] Other anti-Fascist organizations included *Concentrazione Antifascista*, *LaLiberta*, the National Alliance, labor, and various Catholic militants.

It was not surprising that many Italian-Americans should be impressed by Benito Mussolini. They had memories of past nativist attacks and current discrimination. Every day, news of Italy or Mussolini blared across the nation's airwaves. In the United States, Italian-Americans sought acceptance and status by their fellow Americans. Millions of Italians in Italy sought acceptance and status by the international community of nations. For both Italian-Americans and Italians, Mussolini seemed to fulfill these aspirations. One example may be seen in the reminiscence of an Italian-American friend. He recalls his father taking him to the sandy beaches of New Jersey and New York to view pre-announced flights of Italian planes to America. Both cheered wildly. His father was filled with pride and excite-

ment at this outward sign of Italian power and status in the
world. The admiration for Il Duce was not confined to the Italian-
American community. Many segments of American society sang
his praises. Embracing isolationism, they welcomed Mussolini's
call for patriotism among Italians and his utter contempt for the
League of Nations. Former Progressives led the parade of American admirers. Others, including Lincoln Steffens, Thomas Edi-
son, Senator Hiram Johnson, were also impressed with Il Duce.

Following his meeting with Mussolini in 1927, Winston
Churchill declared, "If I were an Italian, I am sure I could
have been with you from beginning to end in your struggle
against the bestial appetites of Leninism."[8] Posing as the savior
of capitalism against communism, Mussolini indeed struck a
responsive chord in the middle-class property owners in America
who were in the throes of a decade of political reaction, nativist
hysteria, and unlimited worship of the world of business.

The popularity of Mussolini among Americans in general
and Italian-Americans in particular extended from 1922 to
1929. The high point of Il Duce's popularity among Italian-
Americans occurred with the signing of the Concordat which
normalized relations between the Vatican and the Italian government.

The Concordat reversed the whole tradition of church/state
separation. It restored the Catholic Church to the position it
had always occupied by the letter of the Italian constitution
as the "sole religion of the state." In the future, Roman Catholic religious bodies would suffer no limitations in their right
to teach and to hold property, and Church marriages would
be legally binding in the eyes of the civil authorities. It was
on the question of marriage that the Pope gained his greatest
victory. Previously in Italy, as in France, a civil marriage ceremony had been obligatory; a Church wedding from the legal
standpoint ranked as no more than an optional supplement.
By the terms of the new Concordat, Italians, like Americans,
might choose whether they wished to be married by a civil ceremony or in church; and in practice, since 1929, most of them
had chosen the latter. Beyond that, however, and here the Concordat diverged from the American example, Mussolini undertook to bring the marriage law of the Italian state into conformity with canon law. Church courts were to have sole jurisdiction
in questions involving the dissolution of the marriage tie.[9]

The wave of pro-Fascist sentiment produced among Catholics
both inside and outside Italy by the settlement of 1929 might
well have raised doubts in the Pope's mind as to the wisdom

of what he had just done, for one of his main purposes in entering into the negotiations had been to prevent Mussolini from smothering the Church with kindness; by regularizing the relations between Catholicism and the Fascist state he had hoped to disentangle the Church from too close an association with Mussolini's regime. The actual effect was nearly the reverse. Whatever doubts about Fascism the Pope himself might have entertained were not shared by most of the Italian clergy. These interpreted the accords of 1929 as a blessing bestowed on all Il Duce's works, as was to be apparent six years later when a number of the highest ranking Italian ecclesiastics actively endorsed Mussolini's war of conquest in Ethiopia.

During the 1920s pro-Fascist and anti-Fascist groups emerged in the United States.[10] Within the Italian-American community, fascism did not have a uniform impact. Those Italian-Americans born in the United States and others who had served in World War I found fascism the least attractive.[11] America produced one of the first anti-Fascist campaigns in the western world, organized and led by segments of the Italian-American community.

American opposition to Mussolini originated in the Italian-American labor movement. After the March on Rome, Italian-American radicals took part in street demonstrations. They went one step further in 1923 by organizing the Anti-Fascist Alliance of North America (AFANA) with Arturo Giovannitti as its secretary.

The radical wing of the press issued a steady stream of anti-Fascist attacks. Such papers as the socialist *La Parola del Popolo,* the Communist *L'Unita del Popolo,* and the liberal *L' Italiano-Americano* took part in the campaign.[12]

AFANA was fragmented among many factions with major doctrinal differences. Some portions of the press attempted to reconcile this factionalism. By 1926, a number of unions seceded from the AFANA, since they felt that Communists were trying to control the Alliance. The seceding groups reorganized under the leadership of the Socialists into the Anti-Fascist League with John Vaccaro as secretary.

In 1926, the anti-Fascist historian Gaetano Salvemini sought political asylum in the United States. There was some question as to whether the American government would grant his asylum. After an intensive investigation, Salvemini was cleared of being either an anarchist or a Communist.

The Coolidge administration negotiated a debt settlement with Italy based to a great extent on Ambassador Richard Child's enthusiastic support of the Italian government. A consortium of Wall Street banks led by J.P. Morgan & Company loaned the Fascist government $100 million to help stabilize the Italian *lira*. At this time, the Italian government decided on a major propaganda campaign in the United States. Attempts were made to establish the Fascist League of North America. The American government did not look unfavorably upon the League, since they viewed it as anti-Communist and dedicated to upholding law and order. Thus, the Italian-American anti-Fascists had the difficulty of overcoming the tacit approval of the Fascist League of North America.

The faction-torn anti-Fascists were also unable to get the support of American labor. In the early 1920s, Samuel Gompers was in awe of the miracle of Italy's progress. The Italian-American labor leadership was opposed to fascism, but a large portion of the Italian-American masses were either uncertain of or highly sympathetic to the charismatic Mussolini during the 1920s. The anti-Fascists, who constituted something like 10 percent of the Italian-American population, risked the image of being un-Italian by attacking Mussolini. Since relations between the United States and Italy were friendly, the anti-Fascists always operated under the threat of an American government crackdown instigated by the Italian government. The Italian government informed the American government through official channels that the anti-Fascists were taking orders directly from Moscow.

Despite these problems, the anti-Fascists waged a relentless campaign. They published articles and journals. They took part in demonstratons and assailed portions of the pro-Fascist Italian-American press. On a number of occasions, they clashed in street demonstrations with pro-Fascist forces.

Professor John P. Diggins, who has studied the anti-Fascist movement in America, asserted in his book *Mussolini and Fascism* that:

> Higher education, always sensitive to the dangers of state control and the erosion of academic freedom, remained on the whole critical of fascism in all phases of Italian life. Columbia University, however, was an exception. Columbia's profascism emanated largely from its Italian Department, which, under the chairmanship of Giuseppe Prezzolini, functioned as something of an overseas branch of Italy's Ministry of Culture and Propaganda.[13]

Diggins contends Columbia University and Casa Italiana were pro-Fascist.

During the 1920s, the *Casa Italiana* of Columbia University was founded. Giuseppe Prezzolini describes the movement to establish the Casa this way:

> It was...a movement prompted by national pride, similar to those prevailing in Italy after World War I, but unlike them in that it was Italian-American. By creating the Casa Italiana, children of Italian immigrants in the United States wished to proclaim the coming of age of a young generation that had begun to forget the parents' Italian dialects and to adopt the language of America's founding fathers. They were the children of poor folk that had become sufficiently rich to be able to pay for their college education and the relative leisure it entailed. These parents were the survivors of wave after wave of Italian immigrants that had left their homeland in search of a livelihood. They were grateful to the country that had sheltered them and given them the opportunity to work. They were not, however, unmindful of the many fellow immigrants that had died, or were in jail or hospitals and insane asylms. At the same time, they were proud of the success of the stronger, hardier, or luckier among them.[14]

In a recently published monograph, Prezzolini effectively refutes Diggins' assertions. Prezzolini had never served as chairman of the Italian Department, and both the Department and the *Casa* had known anti-Fascists within it.

The fact that the *Casa* was devoted to the study of Italian culture and language did not make it a center for Fascist propaganda or a "schoolhouse for budding Fascist ideologues" as Diggins contends. In fact, the *Casa* invited such scholars as Enrico Fermi, Mario Cassela, Arturo Loria, Enrico De'Negri, Alberto Moravia, Emilio Cecchi, and Giorgio Levi Della Vida to take part in programs and to lecture at the *Casa Italiana*. All were anti-Fascist. Prezzolini's own book on fascism was never published in Italy because it was considered dangerous to the government.

The peaceful year of 1929 turned out to be one of the most unforgettable in American history. It was deceptively quiet. The end of the golden dream came abruptly in October 1929 with the spectacular stock market crash. Following the crash, production came to a standstill, and the unemployed were numbered in the millions. Lines of Americans in the streets waited not for seats to the latest film, but for handouts at municipal soup kitchens.

In 1929, an article appeared in Harper's Magazine which unleashed an uproar among Americans. Marcus Duffield, in

"Mussolini's American Empire," stated that "part of Mussolini's empire, from his point of view, lies within the United States.... Fascism, which has seemed remote to the New World, has reached across the seas to fasten its grip upon four million Americans of Italian extraction [whom Mussolini] considers ...as his subjects." Duffield went on to contend that Mussolini sought to conquer the United States and that he could count on Italian-Americans as his vanguard who would serve as soldiers and saboteurs.[15]

The article provoked a State Department inquiry and a subsequent admission by Duffield that much of his evidence was inaccurate. Further investigations were made of the Fascist League of North America. Unwilling to strain diplomatic relations, the Italian government ordered the dissolution of the League.

Duffield began the myth of a monolithic Italian-American Fascist conspiracy. The American public and Washington needed Italian-Americans as scapegoats to excuse their own support and brief marriage with the undemocratic dictatorship of Benito Mussolini.

The anti-Fascists, led by Geatano Salvemni, Carlo Tresca, and Carlo Fama, continued their fight into the 1930s. Italian exiles like Max Ascoli, Giuseppe Borgese, Lionello Venturi, and Enrico Fermi were aided in obtaining teaching positions at American universities. These men formed a nucleus of scholars who were a significant force in the intellectual community. American intellectual support for the anti-Fascists increased during the 1930s, especially with Nazi expansionism; however, Mussolini's prestige in the United States was still high. By the end of 1931, America foundered ever deeper in depression, with little being done about it, yet the nation still was trying to carry on as normally as possible. The year 1932 was the darkest, dreariest, most disastrous year of the Great Depression. Unemployment reached 13 million. In some cities 80 percent of the workers were unemployed. The deepening depression was too much of a political liability for President Hoover, and the 1932 elections brought Franklin D. Roosevelt and his New Deal to power.

The New Deal, in attempting to help all of the disadvantaged, departed in this respect from previous reform movements which had been intended primarily for middle-class native-born Americans. For Italian-Americans, the New Deal provided a channel through which they might gain greater respectability and recognition from American society. The New Deal was a reflection of ethnic America's struggle for recognition and power as well as an attempt at promoting full economic recovery.

The myopia of America's policies toward Europe carried over into President Roosevelt's first administration. The Great Depression profoundly intensified isolationist sentiment. In the 1920s, emphasis had focused on political separation, but after 1929, political separation became strongly and directly linked to economic isolation.

In America, radical movements of all kinds spread during the early and mid-1930s. The followers came mostly from the old lower-middle classes. They were now in an unprecedented stage of frustration and fear and menaced by humiliation, dispossession, and poverty. They came from provincial and nonpolitical groups and, in the main, from the ranks of the self-employed. They felt threatened by organized economic power. To a significant degree, they came from the evangelical denominations. They were mostly men and women of old immigrant stock, such as the Germans and Anglo-Saxons.

In April, 1933, just a few weeks after Roosevelt took office, a new magazine called the *American Review* made its debut. Its editor was Seward Collins, who made the review a forum for "Radicals of the Right." In 1933, Collins called Mussolini "the most constructive statesman of our age." Describing himself frankly as a Fascist, he maintained, "We are offered our choice of communist collectivism or personal liberty under Fascism."[16] The *American Review* became an intellectual forum for American fascism.

The poet Ezra Pound left the United States for Italy and became an international spokesman for fascism. The source of evil to Pound was usury, "the cancer of the world, which only the surgeon's knife of fascism can cut out of the life of the nation."[17] To Pound and other misguided intellectuals, Mussolini offered the twentieth-century way of vindicating the dreams of the founders of the Republic. To Lawrence Dennis, big business had made fascism logical for the United States. Americans, he wrote, were "the most organized, standardized, regimented, and docile people in the world."[18]

Activists in the American fascist movement included other non-Italians, such as General Art J. Smith, a professional soldier. A quasi-veterans organization remained as a sort of illegitimate offspring of the Bonus Expeditionary Force. They maintained their headquarters in Philadelphia under the leadership of Smith. Mussolini had marched on Rome, and Smith proposed to march on Washington.

One of the most influential Fascists was William D. Pelley.

The day after Hitler became Chancellor of Germany, Pelley inaugurated the Silver Shirts. The initials expressed his admiration for the Nazi SS, Hitler's elite guard. From San Diego to Minneapolis to New York City, the Silver Shirts were active and ready for the moment in which their dream would be realized.[19]

One of the successes which was widely publicized by the Fascists was the Treaty of Rome, signed on June 7, 1933. Hitler had attained power in Germany that year, and the time had seemed to come for an agreement among the major European countries for the preservation of peace. This was signed by Italy, Britain, Germany, and France, but was never ratified. Had it been, it might have provided a substitute for the League of Nations, which was unable to cope with the great issues of the times.

Italy and Germany were bound to clash over the problem of Austria. Mussolini and Hitler met in Venice in June 1934 and seemed to have reached an agreement concerning Austria's independence. Yet two months later, a Nazi revolt broke out in Vienna, and the Austrian Chancellor was murdered. The plot had been organized in Germany as a prelude to annexation. Mussolini was quick in mobilizing four divisions and sending them to the Austrian frontier. This meant intervention if annexation took place. As a result, Germany, which was still disarmed under the provisions of the 1919 Peace Treaty, refrained from attempting anything of the kind. Hitler was forced to abandon his plans for a takeover of that country. Mussolini was regarded by Western diplomats as the peacemaker of Europe.

Late in 1935, Mussolini sent his Italian legions plunging across the borders of Ethiopia. Beginning in 1933, the Italian dictator had begun to make preparations for a military campaign in East Africa. Quietly and secretly, these plans were pushed ahead in 1934. A border clash between Ethiopian and Italian troops at Walwal in December gave Mussolini a moral pretext for his act of aggression. Actually, Italy had long been casting envious eyes at Ethiopia from the vantage point of its adjoining colonies, Eritrea and Somaliland. Emperor Haile Selassie of Ethiopia offered to submit the new dispute to arbitration, but Mussolini refused. As a member, Ethiopia then appealed to the League of Nations. The issue quickly became a test of the League's ability to maintain world peace.

Unfortunately, the efforts of the League to take effective action were undermined by France and Britain. The Franco-Italian agreement of January 1935 virtually assured Mussolini that, in return for Italy's cooperation in Europe, France would not interfere in the dictator's colonial affairs. Equally serious was the abortive Hoare-Laval plan. The Foreign Ministers of Britain and France, Sir Samuel Hoare and Pierre Laval, secretly came to an understanding that, in the event of Italian aggression, brakes would be put on the imposition of sanctions by the League. These would be limited to financial and economic measures. They also agreed that Italy could keep most of the territory she had already conquered, while Ethiopia would be given "in exchange" a narrow corridor to the Red Sea. Laval ungraciously published this plan before it was approved by the British Cabinet. Widespread public condemnation in Britain led to Hoare's resignation and the appointment of Anthony Eden to his position.

Despite British and French attempts to sabotage collective action, the League branded Italy an aggressor. It voted for economic sanctions, which proved totally ineffective. Sanctions were to be imposed in successive stages. During the first stage, no restrictions were placed on oil, iron and steel, and coal and coke—items which greased Mussolini's war machine. Moreover, each of the cooperating states was required to enact necessary legislation to enforce the sanctions. None of the powers was anxious to move speedily. This was the first time sanctions had been applied, and because of the depression, few were willing to sacrifice good business. Vigorous action, moreover, was discouraged, since the United States and Germany were not included among the participants in the embargoes. America did place an embargo on shipments of munitions, but not on oil, aviation gasoline, or other military supplies. Oil shipments to Italy were six times greater in 1935 than they had been the previous year. Mussolini, therefore, successfully defined the League "sanctions." After seven months of warfare, he annexed Ethiopia to Italy.

The Ethiopian War was probably the turning point for the American public and the American government. Although many segments of the Italian-American community continued to support Mussolini, ultimately Fascism was abandoned by its Italian-American supporters when it became clearer that Italian diplomacy was venturing upon a collision course with the United States. As Mussolini continued with foreign expansionism, Italians increasingly became disenchanted. His alliance with Adolph Hitler was to be a major turning point in Italian history. Certainly, it marked a turning point in the attitudes of Italians and Italian-Americans.

A source of inspiration for the Italian-American anti-Fascists was Enrico Fermi. Shocked by the racial legislation introduced in Italy by the Fascist regime, Fermi came to the United States in 1938. He accepted a position at Columbia University in 1939 and was invited to join the team of brilliant American and foreign physicists who (in the wake of the discoveries of Rutherford, Einstein, Bohr, and others) were devoting their efforts to the study of nuclear energy.

Fermi, a Roman, born in 1901, was an imaginative theoretical physicist and a patient experimental scientist. Appointed professor of physics at the University of Pisa at the age of twenty-one, he was promoted to the University of Rome in 1927. He studied protons and neutrons; in 1934, he developed the theory of the decay of beta elements; and in 1938, he received the Nobel Prize in physics for discoveries concerning artificial radioactivity induced by neutrons and thermal neutrons.

Mussolini's reckless foreign policy continued, and with Japan's attack on Pearl Harbor, he lost support among Italian-Americans and other Americans. From 1940 to 1941, countless Americans continued to view Italian-Americans as subversives. A ban was placed upon the Italian language.

Developments after 1935—the Spanish Civil War, the Axis Alliance, and the anti-Semitic laws in Italy—caused many Americans and Italian-Americans to turn against Mussolini. These developments produced the conditions for a more broadly based anti-Fascist movement. The Spanish Civil War in particular brought together liberals, intellectuals, socialists, and radical labor groups in the fight against fascism. In the more important realm of political and ideological warfare, the Spanish Civil War was crucially important in forging a sense of unity of purpose among the diverse anti-Fascist movements in Italy and in the United States.

The most important organization to emerge following the Spanish Civil War was the Mazzini Society, which was dedicated to the principles of the Risorgimento. With Italy's attack on France, the anti-Fascists were now regarded as respectable and legitimate. *Il Progresso,* which was published in New York, now made an about face and began to attack Mussolini.[20] The problem arose as to whether the anti-Fascists ought to collaborate with the Communists. The problem of collaboration strained the two principal sources of the anti-Fascist opposition—Italian-American labor and the Mazzini liberals. Luigi Antonini, president of the ILGWU, opposed another Popular Front.

Gaetano Salvemini warned Americans about the rising tide

of hysteria and indiscriminate anti-Italian persecution that was sweeping the nation in 1940. The anti-Fascist forces were to be fragmented during the 1940s. They nonetheless were a potent force of opposition.

In 1942, President Roosevelt entrusted the execution of the Manhattan Project to some of the exiled scientists. Fermi was director of the work that led to the first controlled nuclear chain reaction in Chicago on December 2, 1942, and to the first atomic explosion on July 16, 1945. In 1946, he became director of the Institute of Nuclear Studies (now the Enrico Fermi Institute) at the University of Chicago. The exile of Fermi and the numerous other European scientists who found life under dictatorship intolerable was more than merely a loss to Italy or Germany and a gain for the United States; by stifling their scientists, totalitarian dictatorships lost the military superiority they enjoyed during the first phase of World War II. This sealed the doom of the vast coalition aimed at destroying the democratic way of life.

Ultimately, for all the Fascist proselytizing among the Italian-Americans, fascism was to have little effect on their loyalty to the United States. In truth, the largest and most visible anti-Fascists were the one and one-half million Italian-Americans who served their country in World War II against fascism.[21] Ten Italian-Americans were awarded the Navy Cross, and one, John Basilone, was given the Congressional Medal of Honor.

With its defeat, Italy sought to make a break with its recent past, and that break was total. Fascism, itself, was gone, even if, as an idea, it still lingered for a small minority (about one Italian in twenty, according to election returns from 1948 to 1970). Spokesmen for what had been the dominant majority in pre-Fascist Italy—such as Croce, Orlando, Nitti, Sforza, and De Nicola—were respected, but had a small following, as did many other former prominent liberal and democratic leaders who were not tainted with Fascist sympathies. The ideals and aspirations identified with socialism had gained ground, but their impact on the nation and the state was weakened by the deep cleavage between democratic and authoritarian socialists, between the Socialist and Communist parties. With the Christian Democratic party, political Catholicism, once an opponent of democracy and now a supporter, became the dominant force in Italy.

The referendum of June 2, 1946, had established the Italian Republic. On the same day, elections for a Constituent Assembly were held.[22] The results of the elections for the Constituent

Assembly confirmed the voting patterns of the coalition, which was composed of parties congenial with each other—Christian Democratic, Republican, Liberal, and right-wing (Saragat) Socialist.

Apparently unaware of what was being planned, Togliatti, Communist party leader, continued to stress the importance of maintaining the governing coalition of the three mass parties. He even went so far as to attempt to gain Christian Democratic favor by directing his party to vote for the retention of Mussolini's Concordat with the Vatican in the new constitution that was slowly being elaborated by the Assembly. This vote—which deeply shocked deputies of anticlerical conviction, including Togliatti's own Socialist allies—saved the Concordat for posterity. But it could not save Togliatti himself. De Gasperi simply accepted the communists' pro-Catholic vote in the cynical spirit in which it had been offered and proceeded to carry out his plans. In May, he announced the necessity of enlarging his government both to the Right and to the Left. There followed his own resignation, a feint to put his adversaries off the track, and an interlude occurred in which Francesco Saverio Nitti, another octogenarian from the pre-Fascist era, tried in vain to collect a ministry. Eventually, with all alternative possibilities exhausted, De Gasperi accepted President De Nicola's invitation to form his fourth government. This time, it was to be a frankly conservative ministry, including besides the Christian Democrats only the Liberals and a few eminent personalities like Count Sforza. The Communists and left-wing Socialists had been left outside. Togliatti had lost the game.

In their irritation at being outwitted, the Communists threatened that it would prove impossible to govern against them, against the parties that the elections had shown to represent a third of the Italian nation. Many non-Communists agreed with this estimate of the situation, but the summer and autumn of 1947 proved that DeGasperi's courageous gamble had succeeded.

By the winter of 1947–48 Italy's internal and external position had vastly improved. Inflation had been brought under control, and the economy was reviving appreciably. A peace treaty had been signed and ratified, and its terms could hardly be regarded as vindictive by an objective observer, though the immediate reaction of the Italian people was one of disappointment and bitterness. Another stabilizing factor was the new constitution, which went into effect at the beginning of 1948. Though excessively long, though the product of too many compromises, and though many of its articles were to be inadequately executed (notably regional autonomy), the constitution provided the framework for a renovated and progressive Italy. The stage was now prepared for the general election that would choose the first Senate and Chamber of Deputies under the new republican constitution completed four months earlier.[23]

The first election of a parliament under the new Constitution was scheduled for April 18, 1948. The preceding winter had been bitter. The coup d'etat in Prague, which led to the Communist takeover in Czechoslovakia, had a major impact on the Italian elections. The Italian election was turned into a struggle between Christ and Antichrist, between Rome and Moscow.

Prior to going before the electorate, De Gasperi decided to broaden the base of his government by taking in the Republicans and Saragat's Social Democrats. With all three of the "repectable" minor parties now in his ministry, he could plausibly argue that his government constituted the sole democratic alternative to Communism. Such was also the opinion of the American Embassy. Both the Church and Catholic Action quite naturally felt the same way.

The election witnessed massive intervention on the part of the Church, with important consequences for the future. When the campaign got under way, Pius XII was determined to use his influence to bring about the victory of the Christian Democratic party. In accordance with instructions contained in several pontifical speeches, the 300 bishops and 125,000 members of the secular and religious clergy began, through written and spoken word, to counteract the propaganda organized or inspired by the leftist parties. Italy's potential voters numbered about 29 million; of these, 15 million were women. A determined effort was made to get all women (including cloistered nuns) to vote, on the assumption—and a correct one—that the overwhelming majority of them would vote the Christian Democratic ticket. The incompatibility of Catholicism and materialistic ideologies was repeatedly stressed. Speaking to streetcar conductors on February 22, the Pope stated, "Despite false rumors that have circulated among you, the doctrine of Christian truth and faith is irreconcilable with materialistic maxims, support of which, whether one likes it or not, means to desert the Church and cease being a Catholic."[24] Many Cardinals and bishops ordered their priests not to administer the sacraments to anyone voting for the pro-Soviet slate.

The United States mobilized its economic and political weapons to stem the apparent Red tide. On March 15, 1948, it announced that all economic aid would be cut off if the Communnist/Socialist slate won.

Efforts were made in the United States to mobilize Italian-Americans to influence their friends and relatives in Italy to vote against the Communists. The movement was spearheaded by Generoso Pope. publisher of *Il Progresso,* and Monsignor E. Montelone. A mass campaign of letters, cards, telegraphs, and radio broadcasts was begun. The chief center of this campaign was in New York City.[25]

The Committee to Aid Democracy in Italy distributed a half million postcards to be mailed to Italy. The Italian language radio station WOV made recordings by Italian-Americans to be sent to Italian relatives. Prominent Americans made radio broadcasts on behalf of the anti-Communist cause.

This movement had its origins among a group of Italian-Americans and was accepted and actively advanced by the Catholic Church and Italian-American organizations. It finally received additional endorsement from non-Italian sources.

The following is a portion of a typical form letter distributed by Italian-American anti-Communists designed to be sent to Italian relatives:

> By voting for the Communists you are betraying yourselves, trampling on your forefathers' religion; you will betray... our dear Fatherland; you will betray your families....
>
> If you want the salvation of religion, of the Fatherland... vote for the Christian Democratic party, because then you will be voting for liberty.[26]

In either event, the danger was exaggerated, although many honest and serious people were convinced by its reality. It did serve to commit more American resources to Italy. Internally in Italy, the scare drew large numbers of conservative and moderate voters into the Christian Democratic party. Although the Christian Democratic party had received less than half the popular vote, it had an absolute majority of the seats in Parliament. Italy gradually worked itself back into the community of free nations.

The 1930s and '40s witnessed Italian-Americans organize in opposition to extremism of both the left and the right.

13 Symbol of Amoral Power

In 1970, many law-enforcement officials expressed surprise when Hugh Mulligan was charged with being the key figure in organized crime's successful attempt to corrupt New York City policemen by getting valuable information from them and influencing decisions on personnel assignments, reassignments, and the like.... When Mulligan was finally indicted in 1970, a spokesman for the Manhattan district attorney's office was asked to explain how such an important figure could have concealed his criminal activities so well. The official responded, "We never really heard about him before two years ago. When we went after organized crime, we only went after Italians."[1]

Why would any law-enforcement official in search of organized crime figures look only for Italian-Americans? Had the Italian-American become stereotyped as a criminal in the same way that the Jew was thought to be moneylender, the Indian a treacherous savage, the Irish-American a drunkard, and the black man lazy and stupid? John Mariani observes:

Everybody loves Italians! We're emotional, romantic, sentimental and sing wonderfully; Italian men are all studs, and Italian women are all passionate. If we're sometimes a little slow-witted or vulgar, we have ways of taking care of snobs and getting revenge, and we don't bother with those not of our kind. We're a sweet and peppery people who stay to ourselves. And if you don't believe that, I'll break your arm.

That's how most Americans see Italians, thanks to the kind of stereotypes Hollywood and television have been exhibiting for decades. From organ grinder to mobster to soulful underdog, the Italian on screen has always been cast in a rather shadowy light, a chiaroscuro that can be troubling and intimidating, mysterious, captivating and sensual.[2]

A host of such images have become more or less stable stereotypes in the American mind. They have their origin in the racism and bigotry of the past. The stream of nativist thinking in the late nineteenth century and the early twentieth century was to permeate the American consciousness up to the present. The coming of fascism in Italy and its growing menace to free nations in the 1930s and 1940s was to influence the Italian stereotype in yet another way. Italian-American conservatism was to be equated with fascism and later with right-wing extremism.

In the silent movie era, Italians were depicted as jovial immigrants behind pushcarts. Rudolph Valentino displayed the erotic Latin temperament. But it was in the 1930s that the image of Italians as gangsters took shape in American movies. Edward G. Robinson's Rico Bandello in "Little Caesar" and Paul Muni's "Scarface" were to inspire a succession of films whose characterizations extend from the 1930s to the present.

With the emergence of the mass media, the composite stereotype and the nativist currents were to find new and deadly outlets of expression. Arcangelo R. R. D'Amore, a noted Washington, D.C., psychiatrist explains:

> The romantic Latin lover of pre-World War II fims; and the Italian-American singer on radio and television of the 1950s have faded. In the 1960s and 1970s, the Italian-American is less likely to be portraying tenderness; he is more likely to be seen in roles of violent aggression—as in the Mafia films. He is fixated at an adolescent level of development as a sado-masochistic symbol of amoral power....[3]

Nineteen seventy-two will undoubtedly be recorded as the year of the Peking and Moscow summit meetings and the SALT agreements. It was also the time when the Supreme Court took a significant step backward in the quest for full equality for millions of blacks when it upheld the right of private clubs to exclude them. Equally ominous a development was the coming to the screens of American movie theaters of pictures such as *The Godfather* and *The Gang That Couldn't Shoot Straight*, and to television of *The Super*. *The Godfather* became the film to see, since it had all of the proper ingredients for commercial success: ethnic stereotypes, crime, sex, and violence.

What is instructive about the critical reaction to these productions is that they were either upheld or not on the quality of the performances and the scripts. *The Godfather,* according to most accounts, had some fine performances from some fine actors. This only worsens the situation. It reminds me of the blacks who have been stereotyped for years, making it impossible for black actors to obtain any but stereotyped roles. The crime is that many were so good at it. Is this to be the fate of Italian-Americans?

Let us not even go into the value system of the picture, the exaltation of killers, sadistic preoccupation with blood and violence, and the reactions of the audience which cheered the taking of human life. As columnist William Shannon noted in the *New York Times*:

> In "The Godfather," the exploitation of Catholic rituals and Italian customs—in the wedding and funeral scenes as well as the Baptism—is part of the biggest cultural ripoff that any commercial promoters have gotten away with in years. "The Godfather" stereotypes as gangsters or as the half admiring, half fearful pawns of gangsters. . . .
> The film flatters Italian males by stressing their toughness and sexual prowess. But to what purpose? To end with a hero, the young Godfather, who is—by any decent human standard —a monster. Some flattery.[4]

The Godfather Part I and *Part II* were a shameless romanticization of evil and vicious men. *The Godfather Part II* is not just a cynical attempt to capitalize on the sex and violence that made *Part I* such a tremendous financial success; it purports to be saying something significant about the failure of the great American dream. It is a glossy and shameful rendering of the Italian-American family life and has no relationship to what most Italian-American families have endured and accomplished.

Marlon Brando, upset over the way Hollywood has exploited the American Indians and distorted their image, has expressed no concern for his part in the exploitation and distortion of Italian-Americans.

The success of the godfather films raises an enormous cultural obstacle. To an Italian-American, *compare* means "godfather." It has always been a cultural-religious term of love and respect. Traditionally, a godfather means an alter ego in place of a parent in time of need. The picture *The Godfather* has had the effect of changing the meaning. Henceforth, the term *godfather* will be understood to mean a ruthless Italian killer. Events have consequences, and the consequences of this film cannot be good for Americans of Italian or non-Italian ancestry.

Perhaps the test for making it in Hollywood for a young aspiring Italian-American director is to produce a "Mafia" film.

the enormous success of *The Godfather*, Martin
made his major film debut in *Mean Streets*. Beneath its
appings, *Mean Streets* aims for a "true life" study of
ife in the big city, Scorsese's characters are ethnic stereo-
tage Italians as predictable and as overstated in their
flamboyant gestures and earthy speech as stage Irish or stage
Jewish. "Big City ethnic naturalism set against crime thriller
operatics, the movie ends up as a kind of 'Marty' meets the godfather." *Mean Streets* has no heroes, no values, only corruption.

What about television? "The Super," when reviewed, was
panned because of the poor quality of the scripts and performances. (Richard Castellano in the key role had also appeared
in *The Godfather*.) In other words, if they had been better
executed, "The Super," and, I would suspect, *The Gang That
Couldn't Shoot Straight,* would be wholly acceptable. "The
Super" was followed by another series, the now defunct "Monte-
fuscos." Currently, TV's Fonzi of "Happy Days" and Pinky
Tuscadero of "Laverne and Shirley" epitomize an image of
Italian-Americans as childish, hardworking but ambitionless, parochial, crude, vulgar, and dull.

Guilio E. Miranda, author and intergroup-relations consul-
tant, has observed:

> There is a reflex of racism in America which is too powerful
> to contain. When it is stopped from flowing in one direction,
> its mainstream goes in another. Obviously, the media never
> cared about blacks, Chicanos, or Indians—witness the stereo-
> types. But they are running scared under pressure. They can't
> break the habit, so now it's open season on ethnics.

What values and goals direct the media? The importance
of audience ratings on television programing clearly indicates
that the media are more often guided by the commercial values
of money and profit than by artistic ones. Italian-Americans
as portrayed in television scripts think and act the way TV script-
writers believe Italians look, talk, and act. More recently, the
TV screen became saturated with Italian cops such as Colombo,
Toma, and Barretta. Most of the Italian-ness of the characters
portrayed is superficial or stereotypical. These Italian cops
operate on the fringes of the law enforcement establishment
and frequently engage in tactics that are technically illegal.
Andrew Greeley recently noted:

> By producing a crop of Italian cops, the entertainment in-
> dustry can have it both ways. Italians can continue to be de-
> picted as engaging in illegal and violent behavior, but now

such behavior has been sanctioned because it is serving the cause of good—whatever that is.[5]

The media is indeed a mirror of American society, and the reflections of that society are not attractive ones to many Americans. But the media continue to create and reinforce ethnic and racial stereotypes, the human-rights movement notwithstanding. The Italian-American is able to pick out such subtleties in a way the non-Italian cannot. The only problem is that, when he airs his feelings, he lacks the same legitimacy as blacks or Chicanos. He is dismissed as being overly sensitive and defensive. The media is a reflector and creator of images and perceptions. The danger is that the viewing audience as receivers cannot help but be influenced by a constant bombardment of the same images. Just as many have been concerned about violence on television and its impact, so must we be concerned about the violence committed by stereotypes sent and received. The audience as receivers may tend to think and act in terms of the stereotypes created by the media. Just a cursory exploration of the world of letters—literature and drama and their modern expressions through television and film—will reveal some of the themes and images that daily bombard the American public. What is increasingly clear is that Italian-Americans are used as the referents for organized crime and racial bigotry and as such are blended into an ethnically identifiable cast of characters in the plots of popular books and TV and movie scripts. This is the "Italian-American connection."

The decade of the 1960s was filled with the rhetoric of "radical-liberals" and "hardhats." "Hardhat" became a symbol and synonym for a reactionary, bigoted ethnic. All this was continued in the 1970s when Archie Bunker entered our lives and our vocabulary. What ever would we have done without him? Instead of "hard hat," "Bunker" was now the "in" word. An example of the current application and interchangeability of the term came in the 1970s when a local CBS newscaster felt compelled to refer to areas which were Italian-American neighborhoods on the evening of the New York primaries as Archie Bunker territory. In the Archie Bunker series, there was a familiar bias pointing to white working-class Americans as "the repositories of racial and ethnic bigotry."

A TV pilot series "Every Wednesday" contained the same message. The principal characters are an Italian-American (fully identified by name), a WASP, and a Jew. The script cuts into the lives of each as he prepares for the evening's festivities.

Frank, the Italian-American, is characterized as a male chauvin-
ist, obsessed with his masculinity and his wife's purity of
dress and demeanor. A doctor is called to the gathering when
one of the people becomes ill, but not before Frank has loudly
and frequently referred to "Japs" and "Polacks." To the amazement of all, the doctor turns out to be a woman—and black.
While everyone is stunned by this event, Frank takes center
stage. He gesticulates and verbalizes his bigotry. He does run
a liberal car wash, Frank asserts: Anyone can get a car washed
there regardless of race, color, or creed. His objection to the
black doctor is not her race. It's just that so many people are
passing themselves off as doctors these days. Once again the
ethnic connection is made.

Next to Westerns and sex, probably the chief source of TV,
movie, book plots and newspaper and magazine exposés is the
mafia. Al Capone and Frank Nitti are as familiar to presentday
Americans as Clint Eastwood.

The appeal of using organized crime for plots is especially
strong in today's literature. The mafia is such an important
ingredient that a contemporary novel is hardly successful unless
it contains the appropriate catchwords. There are Ovid Demaris's
books, which include *The Contract,* the lusty violent epic of
Carlo Vincent, godfather of the Syndicate; Al Conroy's *Soldato*
who in this instance is Don Renzo. "The explosive novel of
the Mafia—of a Godson turned Judas for a vengeance"; Peter
Rabe's *War of the Dons,* with Don Pietro Vinciguerra; Charles
Durbin's *The Patriot,* with Raimondo Occhiaccio; Joseph Rosen-
berger's *The Death Machine,* with James Regolanto and deadlier
than the godfather; Peter McCurtin's *Mafioso,* with Nick Lanzetta who wants to become the godfather. Even Noel Clad's
The Savage features a Shoshone Indian who is given a contract
by the Mafia to kill a woman with a sick child. And so it goes,
ad nauseam and *ad infinitum.*[6]

The connection between the nativism of the past with that
of the present becomes more apparent when we consider the
study of Robert Ward. In a study of 118 works of American
fiction, 1890–1919, he found that the Italian figures in the
stories are consistently depicted in a biased light, usually emerging as cowardly, treacherous, and violent.[7]

The association of Italian-Americans with organized crime
is firmly fixed even in hard core pornography. Penelope Ashe
et al in *Naked Came the Stranger* tells the tragic tale of Mario
Vella, the dark handsome owner of the highly successful Bella

Mia Olive Company, who is the son of an organization leader and is now the underboss of a combined organization.[8]

We can get the flavor of the national obsession with the theme and the Italian-American connection with it by looking at the citations for mafia in the *New York Times Index*. In 1950, 5 citations were listed. This jumped to 13 in 1951, 44 in 1966, 278 in 1969 (the year *The Godfather* was published), to over 400 in 1972 (the year of the film version of *The Godfather*). No single theme has been treated more often in *New York Magazine* in 1972 than that of the mafia.

Shortly before Little, Brown and Company published *The Last Testament of Lucky Luciano,* it ran a full page advertisement referring to the book as "packed with revelation after revelation, set against a violent panorama of America's underworld from the twenties to the fifties."[8]

Authors Martin A. Gosch and Richard Hammer received some noteworthy reviews. In *Newsweek,* Peter Prescott noted: "Taken at face value, this would seem the most remarkable of all books on crime in America. . . . Luciano tells all."[9] Yet, Christopher Lehmann-Haupt disagreed in his February 28, 1975 column in the *New York Times,* "Even If It's Real It's Unreal." It is "the nursing home scandal of books—an enterprise with a surface of respectability (a reputable author and a respectable publisher) with all sorts of dirt in its interior, and with hints of skulduggery swirling in the background." Mr. Lehmann-Haupt went on to note:

> An investigation by the *New York Times* has shown, among other things, that no tapes exist . . . although the book had been advertised as based on taped conversations. . . . What remains disturbing about the project, however, is that, even if the book is based on authentic material, it doesn't seem so as one reads it. . . . It deserves the incredulity its publication has provoked.[10]

If one were to administer a rapid word association test on ethnic groups, the Italian-American would be connected most often with crime. On TV's "Hollywood Squares," one of the panelists was given an animal to identify. The host listed the characteristics of the animal concluding ". . . and travels in a mob." "Italians," quipped Jan Murray, the popular comic, as his answer. On a recent Merv Griffin show, Eva Gabor described her travels to an American city which had many Italian restaurants as mafia country. This led to a silly repartee culminating in Griffin's declaring it to be the work of the mafia when the house lights dimmed temporarily. Johnny Carson once informed the audience that a little old man came up to him and kissed him on the cheek. "Are you wishing me good luck for the show?" asked Carson. "No, I come from Sicily," replied the old man.

Martin Karlins, Thomas Coffman, and Gary Walters have researched the stereotypes held by three generations of college students. The image of Italians still was "hot tempered." Forty-four percent characterized Italians as passionate and 28 percent use the words "impulsive" and "quick tempered."[11] Rudolph Vecoli has speculated that over 90 percent of the references to Italians from 1924 to 1974 have connected them with organized crime.[12]

In a *New York Times Magazine* article about Lee Iacoca, president of the Chrysler Corporation, the author discussed the subject's life and his involvement with the automotive company and described Iacoca as leaning back with the "smile of a Mafia don." One wonders if a respected businessman whose name did not end in a vowel would have been described in quite this way. Frank Rizzo, mayor of Philadelphia, was described in a *New York Daily News* article as looking like an "Enforcer."[13] Meyer Lansky, who is considered to be one of the most powerful figures in organized crime (he's not Neopolitan or Sicilian), was treated as a kind of folk hero in a past issue of *Harper's*.[14] In addition, he was quoted on his observations of John Kennedy and sundry other matters. The major organized crime figure in the United States, Lansky staved off two cases against him in Miami (involving taxes and contempt and a final case) and in Las Vegas one alleging the skimming off of $36 million in profits from the Flamingo Hotel. This item was buried in the back pages of the *New York Times*. Why? More to the point, why have not Lansky and others of his ilk been successfully prosecuted?

Crime and its all too frequent association with Italian-Americans follows them even when they try to get away from it all. In the travel section of the *New York Daily News* (August 1, 1972) it was reported that the ethnic quality of the Catskills was changing, becoming more diversified with the rise of ethnic resorts. It went on to describe this process with this cautionary note: "But it's the Italiansissimo-type resorts that have been on the rise in the Catskills. There've been whispers that with the possibility of legal gambling being introduced in the Catskills, a new breed of resort operator is joining the ranks."

Translated into everyday life, Italian-Americans have the experience on a daily basis as that encountered by one of my friends. My friend moved to the suburbs after years of hard work. His next-door neighbor noted he owned a Cadillac, and his opening words of greeting to him after they exchanged names were, "Do you belong to the organization in Brooklyn? You know, the Mafia?" What all this means is that the media has done its job. The ethnic stereotypes it helps to create and perpetuate are immensely harmful to the society at large and Italian-Americans in particular. It does irreparable damage to individuals who become stigmatized by it. I am not here entering the debate whether there is or is not a mafia, but the usage of the term *mafia* is another way of saying Italian-American. After all, the Random House dictionary (1967) defines mafia as, "A secret organization of persons, mostly of Sicilian and Italian origin."

It is small wonder that Italian-Americans have protested the media's stereotypes of them. One recent incident involved a federally funded film, *The Uncle Sam Caper,* starring Telly Savalas. The film was designed to promote the sale of United States savings bonds. The twelve-minute film began with Telly Savalas insulting an Italian-American police officer for being incompetent. All the criminal figures featured bore Italian names, spoke in broken English, and dressed in the stereotyped Italian-gangster image. The movie, which cost the taxpayers $38,000, featured the entire cast of the popular television series "Kojak." It had Savalas trying to convince an Italian gangster that, if he had invested his earnings from his "job" into savings bonds, he would be out of trouble today. It was only after considerable protests by the Italian-American community, spearheaded by Congressman Leo Zefferetti and Mario Biaggi, that Treasury Secretary William Simon ordered the film withdrawn from circulation.

The creation and reflection of negative stereotypes of Italian-Americans are not reserved for newspapers, television, and the movies. They are translated into the very textbooks in our nations' schools. The influence of the textbook on the attitudes of students toward others, *i.e.,* in the way they either accept or reject students who are ethnically different, is significant. In his analysis, "Treatment of Italians in Senior High American History Textbooks," Dr. Thomas Cousins found that authors tend to describe Italian crime more than non-Italian crime and more than multi-ethnic crime.[15] In history, Italian victims of

violence tend not to be identified as Italian, thereby reducing
the effect of understanding the role violence played in Italian-
American history. Cousins concluded:

> The unfortunate association of crime with Italians is clear
> and present in most books. . . . This association is without ques-
> tion one of the most serious in our textbooks. The fact that
> such an association was present in eighteenth-century textbooks
> illustrates how far authors have come in almost two hundred
> years.[16]

So a variety of forces have made the "mafia," i.e. Italians,
synonomous with organized crime. This is artfully done through
the choice use of language. A non-Italian involved in crime
for example is a "leader," or mastermind. His Italian equivalent
is a *capo*. A non-Italian "underling," when translated into mafia
terminology, becomes a "soldier"; a "ring" becomes a "family";
an "underworld figure" becomes a "Godfather," and so on.

Just a cursory examination of recent newspaper accounts
will prove this journalistic dualism and the hypocrisy. In September of 1973, the police smashed "probably the largest" policy
gambling empire in New York City. The initial arrests included
key figures, all non-Italian and all linked to Meyer Lansky.
What was most amazing was the meticulous choice of words.
All accounts referred to the "ring" and Lansky as an "underworld figure"; not one of them used any of the Italian code
words. In July 1974, on the back pages of the newspapers, a
story told of twenty-two people being arrested. The "mob"
did an annual drug business of $32.7 million. Again, no mention
of family or *capo*'s. One of the largest heroin seizures, and
again one of the largest pornography seizures in 1972, bore
none of the associations with organized crime. On November
12, 1976, the top narcotics dealer in the United States was arrested. Not one mention of organized crime or possible links
were made to David T. Stone. A month earlier, Leroy (Nicky)
Barnes, the top narcotics dealer in New York City, was arrested
on the illegal possession of a gun. He was acquitted. On March
17, 1977, Barnes and seventeen others were arrested on the sale
of forty-four pounds of heroin with a wholesale price of almost $1 million. According to the indictment, "A chain of dis-
tribution was established, and the narcotics flowed through
several levels of the conspiracy, and ultimately to narcotics
on the streets of New York City." Not one word on organized
crime was mentioned by the authorities or the media, which
referred to their activities as an "enterprise."[17]

All of the above cases and thousands of others have one

thing in common. The individuals involved bear non-Italian names; hence, a different terminology is used. The usual code names are reserved for individuals with names ending in a vowel. In its October 25, 1976, issue, *Time Magazine* reported a major nationwide raid in thirty-five cities was conducted by the federal Drug Enforcement Administration. The raid was aimed at breaking up the fifty-seven distribution "rings." The article reported:

> Details vary from ring to ring, but DEA cites the methods of the Oakland based organization of Lemmie Daniel Coleman and Los Angeles operation of Henry Cuwayne Watson as typical. According to DEA agents, each man had a connection in a different Mexican border town who picked up the heroin that had been processed from poppies grown in Western Mexico.[18]

Once again there was no mention of organized crime, "Mafia," "family," "*Capo*," "a soldier." They refer to "rings" and "operation." Why? Is it possible, given the supposedly monolithic character of The Mafia, which is synonymous with organized crime, for such "rings," "operations," etc. to exist? Or is it possible that they are part of independent syndicates? Or are they part of the mafia itself? If the answer is yes to any of these queries, then the very conception of organized crime, at least as it is portrayed to the American public, is greatly distorted. Moreover, unless this distortion is corrected, organized crime in this country will never be eradicated.

One can go on and on to catalogue this journalistic sleight of hand. The issue is not to excuse the criminal behavior of any ethnic group; all criminals should be punished to the fullest extent of the law. But why should such detailed knowledge of reputed and alleged organized crime figures not result in their arrest and conviction? The answer may lie in the fact that organized crime runs very deep in the history and fabric of American society. It involves many non-Italian establishment figures in leadership roles. Organized crime is as American as apple pie. It constitutes the illegal end of the free enterprise system. As such, it provides a set of services to the American public that are dispensed and used for profit by the establishment. Witness the link between the CIA and the Mafia.

The issue, I believe, is not whether Italian-Americans have been involved in organized crime in America. Some have, just as other groups before them and groups after them will unfortunately involve themselves in organized crime. The issue is the relationship of organized crime to an American way of life and an urban way of life in America. As such, it is a viable and persistent institution within American society, with its own symbols, its own beliefs, its own logic, and its own means of transmitting these from one generation to the next. It is an integral part of America's economic life. Organized crime is a functional part of the American social system. In addition, increasing evidence points to the fact that there is no formal national monolithic organization which dominates and controls all of organized crime.[19]

The real issue is that the media in many forms has helped to create a stereotype of the overwhelming millions of Italian-Americans based on the activities of a few, and this presents an enormous cultural obstacle. The stereotype which says that Italians are innately dishonest, cunning, violent, or criminal "grates against every nerve ending in the Italian-American ego, which desires respect and honor. Instead not only are they ignored and ridiculed, but they are also held in contempt."[20] The national obsession with the mafia conspiracy is a diversion. It diverts all of us from the real issues, problems, and aspirations of ethnic Americans in general and Italian-Americans in particular. It diverts Italian-Americans from a fuller understanding of themselves and their worth. The term *mafia*, with its Italian connotations, implies that organized crime is essentially something alien to America and not inherent in the American experience. This naturally leads to the next assumption. Organized crime can be expunged from American society only by eliminating the group of essentially alien persons who make it up. This assumption was the underpinning of CBS's *Essay on the Mafia*, which was less an essay on the Mafia than an indictment of Italian-Americans. Aired in the early 1970s, Italian-Americans were being called to board an airline for a flight to Tontitown. En route, they would give up their urbanity and cultural identity (payment for the flight) and thereby their penchant for crime. In return they could acquire the virtues of honesty, civic responsibility, and respectability.

> In an editorial on the CBS network news on October 17, 1976, Eric Sevareid seriously suggested that the Mafia is "genetically a separate race," to be treated like the Nazis of World War II. When one speaks of genetic race, one is talking of women, children—in this case, the entire genetic pool shared by all who derive from Italy. The inescapable conclusion is that, if the Italian-American gangsters Sevareid speaks of are genetically criminal, so are all Italian-Americans. In fact, this is an old idea in the United States that bears a label we can use precisely for once—racism.[21]

In 1971, a memorable event took place when the film *Sacco-Vanzetti* was shown to the American audience. A powerful commentary on America of the 1920s, *Sacco-Vanzetti* is a kind of horror film filled with biased judges, suppressed information, twisted evidence, badgered witnesses resulting in the death of two defendants who were being tried as Vanzetti declared because, "We are Italian and Anarchists," for underlying the mentality of the 1920s was a national hysteria over the conspiracy of foreign radicals. Nativism was running full tilt.

Today, the nation is obviously obsessed with the mafia conspiracy. America, it seems, is in need of conspiracies. What is interesting to note about Sacco-Vanzetti is that it took fifty-two years to make the film. What is more compelling is that it had to be made by an Italian film company. There is no room for complaisance or comfort in this fact, or in the knowledge that television, the movies, newspapers, books, and all are captializing on an ethnic stereotype.

Who controls the media? It is clear that Italian-Americans do not, nor have they been able to influence it in any substantial way. The cries of protest which emanate from the Italian-American community have not been accorded the legitimacy assigned to other causes. When Earl Butz, former Secretary of Agriculture, insulted Catholics, especially those who are Italian, he received a mere slap on the hand. Another "joke" during the 1976 presidential campaign directed against blacks rightly resulted in his firing.

On January 12, 1979, in a meeting of the Urban Development Action Grant staff, the director solicited suggestions for ways to avoid funding projects that are backed by individuals associated with organized crime. The UDAG staff considered having the FBI do background checks on applicant sponsors. The particular check would be any applicant sponsor, living in any state, with an Italian surname. Congressman Andrew Maguire, upon hearing this, wrote Patricia Harris, Secretary of the Department of Housing and Urban Development, noting: "I condemn any process as capriciously and prejudiciously formulated as the one discussed in the meeting. The Italian-American community in this country, and in New Jersey in particular, has already been subjected to an intolerable degree of suspicion.. Certainly as public officials we must not be responsible for perpetuating such attitudes."[22] The nativism unleashed in the post-1880 period has continued in the 1970s and shows no real sign of ending in the 1980s, the civil rights movement notwithstanding.

14 The Red, White, and Greening of America

The need for a secure identity is universal and is expressed in different ways. Where once everyone seemed content to be an ordinary American, now all kinds of groups are claiming the right to be different, unique, particular, special.

Ethnic groups have chafed under what they consider the requirement for a middle-class background or an uncomplicated name in order to "make it" in America. They are now beginning to demand acceptance on their own, not the majority's terms.

In this post "melting pot" era of our society, educators, social scientists, journalists, social philosophers, and human-relations professionals are still groping for new ways to redefine the social realities of America. Finally, we are coming to grips with the fact that ethnic, racial, and cultural differences are, always have been, and surely will continue to be major forces in our society.

The dynamism of the blacks' struggles of the 1960s, along with the parallel identity struggles of Spanish-speaking Americans, American Indians, and Asian-Americans, paved the way for the flowering of the search for identity among white ethnic Americans and for their own struggle to confirm the validity of their different cultural and communal life styles.

In the 1980s, it is widely evident that group differences are in fact continually more accentuated. But what do those differences mean? How do they affect our lives? How can institutions deal with them honestly and openly, while reducing conflict or conflict-producing situations?

The United States, one would think, would be one of the most fertile of all cultures in favoring pluralism. Unfortunately, so fearful of division and so suspicious of "foreigners" were leaders of this New World that acceptance of American citizenship came also to be linked with a social expectation that one would be converted, outwardly and inwardly. One ought to cease being "other" and become "American"; those who would be successful ought to do so at least.

Following the Second World War two great pressures were driving out diversity and praising the homogenized soup of the melting pot. One was the nationalizing and standardizing of American suburban life. The old neighborhoods began to break up (a little). Television imparted national passions, national symbols, national imperatives. Highways and slowly developing affluence added the solvents of mobility. Herculean efforts at mass education extended the power of the centralized corporate culture, and "enlightened" young people complained about how backward their neighborhoods were. The "heavenly city fell; the secular city beckoned."

Liberal and conservative politicians had their own reasons for encouraging the myth of the success of the melting pot. Liberals sought power through the growing professional classes and the ideology of "the end of ideology." Conservatives wanted to woo Democrats away from the largely ethnic machines.

Influenced by a set of institutions and an ethos which demands total absorption, an ethnic identification, to many people, is un-American. Alistair Cooke in the segment of the "America" series entitled, "The Huddled Masses," uses the Italians as an example of the hyphenated Americans who perpetuate their separation by adherence to such ritualistic expressions of ethnic pride as Columbus Day. In other words, what Mr. Cooke, a British journalist drawing from the familiar "Anglo-Saxon" arguments of the 1920s, is saying is that Italians and their fellow ethnics have hyphenated themselves. Such pronouncements will not stand the test of history and are in fact gross distortions of American history. It is a one-sided, blurred, unreal picture of America.

The new ethnicity, or new pluralism, is a social process which accepts individual and group uniqueness. It allows for a balance between identification with a small group and commitment to the society as a whole, and one in which individuals who do not wish to identify with any group are also fully accepted.

There are many people who are uncomfortable with the resurgence of ethnic identity. They view it as a retreat to tribalism and a force for disunity. "Why can't we just all be Americans?" "Why must they call themselves Italian-Americans or Polish-Americans?" These are typical questions asked by a number of people in America. The force of the new ethnicity is not so much a pressure welling up from primordial tribal ties as a pressure rising up in our own individual selves: a need to recognize our own particularity, to place ourselves accurately on the map of human cultures, and to teach us how to discern and interpret cues from others who differ from ourselves.

The "American way of life" in the past has been portrayed across the screens of American television sets. Father is either a doctor or lawyer or business executive. His speech contains no accent; his physical features are keen and flawless; his dress is conventionally perfect. He lives with his wife and two well-mannered bright-looking children in a suburban home with well-manicured lawns.

Mom gets the kids off to school, serves as household peacemaker, organizes the family social calendar, and makes sure everyone is informed on all that passes for culture. Household conversation is restrained and centers on Dad's latest success or the drop in Jim's baseball average. Over all, the atmosphere is restrained and secure.

That's not how many Italian kids grew up! Many lived in the older neighborhoods of Chicago, Buffalo, New York, Boston, New Haven, or Newark. Italian was as likely to be heard as English. In other ethnic communities, the language might be Polish or Yiddish. Their names were Gallo, Bruno, Lepore, Russo, Miele, and their fathers worked at back-breaking labor. My father declared his independence by starting a grocery business, which he built up at great personal and physical cost. He worked fourteen to sixteen hours a day, six days a week till the day of his retirement. He was hospitalized for serious and prolonged illnesses twelve times in an eight-year period. The struggle to make it for his kids caught up with him.

Monsignor Geno Baroni, the Director of the National Center for Urban Ethnic Affairs, recalls his Italian family:

> I came from a working-class family in a company town between Johnstown and Altoona, Pennsylvania. The town is Acosta and the mine is Mine 120. It was one of the last areas in coal country to be organized. We moved from a shack to a company house. The company owned the electricity, the water, the outhouses. We bought everything at the company store. Remember the song "Sixteen Tons"? My father loved that song; he sang it practically every day.
>
> Italian mothers—if not working themselves—were at home cooking and cleaning, waxing, and ironing. They provided the children with love and the security of the family. Though many Italian families were materially poor, they were psychologically and culturally very rich. My family and their friends had stability. My father didn't go past the fifth grade, but after a bottle of wine he thought he was related to Garibaldi. After

that it was Leonardo DaVinci. My father could prune trees and make wine. . . . We also made whiskey and sold it to the Protestants. They called it "bootlegging," but today it would probably be called "income maintenance."[1]

To those of my generation, descriptions of their youth bring to mind a set of common experiences. There are the family gatherings. On Sunday mornings, one awoke to the tantalizing aroma of simmering sauce. By the time we left for church, our mouths were watering. We felt certain that we couldn't survive the wait to the 1:30 P.M. meal. Mama would favor us with a piece of bread on which her magic ragu was spread. Geno Baroni remembers: "My family used to eat mushrooms, snails, gizzard, tripe, brains, and dandelions—Italian soul food. We raised rabbits and caught squirrels. Rabbit was my favorite meat. I ate it because that's what poor people ate. Now if I want these same things, I have to go to a fancy restaurant."[2] Sounds evoke common memories. I would return home from school in the afternoon and hear the captivating voice of Carlo Butti.

What sets the parents of the first generation of Italian-Americans apart from the "all American" family was their firm belief that they were washing out strains of immigrant culture. Hence, their children would be the real Americans. To be sure, Italian parents were conditioned by the dominant culture. Today, second- and third-generation Italian-Americans may be critical of their parents' rush to assimilate. But many now realize that American society left their parents no other choice. Ralph Perrota, former director of the New York Center for Ethnic Affairs, makes the following observation:

> One of my earliest recollections, going back to before I started school, is of my mother's references to the two Irish families on our block as "Americans" as distinguished from us "Italians." I remember asking myself, and my mother, why they were any more American than we were. Although she conceded the technical point of my American birth and citizenship (and hers) she nevertheless clung to her sense of our being more Italian than American.
>   The distinctions were obvious, and I could not gloss them over no matter how hard I tried. "Americans" were fair and "cool," spoke fluent English (albeit with a brogue, but who heard any other kind on my block?), and had a sense of belonging about them that was confirmed by their living in homes of their own. We were mostly brunets (there was one Italian family whose red hair everyone marveled at), passionate and

demonstrative, and lived in flats or tenements. Our parents were immigrants who had come here as children with their parents, and their English was always less than fluent; how much less depended on how facile they were with words and how old they were when they arrived....[3]

Jerre Mangione in Mount Allegro recalls:

My experiences in drawing and music classes were particularly unhappy and fairly indicative of the delusions some of my teachers had of students with Italian blood. In drawing, I surpassed everyone in my gross ineptness.... My landscapes resembled everything else but landscapes. Most of them looked like scrambled eggs mixed with spinach.

But my teacher was not interested in eggs with spinach; she was determined on a landscape. Gerry Amoroso. An Italian, wasn't I? Then, it was silly for me to say I couldn't paint a landscape. "Your parents are Italian. I can tell by your name. Some of the greatest artists the world had ever known were Italian. No reason on earth why you can't paint a simple landscape."[4]

My family did not rush to assimilate. I grew up with a secure and firm appreciation of my Italian roots. Italian was spoken at home, but it was never really taught to my brother and sisters. I was named Pasquale after my grandfather. It was later changed to Patrick by Irish nuns. I recall the efforts of the schools to foster the assimilation of immigrant kids. In an assembly, six of us—Italians, Poles, Jews, blacks—held up the letters which spelled out Yankee! I was the letter Y. How ironic it was for this son of immigrant parents to say, "Y is for Yankee like you and me, the home of the brave and the land of the free." The closest I came to being a Yankee was my passion for the New York Yankees and Joe DiMaggio.

Many of the children of immigrant parents, when they ventured outside of their little Italys, saw the ethnic enclaves their parents had built as isolating them from the larger society outside. Gradually, immigrant parents ventured outside to meet America on its own terms. Because they only vaguely understood the rules of the game called "making it," they compensated by working twice as hard. The kids always grew up helping dad in the store. My brother, who is now deceased, stood on boxes to take care of customers. Without such aid, he was barely able to peer over the counters. I also grew up in the grocery business. In retrospect, it is difficult to imagine how hard I worked, especially from my early teens to my second year in college. Often, I would come home at night with my legs so

numb that I went to sleep from sheer exhaustion. This was
not unusual for kids of my generation. We did not have to
acculturate to the work ethic. Like many of our parents, we
survived the Great Depression and World War II. I was born
in those years. It took a great deal of courage to have children.
My family came to this country with strong family ties, a strong
work ethic, a fantastic culture, and the hope for a new life
in America. People of my generation will tell you now, "I was
poor, but I went through the Depression and made it."

Through it all, Italian parents kept within them the dimly
felt notion that their differences could be a strength as well
as a stigma. When an alien America exhausted them, when
the struggle to make it became too much of a burden, then
they called on their national origins for renewed strength.

Despite all that they gave up, they were still regarded by "old-
stock" white America as being on the fringes of American
life. The hyphenated American was created by the dominant
society because it really regarded such people, the so-called new
immigrants, as being apart from America.

Ralph Perrotta notes:

> School for me was among other things a way to erase these
> distinctions and become American. Most of the teachers then
> ... were Yankee and so even more prototypically American
> than the Irish families. Their names were of the sort I found
> in my schoolbooks, and their demeanor seemed to convey as-
> surance about their right to be here that I never saw in my
> relatives and neighbors. I found myself, with some success, try-
> ing to emulate them.[5]

The critics, the novelist, the social theorists, the men who
articulated and analyzed American ideas, who governed our
institutions, who embodied what we were or hoped to be were
WASPS (white "Anglo-Saxon" Protestants or white gentiles
whose native language is English) : Hemingway, McLeish, Lewis,
Sandburg, Holmes, Dewey, Parrington. The American mind
was the WASP mind. We grew up with them; they surrounded
us; they were the heroes of the history we studied and of the
fantasy life we sought in those Monday through Friday radio
serials.

The history books never mentioned the likes of William
Paca, Vigo, Tonti, Chino, Mazzei. Never were we put in touch
with the real America. History books at school carried glowing
accounts of the great inventions, the entrepreneurial genius of
industrial statesmen, and the economic riches of the industrial

revolution, but at home we saw the sweatshops, black-lung diseases, and the arthritic, crippled hands from years of poor working conditions.

Italian-Americans, like their fellow ethnics, have a different history from that of many white Protestants. For one thing, those people whose origins are mainly in southern and eastern Europe have felt the economic squeeze more acutely than other middle Americans because their neighborhoods have been so hard hit.

Among ethnic Americans, which includes Italian-Americans, there is a more acute feeling of being left out culturally, not just economically. The "middle American" who is Protestant and "Anglo-Saxon" has a sense of proprietorship about the basic American symbols. Even when he is under attack, this gives him a feeling of security that the white ethnic doesn't really have. As one Italian-American noted while celebrating Columbus Day, "Why not? Every day is their [WASP] day!"

The myths of the melting pot and the American dream are no longer functional. What Italians and other immigrants were taught was that everyone was going to make it, everyone was going to be the same. What has happened is that everyone has not made it, and a lot of people have lost a sense of their own heritage and of their own cultures as they have submerged those things in their attempts to become "American." Ralph Perrotta has this poignant recollection:

> All of us paid a psychic price, though it was extracted at different times and in varying measure, and got something in return. Those of us who "assimilated" perhaps made the best bargain. The decision to assimilate added urgency to our efforts to "make it," and when we did the rewards were gratifying not only for their own sake but also because they were—and are—deemed to confer the status and dignity so precious to those uncertain of their place. But our price was a growing unease, generally diffuse and below the surface but periodically becoming focused and breaking through to a conscious level, that we might get too excited, wave our arms too vigorously when we spoke, lose our grip on our speech habits, or otherwise reveal some telltale evidence of our past to American friends.[6]

These are some of the threads woven into the fabric of dissatisfaction which has sparked the new ethnicity and the Italian-American consciousness movement in particular. Italian-Americans are asking a variety of rather significant questions: Who am I? Who are we? What does it mean to be Italian-American?

What are our goals and aspirations? What is America all about? Prior to considering such issues, it would be helpful to answer the following questions: Where do Italian-Americans live? How many of them are there? Including first, second, and third generations of Italian-Americans, there are from 13 to 15 million Italian-Americans in the United States. An average of 23,000 Italian immigrants have come to the United States annually in the years since 1967. During the period from 1958 to 1969, a total of 89,244 Italian immigrants settled in the United States. The total Italian stock which includes the first and second generations was 4,543,935, or 2.53 percent of the total population. The Italians who were born in Italy comprise 0.7 percent of the American population but 13.7 percent of the foreign-born population.

Sixty-nine percent of the total population of the United States resides in urban areas as compared to 91.8 percent of all the Italians. This underscores the urban concentration of Italians.

The regional distribution of Italians is also instructive. The Northeast region contained 70.3 percent of the Italian-born and 69.2 percent of the nativeborn of Italian parentage. Thus, a total of 69.5 percent of persons of Italian stock reside in this region. The persistence of this pattern is made clearer when we consider that Robert Foerester, in his study of the mass immigration period, found that 71.8 percent of all Italians resided in the New England and Middle Atlantic areas.

The area from north of Boston to south of Norfolk, the so-called megalopolis, contains about 20 percent of the total population and 70 percent are Italians. Sixteen states have 94 percent of the Italian stock and 95 percent of the Italian born. These same states contained 96.4 percent of the Italian aliens in 1965. Of the Italian immigrants who arrived between 1960 to 1965, 65 percent preferred the northeast region. A total of 72.6 percent of all the resident Italian aliens in early 1965 were registered in the Northeast.

Furthermore, 82.2 percent of all Italians reside in standard metropolitan areas and 31.6 percent in the smaller cities. This underscores the urban preference of the Italian immigrant. The size of the metropolitan area and its distance from New York are determinants of the degree of urban concentration for Italian immigrants. Twenty-three standard metropolitan statistical areas had more than 25,000 people of Italian stock each, including the cities of the megalopolis. According to Joseph Velikonja: "The numerical size alone permits the estab-

lishment of many Italian cultural and social services and contributes also to the longer survival of the Italian cultural character in cases where the relative position of the Italian group
is not very strong...."[7]

When we compare the total Italian stock with that of the
total population in the major cities, the dominance of New
York and Connecticut becomes immediately apparent, since Italians there are more than 10 percent of the entire population.
New Haven is the highest ranked metropolitan area; Italians
comprise 15.8 percent of the total population. The New York–
New Jersey consolidated area has a total of 10.3 percent while
in many of the cities the number is higher. Jersey City had
13.6 percent. Richmond, Kings, and the Paterson-Clifton-Passaic
area each had 14.1 percent. Of the foreign-born population,
one-eighth were Italian in Fair Lawn, one-third in Paterson,
and one-tenth in Ridgewood, New Jersey. In New York City,
one-sixth of the total foreign-born population is Italian. Approximately 6 percent of the foreign-born population in the
Bronx is Italian, 5 percent in Brooklyn, 10 percent in Manhattan, 5 percent in Queens and 3 percent in Richmond. The heavy
concentration in the New York area was also noted in the mass
immigration era by Foerester:

> In the state of New York were about as many Italians as the
> whole country had contained ten years earlier. Two out of five
> of all the newcomers, in recent years, have gone thither. Of
> those in the state in 1910, nearly two thirds dwelt in its me-
> tropolis, 340,770—such a number as would make one of the
> large cities in Italy; and if their children were added, the colony
> would exceed in population every Italian city, except possibly
> Naples.... About four-fifths of all the Italians were classed by
> the census as urban, twice as high a proportion as that for the
> country's population as a whole.[8]

Today, the Italians continue to live in the central city in
significant numbers. Like Foerester's early description, the
urban concentration of Italians today does not coincide with
the general trend of the American cities which has seen an
increased flight from the central city and a reduced growth
of the entire eastern seaboard. According to Dr. Velikonja the
reason for the high urban concentration is:

> ... the legislative provision for the quota and non quota im-
> migrants which require the sponsorship or the documentation
> of parentage for admission to the United States. The legislative
> restrictions, therefore, aiming to prevent the establishment of

national clusters through national quota restrictions, instead
reinforced these same concentrations by requiring sponsorship
or proof of parentage. Therefore, the general regional pattern
which was established in its essence at the turn of the century
is being unduly perpetrated for much longer than is economically and culturally advisable.[9]

In addition, the early residence patterns of the mass immigrants,
along with the family-linked immigration patterns of the present,
further reinforce the urban preferences of Italian immigrants.
Italian immigration to the United States is part of an overall
rural to urban flow which is affecting Italy so profoundly. It
is likely that, had the immigrants not chosen to come to an urban
area in America, they would have done so in Italy. Italian immigration, then, is another dimension of the Italian rural-urban flow.

Italian-Americans are not highly mobile in the sense of changing their residences either frequently or at great distances from
the point that they either grew up or have family. This relative
residential stability is seen in the first Italian neighborhoods,
which have clung to their identity. East Harlem, Greenwich
Village, Mulberry and Mott Streets, Carrol Gardens, Bay Ridge,
Red Hook—all are Italian neighborhoods. Professor Nathan
Kantrowitz found that, though ethnic segregation has weakened
in New York City, "the reports of its demise are exaggerated."[10]
Moreover, he found a correlation between Chicago and New
York, when each of the twelve ethnicities and races were ranked
in their segregation from the base population. In his view,
neither Chicago nor any other city differs substantially from
New York in the pattern of ethnic segregation. Kantrowitz
observed: "Two ethnicities remain highly segregated from all
others: the Italians and Scandinavians. We might expect that
the Italians, a southern European or new stock, would remain
highly segregated, but we would have no reason to anticipate that
they are more integrated with the 'old' northwestern Europeans
than with the 'new' southern and central Europeans."[11]

In my study, *Ethnic Alienation: The Italian-Americans,* I
found that all of the Italian immigrants I interviewed came
to the United States via a link with a member of either the
nuclear or extended family. This illustrates the importance
of the family in southern Italian society.

All of the immigrant respondents lived with other new arrivals in exclusively Italian neighborhoods. William F. Whyte
has noted this development: "The *paesani* tend to settle in one
area, and those who are members of the same family usually
live close together."[12] Herbert Gans referred to this area as

the urban village. This is an area of first or second settlement for urban migrants who try to "adapt their nonurban institutions and culture to the urban milieu.... Often it is described in ethnic terms: Little Italy, the Ghetto, or Black Belt." Gans proceeds to note their subsequent movement: "Almost all of the West Enders came to the area as part of a group. Even their movements within the West End ... had been made together with other Italians at about the same time."[13] The length of residence of immigrant respondents ranged from two-and-a-half weeks to six years which was also comparable to the time they lived in the neighborhood. Only two of them said they preferred to live in a mixed neighborhood. Their concept of a mixed neighborhood, judging from the examples given, were either Italian-American or ones occupied by immigrants from different regions.

When the immigrants of the mass immigration settled in New York or in the many industrial communities around that city, they tended to congregate with others from the same province or village.[14] This became the basis of the Italian neighborhood which existed almost as a small semi-independent universe of its own. Sometimes, physical lines separated the Italians from the rest of the population. There were also the invisible lines of separation. The family chain of immigration tended to reinforce the formation of the ethnic enclave. In addition, there was the Italian attachment to the town—*campanilismo*. The importance of coming to live with relatives and *paesani* from the same town took on new meaning in a strange environment. The immigrant was accustomed to identifying himself with others of the same village while in Italy, and now he found an increased desire for the same surroundings. In the crowded cities, one could see the transfer of an entire village within a three or four block area. In some cases, there was a block by block separation between Neapolitans, Calabrians, and Sicilians. As Pisani observes: "It was as if part of the old communities had been bodily transplanted to an American street. Signs and posters were in the Italian language, Italian tradesmen set up shop, and peddlers sold Italian food through the streets."[15] Foerester also takes note of this regionalism: "In Briey, in New York, in Buenos Aires, something like a street by street separation of the immigrants according to origin has been ... recognizable ... it is a thing so characteristically Italian that it is best denoted by ... *campanilismo*."[16]

Gans' description of the West End of Boston is an appropriate one relating to the role of the enclave: "The West End was not a charming neighborhood of 'noble peasants' living in an exotic fashion, resisting the mass produced homogeneity of American culture and overflowing with a cohesive sense of community."[17] The original enclave, started in or near the city's core, was characterized by the movement of economically successful newcomers out of the enclave and into the "American" community. "Isolated from the community at large by differences in background and language, by their late arrival, and by their early low economic positions, they had to remain with themselves."[18] The lack of acceptance by the American society, the intense discrimination, the near hysterical outburst of fear of the "Italian problem," the militant nativism, all served to reinforce the ethnic enclave.[19]

The enclave is replete with local merchants, a local club and church, the latter with its bell tower standing symbolically, if not protectively, in the heart of the enclave. While there is modification of the ethnic enclaves from the earlier immigration, it is still identifiable as being Italian.[20]

The existence of a strong community among immigrants and its importance in the process of assimilation has become increasingly recognized. The Italian community is a group of people who follow a distinctive way of life or patterns of behavior which distinguish them from the people in the broader society to which they have come.[21] They are people who generally have come from the same place: most broadly, from southern Italy. Beyond this, there is often the similarity of region, province, and even town. They now are identified with a particular locality in the United States, such as south Brooklyn or Paterson, where they now live or to which they have recently come. They speak the same language and often the same dialect and share the same religion. They tend to stick together to help and support each other. They also have expectations of loyalty to one another.

The distinct social group which assimilates culturally while retaining its distinct social identity is another way of indicating the central role of the immigrant community.[22] It seemed as if three distinguished scholars had given a private lecture on this point to Mario, who, one evening in his usually thoughtful manner, remarked, "I think the Italians who come, the immigrant, needs the tie with other immigrants and being with other Italians... their similar ways and customs." Indeed if the immigrants are torn too rapidly from the traditional cultural framework of their lives and thrown too rapidly as strangers into a cultural environment which is unfamiliar, the danger of social disorganization is very great. The Italian immigrants need the traditional social group in which they are at home and in which they find their psychological satisfaction and security, in order to move with greater confidence toward greater interaction with the larger society.

The impact of the elements of the community are the conscious sharing of common ends, norms, and means which gives the group an awareness of the bonds of membership which constitute its unity.[23] Interaction primarily with others of the same ethnic group is also required. This generally cannot take place at too great a distance from the larger society.

In the case of the Italian immigrants, the active reality which is the community is not the larger society but the Italian subculture of the larger society. The basic area limits are necessary to define community. Gans was able to locate various subcultures in the "urban village" according to different attitudes and values. Gans states:

> The basis of adult life is peer group solidarity... membership in the group is based primarily on kinship. Brothers, sisters, cousins, and their spouses are the core. Godparents and single individuals are also included, the latter because of the sympathy of the Italians for the unattached individual, a role little valued in their culture. Neighbors can be included... people must be relatively compatible in terms of background, interests, and attitudes.[24]

Gans links community with a number of institutions such as the church, parochial school, formal school, political and civic groups, and businesses.[25] According to him, "These institutions —predominantly Italian—exist outside the peer group society but are linked with it if and when they can be used to meet group and individual needs."[26] These constitute the community since they are an accepted part of the life of the people and their functions are often "auxiliary of those of the peer society."[27] Gans uses community in the social sense:

> ... to describe the set of institutions and organizations used by the West Enders to perform functions that cannot be taken care of within the peer group society.
> While these institutions are located in the neighborhood, this only puts them within reach of their users. Their functions otherwise have little to do with the area or neighborhood. For this reason the role of the institutions... can be described almost without reference to the spatial community or neighborhood.[28]

Thus, a major index of community is a knowledge of the neighborhood and those aspects which are the tangible points of identity. A church, a store, a club, a street corner, a place of work are such points of identity since they are the spatial context for the social life of a group of people. Many of the Italian respondents knew each other on a number of different levels. In each case, some aspect of the community brought the immigrants together.

The immigrant community serves as a kind of staging area, a beachhead where Italian immigrants can remain until they absorb new ideas and habits which make their adjustment to an alien environment possible. The ethnic community as a buffer fulfills a vitally important function both to the newcomer and to the receiving society.

The relative stability of residence patterns in the Italian neighborhood becomes more apparent as we take a closer view of the three generational span. Among the first-generation respondents in my study, the average length of residence in the present neighborhood was 8.1 years. Most of the first-generation respondents spent a considerable time in their previous neighborhood, and the movement to their present residence represented their first major move of any kind. Most of them came from exclusively Italian neighborhoods, with many Italian immigrants and Italian-Americans with other groups on the fringes such as Irish or blacks.

In most cases, the movement from their previous residence was due in part to a better economic situation at home. Most of the mixture among the friends of the respondents was on the professional or business level. The most intimate relationships were still confined to Italian-Americans.

Among the second-generation respondents, there was little variation in either their residence or friendship patterns. For most Italian-American respondents, the movement out came after many years in their previous neighborhood. Movement to their present residence was the first major break from the neighborhood for the first- and second-generation respondents. There was no major projection of future movement. The neighborhood of the second generation Italian-American was predominantly Italian with little real mixture. While there is some evidence of more mixture among friends, still the predominant ones, the more social ones were with Italian-Americans. Four of five of the second-generation respondents expressed a desire to live in a mixed neighborhood but were in reality living in one that was Italian-American.

Of the third-generation Italian-American respondents the pattern of the average length of residence in the present neighborhood was in many respects similar to that of the first and second-generation respondents. Most came from heavily Italian-American areas and were currently living in similar ones, with only one major exception. There was a greater mixture with other ethnic groups either within the neighborhood or in the actual dwelling. The mixture is often with the Irish or Jews. All third-generation respondents showed a greater disposition to live in a mixed neighborhood.

In another sense, the residential patterns of Italians can be seen as an element in their assimilation and an indicator of other elements of assimilation. Residential segregation has an important impact on other aspects of their assimilation. Residential segregation is a factor in highlighting differences between groups by making such groups more visible. It also enables the ethnic group, the Italian in this case, to hold on to its peculiar traits and group structure. The more the Italians are physically isolated from the host society, the greater their tendency to maintain links with Italy.[29] The residential patterns that I uncovered would seem to indicate that those living in areas with high concentrations of other Italians would be less well assimilated than those who live in nonsegregated areas.

The ethnic group has a special relationship to the social structure.

> Within the ethnic group there develops a network of organizations and informal social relationships which permit and encourage the members of the ethnic group to remain within the confines of the group for all of their primary relationships and some of their secondary relationships throughout all the stages of the life cycle.[30]

Herbert Gans found that working-class Italian-Americans tended to confine their meaningful social and institutional participation to other working-class Italian-Americans, mostly to the same generation and the same neighborhood.[31] Culturally, he found few traces of the immigrant way of life in these American-born semi-skilled and unskilled workers. I found that, even when the Italian language was retained, it was not spoken fluently. Most second-generation respondents could not read Italian. All of the immigrant and first-generation respondents could speak and read Italian.[32] By the third generation, I found a total absence of an ability either to speak or read the language. Most of the respondents in all three groups, however, felt that they would like to see their children speak the language. Gans' subjects retained their particular dialect as a second language, although their own children, the third generation, are not being taught the language and will grow up knowing only English. All three groups of our Italian-Americans still preferred Italian cooking. While the structural pattern of the peer group society is in many ways compatible with their ancestral Italian social patterns, this emphasis on peer-group sociability is a general working-class cultural pattern and not peculiarly Italian. A number of stimuli and predispositions have served to perpetuate an Italian-American subsociety.

As part of the new ethnicity, the Italian-American consciousness movement is far reaching. The present reassertion of ethnicity in this country is not a fad. It goes much deeper than political motives, convenience in organizing, or intergroup conflict. It is a search for identity. Indeed it is a search for community.

I do not agree with critics who label ethnicity as reversion to tribalism and a demonstration of primordial affinities, nor do I agree with those who view ethnic identity as a crisis or state of confusion. It might be helpful to clarify some often quoted but misused terms. Acculturation and assimilation are often used interchangably. In truth, the former is only one stage in the total process of assimilation.

Milton Gordon has studied the nature and structure of group life and maintains that adequate analytical theory requires a distinction to be made between structure and behavior in dealing with ethnic group adjustment.[33] The United States, according to Gordon, is a multiple melting pot in which acculturation for groups beyond the first generation of immigrants, without eliminating all value conflict, has been massive and decisive. Structural separation on the basis of race and religion has also emerged. This structural pluralism or separation of ethnic groups is brought about partially because of the prejudice of the majority group and partly because an insufficient number of the members of minority groups have wanted assimilation.

By cultural assimilation (acculturation) Gordon means the adoption by the immigrant of those basic values and patterns of behavior of the host society which enable him to function effectively within it.[34] By structural assimilation he means the complete acceptance of the immigrant into primary face-to-face relationships by the members of the host society. Cultural assimilation may and often does take place without the occurrence of structural assimilation.[35] Structural assimilation consists of many levels—from participating in various types of occupation to intermarriage, which is the final stage of structural assimilation. In addition to these, Gordon cites five other variables in the process of assimilation. Once structural assimilation has occurred, either simultaneously with or subsequent to acculturation, all of the other types of assimilation will follow.

While the Italian acculturates rapidly, there is no outright exchange of group identities. The Italian immigrant identifies as an Italian, while those of the first, second, and third generation identify as Italian-Americans. On the whole, the Italian still favors in-group marriages although there is evidence of a predilection to marry non-Italians by the second and third generation.

The Italian has acculturated rapidly, and the process is usually complete by the first generation. The most important level of assimilation finds the Italian structurally unassimilated as evidenced by an occupational, income, and residential differentiation from the core society. Structural separation of the Italian results in the retention and solidification of an Italian identity. It also allows the Italian subsociety to persist.

Ethnicity is another term that has proved elusive. Ethnicity means a sense of commonality or community derived from networks of family relations which have, over a number of generations, been the carrier of common, shared experiences. It means the culture of the people—values, attitudes, orientation to time, needs, modes of expression, behavior. It is behavior without awareness. In the more literal sense, it is identity—who am I?

Between the solitary individual and the bureaucratic power of the large modern state, intermediate social bonds have been weakening—those of family, group loyalties, churches, and neighborhoods, especially. Now that technology has made centralizing forces so powerful, intermediate social bonds are indispensable for the protection of the individual from the state. A healthy society is a system of checks and balances. If some components in the social system fail, others take over their functions and threaten to devour the whole.

The fact is that social and cultural traditions, transmitted largely unconsciously by families, provide individuals with repertories of perception and behavior, and resources of understanding and flexibility, that vary ethnically. In America of the 1980s and beyond, ethnicity has new and perhaps unparalleled meanings. On each of us, our ethnic background, even if it is mixed, has left unmistakable marks; it has colored our experience of family, religion, sex, political values, and occupation.

The sense that one is bound up with "his people" might be called historical identification. In this sense, the ethnic group is the locus of historical identification. A sense of comfort with certain people leading to frequent participation in activities with them and in shared behavioral similarities might be called participational identification. With a person of the same social class but of a different ethnic group, one shares behavioral similarities but not a sense of peoplehood.[36] With those of the same ethnic group but of a different social class, one shares the sense of peoplehood but not behavioral similarities. The only group which meets both of these criteria are people of the same ethnic group and the same social class. American society may be conceived as a mosaic of ethnic groups based on race, religion, and national origins, interlaced by social class stratification to form a characteristic subsocietal unit, the ethniclass.

Each subsociety, as lower middle-class Italians, exists as a reference group in the minds of other Italians. The tangible units of each subsociety are localized in space in particular communities. Thus, one might speak of the lower-middle-class Italians of Paterson or the upper-class, white, "Anglo-Saxon" Protestants of Boston. These subcommunities in the various communities are connected with each other, in part by class and ethnic-typed institutions and organizations which are national in scope, and in part by class and ethnic-typed friendships across community lines. They are more importantly connected by the ability of each person in a given ethniclass to move to another community and take his place within the same segment of the population marked off by ethnic group and social class. The sum of these subcommunities interwoven by the various national institutions and organizations characteristic of that particular ethnic group and social class constitute the subsociety. As Etzioni observes, "A group can maintain its cultural and social integration and identity, without having an ecological basis." The subcommunity is not necessarily a geographical location but rather a social construct in the minds of its residents.[37]

An ethnic group is not monolithic. There are differences according to generation and social class. The Italians in New York City are a case in point. Italian New Yorkers form a fascinating and complex ethnic community.

Like all ethnic communities in the country, the Italian group is united and homogeneous only in the mind of distant observers. It is, in fact, an unfortunate general temptation to simplify our perception of other individuals by stereotyping them into a uniform group. Underneath the surface, the Italian community of New York is complicated and segmented into many subgroups. Each has its own fluctuating alliances, much to the frustration of politicians and social reformers. There is also a scale of visibility in the Italian ethnic community which seems inversely proportional to actual strength. In fact, we may speak of three major subdivisions in the Italian-American population which have different characteristics and symbols of mutual acknowledgment, different dressing styles, different accents and ideas.

The Italian-Americans are among the most visible ethnics in the city together with their counterparts in the Jewish community. This subgroup bears the deepest scars of the assimilation process. They tend to paste the American and Italian flags on their cars, demonstrate at Italian ethnic manifestations, applaud the loudest speakers at banquets, and become members in several very small organizations. There may be as many as half a million of these mostly blue-collar and civil-service workers of Italian-American identity. They are second generation or third generation from families which never moved from Little Italy. They are ambivalent in their feelings toward themselves, America, and their ethnicity. Their frustration and occasional anger are compounded by their economic difficulties and by the lack of services in their neighborhoods.

The Italian-Italians are the recent immigrants who came to America to join relatives and to improve their opportunities in life. This second subgroup of the Italian ethnic community prefers to speak Italian or dialect but can manage to make themselves understood in English. They are aggressive in their work habits, tenaciously saving every penny until, after five or six years, they can afford to buy a house of their own, maybe by paying for it in cash. They have little time for social involvement. Their only participation in community enterprises is going to an agency or an office to straighten out their immigration papers or to prepare those of a relative who is in the process of coming over from the old country. It is not easy to spot them, unless you hear them talking in Astoria, Bensonhurst, Ridgewood, or other sections of Brooklyn.

The American-Italians, the third, most invisible subcommunity, constitutes the largest segment of the Italian-American population. There are over a million in the city alone. Their children are in private colleges like Fordham and St. John's. They form a solid silent middle class which is sensitive to the bad press Italians have received in the city but not sensitive enough to fight back with efficiency. They are willing to organize along ethnic lines but not pressured enough by discrimination and prejudice and self-interest to do so effectively. They accept the individual approach to success and the work ethic. Their presence in business and politics reveals an extraordinary array of names who have achieved the highest positions. They are either third generation or have shaken off the burden of insecurity which annoys children of immigrants who find themselves between two cultures and two worlds. It is impossible to know the exact number or even get a very close figure on the real consistency of the American-Italians. The Census bureau does not keep track of ethnics beyond the second generation. After more than a century since large Italian communities settled in the United States, these people certainly form the majority of all persons of Italian ethnic background in the country.

Italian-Americans, Italian-Italians, American-Italians are three *ideal* subdivisions of the entire ethnic group. Perhaps these subdivisions are a more practical way of speaking about the variety of Italian-Americans than intransigent and meticulous categories. Another two thousand or so representatives of Italy's banking and business community should be added to the New York Italian-American scene. They are persons whose main concern is Italy. They remain in New York a few months or a few years and form a group of their own which contributes to the multifaceted appearance of the Italian-American community of the city.[38]

We have previously noted the attempts made by Italians to re-establish the communities of their homeland in America. While they were largely successful in doing just this, they were unable to transplant their way of life exactly and in every detail. Furthermore, it would be an exaggeration to say it persisted in a vacuum outside the reach of the larger society. Their native ways had to undergo some change. The Italian language underwent a change; what emerged was an Italian-American dialect.[39] By the first generation, and definitely by the second generation, acculturation is complete, and interest in the Italian culture has dropped sharply.[40] Despite cultural assimilation, the Italians have maintained a social substructure which takes into account both their primary and secondary relations. Hence, Italians in particular and the ethnic group in general bear a special relationship to the social structure.[41] Both Whyte and Gans have noted that American styles, language, sports, etc., predominated among the Italian-Americans of Boston, but personal relations and social group structures were almost exclusively Italian-American in both the North End of the 1940s and the West end of the 1960s. We have reached the same conclusion about Italians of the New York metropolitan area. As Parenti observes: "For ethnic social subsystems may persist or evolve new structures independent of the host society and despite dramatic cultural transitions in the direction of the mainstream culture."[42]

There has not been substantial movement by the Italian-American masses into the higher occupational and residential levels. Even if individual Italians may have entered professional and occupational roles beyond the reach of their fathers, the group mobility of the Italians has not been substantial.[43] When we look at the occupational positions of the first and second generation Italians, there is no substantial convergence of intergenerational status levels. The same holds true of a similar generational comparison of other ethnic groups.[44] Thus, ethnic distinctions continue to persist in the stratification system. Movement upward for the Italian-American is less a matter of group mobility than an overall improved standard of living for all Americans. The availability of more white collar jobs for Italian-Americans is due to structural changes in the American economy.

The movement from the central city and the ethnic enclave to the suburbs does not appear to have an integrative effect. The individual Italian can live most of his life aside from work in a subsocietal network of schools, family, church, and recreation.[45] Suburbs tend toward the establishment of ethnic clusters.[46] The movement to the suburbs may create a tension between the native resident and the new arrival which may reinforce ethnic identification. This same tension may reinforce ethnic political alignments. There is some foundation for the assertion that those Italians who were most segregated from the core society in the central city are also most residentially concentrated in the suburbs. Thus, suburban residential patterns follow in the same manner as those found in the central city.

Residential segregation is not a necessary condition for Italians to maintain a subsocial structure. As we have seen, Italians can maintain a social cohesion and identity without an ecological base. While the Italian neighborhood cannot be transplanted exactly as it existed in the city, its features are *adapted* to suburban living, but not eliminated. In-group social patterns reinforce an Italian identification.

While there may be changes in the social patterns of the Italians, it does not seem to indicate structural assimilation into the core social structure. Nor does the movement of Italians from the city to the Far West indicate that this structural assimilation is taking place elsewhere. In fact, their acculturation may lead to a more ethnic political awareness.

Parallel social structures have emerged, encouraged by a greater affluence. Movement to the higher residential and occupational hierarchies for individual Italians often provides the resources for the establishment of parallel subsocietal structures rather than their destruction. For example, Protestant clubs which had been exclusionist have engendered the rise of Catholic ethnic clubs. Marymount College is the Catholic counterpart for upper-class Catholic girls of Sarah Lawrence or Vassar, schools for upper-class Protestant girls. Upper-class Catholic boys might choose Notre Dame University as a counterpart of Yale or Princeton, where they might meet girls from nearby St. Mary's college. Polish-Americans might choose Alliance College. The abortive experiment of Verrazzano College may have been an outlet for Italian-Americans.

What accounts for the persistence of an Italian identification? Parenti has observed:

> Insofar as the individual internalizes experiences from earlier social positions and sub-cultural matrices, his personality may act as a determinant—or character interpreter—of his present socio-cultural world.... Just as social assimilation moves along a different and slower path than that of acculturation, so does identity assimilation, or rather non assimilation, enjoy a pertinacity not wholly responsive to the other two processes.[47]

The early experiences with the Italian culture, the persistence and extension of family attachments, and the Italian name provide constant reminders of one's Italian-ness. Though acculturated, an Italian-American identification provides the individual with an identity which may disappear when he becomes a nonethnic. Such an identity becomes increasingly important with living in an urban environment and in a mass society. Moreover, the acculturated Italian-American may be more acceptable to the core society than the unacculturated, but this acceptance does not mean an incorporation into the primary group relations. Even with acceptance, some kind of stigma may be attached to being Italian. The persistence of an Italian-American identification and a parallel substructure is based on an out-group rejection. The greater the feelings of exclusion among our respondents, the more they will identify as Italian-Americans.

Another factor in the persistence of an Italian-American identification which in turn influences political behavior is the American political system. That system continues to rely on ethnic strategies. The reason that politicians give consideration to ethnic groupings is the fact that ethnic substructures are highly visible. They do exist, and ethnics respond as ethnics.

To the Italian-American, being a member of an ethnic group, produces attitudes which have a bearing on his social and political participation. Among these perceptions is an acute sense of subordinate status, the feeling that society underrates him and his group. This holds true of the Italian as well as other ethnic groups. This is not only grounded in subjective estimates but in objective reality.

While the signs of self-identity are encouraging, the impact of prejudice and discrimination in the form of self-hatred can be seen by Italian-Americans who parade in godfather garb to advertise the opening of an Italian restaurant, or the tossing of *dago* balls at a midwestern carnival, or hucksters at a *festa* exhorting the people to come to the *Guinea* festival.

Recently, a young playwright, Joe Ponzi, attempted to deal with this dimension of negative Italian-American identity. His play *Union Street* was given in Manhattan, the Bronx, and Queens. The play is designed for the street in brevity and relevance. It runs an hour and ten minutes and deals with the tragedy of young lovers trapped in their dilapidated Brooklyn neighborhood of junkies, corrupt policemen, do-nothing welfare workers, and avaricious landlords. At the end, the neighborhood gains cohesion by sharing its concerns.

The play had its premiere at Carroll Park playground in 1976 in Brooklyn. The playwright was a street worker for the Youth Services Agency. It was sponsored by the Park, Recreation and Cultural Affairs Administration's Department of Cultural Affairs, assisted by Joseph Papp's New York Theatre. Much of the play, performed by an enthusiastic young cast of professionals, is taken up with the postures and violence of street behavior.

"There's almost an inferiority feeling among Italian kids in the city," Mr. Ponzi says. "The street bravado is a coverup. It's like we can't admit we're afraid."

Mr. Ponzi got the idea for the play while working with youths, many of them school dropouts, in his old neighborhood around Arthur Avenue in the Bronx.

"You see kids hanging out on the corners talking about the 'things' everybody else is getting," he said. "I thought, why not bring one of the 'things' to them. Maybe they'll say, 'Yeah, we can do that too.' "

I saw one performance of *Union Street*. While an ambulance wailed by on Clinton Street, and dogs and children scampered around the makeshift set, an actor in Brooklyn looked at the lowering sky and mused about "the old days when people had heart." It was an evening performance, an experiment in free outdoor theater that was touring Italian neighborhoods of the city in an effort, according to its author, to "give people pride in being Italian."

As my good friend Giulio Miranda asserts "We will also have to remember that there is no absolute as to what one must be, feel, do, to be acceptably Italian-American. We may be involved parochially in the search for ourselves, but we are also part of a larger search for the new American identity. Nobody can lay down on someone else what or how he should be. What we demand is the right to decide for ourselves."

Roseto, Pennsylvania, which had been the object of study by Dr. Stewart Wolf, is a case in point. He found that few in Roseto had ever died of a heart attack. Dr. John Bruhn, his associate, made this observation: "Our feeling was that Roseto was a very cohesive place with a lot of interrelationships. If you asked the average American how he'd spend his life if he only had a few years to live, he'd talk about economic security. If you asked a Rosetan, he'd talk about spending it with family and friends."[48]

As Robert Oppedisano described it:

> Rosetans have had to make the trade-off between economic success and ethnic identity. But they've managed to sustain a delicate balance between their very real success as Americans and their persistence as Rosetans. They seem to make both cultures work for them; after all, part of the reason they stood strongly attached to a way of life was because it worked for them in the past, as refuge and strength against a hostile society. Although much is gone, although Rosetans now get heart attacks and ulcers just like everyone else, the core of the culture remains.[49]

"It's in their pride as a people," Dr. Bruhn said, "They feel comfortable about themselves. They know who they are."[50] There is a strong and powerfully healthy relationship between ethnicity and mental health. The search for identity is a basic psychological need, and ethnicity is a powerful and subtle influence in determining its shape and form.

Two hundred years after the birth of the Republic, we have

still not discovered America. Many of her citizens are still unknown to her—and perhaps to themselves. Campbell's Soups
and Standard Oil, the Six Million Dollar Man and Coca Cola
prove that we have unity, abundant unity. We do not as readily
or as easily recognize our diversity.

While millions around the world welcome the goods of mass
production, many more are revolted by certain aspects of modern living. Almost everywhere, people see in their own cultural
history—a history which only yesterday some seemed ready to
abandon—a defense against certain evils of modern life. They see
in it the humanistic values that have given life its savor.

The study of one's past is part of self-discovery and self-
understanding. It is part of greater maturity. But the study
of the Italian past in America should not be done in a spirit
of ethnocentrism. It should be part of comprehending the
manner in which the total American pluralistic society has
evolved. As such, the study of the past will help to illuminate
the present and point the way in the future.

As part of the new ethnicity, Italian-Americans are searching
for a new way to define what it means to be American. They
are embracing the American dream as culturally pluralistic—a
nation having unity of spirit and ideal, but diversity of origin
and expression, a nation not of autonomous individuals, but
of dynamic, interacting groups, each of which brings forth its
best to help build a just and equitable society.

The aim of the new ethnicity is cohesive, not divisive; creative,
not destructive; multi-cultural, not chauvinistic. The new
ethnicity encourages others to acquire a more accurate self-
knowledge, especially with respect to the social structure of
the self. It is an affirmation by Italian-Americans of a pride
in heritage. It implies the sense that they don't have to give
up their own culture, their lifeways, their definitions of what
is the good life. As Giulio Miranda has asserted, "We were
put down—first by an uncomprehending segment of the Nordic
world, and then by a self-appointed intelligentsia who decided
we are 'backward,' 'village-oriented,' 'racist' and 'tribal.'" The
Italian-American consciousness movement is related to other
similar movements which are at last asking challenging questions. "What is an American? How much must we melt? Must
we melt at all? What do we owe to God, and what to Caesar?"
If diversity was once a luxury we could not afford, now it
is a reality we can no longer avoid. Since the civil rights struggle
of the 1960s, we can no longer insist on any one version of what
it means to be American nor any one vision of what it ought
to mean.

15 Italian-Americans and the Urban Crisis

One day in 1975, City Hall Plaza in New York City became an Italian palazzo bedecked with banners and garlands of laurel as two thousand recipients of invitations and city officials united in celebrating Italian Culture Week. The City Hall event initiated a festival and trade fair that extended from the harbor with a "celebration sail" to Fifth Avenue, appropriately hung with Italian flags and gleaming with window displays of the latest Italian fashions.

Mayor Abe Beame, wearing a broad green, white, and red sash and sipping vino, proclaimed the week "for my fellow Italians" and made the usual flattering rhetorical remarks about New York being "the second largest Italian city in the world."

It was enjoyable, though, to see the decorations, the opera troupe, and the sidewalk umbrella stands offering expresso and pastry. It stirred ethnic pride.

But there was no festive atmosphere in many of the other Italian-American neighborhoods in cities throughout the United States. There, life for the poverty stricken, the aged, the new immigrant went on as usual. These *paesani* were not invited to City Hall, nor to the boat ride, nor were Fifth Avenue fashions high on their shopping list.

A few months before Italian Culture Week, it took a television exposé to provide hospital treatment and public assistance to one Mulberry Street resident who, it was reported, had little to eat, was ill and unable to walk, and had not left her room in three years. Officials rushed to her aid, but only after her situation was flashed on the screen for all to see. It was a crisis focused on this single Italian-American woman.

Take the case of Mrs. Ferrara, who is eligible for welfare aid and at this stage in life not opposed to taking some of it, but her married daughter will not let her—pride. The eighty-six-year-old widow lives alone in a tiny apartment in Greenwich Village. Though the apartment is spotless, the building is in disrepair. It has no running water because of broken pipes the landlord refuses to fix. There are upwards of 400,000 Mrs. Ferraras living in New York City. They live on an annual income of $4,300 or less but are unrecognized by the poverty programs.[1]

Multiple crises have characterized the past fifteen years. The overarching umbrella became the "urban crisis." Much has been written about this subject. What is increasingly apparent is that millions of ethnic Americans were never included in the urban crisis equation. When they were included, they were viewed as the cause and not a part of our urban dilemma.

To many social scientists, Italian-Americans were seen as not having problems as a result of living in urban America. Italian-Americans were included among those unable to have their concerns and problems placed on the agenda of national policy. Their cause was not accorded the same legitimacy as that of other minorities.

Much of the social and political research concluded that Italians were upwardly mobile. They had made it. Italian-Americans were moving to the suburbs; hence, urban living constituted no difficulty for them. Many of these value-laden premises continue to this day.[2]

An astonishing declaration was made early in the Ford administration. What had been called the "urban crisis" was unilaterally declared to be at an end, despite the fact that 125,000 people continued to leave New York City annually. New York City lost one million residents between 1960 and 1970. For millions of ethnic Americans, the urban crisis had passed them by. Shortly after the Ford declaration, New York City was on the brink of financial ruin.

The 1970 census indicates that a greater proportion than ever of the nation's people live in 230 metropolitan areas. For the first time, the number living in the suburbs is greater than that in the central cities. In some instances, the decline of city population has been dramatic, while the metropolitan area has grown substantially.

The urban preference of Italian-Americans is greater than it is for the United States population as a whole: 73 percent of Americans live in urban areas, while the percentage for Italian-Americans is over 92 percent. This illustrates a major dimension of the relationship of Italian-Americans to urban areas. It reflects the strong attachment many Italian-Americans have to their neighborhoods and their reluctance to join the mass flight to the suburbs. Whatever the cause of this reluctance, Italian-Americans have a certain staying power in the cities. This accounts in part for the large proportions of central-city populations comprised of Italian-Americans in the large cities of the United States, such as Philadelphia, Chicago, Cleveland, New York, Detroit, Newark, Buffalo, New Haven, Baltimore, Rochester, Boston, and Providence.[3] In these and many smaller cities in the Northeast, that proportion is increasing, as other whites continue to leave the cities for the suburbs.[4] As Joseph Conforti put it:

> This places Italian-Americans in the position of increasingly becoming *the* whites in central cities, thus putting them at the cutting edge of the urban crisis. It is in fact difficult to separate this relationship of Italian-Americans to the urban crisis from the urban crisis itself, for the term summarizes a range of specific problem manifestations resulting from and reflecting the movement of population groups and their activities.[5]

The tax burden has inevitably shifted more heavily to the city's residents, in terms of increased property, sales, and income taxes. With out-migration to the suburbs dominated by the city's most affluent residents, this also means the increasing tax burden is borne by an ever poorer resident population. To compound the situation further, an increasing proportion of the central city's population is economically disenfranchised, helplessly dependent upon unemployment or welfare payments and a broad array of public services. This can be quite dramatic. New York City has nearly 1.5 million residents who are either unemployed or on welfare. Newark presents the dramatic phenomenon of a city in which approximately half the resident population is either unemployed or on welfare.

It should not be necessary to catalog all the specific problems that comprise the urban crisis of the central cities. The physical deterioration, crime, declining quality of education and educational opportunities, filth, corruption, and inadequate housing have all been widely reported through the mass media. The specific problem manifestations that comprise the urban crisis and bear directly on Italian-Americans, and ethnic Americans in general, include the following: economic insecurity, limited group mobility, unfair tax burdens, discrimination, jobs, education, inadequate housing, physical deterioration of the cities, crime and violence, poverty, the aged. What is important to note is that, while these problems have received national attention where blacks and Spanish-speaking people are concerned, white ethnics have been viewed as not suffering from the urban malaise. Responsibility for dealing directly with these problems has remained primarily at the local level. It is such local responsibility that makes the urban crisis of particular importance to Italian-Americans, since they make up an increasing proportion of the central city's white population.[6]

Even the means of identifying the problem has value-laden assumptions. Take the use of the "ethnic" survey as a means of determining job discrimination, housing needs, or whatever. Such surveys mandated by federal or state agencies invariably have had categories such as: White, Black, Hispanic, or Other. Rarely is there a breakdown of the "white" category. Such a breakdown would be revealing in terms of job discrimination against Polish-Americans, Italian-Americans, Jewish-Americans, and other ethnic groups. Hence, what many people detected in the surveys was social planners using reverse quotas to determine job discrimination for one or two groups. In the past, the revelation of such information was used against a number of ethnic groups such as Jews and Italian-Americans. Moreover, there is the feeling among some ethnic groups that qualification and merit are being disregarded in hiring. White ethnic groups sense that the rules of the game are being changed while the game is still being played.

The affluent society is a cruel delusion for many white working and lower-middle-class people. The affluent can buy their way out of unwanted social situations; most blue-collar workers cannot. In more than half of all ethnic families, both husband and wife are working. Yet the typical family is likely to be making somewhere between $9,000 and $14,000 a year, with the median likely to be somewhere around $11,000 or $12,000.

In 1970, the Census Bureau released a report titled "Characteristics of the Population by Ethnic Origin," which drew on a special survey done in 1969. In five ethnic groups, which included Italian-Americans, nearly 20 million people lived in families with $5,000–$10,000 annual incomes. Six million males over age sixteen were employed in blue-collar jobs, with another 1.5 million in sales, clerical, and service work.[7]

Former Assistant Secretary of Labor Jerome Rostow, in his "Blue Collar Memorandum" to the President, estimated that 70 million Americans make up the $5,000–$10,000 income group, of whom 10–15 million are nonwhite minorities. The 20 million figure cited by the Census for portions of only five ethnic groups supports the notion that a very large proportion of the urban working class in America is ethnic.

According to a National Opinion Research Center survey, the family income of Italian-Americans was $7,979. The NORC data show that 20 percent of Italian-Americans have family income under $4,000 annually, while 50.9 percent have income between $4,000 and $9,999. An additional 18.7 percent of Italian-Americans have incomes between $10,000 and $14,999. Only 9.8 percent have family incomes above $15,000.[8] In an era of recession and high inflation, that leaves little margin when inflation is unchecked. Despite overtime, moonlighting, and working wives, the typical family is overburdened with install- ment debts and mortgages. Against this economic picture, one can understand the deep resentment of a rising burden of taxes and erosion of income by inflation. This has triggered protests against welfare, poverty programs, and social experiments, particularly when these do not seem to provide any benefits to ethnic Americans themselves. As one ethnic leader noted, "We, urban ethnic working people, feel we pay the largest percentage of local and federal taxes and we get the least in return in terms of goods and services. We need tax reform which will put the burden on those who can afford to pay."[9]

It is a hard squeeze, and it is causing a great deal of hardship and even bitterness. Many Italian-Americans have been working for three generations for a chance to get ahead. Some were wiped out by the Depression. Some of the brightest were then encouraged to go into engineering and aerospace in the 1950s, which is now a disaster area economically. Many parents make too little to send three or four kids to college, but earn too much to qualify for scholarships according to the federal guidelines.[10]

One private report published in 1975 concluded that Italian-Americans in New York City made up at least 50 percent of the population, yet 10 percent of all Italian-American families live under the federally established poverty level. Of these, only 15 percent received the public assistance to which they are entitled. The study notes further that, in the city's 26 desig- nated poverty areas, less than one quarter of poor Italian fami- lies residing there receive public assistance. The report called upon the city to redefine the concept of poverty based on geography.[11]

In the late sixties and early seventies, New York City doled out in excess of $60 million of Federal funds to community groups seeking to create neighborhood self-help programs. In 1970, a list of almost two thousand beneficiaries did not reveal the name of a single Italian-American organization. Of the more than one thousand special projects for the poor carried on in 1970, none were aimed at meeting Italian-American needs. Of New York City's 250 on-going, year-round, fully funded delegate agencies, none concerned themselves with the Italian poor or disadvantaged. It was only after considerable pressure and a lawsuit that City Hall was moved to channel limited funding for such self-help programs.

Despite the presence of community groups and socially active Italian-Americans who sincerely want to help their communities, Italian-Americans were unable to receive a fair share of funding from either their city, state, or federal governments. When funding did emerge, it was to be cut severely later, as all levels of governments faced budget crises. There is a cruel irony to all of this. Given little and belated recognition, Italian-Americans, like other white ethnic groups, have been among the first to have their funding cut. One case in point is the effort by medical researchers and Italian-Americans to receive full funding for research on Cooley's anemia. Cooley's anemia is one of the most common of the inherited diseases of the blood. It causes a lifelong disability which must be treated with blood transfusions to sustain life. In the United States, close to a quarter of a million people are carriers of Cooley's anemia, and thousands of children have been afflicted with the disease. Many of these individuals trace their ancestry to the Mediterranean region. Most are of Italian or Greek descent. In August of 1972, the National Cooley's Anemia Control Act was signed into law after many months of lobbying. As time passed, it was learned that, in the legislative process, authorization did not mean appropriation. No funds were made available nor were any requested by the Nixon administration. Attempts to remedy this situation were met, in one case, by an acknowledged liberal Senator who referred to Cooley's anemia as "the disease of the month." Finally, after considerable pressure, a Health, Education and Welfare Department bill provided for appropriations to the National Institute of Health. The bill was subsequently vetoed by President Ford and overridden by the Senate on September 30, 1976. Until this action was taken, one can conclude that at minimum not enough emphasis or real concern was exhibited by the President or Congress.

There is a further irony in the fact that "welfare for the rich" has not been faced with the same budget limitations as that for the middle and lower classes of Americans. In any given year, the U.S. Treasury distributes about $10 billion in direct payments to various enterprises to enhance their profits and diminish their losses. The federal government maintains prices at noncompetitive high levels in regulated areas of the economy, at a multibillion dollar cost to consumers and to the lasting advantage of established producers. The federal government gives private corporations the use, profit, and sometimes ownership of new technologies developed at public expense.[12] It is this growing realization of paying a disproportionate amount of the tax burden without a commensurate return in government assistance and services that has led to the growing sense of alienation. As one observer of the urban scene noted, "He [ethnic] pays the bill for every major government program and gets nothing or little in the way of return. . . . He himself is the victim of class prejudice. . . . He has worked hard all his life to become a "good American" . . . [but] in many instances he is treated like the machine he operates."[13]

In the past, a middle-income American in the $7,000 to $20,000 range paid a higher percentage of his income for taxes than the richest 1 percent of Americans. One calculation estimated that families with yearly incomes of $100,000 and above—about 0.3 percent of the population—receive tax preferences of more than $11 billion annually.

One percent of the nation's families, those with incomes of $50,000 or more a year, own 51 percent of the stock and collect almost 47 percent of the dividends.[14] This growing gap between income distribution, tax burdens, and return of services has been the basis of growing alienation among white ethnic Americans.[15] With regard to Italian-Americans, there is the added fact that increasing education is not being translated into movement into the higher income and occupational categories.

As far as education is concerned, Italian-Americans are at the national average. According to the NORC data, 17 percent of Italian-Americans are likely to have gone to college. Italian-Americans have reached the national average in the percentage of those who have become managers or owners or professional or technical workers (26 percent). Nearly 26 percent are likely to be service, sales, or clerical workers.[16]

Among ethnic Americans, and Italian-Americans in particular, there is the growing perception that they are excluded from the dominant institutions and organizations of American society.[17] The more affluent Italian-Americans who have "made it" refuse to admit that discrimination against Italian-Americans still exists. This is often due to a rejection of ethnic identity on one hand and a "we made it; why can't they?" mentality on the other.

One study attempted to determine the extent to which varying minorities have penetrated the centers of power and influence in Chicago-based corporations. This was done by determining how many of the groups either serve on the board of directors or occupy the highest executive positions in Chicago's largest corporations. While Italian-Americans made up 4.8 percent of the population, only 1.9 percent of the directors of the 106 largest corporations were Italian. The same pattern holds if one looks at executive officers. Italian-Americans accounted for 2.9 percent. Eighty-four out of 106 corporations still had no directors who were Italian-American, and 75 out of 106 corporations had no officers who were Italian-American.[18]

A similar study of the 100 largest corporations was completed in Detroit. Twenty-seven of these corporations are among the 100 largest industrial corporations or the largest nonindustrial firms in the United States; 80 of the 100 corporations had firms in the United States; 80 of the 100 corporations had no Italian-American directors; 78 had no Italian-American officers. Often one or two persons in the study occupied executive positions in more than one corporation.[19]

James Polk, writing in the *New Republic,* states that "for many years the boards of American business have been a closed shop, a system of ingrown groups in which the controlling management would choose its own watchdogs, with an occasional minority mascot named to blunt the winds of public opinion."[20] Professor Barta makes the following observation about the situation in Chicago. "As such studies accumulate, the result may be a national profile for each of America's ethnic groups showing precisely the extent to which each of them shares in the power and affluence of the nation."[21] In the process, the nation will learn to what extent the American corporation is a "truly public institution bound to the same criteria of selection that today affect government service—freedom from bias, and the requirement at the same time to represent and reflect all parts of the American population."[22]

As one white ethnic has remarked, "Nobody has done anything for ethnics since Social Security. . . . Yet here they are being blamed for white racism. But they're not the people in the executive suites who would not hire a single Jew or Negro for so long."[23]

There are other levels of discrimination which exclude and

are sensed by Italian-Americans. Dr. Ermanno Trabucco was
a clinical assistant in surgery at Flushing Hospital and Medical
Center for five years before being granted a voluntary leave
of absence in 1968 to establish a charitable hospital in Rome.
When he tried to return to his former position in July 1970
he was told his leave had expired and he would have to reapply.
In August of 1970 he was told he would not be reappointed.
In September 1970, the director of surgery called Trabucco
a "guinea" and told him "that he should go back to Italy where
he belonged; that he believed the complainant's project in Rome
to be a mafia-financed hospital; and that the complainant
organized a mafia group at Flushing Hospital."[24] Trabucco
had organized a local chapter of Graduates of Italian Medical
Schools, an American organization open to qualified doctors
regardless of national origin. The New York State Division
ruled in 1973 that Trabucco had been discriminated against
because of his Italian background. It ordered his reinstatement
and damages of $100,000.

Matthew and Maureen DiTeresa applied for membership
three times in fourteen years to the Lake Tamarack Association,
a private recreational club. They were rejected each time. The
State Division of Civil Rights of New Jersey ordered the private
club to open its door to all people who meet its residency requirements. They upheld the complaint of discrimination against
Italian-Americans.

There is a keen awareness of exclusion from the dominant
institutions in American society. And this exclusion is viewed
as being a result of ethnic barriers as well as economic ones.

Another dimension of discrimination is evident in academic
life. The Association of Italian-American Faculty, in a report
"Status of Italian-Americans in the City University of New
York," charged the City University that Italian-Americans had
been subjected to *de facto* discrimination. As of 1973, the report
showed that, of five university chancellors, none were of Italian
background; of 21 college presidents there was only of 1 of
Italian background; only 11 of 126 deans were Italian-American;
of 27 division directors, only 1; of 406 department chairmen,
only 28; of 405 higher education officers, only 11; of 98 regis-
trars, only 3; of almost ten thousand professors of all ranks,
instructors and full-time lecturers, never did the Italian-Americans reach beyond 6.9 percent in any category.[25] There were
only 475 of Italian background or 6.4 percent in a total CUNY
teaching staff of 7,398. The faculty association report goes
on to cite two specific instances in detail. "Looking at two large,

typical colleges, one a senior college located in the borough that has the highest Italian-American population in the City, and one a junior college located in the borough of second highest Italian-American population," the document draws clear implications. At Brooklyn College, serving an estimated Italian-American borough population of 691,900, only five of the forty-five member administration are of Italian background. Counted in this number is a security officer and the building superintendent. Of thirty-four departmental chairmen, there are no Italian-Americans. Out of a total of 991 full-time faculty, only 68 are of Italian background.

At Queensborough Community College, serving an estimated Italian-American borough population of 494,700, only four members of the thirty-nine member administration are of Italian background. Both are departmental chairmen, two out of seventeen. Of a total faculty of 546, only 46 are of Italian background.[26]

These low figures are cited in spite of documentation that fully one-quarter of the student population in the city university system is of Italian background. The report concluded "City University, with approximately a one-half million dollar budget from municipal and state taxes, has historically practiced de facto discrimination against the Italian-American."

The charges leveled at City University and the issues are not uncommon to other institutions of higher education. Similar charges with supporting data were made against the State University of New York at Purchase in 1975 by Italian-Americans.[27]

Quotas have been inimical to the heritage of a number of ethnic groups. The sense of exclusion can again be illustrated in a case involving two Italian-American students who sought admission to City University's bio-medical program. The program, begun in February 1973, "is designed to increase the minority physicians practicing in urban areas."[28] It combines undergraduate and medical studies in an accelerated six-year course of study.

The program prompted charges of reverse discrimination when Michael Scognamiglio, a senior at the top-rated Bronx High School of Science with a scholastic average of over 95, was refused admission. Subsequently, Robert Trotta, a state regents scholarship winner at John Dewey High School, was also refused, despite a 91-plus average. Both students filed complaints alleging disparate treatment because of their race and national origin.

While denying that the ethnicity of candidates was considered during admission interviews, it was conceded by CUNY officials and reported by the State Division of Human Rights that four separate lists were compiled on an ethnic basis: black, Spanish, Asian, and others. Replacements for those applicants who had been accepted but who declined were chosen from these lists on a one-for-one basis, clearly a legal inpropriety. Also considered for admission were high school averages, community activity, and intent to practice in urban New York. It is strongly suspected that the weight assigned to each factor differed according to the race or national origin of the applicant. The Division of Human Rights in its inquiry received limited cooperation from City University. These two bright high-school students were caught in the vortex of a storm raging in this country—the quota system versus the merit system, better known as reverse discrimination. These terms mean simply that otherwise qualified white ethnics are cast aside in favor of other minority groups. In effect, the quota system, in seeking to create a better ethnic and racial balance in the professions, has rejected an important American principle—that opportunity shall be afforded to all equally, and those best qualified shall prevail. Instead, the theory is being advanced that we can be made to qualify if enough preferential treatment is given to some. It could hardly apply to training medical doctors, in particular when such training is accelerated to the point where the course of study is shortened by two years. The cases of Robert Trotta and Michael Scognamiglio are among the thousands which have occurred daily involving the issue of quota and merit.[29]

Outside of the academic world, there are other such instances of reverse discrimination. One such case involves Elizabeth Talmo, who was told by the New York State Department of Labor she would no longer be needed in her $10,350-a-year job as an employment interviewer. Ms. Talmo, who had worked her way through Hunter, gained what she needed as necessary experience teaching school in the South Bronx, and had passed the Civil Service examination, was displaced because of a special program designed to get more members of "minority groups" into state jobs. Ms. Talmo was not considered to be in one of the groups needing special help.[30]

In December of 1974, the State Human Rights Commission found that "probable cause exists to believe that the Department of Labor had engaged in an unlawful and discriminatory practice."[31]

The combination of inflation and recession is taking its

toll on upwardly mobile Italian-Americans. Certain areas have recently witnessed Italian-Americans making inroads. These areas such as higher education are precisely those in which "last hired and first fired" principle is in operation.

Young second and third generation students are also being affected by the budget crunch. Since many of them do not qualify for financial assistance, the financial situation at home because of recession and inflation has cast a pall of gloom on their college futures. White ethnics are the group most affected by budget cuts and policy changes.

Increasingly, Italian-Americans and their organizations are becoming more vocal and militant about what they see as an impediment to their upward mobility and their growing desire to enter colleges and the professions. In short, they do not want to be kept out of jobs or schools or be denied promotions or access to special programs because they are not black, Puerto Rican, or part of a special interest group. A growing number of them—especially, the young—are claiming this is precisely what is happening. To many of them, the official and unofficial quotas undercut the tradition of advancement by merit and even work against the very people they are meant to aid, since these people will ultimately be unable to get jobs if their quotas are filled. Among the Italian-American students on campus, the vast majority have not come to realization that a basic inequity is at work and will affect their future advancement. In a recent study of the Italian-American student body at Brooklyn College, conducted by Professor Vincent Fucillo and Professor Jerome Krase, 39.3 percent perceived no obstacles to attaining their career or professional goals. Among the Italian-American student sample, 16.2 percent saw their ethnicity as an obstacle.[32]

There is a cruel irony in all of this. Precisely when large numbers of Italian-Americans are beginning to enter college, they are facing job quotas, little scholarship aid because their incomes disqualify them, a cut in college services and more fundamentally a recession which is changing the job market so dramatically that counseling takes on a greater importance for them. Many remain confused and unaware of these forces which are affecting their present lives and their future careers.

This is occurring when their expectations for advancement are rising. According to the Fuccillo and Krase study, "The heightened aspirations of our Italian-American students for professional and managerial positions is tied in part to the availability of college education."[33] About three-quarters of the Italian-American students at Brooklyn College aspire to a professional or managerial career, whereas a small percentage of their parents are currently employed in such occupations. About 63.3 percent of the students surveyed have fathers whose occupations are currently in the blue-collar category, with 27 percent employed in craft occupations. Higher education for them is the ticket into white-collar, professional, semi-professional, and managerial occupations. Half of the sample are employed during the academic year and need to work in order to stay in college. The parents of the vast majority of students have never attended college, but 61.4 percent of the fathers and 69 percent of the mothers have completed at least a high school education. Thus, these students are often the first in their families to pursue a higher education.[34]

The Italian-American students studied by Fuccillo and Krase are job-oriented and view their education principally from a vocationally and career based perspective. In their study they conclude:

> The counseling services of the college must be made more responsive to the needs and special interests of our Italian-American students.... It is also important to provide visible recognition of the presence and legitimate status of the Italian-American students, although this matter is equally pressing in other areas of college activity. The assignment of a number of Italian-Americans to prominent positions within the counseling program is not unimportant....[35]

In their report "Status of Italian Americans in the City University of New York," the Association of Italian-American Faculty noted that only 8 of the 398 student counselors were of Italian background, confirming the assumption that "qualifying Italian-American students are not being informed of the availability of programs, nor are their particular academic and emotional needs being met...."[36]

Particularly discriminatory to the poverty-level Italian-American students was the special program requirement that one must come from a designated poverty area of the city. These areas do not coincide with the areas of greatest Italian-American concentrations in all five boroughs.

By 1973, Italian-Americans comprised 25 percent of all CUNY students. According to the 1975 study of Fuccillo and Krase, 11 percent of the student body at Brooklyn College in all divisions were Italian-Americans. Whether the university expected Italian-American students or not, it has shown little evidence that it recognizes their specific needs, problems, or even presence. Despite the fact that many of them need academic aid and counseling, they are expected to make it on their own.

The SEEK program is CUNY's largest effort to aid underprepared students. Presently, it serves about eighty-four hundred students. In 1973, forty-two were Italian-Americans. Of the more than nine thousand students in CUNY's other programs of similar academic help, about one hundred sixty are Italian-Americans. All of this led to a hearing by the State of New York to probe charges of discrimination.[37] The hearing concluded that *de facto* discrimination did exist. In 1970, one Italian-American staff member of CUNY won his discrimination case against that institution before the New York State Division of Human Rights.

The deterioration of American's cities is related to the destruction of neighborhoods. Yet, neighborhood is important to the reconstruction of urban America. Neighborhood is an important ingredient in Italian-American life.

An interesting organization was established on the Lower East Side of Manhattan called the Little Italy Restoration Association. By the time it was little more than a year old, it had ambitiously undertaken the stimulation and coordination of a variety of rehabilitative and developmental endeavors in New York's historic Little Italy. The reason for such an effort are fairly simple: the area has been intensely used, with little new development, since the nineteenth century. It contains an aging, low-income population in need of services only limitedly available; and there is a problem with the aging, contracting Italian population, relative to the growing and expanding Chinese community.

More surprising, there are families and individuals who have expressed interest in acquiring apartments in either new or rehabilitated residential buildings in the area. In addition to people already living there who are seeking to upgrade their living conditions, there are many interested Italian-Americans who had moved from the area to gain better housing in New York's outer boroughs or suburbs. There are also many who have never lived on the Lower East Side. The reasons given by these latter groups reportedly include the attractiveness of safer streets, a friendly neighborhood, a compatible way of life, and a general expectation that they would feel comfortable living there.[38]

That people who long ago moved from the Lower East Side should want to move back certainly goes counter to the American notion of progress. That people who never lived there would express a desire to live in an old, deteriorating tenement district runs counter even more emphatically to American notions of progress. Yet this illustrates a major dimension of the relationship of Italian-Americans to urban areas. It reflects the strong attachment many Italian-Americans have to old city neighborhoods and the reluctance of many to move from them unless pushed to join the exodus to the suburbs. It is this loss of commitment to neighborhood that has made many of our cities unlivable. In Newark, New Jersey, like other cities, only the Italians are staying on as the black population has increased.

It is increasingly clear that Italian-Americans tend to be more willing to stay in the central city neighborhoods than members of other ethnic groups. This accounts in part for the large proportions of central city populations comprised of Italian-Americans in large northeastern cities of the United States.[39]

Just before New York announced that it was on the brink of financial catastrophe, the city government announced plans to restore the Little Italy section of New York with increased housing, a new school, increased social services, and the preservation of historic storefronts. This happened after much time spent pressuring the city government to respond to the needs of Italian-Americans. Among the old-time residents there was skepticism born out of bitter experience. Some took a wait-and-see attitude. Now fiscal crisis has entered to deny again the meeting of real needs too long ignored.

While most community organizations worry about the future because of the lack of money, the Little Italy Restoration Association says that it has no plans to roll over and die. It is currently seeking new funding elsewhere. The plan was intended to revitalize the Little Italy community, the spiritual heart of the city's Italian-American population. As Theodore Tarrantini, the former director of LIRA noted, "Our aim now is to show the federal government and the Housing and Urban Development Administration why the job should be done. This is a prime area for redevelopment even if it is done on a small scale."[40] The Italian-Americans, like their neighbors in Chinatown, are by nature self-helpers. Tarrantini went on to observe:

> They want jobs and opportunities, but most of all they want the area redeveloped on a real economic tax base. The faith that they have demonstrated in the restoration program has been fantastic. These people have been picked up and let down too often. If the city is ever going to turn around it has got to start somewhere. This is a good place to start.[41]

The Italian-American values of neighborhood, self-help, and independence may be seen in "The Hill," a fifty-six-block, largely Italian area on the south side of St. Louis. This community has successfully resisted the encroachment of urbanization. After a fierce, emotion-charged battle with local, state, and federal officials, the Italian-American residents of The Hill boast a model community that has the lowest crime rate and the highest property values in the city. There is a strong sense of ritual and community on The Hill, where 90 percent of the population of sixty-five hundred are Italian-Americans and 95 percent are Catholics. Life on The Hill is tightly and finely woven. There is pride in the rows of narrow, clean houses and family-run stores.

This was not always the case. During the 1960s, government officials planned Interstate Highway 44 to run straight through an area on The Hill. Many fearful homeowners stopped improvements on their homes. The Hill began to deteriorate.

Interestingly enough, a priest, Father Salvatore Polizzi, now fifty-one years old, associate pastor of St. Ambrose Roman Catholic Church, was to play a key role in changing things. He followed the tradition of many Italian-American priests before him in shaping the lives of their communities. From the pulpit he implored the residents to regain their sense of pride. Polizzi also made contact with the local Democratic organization. Soon, he mobilized Italian-Americans to resist the construction of a drive-in theater. They literally lay down in front of the bulldozers. The construction stopped. Then an ordinance was passed prohibiting the construction of any drive-in within five hundred feet of a residential area.

The next big battle was the construction of Highway 44 which would have cut off a segment of the community and isolated one hundred fifty families. In protest, hundreds of citizens, packed in buses, traveled to the state capital to argue for the construction of an additional overpass which would leave the homes intact. The commission responded with a firm no. Polizzi contacted Secretary of Transportation John Volpe for help. Polizzi led a Hill delegation to Washington with a check for $50,000 raised by the community to pay for the overpass themselves. The Hill got its bridge, and the bells of St. Ambrose rang out the good news.[42]

Father Polizzi joined eleven hundred families to form a nonprofit corporation. Money raised from an annual summer festival draws 100,000 tourists. In short order, the corporation found numerous jobs for the residents and set up a youth program which hired students to clean up the area and plant trees. When houses become vacant, the corporation buys them, refurbishes them, and resells them at low cost to young couples. This is just one example of an effort to preserve what is dear to people through leadership and community mobilization. Self-respect and independence are ingrained among Italian-Americans.

The fastest growing component of the central city population in the northeast is comprised of blacks and Hispanics, who also make up the largest part of the economically disenfranchised population. Many of the central city's problems and the efforts to resolve them are necessarily endeavors to overcome such economic disenfranchisement. In the arena of a decreasingly viable central city, this means scrambling for ever-scarcer resources and the likelihood of competition and conflict with the city's remaining whites, who are often only slightly better off and who are fearful of losing ground.

This casts Italian-Americans in a role and defines their relationship to the urban crisis largely in terms of conflict. One area of conflict is the worsening imbalance between a shrinking tax base and a constantly increasing demand for public services. Since Italian-Americans are not generally considered among the economically disenfranchised and tend to avoid involvement with public agencies if at all possible, it is unlikely that they are contributing much to the increasing demand for public services. Rather, they are on the other side of the imbalance. They are paying for those services through a variety of taxes. This easily becomes a source of hostility when Italian-Americans view blacks and Hispanics as the source of an increasing tax burden. Some Italian-Americans are not particularly sympathetic to arguments stressing the lack of opportunity or the effects of discrimination suffered by blacks and Hispanics. The harsh immigrant experience is too recent for Italian-Americans, who say nobody ever gave us anything; we had to work for what we got; why shouldn't they?

Since there cannot be enough recognition and resources to go around for all groups, the question of which groups are to get the available resources leads to ethnic conflict.[43] One advantage, however, is the greater the ethnic conflict in a community, the greater the rates of political participation of the conflicting groups.

One view of the Italian-Americans in the 1960s is that they were part of a "blacklash." Other studies show significant levels of tolerance among Italian-Americans for other ethnic and religious groups.[44]

The term *conservative* applied to white ethnics including Italian-Americans is misleading. White ethnics are the most solid bloc of progressive voters in the whole country on a broad variety of issues—from labor through Social Security and medical and civil rights. On family matters, they are out of tune with the affluent left. Their feeling is much more antiliberal than it is anti-civil rights. The great votes piled up for civil-rights legislation came from lawmakers representing the white ethnics. Ethnics want the same laws and standards of help and protection applied to them.

One of the central issues in the central cities which affect a variety of values, including neighborhood and merit, is the issue of busing. On its face, busing has racist presuppositions. The assumption behind busing is that blacks, unlike Catholic immigrants, cannot learn in largely separate environments. They need an infusion of "white magic."

Let us look at a number of factors which shed light on recent court rulings. Traditional residential patterns of northern cities have always involved *de facto* ethnic segration, not only for blacks, but for almost every ethnic group over the past century. In some instances, more financial resources have been directed to predominantly black schools than predominantly white ethnic schools.

Before 1900, 90 percent of all blacks lived in the South; and 90 percent of the white ethnics who now live in the northern cities had not yet arrived. These two great migrations were not linked by slavery, were culturally almost totally unprepared for their future meeting, and came to their rendezvous with some different social skills, family traditions, disciplines, needs, and aspirations.

The role of the family or family-substitute in bringing about certain kinds of attitudes, behavior, and academic success is undoubtedly the greatest single factor influencing the classroom. The family is a more basic social unit than the school. According to Michael Novak, class factors influence dramatically the attitudes, behaviors, aspirations, and educational success of students in school. Families choose their place of residence—or judge its merit—by their preference for its neighborhood school as much as, or more than, by any other factor.

If these propositions are true, then it must surely be predictable that 96 percent of the whites and 91 percent of the blacks would find busing a poor instrument for what a great majority, both black and white, also desire—a genuinely, peacefully integrated society.

What seems to have been forgotten is that busing is merely an instrument, a tool—a method, not an end. The most appropriate question with respect to busing, as for any instrument, is, Does it work? What are its effects? is the central moral question.

Michael Novak contends:

> In my view, busing of the Boston and Detroit sort is an immoral policy. It goes against the basic social principles of American life; against family, neighborhood, class, ethnic, and even educational realities which are so basic they are seldom even voiced.... Forced busing will set back the advances of civil rights made during the past generation by twenty years. ... Busing is to black equality what Prohibition was to the moral crisis of the Depression. It is a flaming moral issue of dubious social judgment.... Now, as then, the fundamental problem is economic.[45]

These are the principal forces on the urban scene which are producing a sense of alienation among Italian-Americans. One of the components of political alienation is a sense of political powerlessness—a feeling that one cannot affect the actions of government, that the authoritative allocation of values which is at the heart of the political process is not subject to the person's influence. Among Italian-Americans, a sense of powerlessness is greatest through the second generation but declines significantly, though it is not eliminated, in the third generation. A sense of political powerlessness will be associated with the feelings that the political processes do not involve and have no impact on the respondent. Moreover, the individual feels that he cannot influence the government in any meaningful way.[46]

Most first, second, and third generation Italian-Americans show the impact of American political culture by viewing the operation of government from the standpoint of intermediaries or representatives. Those representatives, however, may be more responsive to the more influential individuals or groups.[47]

As the Italian becomes conscious of his ethnic identity and his place in society, he will be more sensitive to the politics of recognition.[48] The locus of Italians' political interests is most often on the local level. This may be due to the historic role of community and region in the Italian past which persists among succeeding generations of Italians in America.

American cities, on the other hand, have not developed an impartial nonpolitical bureaucracy or local magistracy. This results in a mutual reliance between public officials and voter.

Rewards are distributed in relation to the voting strength of various groups, ethnic included.[49] During the New York mayoralty campaign of 1969, John Lindsay sought to capture the loyalty of the voters of Queens by pressing physical and service improvements for the residents. The area, heavily Italo-American, had severely criticized the mayor for his apparent mishandling of a snow emergency. In December, 1969, following months of stormy protests by homeowners in Queens over the planned construction of a school, Mayor Lindsay, with an eye for the political support of the Queens residents, removed the chairman of the planning commission and appointed an Italian-American.[50]

The relationship of political strength and distribution of rewards becomes more important with residential segregation, since issues such as welfare, crime, and so on, become ethnically related matters. If, as I contend, an Italian substructure need not have an ecological base, then the transfer of such ethnically related issues takes place with movement to the suburbs. Some of the rewards and services of local government in particular lead to group patronage; i.e., certain rewards go to a member of a group rather than to the individual.[51] As the positions at stake involve higher status rather than economic motives, the Italians' quest for rewards is transferred to one of seeking a go-between and intermediary. The intermediary will serve as protector and as a symbolic recognition of the Italians' worth and dignity.[52] In a sense, the selection of John Volpe as United States Secretary of Transportation was for this purpose. At the same time, the intermediary is used for political purposes. In October of 1970 Volpe appeared before an Italian-American dinner honoring him. His other mission was to show his support for the Republican candidate, Nelson Gross. Referring to the issues of disorder and permissiveness in America, Volpe went on to say that many in his audience like himself were brought up by Italian-American parents "who were not afraid to use a little discipline."[53]

Italian-Americans in the past have been mobilized by intermediary leaders. Predominantly Italian leadership patterns have in the past been molded by occupational choices and social organization of Italians.[54] The concentration of Italian leadership in building and construction, with its close political ties, has led to the political arena. For the Italians, the undertaker was often an important political person in the community, with leisure for politics and the incentive of operating a regulated trade.[55]

Not all of Italian-American intermediaries have served the community well. On the local level, some Italian-American politicians have cast themselves in the role of political *padroni*. In fact, this may account in part for the inability of the Italian-American community to have its concerns placed on the public agenda.

My friend Phil Foglia, a political and social activist, has discerned a number of types of political *padroni*.[56] There are several different breeds of political *padroni*. The first is the elected *padrone*. He is the politico who is elected from districts that are predominantly Italian. He spends most of his time on projects or legislation that is designed to win over the non-Italian segment of his district. The Italian constituency is given lip service and moving speeches on holidays and during *festas*. Never, however, does he formulate a strategy to attack the problems of his Italian constituents. That would be too parochial. After all, Italians are resigned to receiving no help from the government and will ultimately vote for an Italian incumbent under any circumstances. Accordingly, this *padrone* keeps a public posture that is far removed from Italian concerns so as to avoid conflicts with other ethnic or minority groups. He is, in essence, a coward.

Another type of *padrone* is the appointed *padrone*. He is usually an Italian-American who is qualified within a given area and sufficiently identifiable as an Italian-American as to be politically operative for the administration which he serves. The problem with this appointment level *padrone* is that he doesn't serve Italian-Americans but merely serves as *an* Italian-American, much the same way the old labor agents did. Government administrations, as well as corporate and institutional administrations for that matter, are careful to select "safe" Italians who will not make waves or create disturbances in the quest for justice for their people. This kind of cooperation permits neglect of the Italian community to be perpetuated while the problems become more severe.

Another *padrone* is the politically ambitious comer who wants to be the number-one Italian in the city or state, to balance every ticket or fill any position where it is advantageous to have an Italian-American. By undercutting his fellow Italian-Americans and pitting himself against them, he limits the range of achievement for Italian-Americans generally. As Phil Foglia observes, "These people must be made to understand that this kind of activity is not acceptable and will no longer be tolerated. If Italian-American politicos cannot cooperate and work with

other brothers, then they do not deserve the support of the community and should be actively opposed. Caucuses, alliances, and
coalitions of Italian-American leadership are essential before we
can begin to solve the problems that have been neglected for so
long in our communities as a result of *padronism* and the vacuum
of leadership created by it."

All this is not to say that the Italian community does not
have excellent individual leaders. It does, but the *padrone*
syndrome has created great obstacles to the development of
leadership in general. The political *padroni* have to be put
in their proper perspective before Italian-Americans as a group
can move ahead.

For the 1980s and beyond, the Italian-American community
has to make its move on the political level. The move has to
come in the arena of public policy and in areas concerning
the quality of life. It must be based on real issues which affect
the community in particular and those social policies which
have an impact upon the values of life in the city and suburb.

A case in point is the presidential election of 1976. The Italian-
Americans rightly could have claimed a major role in the election of President Carter in 1976. Precinct returns show that
Italian-Americans voted overwhelmingly for the Democratic
party in 1976. In addition, an analysis of New Jersey, New
York, Pennsylvania, Connecticut, Massachusetts, and Rhode Island indicate that Italians constitute such an important portion
of the total population that it can be stated that their support
was crucial to Carter's victory. Salvatore LaGumina concluded,
"Realization of this role ought to be reason enough for Italian-
Americans to make their just claims on the Carter administration. With Italian-Americans still establishing a third generation,
it ought to demonstrate the potential impact this group can
have in major elections in the future."[57]

A number of forces have converged to produce a widespread
sense of alienation among ethnic groups in America. The past
fifteen years has witnessed assassinations, an unpopular and
unsuccessful war, racial and generational turmoil, inflation,
unemployment, grave political scandals, and increasing stan-
dardization of American life. The effect of all of this has
been to quicken the velocity of pessimism in America. Popular
belief in the integrity, responsiveness, and competence of the
presidency and Congress has declined markedly. Respect for
the military, corporations, and trade unions has decreased. For
ethnic Americans, group mobility has not materialized to the
extent previously assumed.

There is a message in all of this for Americans in general and Italian-Americans in particular. Disillusionment expresses itself politically in an antigovernment style. In many respects, this comes naturally to Italian-Americans. This antigovernment style of politics, which is so pervasive, is more significant for what it tells about the mood of the electorate than for what it forecasts about the nature of government. Government is not going to wither away or even to diminish. Rather than a withdrawal from politics, Italian-Americans need to be more actively involved. They need to develop a national pressure group capable of support of the entire Italian-American community in order to place its concerns on the agenda of national policy.[58]

16 From Columbus to Watergate

In 1972, the ethnics, hitherto relatively quiet and complacent and predictably Democratic, organized, and rebelling prepared to vote for Richard Nixon in massive numbers. The switch in the ethnic vote was one of the most striking phenomena of the 1972 election, since it was an important element in labor's defection from the Democrats, as many in the trade unions' rank and file are blue-collar ethnics.

Their expression of ethnicity was a display of pride and belligerence along with a sense of grievance and loss: ethnics were just not as happy as they used to be. They came full of hope to their adopted land; without forfeiting their heritage or giving up all their lifestyles, they wanted to assimilate, the sooner the better. As Geno Baroni, director of the Center for Urban Affairs in Washington, D.C. notes:

> We thought the way to become real Americans was to be more patriotic—be better Americans than anyone else. We flocked to American Legion oratorical contests and gave speeches on the flag and the Constitution. And we had to prove something. We had to march [like] the Italians on Columbus Day. We never realized that the WASPs never marched. Every day was their day.[1]

Michael Novak makes this observation:

> The flag to ethnic Americans is not a symbol of bureaucracy or system. . . . It is a symbol of spiritual and moral value. . . .
>
> To ethnics, America is almost a religion. The flag alone proves that they are not stupid, cloddish, dull, but capable of the greatest act men can make: to die for others. The flag is not a patriotic symbol only. It is the symbol of poor wretched people who now have jobs and homes and liberties. It is a symbol of transcendence. . . . When that flag flaps, their dignity is celebrated.
>
> "I am an American!" How many humiliations were endured

until one could say those words and not be laughed at by
nativists.

Where has the dream led, in reality?[2]

By 1972, the ethnics sensed that their values were under assault, the institutions they cherished—church, family, labor
union—were under a cloud. They watched helplessly as the
more affluent whites fled the cities and poor blacks took their
place. Though the affluent limousine liberals moved out to
the safety of the suburbs, the ethnics were expected to bear
the full brunt of the urban crisis. They felt they were being
deserted by those who were making them bear the brunt of
social change. Limousine liberals and the radical chic called for
open housing and integrated schools while their own kids enrolled in private schools and they themselves lived on estates
with high fences miles away from the inner city. The combined
recession and inflation hit ethnics hard. Baroni observes, "The
ethnic worries how he is going to get the money to send his
kid to Penn State and pay for his mother's cortisone shots and
keep up the payments on the house and car."[3] The ethnics
felt left out and looked down upon, confused and angry.

For ethnics, George McGovern was to symbolize everything
that was wrong with the Democratic party in 1972. From their
point of view, he made his first critical mistake when he permitted Mayor Daley's delegation to be thrown out of the Democratic Convention. Though liberals may have been delighted,
the ethnics saw only that a delegation of democratically elected
Polish-Americans, Czech-Americans, Italian-Americans, and others
had been rejected. McGovern instituted quotas at the convention which forced the traditional New Deal coalition out of the
convention. Quotas seemed to go against everything that ethnics
had learned about America. It frightened all of them who now
sensed the rules of the game were being changed while the game
was still being played. McGovern's manner was also not reassur-
ing. As one political pro said at the time, "He comes on like a
soft spoken preacher from South Dakota. That style is hard to
comprehend in a working-class neighborhood." An aide to Mayor
Daley elaborated: "McGovern is the kind of guy who doesn't
sweat. No one is more difficult for an Irish-Catholic to get along
with than one of the nonsweating Methodists." The ethnics
wanted a candidate who shared their sweat and was not put off
by it. The ethnics were attracted to the Republican party
because they were repelled, doubtless against their wishes, by
the Democratic party. It no longer seemed to fit them comfort-
ably in 1972. It used to be the home of the working man, but

they no longer felt welcome. The ethnics viewed the forces behind McGovern as elitist, overly ideological, antilabor, and oblivious to their needs. They saw the Democratic Convention and watched all those people running it who never had a callus in their lives.

No one paid more attention to these developments than Richard Nixon. The Republican campaign was highly organized in its efforts to court the ethnic vote. At the Heritage Groups Division in Washington, contact was maintained with thirty-two ethnic groups. A G.O.P. newsletter reported on all ethnic activities, applauded their accomplishments, and noted the appointment of every ethnic to a federal post. Nothing as elaborate was undertaken by the Democrats. When Nixon was running in 1968, only seven thousand ethnic volunteers helped in his campaign. In 1972, that number dramatically jumped to seventy-five thousand.[4]

On Labor Day, the President made his most vigorous attack on quotas, a direct appeal to ethnic voters. Paul Asciolla describes Nixon's appeal to the resentment among ethnics this way:

> The blacks became the darlings of the 60s, and the ethnics the niggers of the North. They learned the Puritan work ethic and the system of meritocracy, and now they're caught in a game where the rules are changing. They were just about to cross the goal line with the football when they were tapped on the shoulder and told to give the ball back to a black to carry over. They know God is a Democrat, but this year they're voting Republican.[5]

On September 17, 1972, President Nixon flew in by helicopter to Mitchellville, Maryland, just outside of Washington, D.C., where a crowd of some twenty thousand people were celebrating the Twelfth Annual Festival Italiano. He made all of the right moves to appeal to the ethnic votes. Mr. Nixon was met by Secretary of Transportation John Volpe and John Scali, White House aide and former ABC-TV newsman. The President delighted everyone by declaring, "Every time I'm at an Italian-American picnic, I think I have some Italian blood." In addressing the crowd, Nixon praised Italians because "they believe in hard work." He also said that they were religious, loved their families, and gave older people "the respect that they deserve." He went on to say Italians are proud of their heritage, but they are also proud of being Americans. Before leaving, the President presented his donation to the festival to Rev. Anthony Dal Balcon,

Administrator of the Villa Rosa Home for Aged, which he visited before taking off.[6]

While all this was going on, Mike Balzano, President Nixon's White House advisor on ethnic affairs, turned up in Fraser just outside of Detroit for an ethnic salute to Republican Senator Robert Griffin. Balzano was a former garbageman turned businessman who had worked his way up the ladder. He earned his Ph.D. at Georgetown University after having become a successful optician. Here was a living symbol to all ethnics.

Less than a week later, Senator McGovern took his campaign for the presidency to New York's San Gennaro Festival. McGovern paid the usual compliments to his Italian audience. He said, "When other Americans think of their fellow citizens of Italian heritage, these are contributions to be honored and respected. And I, for one, personally deplore unfair and defamatory depictions of Italian-Americans, especially the criminal stereotype too often presented by the entertainment idustry, that distorts and dishonors those contributions to life in our country." Senator McGovern pinned a cash donation on the statue of San Gennaro before leaving New York's Italian community.

On September 26, 1972, President Nixon officially opened the American Museum of Immigration on Liberty Island. The governors of New York and New Jersey were there in the unusually warm sun together with over five thousand people. Mrs. Nixon, Secretary of the Interior Morton, and others with resounding WASP names were seated on the platform while enthusiastic Italians, Poles, Ukranians, Greeks, and Jews, as well as other representatives of ethnic groups in the audience served as a decorative setting. This was another in the President's campaign stops seeking the ethnic vote.[7]

Ironically, the museum opened in the midst of a storm of controversy. The museum's exhibits were to emphasize the so-called old immigration and it slighted those of the post-1880 period. The museum reaffirmed implicitly and explicitly that some American groups were more American than others. The Italian exhibit consisted of a rolling pin, a bible, and a piece of lace. This was the organizers' conception of the Italians' contribution to America. Mexicans have settled in the United States by the thousands, but there was no sign of them in the museum. Perhaps they made the mistake of settling too far south. French-Canadians have populated entire towns in New England, but there was no sign of them either. In fact, most of the groups rooted in a Catholic tradition and culture could not find a parallel expression of recognition in the museum.

On October 12, 1972, McGovern blundered badly on Columbus Day in New York City when he failed to control his supporters. Chanting "We want George!" they held up festivities for fifteen minutes, not realizing what the parade meant to its Italian-American participants.

When McGovern pinned his dollar bill on the statue of San Gennaro for the benefit of the cameras, he was as convincing as Nixon addressing ethnic gatherings or dedicating the Museum of Immigration. Nixon noted the unique importance of the ethnic heritage while vetoing appropriation of moneys legislated by Congress under the Ethnic Heritage Studies Act. As Irving Levine, the Director of the National Project of Ethnic America of The American Jewish Committee, said:

> I thought it was ironic and I was greatly angered that, on Columbus Day of all days, we were informed by government officials that the White House had failed to recommend any funding for the Ethnic Heritage Studies Act. Perhaps the time has come to say to politicians that we have had enough of ribbon cutting, food munching, and parade viewing. We now want substantial funding to help maintain our identity and to help our people make a contribution to the common culture.[8]

But ethnics did not heed Levine's advice, and millions crossed over to the party which they had long identified as that of the WASP establishment. Viewed over a time span extending back to 1964, there was a general defection of American voters from the Democratic coalition to the Republican party. In 1972, ethnics joined this voter defection and pulled the Republican lever under protest. Over 60 percent of Italian-Americans cast their vote for Nixon, while less than 29 percent went for McGovern. In New York City, the Nixon vote among Italian-Americans exceeded 70 percent.[9]

In June 1972, a group consisting mostly of ex-CIA agents, some of whom were associated with President's Nixon's campaign staff, were caught breaking into the Democratic party headquarters in the Watergate building in Washington. Subsequent investigations revealed that the burglary was only a small part of an extensive campaign involving political espionage, campaign sabotage, wire tapping, illegal entry, theft of private records, destruction of campaign finance records, illegal use of funds, perjury, conspiracy to obstruct justice, and other such acts, planned and directed by White House officials and

members of President Nixon's campaign staff. Directly implicated were the President's former Attorney General and closest
political adviser, the President's personal appointments secretary,
the President's personal lawyer and political confidant, the
President's White House counsel, his two top staff members,
and more than a dozen other members of his White House
staff and an equal number of his campaign staff.

President Nixon himself miraculously knew nothing about
it, he insisted, although in subsequent statements he admitted
having suppressed certain parts of the investigation, specifically
an FBI probe into G.O.P. campaign funds that had been di-
verted to a Mexican bank and had been linked to the Watergate
conspirators—an action he said he took because "national security" might have been involved. Nixon also admitted having
authorized break-ins and acts of espionage by White House
intelligence units—although he contended that Watergate occurred without his specific authorization or knowledge. Testimony by others close to the President alleged that for a month
Nixon withheld evidence of a break-in at the office of Daniel
Ellsberg's psychiatrist and may have even ordered it, that he
tampered with the judge presiding over the "Pentagon Papers"
trial of Ellsberg and Russo by offering him the directorship
of the FBI while the trial was still in progress, that he failed
to respond to warnings from his acting FBI director, Patrick
Gray, who informed him of cover-up efforts by highly placed
members of the White House staff, and that he, himself, had
engaged in cover-up activities.[10]

President Nixon most likely would have remained in office
had it not been discovered that there were tapes of all White
House conversations. These revealed that Nixon had known
all along about the Watergate cover-up, had been engaging in
cover-up activities, and had been lying to the public. In August
1974, facing impeachment proceedings in the House of Representatives, Nixon resigned from office. Gerald Ford, the man
picked as Vice President, succeeded to the presidency and, after
some painstaking deliberation, pardoned Nixon.

A very tough Italian-American judge with an inbred hatred
of whitewash was the man who was to pull the plug on the
Watergate affair. There is little doubt that, had Chief Judge
John Sirica not swung a heavy judicial club at defendants in
the Watergate case, the deep involvement of some of President
Nixon's aides and staff members would have remained obscured
if not buried. Sirica made it clear that he would not stand for
a judicial whitewash.

During the courtroom action, Sirica was reluctant to accept the guilty plea from the Watergate burglars. Sirica was visibly impatient with the burglars and was not about to accept their stories. On the last day of their trial, one of the defendants' attorneys complained that Sirica "did not limit himself in acting like a judge. He has become, in addition, a prosecutor and an investigator. Not only does he indicate that the defendants are guilty, but that a lot of people are guilty."[11]

Sirica did exactly that. He left little doubt in the minds of many that the penalties imposed on the defendants would be tempered by their willingness to cooperate with the grand jury and with the Senate investigating committee. And that was what pulled the plug on the Watergate affair. James McCord handed over his now famous letter in which he said that he would talk.

No one should have been surprised at Sirica's conduct of the Watergate trial, at his expression of belief that perjury had been committed before him, at his unconcealed determination to pin responsibility where it belonged.[12] In 1944, he had voiced his opposition to another whitewash.

On November 28, 1944, with a ringing denunciation of the inquiry, Sirica resigned as chief counsel to a House Select Committee probing kickback charges against the FCC. He would be no party to a whitewash, Sirica said of the investigation, "and I submit there is no other word you can use for it than that."[13]

The roots of this man's tough-mindedness and unshakable honesty lie in his family. Fred Ferdinand Sirica was seven years old when he came to this country with his father and mother from the village of San Valentino near Naples. He settled with relatives in Waterbury, Connecticut. Later, he learned to be a barber, and he married Rose Zinno, who was born in New Haven. Their two children Andrew and John were born in Waterbury. But Fred Sirica, perhaps with some vague longing for the Neapolitan sun of his childhood, was always sick in the colder climate.

Life in those early 1900s was a struggle. "In Waterbury," John recalls, "my dad was making $15 or $16 a week as a barber." His father told him, "If you ever learn the barber trade, I'll break your arm." "My mother ran a grocery store and we all lived in one room in the back."[14]

In 1911, Fred Sirica and his young family did something bold and maybe crazy. They just packed up and headed south, with no firm destination in mind. John Sirica recalls little of the journey, but he does remember the mother and the two boys, with their scant possessions, waiting in a railroad station in Atlanta while the father talked to a man about a business venture in Dayton, Ohio.

Off they went to Dayton; but it wasn't the last such odyssey. In the years to come, a more attractive city, a restaurant or grocery business, or some other deal always beckoned, and the trusting Fred Sirica was most of the time taken in, deceived by partners.

They moved to Jacksonville, where the family's circumstances and his father's health improved, although Fred Sirica still had a hacking cough from cigarette smoking. He cut hair, and his wife worked in a little delicatessen, and the boys began to work, too. For a time, "Johnny" was a waiter in an ice-cream parlor by the beach. They lived in Jacksonville for several years, with an interlude in New Orleans; then they came to Richmond, Virginia, and finally to Washington, on the eve of the American entry into World War I, when John was fourteen.

What held this restless family together, as John Sirica tells it, was an abiding affection, the self-sacrificing mother who kept the boys spotless no matter how bad times were, the father who always took them aside to explain the lesson when he was deceived. Also, it seems, a dream. The dream of an immigrant father roving a vast land in search of roots, the paths strewn with treachery, in hope of bettering himself and enabling his boys to get an education and travel farther.[15]

"He had one trait I'll always remember," John Sirica says today about his father, who died in 1940. "He could never understand why people lied to him. He was disappointed when they did. But it didn't make him callous. I like to feel as my father did, when I meet someone for the first time, that I am meeting an honest person."[16]

Active in Republican politics and a frequent advocate before Italian groups for a number of presidential candidates, Sirica was appointed a federal judge by Dwight Eisenhower in 1957. "Hell, yes, I'm a Republican," he still says. "You can't change a fellow's feelings just because you give him a judicial robe. But when I get on the bench then I'm nothing. Politics is out then. Then, it's my duty to search for truth."

Exposure of wrongdoing is the first requisite in achieving justice, and John Sirica deserves the prime credit for taking those vital steps in the Watergate affair. He set the tone and direction for members of Congress, the government prosecutors, judges, jurors, the vast public jury to try to emulate the nonpartisan tough determination and faith of Judge John Sirica who insisted with simple sincerity that, "if the truth just comes out, we'll all be right."[17]

The Watergate affair moved inexorably toward impeachment when the existence of White House tapes was disclosed by Alexander Butterfield before the Senate investigating committee. It was at this point another Italian-American was to take center stage. Peter Rodino, a congressman from Newark, New Jersey, and Chairman of the House Judiciary Committee, was to guide the delicate impeachment hearings in one -of the darkest days of our republic. Until the impeachment proceedings began, Rodino was a little-known congressman from Newark, a big-city liberal who learned the ropes of congressional politics during his twenty-five years of service.

The silver haired and raspy voiced Peter Rodino was born on June 7, 1909, in a tenement on "Drift Street," the title of his unpublished novel. His father was an Italian immigrant who came to the United States when only sixteen years old. His mother died when he was four. Rodino remembers, "She would tell my father, 'Look after him; he's going to amount to something.' "[18]

At one time, Rodino had hopes of becoming a poet—he still loves to recite Shakespeare, Byron, Shelley, and Keats—but he diligently worked his way through the Rutgers University Law School. Rodino was first elected to Congress in 1948. As a congressman, he concentrated on ethnic issues and rose to the chairmanship of the prestigious Judiciary Committee in 1973. As an Italian-American, it did not take long for innuendos to circulate that he was associated with organized crime.

When impeachment became a possibility, House Speaker Carl Albert pointedly suggested to Rodino that, instead of giving the matter to the Judiciary Committee, the House should perhaps set up a special select body to conduct the inquiry. Rodino flatly refused to go along, and Albert gave way.[19]

Rodino did not relish the job of conducting the impeachment inquiry. He had a friendly relationship with Nixon over the years and, he says, "I'd rather find the good in people than the bad."[20]

Promised an unlimited budget by Speaker Albert, Rodino began assembling a separate impeachment staff—which was to grow to 105, nearly half of them lawyers—and started looking for a chief counsel. To avoid any charge of partisanship, Rodino wanted an outsider and a Republican. For two months, while the Democratic leadership squirmed at the delay, Rodino consulted deans of law schools, judges, bar-association officials, and leading attorneys before choosing John Doar in December.

From the start, Rodino recognized the danger that the inquiry would blow up in the hands of the Democrats if the nation perceived it to be a partisan vendetta against the President. Even so, Rodino was charged with partisanship himself early on when he gaveled through decisions on party-line votes to give himself sole subpoena powers. Later, Rodino gave up that right and got strong bipartisan support for the eight subpoenas for presidential tapes, all of which Nixon refused to honor.

Assiduously, Rodino backed off on other matters. Against the advice of Doar, Rodino decided in fairness to allow Presidential Counsel James St. Clair not only to attend the sessions but to question witnesses and to call all six of the witnesses he wanted. And all the while, the chairman was urging the Democratic firebrands to stop calling for impeachment. "I told them that the ultimate judgment was going to be the people's and our performance was going to be so judged," said Rodino. The members went along with Rodino, although not always happily. Snapped Detroit's John Conyers, "I just want to make sure he's not too damn fair."[21]

Rodino steered his faction-torn committee to the goal he had been striving for so diligently all along. Through it all—the proddings from his own leaders and the cries from the White House that he was conducting a "kangaroo court"—Rodino remained collected. As his congressional colleagues acknowledged, Chairman Rodino could say with pride and justification, "We have deliberated, we have been patient, we have been fair."[22]

When the judiciary voted articles of impeachment, he left the committee chambers to talk with the impeachment counsel, John Doar. Rodino was so overwrought "I was making no sense," Rodino rememberd. He then went into a smaller room to call his wife in Newark. "Well, we did it," he managed to say before he broke down in tears.[23]

Watergate was not in the tradition of the rough and tumble American politics, of politics as usual. Spiro Agnew's crimes are in that tradition; they were old-fashioned ones. He simply wanted to live in an expensive house and travel in certain expensive circles. His sins were not mortal sins; they were venial.

Harold Abramson contends that there was something singular in Nixon's crimes. Watergate had been an attempt to corrupt institutions and society. Nixon was unique in political annals in American history because he was rootless, a leader with no sustained ties to ethnic groupings in the American mass. He had no ties to segments of the American people which could furnish him not only with an identity, but also with a moral code, a group conscience, and an anchor for stability.

Nixon, as Abramson views it, derived no consistent solidarity from the Quakers, the religion of his mother and his upbringing. He derived no support from ties with Orange County and southern California. And unlike other politicians, he gained no "ethnic" solidarity with fellow Republicans across the country.

"UnEthnic Man," according to Abramson, lacks identity as well as ethnicity. He does not know who he is in the American mass. It is not enough, really, to be just American. What is frightening about the people who surrounded President Nixon was their lack of any moral fiber. "UnEthnic Man" has no group constraint, no intermediating or tempering moral code, to restrain his mobility. He has nothing to guide his behavior in crisis either.[24]

After the October 1973 Saturday Night Massacre, in which Archibald Cox and William Ruckelshaus were fired and Elliot Richardson resigned, Carl Albert, the Speaker of the House, quietly channeled the impeachment inquiry to Peter Rodino's Judiciary Committee. Rodino moved quickly but prudently into the settling of an impeachment timetable. The White House tapes were to seal the President's fate. Months after the President had resigned, the nation learned about certain portions of the tapes. Rodino had heard one in particular with dismay and got his committee's ranking Republican, Edward Hutchinson, to agree to its suppression. It was too inflammatory and too divisive. This is what Nixon told Ehrlichman:

> NIXON: The Italians. We mustn't forget the Italians. Must do something for them. The, ah, we can't forget them. They're not, we, ah they're not like us. Difference is, the ... they smell different, they look different, act different. After all, you can't blame them. Oh, no. Can't do that. They've never had the things we've had.
>
> ERLICHMAN: That's right.
>
> NIXON: Of course, the trouble is ... you can't find one that's honest.[25]

To his sorrow, the President ran into not one Italian, Rodino, but a second, John Sirica, who from Nixon's point of view were fatally honest. Beyond them were the millions of other

Italians, Poles, Jews, and other ethnics who were honest. It is a supreme irony of history that the man of law and order was to countenance the breaking of the law. The people who were some of the principal actors in the Watergate drama had names like Rodino, Sirica, Gagliardi, Jaworski, Ben Veniste. They upheld the law and our constitutional system and dealt with Nixon's "breach of faith," openly, fairly, and honestly.[26]

Eril Amfitheatrof, in a poignant conclusion to *Children of Columbus,* asserted, "The Italians who reached the New World, starting with Columbus, were usually outsiders struggling against great odds, and the best of them were brave, beautiful human beings full of warmth and a large-hearted concern for humanity."[27] The Italian-American experience is a portrait of courage, hard work, love, and humanity. As such, it is a source of self-awareness, pride, and strength for future generations.

My dear friend, Rose Basile Green, captured the essence of the Italian-American in "Primo Vino":

> Italians here are like the flow of wine,
> The Primo Vino that ferments the grape;
> Like pristine truths the oracles define,
> They tap the source that gives the vision shape.
> From grapes they press three grades of wine are drawn:
> The first, the elixir of virgin birth;
> The second, juiced until the skins are gone;
> The third, a watery sludge of little worth.
> In company, they celebrate the best,
> For each the other values by his cup;
> At home, the lesser is enough to rest;
> While for the crowd the dredge is measured up.
> They brought the cup to toast the new land's vine;
> They broke the maidenhead, made first the wine.[28]

Notes

Preface

1. Maldwyn Jones, *American Immigration* (Chicago: University of Chicago Press, 1960), p. 1.
2. Oscar Handlin, *The Uprooted* (New York: Grosset and Dunlap, 1951), p. 3.

1. From Columbus to Colombo

1. Samuel Eliot Morison, *Christopher Columbus, Mariner* (New York: New American Library, 1956), p. 35.
2. Ibid.
3. Ernle Bradford, *Christopher Columbus* (New York: Viking Press, 1973), pp. 94–141. See also Samuel E. Morison, *Admiral of the Ocean Sea* (New York: Oxford University Press, 1910).
4. "Vineland Map a Forgery," *Italo-American Times*, February 1974, p. 1.
5. Ibid.
6. "Italians Downgraded," *Bergen Evening Record*, February 3, 1977, p. 3.
7. Denys Hay, *The Italian Renaissance* (London: Cambridge University Press, 1961), pp. 10–25, 101–49.
8. Morison, *Christopher Columbus*, p. 148.
9. Michael Novak, *The Rise of the Unmeltable Ethnics* (New York: Macmillan, 1971), p. 4.
10. Patrick Gallo, *Ethnic Alienation: The Italian-Americans* (Cranford, N.J.: Fairleigh Dickinson University Press, 1974).

2. Destiny

1. Rose Scherini, "Ethnicity Maintenance in the Italian-American Community of San Francisco, 1940–1975," in Patrick Gallo, ed., *The Urban Experience of Italian-Americans* (New York: American Italian Historical Association, 1977), pp. 36–51.
2. There are a number of excellent works which chronicle the early

history of Italians in America. See Alexander DeConde, *Half Bitter, Half Sweet* (New York: Scribner's, 1971); Erik Amfitheatrof, *The Children of Columbus* (Boston: Little, Brown, 1973); Luciano Iorizzio and Salvatore Mondello, *The Italian-Americans* (New York: Twayne, 1971); Andrew Rolle, *The American Italians* (Belmont, Cal.: Wadsworth, 1972); Margherita Marchione, *Philip Mazzei; Jefferson's Zealous Whig* (New York: American Institute of Italian Studies, 1976).

3. Joanne Pellegrino, "An Effective School of Patriotism," in Francesco Cordasco, ed. *Studies in Italian-American Social History* (Totowa, N.J.: Rowman and Littlefield, 1975), pp. 84–104. See also Giorgio Spini, "The Perceptions of America in Italian Consciousness," in Humbert Nelli, ed., *The United States and Italy: The First Two Hundred Years.* (New York: American Historical Association, 1977), pp. 49–59.

4. Gallo, *Ethnic Alienation,* pp. 43–72.

5. *Summary of Italian Statistics, 1861–1955* (Rome, Italy: Central Institute of Statistics, 1968), p. 14.

6. Joseph Lopreato, *The Italian-Americans* (New York: Random House, 1970), p. 35.

7. Joseph LaPalombara, "Italy: Fragmentation, Isolation, Alienation," in Lucian Pye, *Political Culture and Political Development* (Princeton, N.J.: Princeton University Press, 1965), pp. 282–329.

8. René Albrecht-Carrié, *Italy from Napoleon to Mussolini.* (New York: Columbia University Press, 1950), pp. 5–9.

9. Robert Ardrey, *The Territorial Imperative* (New York: Dell Publishing Co., 1966), p. 184.

10. Albrecht-Carrié, "Italy," p. 9.

11. The capital was changed from Reggio Calabria to Catanzaro. *New York Times,* October 17, 1970.

12. Massimo Salvadori, *Italy* (Englewood Cliffs, N.J.: Prentice Hall, 1965), pp. 81–98. See also Dennis M. Smith, *The Making of Italy, 1796–1870* (New York: Walker & Co., 1968) pp.12–55.

13. Ibid., p. 89. See also Giuseppe di Lampedusa, *The Leopard* (New York: Pantheon Books, 1960).

14. Luigi Barzini, *The Italians* (New York: Atheneum, 1965), p. 157.

15. Ibid., p. 165.

16. Smith, *Making of Italy,* pp. 223–35. See also Eric Whelpton, *A Concise History of Italy* (New York: Roy Publishers, 1964), pp. 174–83.

17. Smith, *Making of Italy,* pp. 214–27. See also Robert Katz, *The Fall of the House of Savoy* (New York: Macmillan, 1971).

18. Albrecht-Carrié, "Italy," p. 7.

19. Ibid., pp. 36–43.

20. Ibid., pp. 48–66. See also Salvadori, *Italy,* pp. 107–11; Dennis Mack Smith, *Italy: A Modern History* (Ann Arbor: University of Michigan Press, 1968), pp. 49–51.

21. Ibid.

22. Instituto Centrale di Statistica, *Annuario Statistico Italiana, 1886,* p. 954.
23. Luigi Barzini, "Italy: The Fragile State," *Foreign Affairs* (April 1968), p. 564.
24. A. C. Jemolo, *Church and State in Italy 1850–1950* (Oxford, Eng.: Beauchurd, 1960).
25. Ibid., pp. 319–35.
26. LaPalombara, *Italy,* p. 302.
27. Amfitheatrof, *Children of Columbus,* p. 147.
28. Carlo Levi, *Christ Stopped at Eboli,* trans. Frances Fenaye (New York: Farrar, Straus, and Giroux: Noonday Press, 1969), p. 4.
29. Leonard Covello, *The Social Background of the Italo American School Child* (Leiden: E. J. Brill, 1969), pp. 34–64.
30. Ibid., pp. 66–67.
31. Ibid.
32. Ignazio Silone, *Fontamara* (London, Eng.: Methuen Publishers, 1934), p. 30.
33. Lopreato, *Italian-Americans,* pp. 27–31.
34. DeConde, *Half Bitter, Half Sweet,* p. 79.
35. Barzini, *Italians,* p. 165.
36. Grazia Dore, "Some Social and Historical Aspects of Italian Emigration to America," *Journal of Social History* (Winter 1968), pp. 109–10.
37. Edward Stibili, "The Interest of Bishop Giovanni Battista Scalabrini of Piacenza in the Italian Problem," in Silvano Tomasi, ed., *The Religious Experience of Italian-Americans* (New York: American Italian-Historical Association, 1975), pp. 13–17.
38. Ann Novotny, *Strangers at the Door* (New York: Bantam Books, 1972), p. 9.
39. Ibid., p. 11.
40. Ibid., p. 15.
41. Ibid., p. 18.
42. Ibid., pp. 18–19.
43. *Mental Examination of Immigrants, Administration and Line Inspection at Ellis Island,* quoted in Giulio Miranda, "Stereotypes," *Italo-American Times,* March 1, 1976, p. 5.
44. Ibid.
45. Novotny, *Strangers at the Door,* p. 28.
46. Gino Speranza, "Handicaps in America," in Lydio F. Tomasi, ed., *The Italian in America: The Progressive View* (New York: Center for Migration Studies, 1972), p. 67.

3. We Have Arrived

1. Rudolph Bell, "Emigration from Four Italian Villages: Strategy and Decision," in Gallo, ed., *The Urban Experience of Italian-Americans,* pp. 9–35. See also Harry Jebsen, Jr., "Assimilation in a Working Class Suburb: The Italians of Blue Island, Illinois," in

Gallo, ed., *The Urban Experience of Italian-Americans,* pp. 64–84; Paul Loatman, Jr., "Contadini in the New World Paese," unpublished paper delivered at the American Italian Historical Conference, "The Urban Experience of Italian-Americans," held at Queens College, New York, November 14-15, 1975.

2. Iorizzio and Mondello, *Italian-Americans,* pp. 87–108.
3. Antonio Mangano, "The Associated Life of Italians in New York City," in Tomasi, *The Italian in America,* p. 107.
4. Viola Roseboro, "The Italians in New York," *Cosmopolitan* (January 1888)., p. 3.
5. Gallo, *Ethnic Alienation,* p. 106.
6. Mangano, in Tomasi, ed., *The Italian in America,* p. 106.
7. Emily W. Dinwiddie, "Some Aspects of Italian Housing and Social Conditions in Philadelphia," in Tomasi, ed., *The Italian in America,* pp. 120–23.
8. Antonio Stella, "Tuberculosis and the Italians in the United States," in Tomasi, ed., *The Italian in America,* pp. 116–19. See also Rocco Brindisi, "The Italian and Public Health," in Tomasi, ed., *The Italian in America,* pp. 113–15.
9. DeConde, *Half Bitter, Half, Sweet,* p. 85.
10. Silvano Tomasi, "Militantism and Italian-American Unity," in Frances X. Femminella, ed., *Power and Class* (New York: American Italian Historical Association, 1973), p. 21. See also Iorizzio and Mondello, *Italian Americans,* pp. 87–107; Mangano, in Tomasi, ed., *The Italian in America,* pp. 87–107.
11. Jebsen, in Gallo, ed., *The Urban Experience of Italian-Americans,* p. 70.
12. Loatman, in Gallo, ed., *The Urban Experience of Italian-Americans,* p. 10.
13. Covello, *Social Background,* p. 365.
14. Leonard Covello, *The Heart Is the Teacher* (New York: McGraw Hill, 1958), pp. 43–44.
15. Sister Mary Fabian Matthews, "The Role of the Public Schools in the Assimilation of the Italian Immigrant Child in New York City, 1900–1914," in S. Tomasi and M. Engel, eds., *The Italian Experience in the United States* (New York: Center for Migration Studies, 1970), pp. 129–41.
16. Covello, *The Heart Is the Teacher,* p. 43.
17. Nathan Glazer and Daniel Moynihan, *Beyond the Melting Pot* (Cambridge, Mass.: M.I.T. Press, 1963), p. 200.
18. Phyllis H. Williams, *South Italian Folkways in Europe and America* (New Haven, Conn.: Yale University Press, 1938), pp. 132–33.
19. Frederic J. Haskin, *The Immigrant: An Asset and a Liability* (New York: Fleming H. Revell Co., 1913), p. 141.
20. John H. Mariano, *The Second Generation of Italians in New York City* (Boston: Christopher Publishing House, 1921), pp. 63–64.
21. Covello, *The Heart Is the Teacher,* pp. 75–76.

22. Grace Abbott, *The Immigrant and the Community* (New York: The Century Co., 1917), p. 223.
23. Ibid.
24. Caroline Ware, *Greenwich Village, 1920–1930* (Boston: Houghton Mifflin Co., 1935), p. 131.
25. Eugene Mullan, "Mentality of Arriving Immigrants," Public Health Bulletin #9 (Washington, D.C.: U.S. Government Printing Office, 1917), pp. 118–19. See also Benjamin Fine, *The Stranglehold of the I.Q.* (New York: Doubleday, 1975).
26. Bernard Rosen "Race, Ethnicity and Achievement Syndrome," *American Sociological Review* 24 (October 1959), pp. 47–60.
27. Ibid., p. 48.
28. As Lopreato points out with regard to these three aspects, "Equipped with this conceptual scheme, Rosen turned to his students enrolled in two sociology classes who, with instructions never made public, spent their Christmas vacation in sixty-two communities in four states in the Northeast interviewing pairs of mothers and sons belonging to different nationality and racial groups." "Social Science Achievement Motivation Among Italian Americans," in Frank Femminella, ed., *Power and Class: The Italian American Experience Today* (New York: American Italian Historical Association, 1973), pp. 1–11.
29. Rosen, "Race, Ethnicity and Achievement Syndrome," p. 60.
30. Ibid., p. 6.
31. Ibid., p. 7.
32. Fred Strodtbeck, Margaret McDonald and Bernard Rose, "Evaluation of Occupation: A Reflection of Jewish and Italian Mobility Differences," *American Sociological Review,* 22 (October 1957), pp. 546–53.
33. Fred Strodtbeck, "Family Interaction, Values and Achievement," in Marshall Sklare, ed., *The Jews: Social Patterns of an American Group* (New York: Free Press, 1958), p. 150.
34. Joseph Lopreato, *The Italian Americans* (New York: Random House, 1970), p. 154.
35. This is not an uncommon practice today in many of our urban schools.
36. Lopreato, *Italian Americans,* p. 160.
37. Ibid., p. 164.
38. Ibid., p. 165.
39. Ibid., pp. 164–65.
40. Ibid., p. 165.
41. Sarah Wool Moore, "The Teaching of Foreigners," in Tomasi, ed., pp. 57–63.
42. Melvyn Dubofsky, "Education and the Italian and Jewish Community Experience," in Jean Scarpaci, ed., *The Interaction of Italians and Jews in America* (New York: American Italian Historical Association, 1975), pp. 57–61.

43. Hutchins Hapgood, "The Italian Theatre of New York," in *The Bookman* (August 1900), pp. 8–12.
44. Maxine Seller, "Theater and Community: The Popular Theater of San Francisco: 1905–1925," in Patrick Gallo, ed., *The Urban Experience of Italian-Americans*, pp. 52–63.
45. Ibid.
46. Mangano, in Tomasi, ed., *The Italian in America*, p. 110.
47. Rose Basile Green, "The Italian-American Novel in the Main Stream of American Literature," J. Cammet, ed., *The Italian American Novel* (New York: American Italian Historical Association, 1969), pp. 1–5. See also Rose Basile Green, *The Italian-American Novel* (Cranbury, N.J.: Fairleigh Dickinson University Press, 1974).
48. Green, in Cammet, ed., *The Italian-American Novel*, p. 1. For the image of Italian-Americans in modern drama, see Peter Ventimiglia, "Through Other's Eyes: The Image of Italian Americans in Modern Drama," *Italian-Americana* 2 (Spring 1976), pp. 226–39.
49. Mario Puzo, "Choosing a Dream," in T. Wheeler, ed., *The Immigrant Experience* (Baltimore, Md.: Penquin Books, 1971), p. 47.
50. Robert Oppedisano, "Roseto Revisited," I-AM, February 1977, p. 35.
51. Bill Beeney, "Paying Tribute to a Patriarch in Italian Style," *Democrat and Chronicle*, November 20, 1975, p. 2.
52. Cuomo, in Gallo, ed., *Experience of Italian-Americans*, pp. 3–4.

4. The Rich Have It All But Accomplish Little

1. Frank Capra, *The Name Above the Title*, (New York: Macmillan, 1971), p. 15.
2. Ibid., p. 16.
3. See Giovanni Schiavo, *Antonio Meucci: Inventor of the Telephone* (New York: The Vigo Press, 1958).
4. *New York Times*, September 27, 1884.
5. *New York World*, October 8, 1885.
6. "Amadeo P. Giannini and the Bank of America," *Italo-American Times*, February 1975, p. 13.
7. Ibid., p. 13.
8. DeConde, *Half Bitter, Half Sweet*, pp. 88, 239, 276–77. See also Iorizzio and Mondello, *The Italian Americans*, p. 113; Rolle, *The American Italians*, pp. 90–91; Joseph Giovianco, "Democracy and Banking: The Bank of Italy and California's Italians," *California Historical Quarterly*, 47 (September 1968), pp. 195–218.

5. Bread! Work! Justice!—From Salem to Paterson

1. Thomas Cousins, "Analysis of the Treatment of Italians in Senior High School American History Textbooks," in P. Gallo, ed., *The Urban Experience of Italian Americans*, pp. 159–72.
2. Robert Foerester, *The Italian Emigration of Our Times* (Boston: Harvard University Press, 1919), p. 401.

3. Rolle, *American Italians,* pp. 92–93. See also Andrew Rolle, *The Immigrant Upraised* (Norman: University of Oklahoma Press, 1968), pp. 110–25.
4. Oscar Handlin, *Race and Nationality* (New York: Doubleday, 1957), pp. 74–140.
5. Maldwyn A. Jones, *American Immigration* (Chicago: University of Chicago Press, 1960), pp. 177–83.
6. Ibid.
7. Luciano Iorizzo, "The Padrone and Immigrant Distribution," in Tomasi and Engel, *The Italian Experience in the United States,* p. 57.
8. Humbert Nelli, "The Italian Padrone System in the United States," *Labor History* 3 (Spring 1964), pp. 153–67.
9. Tomasi, *Italians in America,* p. 88.
10. Rolle, *American Italians,* pp. 61–62.
11. Richard Hofstadter, *The Age of Reform* (New York: Vintage, 1960), pp. 179–80.
12. Edwin Fenton "Italian Immigrants in the Stoneworkers Union," *Labor History* 3 (Spring 1962), pp. 188–207.
13. Jones, *American Immigration,* pp. 207–23.
14. Edwin Fenton, "Immigrants and Unions: A Case Study, Italians and American Labor, 1870–1920." See also Edwin Fenton, unpublished Ph.D. dissertation, Harvard University, 1957; "Italians in the Labor Movements," *Pennsylvania History* 26 (April 1959), pp. 133–48.
15. Mario De Ciampis "Storia del Movimento Socialista Rivoluzionario Italiano," *La Parola del Popolo, Cinquantesimo Anniversario, 1908–1958* 9 (December 1958-January 1959), pp. 136–63.
16. Fenton, "Italians in the Labor Movements," pp. 133–48.
17. Nunzio Pernicone, "Anarchism in Italy, 1872–1900," in P. Vecoli, ed., *Italian American Radicalism: Old World Origins and New World Developments* (New York: American Italian Historical Association, 1972), pp. 1–29.
18. Patrick J. Gallo. *Political Trials in America* (Boston: Allyn & Bacon, forthcoming).
19. DeCiampis, *La Parola del Popolo,* pp. 136–63.
20. Pernicone, *Italian-American Radicalism,* pp. 1–29.
21. DeCiampis, *La Parola del Popolo,* pp. 136–63.
22. Samuel L. Baily, "The Italians and Organized Labor in the United States and Argentina, 1880–1910," *The International Migration Review* (1967), pp. 56–66.
23. Patrick Renshaw, *The Wobblies* (Garden City, N.Y.: Doubleday, 1968), pp. 21–41. See also Philip Foner, *The IWW, 1905–1911* (New York: International Publishers, 1965).
24. Ibid., pp. 97–117.
25. Philip Foner, *History of the Labor Movement in the United States* (New York: International Publishers, 1963), p. 314.
26. Ibid.

27. James Heaton, "The Salem Trial," in Tomasi, *Italians in America*, p. 220.
28. Ibid., p. 221.
29. Ibid., p. 218.
30. Renshaw, *The Wobblies*, p. 106.
31. Renshaw, *The Wobblies*, pp. 141–42.
32. Ben Aronowitz quoted in Mel Most, "The 1913 Silk Terror," *The Sunday Record Magazine*, September 30, 1975, p. 12.
33. Pernicone, *Italian-American Radicalism* pp. 24–29.
34. Gallo, *Political Trials in America*, pp. 38–42.
35. John Crawford, *Luigi Antonini, His Influence on Italian-American Radicals* (New York: ILGWU, 1959).

6. "The Dagoes Shot Me"

1. De Conde, *Half Bitter, Half Sweet*, pp. 18–35. See also H. R. Marraro, "Italian Americans in Eighteenth Century New York," *New York History* 21 (July 1940), pp. 316–23.
2. John Higham, *Strangers in the Land* (New York: Atheneum, 1963), p. 3.
3. Ibid., pp. 3–11.
4. Iorzzio and Mondello, *The Italian-Americans*, pp. 87–89, 109–11.
5. Hofstadter, *Age of Reform*, p. 135.
6. Ibid., p. 137.
7. Ibid., pp. 137, 181–82.
8. Higham, *Strangers in the Land*, p. 78.
9. Ibid., p. 47.
10. Ibid., p. 48.
11. "To Prohibit the Immigration of Foreign Contract Labor into the United States," House Report No. 444, *Congressional Record* 48th Cong., 1st sess., 1883, pp. 5349–50.
12. Higham, *Strangers in the Land*, p. 181.
13. Ibid., p. 90.
14. Salvatore Mondello, "The Italian Immigrant in Urban America, 1880–1920, as Reported in the Contemporary Periodical Press," unpublished Ph.D. dissertation, New York University, 1960.
15. Iorizzio and Mondello, *The Italian-Americans*, p. 74.
16. *Detroit Plaindealer*, May 29, 1891.
17. Ibid., June 26, 1981.
18. *Washington Colored American*, April 18, 1903.
19. Anthony Margavio, "The Reaction of the Press to the Italian-Americans of New Orleans, 1880 to 1920," *Italian Americana* (Fall/Winter 1978), pp. 72–83.
20. *Times Democrat*, October 16, 1890.
21. E. J. Hobswan, *Primitive Rebels* (New York: W. W. Norton, 1965), pp. 42, 92–107.

22. DeConde, *Half Bitter, Half Sweet,* p. 122. See also Richard Cambino, *Vendetta* (Garden City, N.J.: n.p., 1977).

23. Ibid., p. 123.

24. Arnold Shankman, "The Image of Italians in the Afro-American Press, 1886–1936," *Italian Americana* (Fall 1978), p. 33.

25. Jean Scarpaci, "Immigrants in the New South: Italians in Louisiana's Sugar Parishes, 1880–1910," in F. Cordasco, ed., *Italian Social History,* p. 138.

26. Roger Shugg, *Origins of the Class Struggle in Louisiana* (Baton Rouge: Louisiana State University Press, 1953), p. 240.

27. George Cunningham, "The Italian: A Hindrance to White Solidarity in Louisiana," *Journal of Negro History,* 50 (1965), pp. 23–25.

28. Iorizzio and Mondello, *The Italian-Americans,* pp. 113, 136.

29. *New Orleans Daily Picayne,* November 12, 1890.

30. Luciano Iorizzio, "Italian Migration and the Impact of the Padrone System," Ph.D. dissertation, Syracuse University, 1966, p. 238.

31. *New Orleans Times Democrat,* October 21, 1890. See also John E. Coxe "The New Orleans Mafia Incident," *Louisiana Historical Quarterly,* 20 (1937) pp. 1070–73; John S. Kendall, "Who Killa da Chief?" *Louisiana Historical Quarterly,* 22 (1939) pp. 492–530.

32. C. Vann Woodward, *Origins of the New South* (Baton Rouge: Louisiana State University Press, 1951), pp. 230–60; T. Harry Williams, "The Louisiana Unification Movement of 1873," *Journal of Southern History* 11 (1945), pp. 356–68.

33. Williams, "Louisiana Unification Movement," pp. 356–68.

34. John F. Carr, "The Coming of the Italians," *The Outlook* 82 (1906), pp. 418–31.

35. Cunningham, "The Italian," pp. 28–35. Robert L. Brandfon, "The End of Immigration to the Cotton Fields," *The Mississippi Valley Historical Review* 50 (1964), pp. 591–610. Brandfon explains that "the Italians assumed the status of Negroes. One blended into the other, and Southern thinking made no effort to distinguish them." The conflict that followed should be viewed in the light of one group attempting to impose (utilizing its traditional method, lynching) its perceptions upon the "other."

36. Alice Fortier, *A History of Louisiana* (Baton Rouge, La.: Glaitors Publishing Div., 1940), pp. 153–56. See also Melvin J. White, "Populism in Louisiana During the Nineties," *Mississippi Valley Historical Review* (June 1918), pp. 7–10.

37. Cunningham, "The Italians," p. 25.

38. Woodward, *Origins of the New South,* pp. 255–57.

39. Kendall, "Who Killa da Chief?" p. 508.

40. Cunningham, "The Italians," p. 34.

41. Sheldon Hackney, "Southern Violence," *American Historical Review* 74 (1969), pp. 906–25.

42. Joseph Albini. *The American Mafia* (New York: Appleton Century Crofts, 1971), pp. 175–200.
43. Coxe, "New Orleans," p. 1072. See also Kendall, "Who Killa da Chief?" pp. 509–11; *New Orleans Times-Democrat*, October 21, 1890.
44. Coxe, "New Orleans," pp. 1072ff. The *New Orleans Times-Democrat*, October 19, 1890, carried the story, as provided to the paper by the Provenzanos.
45. Ibid., pp. 1069–73; Kendall, "Who Killa da Chief?" pp. 503–10.
46. Kendall, "Who Killa da Chief?" p. 514. See also the *New Orleans Times-Democrat*, October 19, 1890.
47. *New Orleans Daily Picayune*, March 14, 1891.
48. Kendall, "Who Killa da Chief?" p. 514.
49. It has been suggested to me that the yellow fever epidemic of 1905, which originated in the Italian Quarter, may also have been a factor in heightening prejudice against the Italian colony. While this may have been the case, I have been unable to find any documentary evidence to substantiate such an assumption.
50. *The New Orleans Item*, June 6, 1937, p. 10.
51. *L'Italiano-Americano*, October 5, 1912, p. 3.
52. Bruno Roselli, *Let the Dead Speak!* (Poughkeepsie N.Y.: Artcraft Press, 1929), p. 2.
53. *L'Italiano-Americano*, October 5, 1912, p. 3.
54. U.S. Bureau of the Census, *Fourteenth Census of the United States: Abstract*, p. 432. It should be noted that these figures are for the entire state, rather than for just the city of New Orleans.
55. Ibid., p. 437.
56. The *New Orleans Times-Picayune*, June 11, 1916, Section 5, p. 1.
57. *La Voce Coloniale*, September 30, 1922, p. 1.
58. Actually, the Italians did not achieve any notable political success until much later. The breakthrough came with the election of Mayor Maestri to office.
59. A. Frangini, *Italians in New Orleans, Louisiana* (New Orleans: Italo-Americana Press, 1912), pp. 53–54.
60. *New Orleans Item*, June 6, 1937, p. 10.
61. Roselli, *Let the Dead Speak*, p. 3.
62. *La Voce Coloniale*, September 30, 1922, p. 2. Andrea Schiro was the father of Victor Schiro, who later became mayor of New Orleans.
63. *New Orleans Times-Picayune*, March 22, 1922, p. 7.
64. *New Orleans Item-Tribune*, July 11, 1926, p. 6.

7. That Agony Is Our Triumph

1. Madison Grant, *The Passing of the Great Race; or The Racial Basis of European History* (New York: Charles Scribner's Sons, 1916), pp. 229–30.

2. Arnold Shankman, "The Image of the Italian," *Italian-Americana* (Autumn 1974), pp. 30–31.
3. Iorizzio and Mondello, *The Italian Americans*, p. 159.
4. Theodore Bingham, "Foreign Criminals in New York," *North American Review* (1908) pp. 383–94.
5. Theodore Bingham, "How to Give New York the Best Police Force in the World," *North American Review* (1908), pp. 702–11.
6. George Pozzetta, "Another Look at the Petrosino Affair," *Italian-Americana* (Autumn 1974), pp. 81–89.
7. Joseph Petrosino to Theodore Bingham, Feb. 24, 1909, New York City Police Department Archives, "Petrosino File" (New York, N.Y.). See also William Henry Bishop to Professor Rallo, March 6, 1909, "Papers on Petrosino Murder Case, Palermo Consulate, 1905–1912," Box I (Yale University Library, New Haven, Connecticut).
8. Pozzetta, "Petrosino Affair," pp. 85–87.
9. Oscar Handlin, *Race and Nationality* (Garden City, N.Y.: Doubleday, 1957), pp. 78–79.
10. Ibid., p. 81.
11. Ibid.
12. Ibid., p. 84.
13. Woodrow Wilson, quoted in Jones, *American Immigration*, p. 239.
14. Woodrow Wilson, in *The Immigrants Experience* (Middletown, Conn.: Xerox Corp., 1967), p. 36.
15. Robert Murray, *Red Scares: A Study in National Hysteria, 1919–1920* (New York: McGraw-Hill, 1955), p. 67.
16. Higham, *Strangers at the Door*, pp. 228–31.
17. Murray, *Red Scares*, pp. 92–104, 224–25. For an historical analysis of the period from 1898 to 1924, see Patrick Gallo, *Swords and Plowshares—The United States and Disarmament, 1898–1963* (Manhattan, Kansas: Military Affairs/Aerospace Historian Publishing, 1980).
18. Gallo, *Political Trials*, pp. 126–27.
19. Frances Russell, *Tragedy in Dedham* (New York: McGraw-Hill, 1962), pp. 68–69.
20. Ibid., p. 65.
21. Ibid., p. 110.
22. Felix Frankfurter, *The Case of Sacco and Vanzetti* (New York: Little, Brown, 1961), pp. 47–58.
23. Russell, *Tragedy in Dedham*, p. 207.
24. From the Sacco Vanzetti Case, Transcript of the Record of the Trial in the Courts of Massachusetts, Vol. V., pp. 4896–904.
25. Clay Burton, "Italian American Relations and the Case of Sacco and Vanzetti," in Vecoli, *Italian American Radicalism*, pp. 65–80.
26. Russell, *Tragedy in Dedham*, p. 8.
27. *New York World*, May 13, 1927. See also David Felix, *Protest: Sacco and Vanzetti and the Intellectuals* (Bloomington: Indiana University Press, 1965).
28. See Louis Joughin and Edmund M. Morgan, *The Legacy of Sacco and Vanzetti* (Princeton, N.J.: Princeton University Press, 1948).

324   NOTES

29. "Sacco-Vanzetti Win Vindication," *Bergen Evening Record*, July 28, 1978, p. A-4.
30. Ibid.
31. Ibid.
32. Walter Goodman, "Sacco, Vanzetti and Me," *New York Times Magazine*, August 22, 1976, p. 7.

8. La Famiglia

1. Barzini, *The Italians*, p. 190. See also Aubrey Menen, "The Italian Family Is a Commune," *New York Times Magazine*, March 1, 1970, pp. 22–23, 77–83.
2. Anthony Polizzi, "Southern Italy: Its Peasantry and Change," Ph.D. dissertation, Cornell University, 1958, p. 22.
3. Richard Gambino, *Blood of My Blood* (New York: Doubleday, 1974), pp. 1–38.
4. Covello, *The Social Background of the Italo-American School Child*, p. 151. See also Francis Femminella, "The Italian American Family," in M. Barashand and A. Scourby, *Marriage and the Family* (New York: Random House, 1970).
5. Jerre Mangione, *Mount Allegro* (Boston: Houghton, Mifflin, 1943), pp. 24–25.
6. Barzini, *The Italians*, p. 190.
7. Edward Banfield, *Moral Basis of a Backward Society* (Glencoe, Ill.: Free Press, 1958), pp. 103–20.
8. Polizzi, *Southern Italy*, p. 71.
9. Ibid., pp. 74–75.
10. Ibid.
11. Covello, *Social Background*, p. 161.
12. Banfield, *Moral Basis of a Backward Society*, pp. 82–85.
13. Covello, *Social Background*, p. 162.
14. Mangione, *Mount Allegro*, p. 25.
15. Clement L. Valletta, "Family Life—The Question of Independence," in Cordasco, *Studies in Italian American Social History*, p. 154.
16. Menen, "The Italian Family Is a Commune," p. 78.
17. Banfield, *Moral Basis of a Backward Society*, p. 83.
18. Leonard Moss, "The Family in Southern Italy: Yesterday and Today," in Nelli, *United States and Italy*, p. 185.
19. Moss, quoted in Nelli, *United States and Italy*, p. 185.
20. Sydel Silverman, "Amoral Familism Reconsidered," *American Anthropologist* (February 1964), p. 3.
21. The term *community* in Italian does not stand for national or public mindedness, but rather for the comunity that exists in the monastery.
22. Silverman, "Amoral Familism Reconsidered," p. 3.
23. Vincenzo Cezaro, "Immigranti e associacizionismi voluntaria," *Studi Emigrazioni* (October 1966), pp. 29–50. See also Pier Gio-

vanni Grasso, *Personalita Giovaniti in Tranzione: Del Familismo al Personalismo* (Zurich: Pas Verlag, 1964).
24. Francis Ianni, "The Italo American Teenager," *The Annals* (November 1961), p. 74.
25. Paul Campisi, "Ethnic Family Patterns: The Italian Family in the United States," *American Journal of Sociology* (1948), pp. 434–47.
26. Bartolomeo Palisi, "Patterns of Social Participation in a Two Generation Sample of Italian Americans," *Sociological Quarterly* (Spring 1966), pp. 167–78. See also Virginia Yans-McLaughlin, *Family and Community—Italian Immigrants in Buffalo, 1880–1930* (Ithaca, N.Y.: Cornell University Press, 1977).
27. Ibid., pp. 167–78.
28. Campisi, "Ethnic Family Patterns," pp. 444–49.
29. Francis A. J. Ianni, "Residential and Occupational Mobility as Indices of the Acculturation of an Ethnic Group," *Social Forces* (October 1957), pp. 65–72.
30. Palisi, "Patterns of Social Participation," p. 50.
31. Valletta, "Family Life," pp. 156–57.
32. Michael Novak, "The Family People," *Newsletter of Empac* (September 1975), p. 1.
33. Colleen L. Johnson, "The Maternal Role in the Contemporary Italian-American Family," in L. Tomasi, R. Harney, and B. Caroli, *The Italian Immigrant Woman in North America* (Toronto, Can.: Multicultural History Society on Ontario, n.d.), pp. 234–45. See also Hugh Carter and Paul Glick, *Marriage and Divorce: A Social and Economic Study* (Cambridge: Harvard University Press, 1976).

9. Cabrini and Covello

1. Pietro DiDonato, *Immigrant Saint* (New York: McGraw-Hill, 1960), pp. 1–110.
2. Edward E. Stibili, "The Interest of Bishop Giovanni Battista Scalabrini of Piacenza in the Italian Problem," in Tomasi, *Religious Experience of Italian-Americans,* pp. 13–30.
3. DeConde, *Half Bitter, Half Sweet,* p. 93.
4. DiDonato, *The Immigrant Saint,* pp. 115–65.
5. Iorizzio and Mondello, *The Italian-Americans,* p. 181.
6. *Italo American Times,* February 1974.
7. Covello, *The Heart Is the Teacher,* p. 107.
8. Leonard Covello, "A High School and Its Immigrant Community: A Challenge and an Opportunity," *Journal of Educational Sociology* (February 1936), pp. 1, 340.
9. Nicholas Mills, "Community Schools: The Italian Example," *Italo-American Times,* June 1974, p. 8.
10. Covello, *The Heart Is the Teacher,* p. 105.
11. Ibid., p. 107.
12. Ibid., p. 65.

13. Mills, "Community Schools," p. 8.
14. Covello, *The Heart Is the Teacher*, p. 197.
15. Maurie Hillson, *The Record* (November 1967), pp. 191–92.
16. Francesco Cordasco, ed., "Introduction," *Studies in Italian American Social History*, pp. xi–xii.
17. Teachers College, Columbia University (June 2, 1970).
18. Mangione, in Cordasco, *Studies in Italian American Social History*, p. xiii.

10. The Saints Are Older Relatives and Friends

1. Covello, *The Social Background of the Italo-American School Child*, p. 105.
2. Gambino, *Blood of My Blood*, pp. 209–16.
3. Lawrence Pisani, *The Italians in America* (New York: Exposition Press, 1957), pp. 165–71.
4. Ibid., p. 126. See also Francis Femminella, "The Impact of Italian Migration and American Catholicism," *American Catholic Sociological Review*, 23 (Fall 1961), pp. 233–41.
5. Iorizzio and Mondello, *The Italian-Americans*, pp. 184–85.
6. Richard Varbero, "Philadelphia's South Italians and the Irish Church," in Tomasi, *The Religious Experience of Italian Americans*, pp. 41–42.
7. Tomasi and Engel, *The Italian Experience in the United States*, p. 167.
8. Ibid.
9. Iorizzio and Mondello, *The Italian-Americans*, p. 83.
10. Michael Novak, "Ethnic Whites: Where the Action Is" *National Catholic Reporter* (December 3, 1971), p. 7. See also Leo Carroll, "Irish and Italians in Providence Rhode Island 1880–1960, *Rhode Island History*, 28 (1969), pp. 67–74.
11. See Silvano Tomasi, *Piety and Power* (New York: Center for Migration Studies, 1975).
12. Varbero, "Philadelphia's South Italians," p. 47.
13. Jebsen, in Gallo, *The Urban Experience of Italian-Americans*, pp. 69–70.
14. Jacob Riis, "Feast Days in Little Italy," *Italo-American Times* (April 1975), p. 13.
15. Tomasi and Engel, *The Italian Experience in the United States*, p. 193.
16. See Tomasi, *Piety and Power*.
17. Nicholas Russo, "Brooklyn's New Italian Immigrants," *Migration Today* (January 1974), pp. 1, 5.
18. Ibid., pp. 1, 5.
19. Harold Abramson, "The Social Varieties of Catholic Behavior: The Italian Experience Viewed Comparatively," in Tomasi, *The Religious Experience*, pp. 55–62.

20. See Will Herberg, *Protestant, Catholic, Jew* (New York: Double-day, 1955).
21. The proportion of those having a mixed parentage would seem to be inversely related to magnitude of the Italian immigrants' segregation from the native white population. The more segregated the Italian population, the more likely a greater proportion of in-group marriages.
22. B. R. Bugelski, "Assimilation Through Intermarriage," *Social Forces* (December 1961), p. 147.
23. Ruby Jo Reeves Kennedy, "Single or Triple Melting Pot? Inter-marriage Trends in New Haven, 1870–1940," *American Journal of Sociology* (January 1944), p. 56.
24. In a larger sample we would suspect that the proportion of second and third generation people having mixed parentage would be inversely related to the extent they are segregated from the native white population. See also Nicholas John Russo, "Three Generations of Italians in New York City: Their Religious Acculturation," in Tomasi and Engel, *The Italian in the United States.* Russo supports Bugleski's findings in concluding that there was an increasing number of outgroup marriages across a three-generation span.
25. Glazer and Moynihan, *Beyond the Melting Pot*, pp. 202–5.
26. Abramson in Tomasi, *Religious Experience of Italian-Americans*, p. 60. See also Harold J. Abramson, *Ethnic Diversity in Catholic America* (New York: Wiley Interscience, John Wiley and Sons, 1973).
27. Ibid.
28. Paul Asciolla, *Italo-American Times* (August 1974), p. 6.
29. Novack, "Ethnic Whites: Where the Action Is," *National Catholic Reporter,* December 31, 1971, p. 7.

11. LaGuardia and Marcantonio

1. Arthur Mann, *LaGuardia: A Fighter Against His Time, 1882–1947* (N.Y.: J. B. Lippincott, 1959), pp. 25–26, 28.
2. Amfitheatrof, *Children of Columbus,* pp. 250–51.
3. Ibid., p. 261.
4. Mann, *LaGuardia,* p. 59.
5. Salvatore LaGumina, "Case Studies on Ethnicity and Italo-American Politicans," in Tomasi and Engel, *The Italian Experience in the United States,* p. 147.
6. Alan Schaffer, *Vito Marcantonio: Radical in Congress* (New York: n.p., 1966), pp. 18–24.
7. Edward Corsi, "My Neighborhood," *Outlook* (September 16, 1925), pp. 90–91.
8. Salvatore LaGumina, *Vito Marcantonio: The People's Politician* (Dubuque, Iowa: Kendall Hunt, 1969). See also Michael Waltzer, "Vito Marcantonio and the Politics of East Harlem," paper de-

livered at the Eighth Annual Conference of the American Italian
Historical Association, November 14, 1975.

9. Covello, *The Heart Is the Teacher,* p. 180.
10. Ibid., p. 153.
11. Mann, LaGuardia, pp. 171–73.
12. Ibid., pp. 241–44.
13. Waltzer, "Vito Marcantonio," p. 6.
14. LaGumina, "Case Studies," in Tomasi and Engel, *The Italian Experience in the United States,* pp. 143–61.
15. Mann, LaGuardia, p. 188.
16. Howard Zinn, *Fiorello LaGuardia in Congress,* Ph.D. dissertation, Columbia University, 1958, p. 187.
17. Mann, *LaGuardia,* p. 246.
18. Ibid., pp. 245–50.
19. John D. Hicks, *The Republican Ascendancy* (New York: Harper & Row, 1960), p. 229.
20. Zinn, *Fiorello LaGuardia in Congress,* p. 248.
21. Mann, *LaGuardia,* pp. 18, 135.
22. Federal Writers Project, Works Progress Administration in the City of New York, *The Italians of New York* (New York: Random House, 1938), p. 97.
23. Rolle, *American Italians,* p. 88.
24. Arthur Schlesinger, Jr., *The Politics of Upheaval* (Boston: Houghton-Mifflin, 1960), p. 131.
25. Ibid.
26. LaGumina "Case Studies," in Tomasi and Engel, *The Italian Experience in the United States,* p. 148.
27. Shaffer, *Vito Marcantonio,* p. 23.
28. Ibid., pp. 66–73. See also Vito Marcantonio, *Debates, Speeches, Writings* (Clifton, N.J.: Augustus Kelley, 1956).
29. Ibid.
30. LaGumina "Case Studies," in Tomasi, *The Italian Experience in the United States,* pp .155–56.
31. Ronald Bayor, "Italians and Jews in New York: The LaGuardia Elections," in Scarpaci, *Interaction of Italians and Jews in America,* p. 6.
32. Theodore J. Lowi, *At the Pleasure of the Mayor* (New York: Free Press of Glencoe, 1964), pp. 41, 118.
33. Schaffer, *Vito Marcantonio: Radical in Congress,* pp. 160–65. See also LaGumina, *Peoples Politican,* pp. 90–92.

12.   Neither Black nor Red

1. John Thayer, *Italy and the Great War: Politics and Culture* (Madison: University of Wisconsin Press, 1964).
2. Albrecht-Carrié, *Italy,* pp. 110–24.
3. Ibid., p. 144.

4. Luigi Barzini, *From Caesar to the Mafia* (New York: Library Press, 1971), p. 139.
5. Gaetano Salvemini, *The Fascist Dictatorship in Italy* (New York: Henry Holt, 1927).
6. H. Stuart Hughes, *Italy and the United States* (Cambridge: Harvard University Press, 1965), pp. 59–65.
7. Frank Rosengarten, *The Anti-Fascist Press, 1919–1945* (Cleveland, Ohio: Case Western Reserve Press, 1966), pp. 33–85, 90–121.
8. Amfitheatrof, *Children of Columbus,* p. 286.
9. Hughes, *Italy and the United States,* pp. 96–97.
10. John Diggins, "The Italo-American Anti-Fascist Opposition, " *Journal of American History* (December 1967), pp. 579–98. See also Gaetano Salvemini, *Italian Fascist Activities in the United States,* (New York: Center for Migration Studies, 1977).
11. John Norman, "The Repudiation of Fascism by the Italo American Press," *Journalism Quarterly* (March 1944), pp. 1–10.
12. Diggins, "Italo-American Anti-Fascist Opposition," pp. 579–98.
13. John Diggins, *Mussolini and Fascism: The View from America* (Princeton, N.J.: Princeton University Press, 1972), p. 255.
14. Giuseppe Prezzolini, *The Case of the Casa-Italiana* (New York: American Institute of Italian Studies, 1976), p. ix.
15. Marcus Duffield, "Mussolini's American Empire," *Harpers* (November 1929), pp. 661–772.
16. Schlesinger, *Politics of Upheaval,* p. 71.
17. Ibid., pp. 72–73.
18. Ibid., p. 75.
19. Ibid., pp. 68–95.
20. Diggins, "Italo-American Anti-Fascist Opposition;" C. F. Delzell, "The Italian Anti-Fascist Emigration, 1922–1943," *Journal of Central European Affairs* (April 1957), pp. 30–55.
21. Joseph Roucek, "Italo Americans and World War II," *Sociology and Social Research* 29 (July 1945), pp. 465–71.
22. Norman Kogan, *A Political History of Postwar Italy* (New York: Praeger, 1966), pp. 28–56.
23. Ibid.
24. Quoted in *Civilta Cattolica* 99 (January-June 1948), p. 551.
25. C. Edda Martinez and Edward Suchman, "Letters from America and the 1948 Elections in Italy," *Public Opinion Quarterly* (Spring 1950), pp. 111–25.
26. Ibid., p. 115.

13. Symbol of Amoral Power

1. Luciano Iorizzo and Salvatore Mondello, "Origins of Italian-American Criminality: From New Orleans Through Prohibition," *Italian Americana* (Spring 1975), p. 217.

2. John Mariani, "Hollywood's Favorite Ethnic Group," *New York Times,* June 4, 1978 Section 2, pp. 1, 26.
3. Arcangelo D'Amore, "A Psychological Commentary on Italian-Americans," in Nelli, *Italy and the United States,* pp. 225–27.
4. William Shannon, "The Godfather," *New York Times,* August 1, 1972, p. 35.
5. Andrew Greeley, "TV's Italian Cops—Trapped in Old Stereotypes," *New York Times,* July 27, 1975, Section 2, pp. 1, 17.
6. See Dwight Smith, *The Mafia Mystique* (New York: Basic Books, 1975).
7. Robert J. Ward, *Europe in American Fiction: The Vogue of the Historical Romance, 1890–1919* (Missouri, 1967), cited in "Doctoral Dissertations on the Italian-American Experience, 1921–1975," by Remigio U. Pane, *International Migration Review* 10 (Fall 1976), p. 399.
8. *New York Times Book Review,* February 21, 1978, p. 6.
9. Peter Prescott, *Newsweek,* March 29, 1979, p. 24.
10. Christopher Lehmann-Haupt, "Even If It's Real It's Unreal," *New York Times,* February 28, 1975, p. 31.
11. Marvin Karlins, Thomas Coffman, and Gary Walters, "On the Fading of Social Stereotype: Studies in Three Generations of College Students," *Journal of Personality and Social Psychology* 13 (1969), pp. 1–16.
12. Rudolph Vecoli, "The Italian-Americans," *The Center Magazine* 7 (1974), p. 39.
13. Jerry Lisker, "Philadelphia's Mayor Frank Rizzo: A Man Who Means Business," *Daily News,* July 23, 1972, pp. 94–95; William Serrin, "Ford's Iacocca—Apotheosis of a Used Car Salesman," *New York Times Magazine,* July 18, 1971, pp. 8–9, 21–25.
14. S. Zion, "Once a Jew, Sometimes a Jew," *Harpers,* August 1972, pp. 70–73.
15. Thomas Cousins, "The Treatment of Italians in Senior High School American History Textbooks," in Gallo, *The Urban Experience,* pp. 159–72.
16. Ibid., pp. 168–69.
17. "Bad, Bad Leroy Barnes," *Time,* December 12, 1977, p. 21.
18. *Time,* October 25, 1976, p. 75.
19. Albini, *American Mafia.* See also Francis A. J. Ianni, *The Myth of the Mafia* (Detroit, Mich.: Wayne State University Press, 1970); Francis A. J. Ianni, *A Family Business* (New York: Basic Books, 1972); Francis A. J. Ianni, *Black Mafia: Ethnic Succession in Organized Crime* (New York: Simon and Schuster, 1974).
20. Richard Gambino, "What's a Myth?" *I-Am,* April 1977, p. 25.
21. Ibid.
22. Letter from Congressman Andrew Maguire to Patricia Harris, February 14, 1979.

14. The Red, White, and Greening of America

1. Geno Baroni, "I'm a Pig Too," *Washingtonian,* July 1970, pp. 1–2.
2. Ibid., p. 2.
3. Ralph Perrotta, "As Italian as Apple Pie and Baseball," *New York Times,* January 5, 1974, *Op-Ed* page.
4. Jerre Mangione, *Mount Allegro,* pp. 216–17.
5. Perrotta, "As Italian as Apple Pie."
6. Ibid.
7. Joseph Velikonja, "Italian Immigrants in the United States," *International Migration Review* (Summer 1967), p. 33.
8. Foerester, *Italian Immigration of Our Times,* p. 329.
9. Velikonja, "Italian Immigrants," p. 33.
10. Nathan Kantrowitz, "Ethnic Segregation in New York City," *American Journal of Sociology* (May 1969), pp. 685–95.
11. Ibid., pp. 685–95.
12. William F. Whyte, *Street Corner Society* (Chicago: University of Chicago Press, 1943), p. 208.
13. Herbert Gans, *The Urban Villagers* (New York: The Free Press, 1962), p. 4.
14. Pisani, *Italians in America,* p. 125.
15. Ibid., p. 61.
16. Foerester, *Italian Immigration of Our Times,* p. 431. See also Humbert Nelli, "Italians in Urban America: A Study in Ethnic Adjustment," *International Migration Review* (Summer 1967), pp. 38–55. Professor Nelli contends that it is an error to conclude that certain districts were either inhabited exclusively or even predominantly by Italians. Urban areas according to this view had few solidly Italian blocks or Italian neighborhoods.
17. Gans, *Urban Villagers,* p. 16.
18. Pisani, *Italians in America,* p. 125.
19. Salvatore Mondello, "The Italian Immigrant in Urban America as Reported in American Magazines, 1880–1920, *Social Science* 39 (June 1964), pp. 131–42. Professor Mondello concludes that a considerable number of the articles concerning Italian immigration were unfavorable to them causing the deterioration of relations between the native born and the Italian immigrants. This retarded the immigrants' assimilation. See also Higham, *Strangers in the Land,* pp. 158–234.
20. Whyte, *Street Corner Society,* p. 273.
21. Joseph Fitzpatrick, "The Importance of Community in the Process of Immigrant Assimilation" *International Migration Review* (Fall 1966), pp. 5–16. See R. Brenton, "Institutional Completeness of Ethnic Communities and the Personal Relations of Immigrants," *American Journal of Sociology* (September 1964).
22. Gino Germani, "Migration and Acculturation," in Philip Hauser, ed., *Handbook for Social Research in Urban Areas* (New York:

Unesco, 1965), pp. 159–78. See also S. N. Eisenstadt, *The Absorption of Immigrants* (London: Routledge & Kegan Paul Ltd., 1954), pp. 2–7.

23. Fitzpatrick, "The Importance of Community," p. 9.
24. Gans, *Urban Villagers,* pp. 74, 76.
25. Ibid.
26. Ibid., p. 105.
27. Fitzpatrick, "The Importance of Community," p. 13.
28. Gans, *Urban Villagers,* p. 104.
29. Stan Lieberson, "The Impact of Residential Segregation on Ethnic Assimilation," *Social Forces* (October 1961), pp. 52–57.
30. Gordon, *Assimilation in American Life,* p. 34.
31. Gans, *Urban Villagers,* p. 106.
32. Segregation and the ability to speak English are in part functions of length of residence. But the persistence of this association is evident even after length of residence is considered.
33. Gordon, *Assimilation in American Life,* p. 131.
34. Ibid., pp. 71–83.
35. Erich Rosenthal, "Acculturation Without Assimilation?: The Jewish Community of Chicago, Illinois," *American Journal of Sociology* (November 1960), pp. 23–31.
36. A sense of peoplehood might be called ethnicity. A group with a shared feeling of peoplehood is an ethnic group.
37. Amitai Etzioni, "The Ghetto—a Re-Evaluation," *Social Forces* (March 1959), pp. 255–62.
38. Gallo, *Ethnic Alienation,* pp. 43–82.
39. Words like *cake* became *caka; street—stritto; car—carro; store—storo.* See Josephine Butera, "A Study of the Italo-American Dialect; Adaptation into the Italian Language or Dialects for the Purpose of Adjustment in an Italo-American Environment." Master's thesis, New York University, 1941.
40. See Oscar Handlin, *Boston's Immigrants: A Study in Acculturation* (Cambridge: Harvard University Press, 1959); W. L. Warner and Leo Strole, *The Social Systems of American Ethnic Groups* (New Haven: Yale University Press, 1945); Fred Milano, "The Italian-American Working Class and the Vietnam War," in George Pozzetta, *The Italian-American Working Class* (New York: American Italian Historical Association, 1980), pp. 1–25.
41. Social structure is employed here to mean man's crystallized social relationships. See Gordon, "Assimilation in American Life," p. 31.
42. Parenti, "Ethnic Politics," pp. 718–19.
43. Warner and Srole, *Social Systems of American Ethnic Groups,* pp. 102, 285–96.
44. U.S. Census of Population, 1960.
45. Scott Greer, "Catholic Voters and the Democratic Party," *Public Opinion Quarterly* 25 (1961), p. 624.
46. Robert Wood, *Suburbia: Its People and Their Politics* (Boston: Houghton Mifflin, 1958), p. 178.

47. Parenti, "Ethnic Politics," pp. 722–23.
48. Oppedisano, "Roseto Revisited," p. 40. See also Carla Bianco, *The Two Rosetos: Italian Americans in Roseto, Pennsylvania* (Bloomington: University of Indiana Press, 1974).
49. Ibid.
50. Ibid.

15. Italian-Americans and the Urban Crisis

1. Josephine Casalena, "A Portrait of the Italian-American Community in New York City," Congress of Italian American Organizations, New York, 1975, pp. 1–71. See also Edward J. Miranda and Ino Rossi, "Preliminary Profile of Italian Americans Living in New York City," Italian-American Center for Urban Affairs, Inc., New York, 1973 pp. 1–25; Andrew Greeley, *Ethnicity in the United States* (New York: Wiley, 1974).
2. Gallo, *Urban Experience of Italian-Americans*, p. 2.
3. Gallo, *Ethnic Alienation*, pp. 43–50.
4. Joseph Conforti, "The Italian-Americans and the Urban Crisis: A Sociological Perspective," in Gallo, *Urban Experience of Italian-Americans*, pp. 95–106.
5. Conforti, "The Italian-Americans and the Urban Crisis," pp. 95–106.
6. Ibid.
7. United States Census of Population, 1970, "Characteristics of the Population," United States Department of Commerce, Vol. I.
8. Greeley, *Ethnicity in the United States*, p. 56.
9. Jack Rosenthal, "Angry Voices Decry a 'Racist and Dullard' Image," *New York Times*, June 17, 1970, p. 31.
10. Vincent Fuccillo and Jerome Krase, "Italian-Americans and College Life: A Survey of Student Experiences at Brooklyn College, 1975," Center of Italian-American Studies, Brooklyn College, 1975, pp. 5–16. See also Richard Ulin, "Ethnicity and School Performance: An Analysis of the Variables; Italo Americans," *California Journal of Educational Research* (September 1968), pp. 190–97.
11. Casalena, "A Portrait of the Italian-American Community," pp. 1–71.
12. Michael Parenti, *Democracy for the Few* (New York: St. Martin's Press, 1974), pp. 69–72.
13. Gallo, *Ethnic Alienation*, p. 208.
14. Clem Morgello, "Who Owns What," *Newsweek*, December 23, 1974, p. 68.
15. Gallo, *Ethnic Alienation*, pp. 135–74.
16. Greeley, *Ethnicity in the United States*, pp. 52–62.
17. Gallo, *Ethnic Alienation*, pp. 135–74.
18. Russell Barta, "The Representation of Poles, Italians, Latins and Blacks in the Executive Suites of Chicago's Largest Corporation," *The Minority Report* (Chicago: Institute of Urban Life, 1974), pp. 1–2.

334   NOTES

19. Gerald E. Diggs, *Economic Elite Study, Detroit 1975* (Detroit: Michigan Ethnic Heritage Studies Center, 1975), pp. 1–8.
20. James R. Polk, "Slush-Bribery and Other Costs of Doing Business Abroad," *New Republic,* May 17, 1975, p. 23.
21. Barta, *Minority Report,* pp. 1–2.
22. Ibid.
23. Rosenthal, "Angry Voices," p. 31.
24. "Mafia Slur Costly to Flushing Hospital Center," *Italo-American Times,* May, 1974, p. 1.
25. "Status of Italian-Americans in the City University of New York," Association of Italian American Faculty, Italian American Center for Urban Affairs, 1976, pp. 1–25. See also John Calandra, *A History of Italian-American Discrimination at CUNY* (Albany, N.Y.: New York State Senate, 1978), pp. 1–43.
26. Ibid.
27. "Anti-Italian Bias Is Charged to State College at Purchase," *New York Times,* July 17, 1975.
28. "State Cautions CUNY on Racial Quota Charges," *Italo-American Times,* September 1974, pp. 1–2.
29. Shelia K. Johnson, "It's Action, But Is It Affirmative?" *New York Times Magazine,* May 11, 1975, pp. 18–24, 30, 33. See also Robert Lindsey, "White-Caucasian and Rejected," *New York Times Magazine,* April 3, 1977, pp. 42–46, 95–96; Nathan Glazer, *Affirmative Discrimination* (New York: Basic Books, 1975), pp. 3–75.
30. Richard Severo, "Italian-Americans Here Unite to Fight Reverse Racial Bias," *New York Times,* June 28, 1974, p. 35.
31. Ibid.
32. Fuccillo and Krase, "Italian-American and College Life," p. 28.
33. Ibid., p. 5.
34. Fuccillio and Krase, "Italian-Americans and College Life," p. 6.
35. Ibid., p. 13.
36. "Status of Italian-Americans in the City University of New York, pp. 1–25.
37. Ibid.
38. Conforti, "The Italian-Americans and the Urban Crisis," in Gallo, p. 95.
39. Gallo, *Ethnic Alienation.* See also Greeley, *Ethnicity in the United States,* pp. 52–62; Conforti, "Italian Americans and the Urban Crisis," pp. 90–95.
40. "City to Revive and Refurbish Little Italy," *New York Times,* May 1, 1977, pp. 1, 78.
41. Ibid.
42. "St. Louis: Pride on 'the Hill,'" *Time,* April 29, 1974, p. 27.
43. Gallo, *Ethnic Alienation,* pp. 125–29.
44. Ibid., p. 124.
45. Michael Novak, "Busing—The Arrogance of Power," *A New America,* November 5, 1975, p. 6.
46. Gallo, *Ethnic Alienation,* pp. 135–74.

47. Wolfinger, *Electoral Process*, Chapter 3.
48. Edward H. Litchfield, *Voting Behavior in a Metropolitan Area* (Ann Arbor, Michigan: University of Michigan Press, 1941).
49. Gallo, *Ethnic Alienation*, pp. 135–74.
50. *New York Times*, October 19, 1969, pp. 1, 72.
51. *New York Times*, October 19, 1969, pp. 1, 72.
52. Banfield, *City Politics*, pp. 41–43.
53. Newark *Evening News*, October 7, 1970, p. 15.
54. Banfield, *City Politics*, pp. 50–51.
55. Humbert Nelli, "John Powers and the Italians: Politics in a Chicago Ward 1896–1921," *Journal of American History* (June 1970), pp. 67–84. Certain occupations have permitted those in other ethnic groups to serve as political intermediaries, e.g., tavern owners for the Irish.
56. Philip Foglia, "The Padrone Is Alive and Well...Politically," *Italo-American Times*, April 1975, p. 2.
57. Salvatore La Gumina, "Inauguration Day: Some Thoughts for Jimmy Carter," *Identity*, February 1977, p. 71.
58. Gallo, "Italian-Americans in the America of the Seventies," in Nelli, *United States and Italy*, pp. 237–42.

16. From Columbus to Watergate

1. "God May Be a Democrat: But the Vote Is for Nixon," *Time*, October 30, 1972, p. 22.
2. Novak, *Rise of the Unmeltable Ethnics*, pp. 64–65.
3. *Time*, October 20, 1972, p. 22.
4. "Catering to Azerbaijanis," *Time*, September 18, 1972, p. 17.
5. *Time*, October 30, 1972, p. 23.
6. Ibid.
7. "Nixon Bids for Ethnic Vote in City Visit," *New York Times*, September 27, 1972, pp. 1, 35.
8. Ibid.
9. George Gallup Survey, August 20-September 1, 1972.
10. Michael Parenti, *Democracy for the Few*, pp. 164–65.
11. "The Making of a Tough Judge," *Time*, January 7, 1974, p. 12.
12. Carl Bernstein and Bob Woodward, *All the President's Men* (New York: Warner Books, 1975), pp. 365–66.
13. "The Making of a Tough Judge," pp. 12–13.
14. Howard Muson, "A Man for This Season," *New York Times Magazine*, November 4, 1973, p. 106.
15. Ibid., pp. 34, 105–6.
16. Ibid., p. 106.
17. "The Making of a Tough Judge," pp. 12–13.
18. "House Judiciary Chief," *New York Times*, October 24, 1973, p. 34.
19. "The Man With the Judicious Gavel," *Time*, August 5, 1974, p. 14.
20. Ibid., p. 15.
21. Ibid.

22. Ibid., p. 14.
23. Ibid.
24. Harold Abramson, "The Social Varieties of Behavior: The Italian Experience Viewed Comparatively," in Tomasi, *Religious Experience of Italian-Americans,* pp. 63–67.
25. Jimmy Breslin, *How the Good Guys Finally Won* (New York: Viking Press, 1975).
26. Theodore White, *Breach of Faith* (New York: Atheneum-Readers Digest Press, 1975).
27. Amfitheatrof, *The Children of Columbus,* p. 324.
28. Rose Basile Green, *Primo Vino* (Cranbury, N.J.: A. S. Barnes, 1974), p. 15.

Bibliography

Documents and Dissertations

Abramson, Harold J. "The Ethnic Factor in American Catholicism." Ph.D. dissertation, University of Chicago, 1969.

Alissi, Albert S. "Boys in Little Italy: A Comparison of Their Individual Value Orientations." Ph.D. dissertation, Case Western Reserve University, 1967.

Butera, Joseph. "A Study of the Italo American Dialect: Adaptations into the Italian Language of Dialects for the Purpose of Adjustment in an Italian American Envronment." M.A. thesis, New York University, 1941.

Dyson, James. "Political Alienation: A Study of Apathy, Discontent and Dissidence." Ph.D. dissertation, Indiana University, 1964.

Iorizzo, Luciano. "Italian Immigration and the Impact of the Padrone System." Ph.D. dissertation, Syracuse University, 1966.

Fenton, Edwin. "Immigrants and Unions, A Case Study: Italians and American Labor, 1870–1920." Ph.D. dissertation, Harvard University, 1957.

Ferroni, Charles D. "The Italians in Cleveland: A Study in Assimilation." Ph.D. dissertation, Kent State University, 1969.

Matthews, M. F. "The Role of the Public School in the Assimilation of the Italian Immigrant in New York City." Ph.D. dissertation, Fordham University, 1966.

Mondello, Salvatore. "The Italian Immigrant in Urban America 1880–1920." Ph.D. dissertation, New York University, 1960.

Parenti, Michael. "Ethnic and Political Attitudes: Three Generations of Italian Americans." Ph.D. dissertation, Harvard University, 1950.

Polizzi, J. A. "Southern Italian Society: Its Peasantry and Change," Ph.D. dissertation, Cornell University, 1968.

Pozzetta, George. "The Italians of New York City, 1890–1914." Ph.D. dissertation, University of North Carolina, 1971.

Rossili, V. R. "A Study of the Effect of Transplantation upon the Attitudes of Southern Italians in New York City as Revealed by Survivors of the Mass Migration 1887–1915." Ph.D. dissertation, New York University, 1967.

Tait, Joseph W. "Some Aspects of the Effect of the Dominant American Culture upon the Children of Italian Born Parents." M.A. thesis, Teachers College, Columbia, 1942.

Articles and Pamphlets

Aho, William. "Ethnic Mobility in Northeastern United States: An Analysis of Census Data." *Sociological Quarterly* (Fall 1966), pp. 512–26.

Barta, Russell. "The Representation of Poles, Italians, Latins and Blacks in the Executive Suites of Chicago's Largest Corporations." Institute of Urban Life, 1974, pp. 1–2.

Bugleski, B. R. "Assimilation Through Intermarriage." *Social Forces* (December 1961), pp. 149–54.

Campisi, Paul J. "Ethnic Family Patterns: The Italian Family in the U.S." *American Journal of Sociology* 53 (1948), pp. 434–47.

Casalena, Josephine. "A Portrait of the Italian American Community in New York City." Congress of Italian American Organizations, 1975, pp. 1–71.

Cezaro, Cincenzo. "Immigrati e Associocizionismi voluntario." *Studi-Emigrazione* (October 1966), pp. 29–50.

Cornwell, Elmer. "Party Absorption of Ethnic Groups: The Case of Providence, Rhode Island." *Social Forces* (March 1960), pp. 205–10.

Coxe, John. "The New Orleans Mafia Incident." *Louisiana Historical Quarterly* 20 (1937), pp. 1070–73.

Cunningham, George E. "The Italian: A Hindrance to White Solidarity in Louisiana, 1890–1898." *Journal of Negro History* (January 1965), pp. 23–35.

Diggins, John P. "Flirtation with Fascism: American Pragmatic Liberals and Mussolini's Italy." *American Historical Review*, 7 (January 1966), pp. 487–536.

Diggins, John P. "The Italo-American Anti-Fascist Opposition." *Journal of American History* 54 (December 1967), pp. 579–98.

Diggs, Gerald. "Economic Elite Study, Detroit 1975." Michigan Ethnic Heritage Studies Center, 1975, pp. 1–8.

Femminella, Francis X. "The Impact of Italian Migration on American Catholicism." *American Catholic Sociological Review* (Fall 1961), pp. 233–41.

Fitzpatrick, Joseph. "The Importance of Community in the Process of Immigrant Assimilation." *International Migration Review* (Fall 1966), pp. 5–16.

Fried, R. C. "Urbanization and Italian Politics." *Journal of Politics* (August 1967), pp. 505–34.

Gallo, Patrick J. "Italy and the United Nations." *Rivista Di Studi Politici Internazionali* (April-June 1968), pp. 290–306.

Gallo, Patrick J. "Student Alienation at an American University." *Rassegna Italiana di Sociologia* (April-June 1970), pp. 295–310.

Gambino, Richard. "What's a Myth." *I-AM*, April 1977, pp. 23–25.

Gordon, Daniel. "Immigrants and Urban Governmental Forms in

American Cities, 1933–1960." *American Journal of Sociology* (September 1968), pp. 158–71.

Grazia, Dore. "Some Social and Historical Aspects of Italian Immigration." *Journal of Social History* (Winter 1968), pp. 107–10.

Greeley, Andrew. "TV's Italian Cops—Trapped in Old Stereotypes." *New York Times,* July 27, 1975, pp. 1, 17.

Hazelrigg, L. "Religious and Class Bases of Political Conflict in Italy." *American Journal of Sociology* (January 1970), pp. 496–510.

Heiss, Jerold. "Factors in Immigrant Assimilation." *Social Forces* (June 1969), pp. 422–28.

Heiss, Jerold. "Residential Segregation and the Assimilation of the Italians in an Australian City." *International Migration Review* (1966), pp. 165–71.

Hodge, Robert and Treiman, Don. "Class Identification in the U.S." *American Journal of Sociology* (March 1968), pp. 535–47.

Ianni, Francis. "Residence and Occupational Mobility. The Italian American Colony in Norristown." *Social Forces* (October 1957), pp. 65–72.

Ianni, Francis. "The Italo-American Teenager." *The Annals* (November 1961), pp. 70–78.

Juliani, Richard. "American Voices, Italian Accents: The Perception of Social Conditions and Personal Motives of Immigrants." *Italian Americana* 1 (Autumn 1974), pp. 1–26.

Kantrowitz, Nathan. "Ethnic and Racial Segregation in the New York Metropolitan Area, 1960." *American Journal of Sociology* (May 1969), pp. 685–95.

Karlins, Marvin, Thomas Coffman, and Gary Walters. "On the Fading of Social Stereotypes: Studies in Three Generations of College Students." *Journal of Personality and Social Psychology* 13 (1969), pp. 1–16.

Kennedy, Ruby Jo. "Single or Triple Melting Pot? Intermarriage Trends in New Haven, 1870–1940." *American Journal of Sociology* (January 1944), pp. 313–20.

Krickus, Richard. "The White Ethnics: Who Are They and Where Are They Going?" *City Magazine* (June 1971), pp. 1–5.

Lindsey, Robert. "White Caucasian—And Rejected." *New York Times Magazine,* April 3, 1977, pp. 42–46.

Lopreato, Joseph. "Economic Development and Cultural Change." *Human Organization* (Fall 1962), pp. 95–96.

Lopreato, Joseph. "Social Mobility in Italy." *American Journal of Sociology* (November 1965), pp. 311–14.

Mailey, Hugo. "The Italian Vote in Philadelphia, 1928–46." *Public Opinion Quarterly* (Spring 1950), pp. 48–57.

Margavio, Anthony. "The Reaction of the Press to the Italian-Americans of New Orleans, 1880 to 1920." *Italian Americana* (Fall/Winter 1978), pp. 72–83.

Mariani, John. "Hollywood's Favorite Ethnic Group." *New York Times,* June 4, 1978, pp. 1, 26.

Martinez, C. and Edward Suchman. "Letters from Americans and the

1948 Elections in Italy." *Public Opinion Quarterly* (Spring 1950), pp. 111–25.

Menen, Aubrey. "The Italian Family Is a Commune." *New York Times Magazine*, March 1, 1970, pp. 22–23, 77–79, 83.

Miranda, Edward and Ino Rossi. "A Preliminary Profile of Italian Americans Living in New York City." N.Y. Italian-American Center for Urban Affairs, 1973, pp. 1–25.

Miranda, Giulio. "From the Italo Think Tank." *Italo-American Times*, September 1972, p. 8.

Moss, Leonard and Walter Thompson. "The South Italian Family: Literature and Observation." *Human Organization* (Spring 1969), pp. 287–300.

Moss, Leonard, Walter Thompson and Stephen Cappannari. "Estate and Class in a South Italian Hill Village." *American Anthropologist* (1962), pp. 287–300.

Muson, Howard. "A Man for This Season." *New York Times Magazine*, November 4, 1973, pp. 34 ff.

Nelli, Humbert. "Italians in Urban America: A Study in Ethnic Adjustment." *International Review* (Summer 1967), pp. 38–55.

Norman, John. "The Repudiation of Fascism by the Italo-American Press." *Journalism Quarterly* (March 1964), pp. 1–10.

Palisi, B. J. "Ethnic Generation and Family Structure." *Journal of Marriage and the Family* (Fall 1966), pp. 49–50.

Palisi, B. J. "Patterns of Socio-Participation in Two Generations of Italian Americans." *Sociological Quarterly* (Spring 1966), pp. 167–78.

Parenti, Michael. "Ethnic Politics and the Persistence of Ethnic Identification." *American Political Science Review* (September 1967), pp. 717–26.

Perrotta, Ralph. "As Italian as Apple Pie and Baseball." *New York Times,* January 5, 1974, p. 43.

Plax, M. "On Studying Ethnicity." *Public Opinion Quarterly* (Spring 1972), pp. 99–104.

Pozzetta, George E. "Another Look at the Petrosino Affair." *Italian Americana* 1 (Autumn 1974), pp. 81–91.

Rosen, Bernard. "Race Ethnicity and the Achievement Syndrome." *American Sociological Review* (February 1959), pp. 47–50.

Rosenthal, Erich. "Acculturation Without Assimilation?: The Jewish Community of Chicago, Illinois." *American Journal of Sociology* (November 1960), pp. 23–31.

Severo, Richard. "Italian Americans Here Unite to Fight Reverse Racial Bias." *New York Times,* June 28, 1977, p. 35.

Shankman, Arnold. "The Image of the Italian in the Afro-American Press." *Italian Americana* (Fall/Winter, 1978), pp. 30–49.

Silverman, Sydel. "Prestige in a Central Italian Community." *American Anthropologist* (August 1966), pp. 899–921.

Silverman, Sydel. "Amoral Familism Reconsidered." *American Anthropologist* (Fall 1968), pp. 1–19.

Strodtbeck, Fred, et al. "Evaluation of Occupation: A Reflection of Jewish and Italian Mobility Differences." *American Sociological Review* (October 1957), pp. 546–53.

Tarrow, Sidney. "Political Dualism and Italian Communism." *American Political Science Association* (March 1967), pp. 39–53.

Veccoli, Rudolph. "Contadini in Chicago: A Critique of the Uprooted." *Journal of American History* (December 1964), pp. 404–17.

Veccoli, Rudolph. "Peasants and Prelates." *Journal of Social History* (Spring 1969), pp. 217–68.

Velikonja, Joseph. "Italian Immigrants in the U.S. in the Mid-Sixties." *International Migration Review* (Summer 1967), pp. 25–37.

Wolfinger, Raymond. "The Development and Persistence of Ethnic Voting Groups." *American Political Science Review* (December 1965), pp. 896–908.

Books

Abramson, Harold J. *Ethnic Diversity in Catholic America.* New York: John Wiley & Sons, 1973.

Adams, John and Paolo Barile. *The Government of Republican Italy.* Boston: Houghton Mifflin, 1961.

Albini, Joseph L. *The American Mafia.* New York: Appleton Century Crofts, 1971.

Albrecht-Carrié, René. *Italy: From Napoleon to Mussolini.* New York: Columbia University Press, 1950.

Almond, Gabriel and Verba, Sidney. *The Civic Culture.* Princeton: Princeton University Press, 1963.

Amfitheatrof, Erik. *Children of Columbus.* New York: Little, Brown & Co., 1973.

Bailey, Harry and Ellis Katz. *Ethnic Group Politics.* Columbus, Ohio: Merrill Publishing Co., 1969.

Baltzell, Digby E. *The Protestant Establishment.* New York: Random House, 1964.

Banfield, Edward C. *The Moral Basis of a Backward Society.* Glencoe, Ill.: The Free Press, 1958.

Banfield, Edward C. and James Q. Wilson. *City Politics.* Cambridge, Mass.: Harvard University Press, 1966.

Barrie, W. D. *Italians and Germans in Australia: A Study of Assimilation.* Melbourne: Australian National University, 1954.

Barzini, Luigi. *The Italians.* New York: Atheneum, 1965.

Bianco, Carla. *The Two Rosetos, Italian Americans in Roseto, Pennsylvania.* Bloomington: Indiana University Press, 1971.

Bradford, Ernle. *Christopher Columbus.* New York: Viking Press, 1973.

Brandenburg, Broughton. *Imported Americans.* New York: Fred Stokes Co. Publishers, 1904.

Bucci, Vincent. *Chiesa e Stato.* The Hague: Martinus Nijhoff, 1969.

Calandra, John. *A History of Discrimination at CUNY.* Albany, N.Y.: State Senate, 1978.

Cammet, John, ed. *The Italian American Novel.* Staten Island, N.Y.: American Italian Historical Association, 1969.

Caroli, Betty. *Italian Repatriation from the United States 1900–1914.* New York: Center For Migration Studies, 1974.

Chapman, Charlotte. *Milocca: A Sicilian Village.* N.p.: Shenkman, 1971.

Child, Irwin. *Italian or American?* New Haven: Yale University Press, 1943.

Cilento, Nicola. *Italian meridionali longoburda.* Milan: R. Riccardi, 1966.

Cingari, Gaetano. *Il Mezzogiorno e Giustono Fortunato.* Florence: Parenti, 1954.

Cordasco, Francesco, ed. *Studies in Italian American Social History.* N.p.: Rowman and Littlefield, 1975.

Cordasco, Francesco and E. Bucchioni. *The Italians: Social Backgrounds of an Ethnic Group.* Fairfield, N.J.: Augustus M. Kelley Publishers.

Covello, Leonard. *The Social Background of the Italo-American School Child.* Leiden: E. J. Brill, 1967.

Covello, Leonard. *The Heart Is the Teacher.* Totowa, N.J.: Littlefield, Adams, 1958.

Crawford, John S. *Luigi Antonini, His Influence on Italian-American Relations.* New York: ILGWU, 1959.

DeConde, Alexander. *Half Bitter, Half Sweet.* New York: Charles Scribner's Sons, 1971.

DiDonato, Pietro. *Christ in Concrete.* N.p.: n.p., 1977.

DiDonato, Pietro. *Immigrant Saint.* New York: McGraw-Hill, 1960.

DiPalma, Giuseppe. *Apathy and Mass Participation.* Berkeley, Calif.: University of California Press, 1966.

DeGrazia, Sebastian. *The Political Community: A Study in Anomie.* Chicago: University of Chicago Press, 1948.

Diggins, John P. *Mussolini and Fascism.* New Jersey: Princeton University Press, 1972.

Dogan, Mattei and O. Petracca. *Parti politici e strutture sociali in Italia.* Milan: Edizioni di Communita, 1968.

Dolci, Danilo. *Report from Palermo.* New York: Orien Press, 1956.

Domhoff, William G. *Who Rules America?* Englewood Cliffs, N.J.: Prentice Hall, 1967.

Dore, Grazia. *La democrazia Italiana e l'emigrazione in America.* Brescia: Morcelliani, 1964.

Ehrmann, Herbert. *The Case That Will Not Die: Commonwealth v. Sacco and Vanzetti.* Boston: Little, Brown & Co., 1969.

Eisenstadt, S. N. *The Absorption of Immigrants.* London: Routledge & Kegan Paul Ltd., 1954.

Ellis, John R. *American Catholicism.* Chicago: University of Chicago Press, 1956.

Federal Writers Project. *The Italians of New York.* New York: WPA, 1936.

Felici, Icilio. *Father to the Immigrants: The Life of John Baptist Scalabrini.* New York: P. J. Kennedy & Sons, 1955.

Felix, David. *Protest: Sacco and Vanzetti and the Intellectuals.* Bloomington, Ind.: Indiana University Press, 1965.

Femminella, Frank. *Power and Class: The Italian-American Experience,* Staten Island, N.Y.: The American-Italian Historical Association, 1973.

Fermi, Laura. *Illustrious Immigrants.* Chicago: University of Chicago Press, 1968.

Fine, Benjamin. *The Stranglehold of the IQ.* Garden City, N.Y.: Doubleday, 1958.

Foerester, Robert. *The Italian Immigration of Our Times.* Cambridge, Mass.: Harvard University Press, 1919.

Foner, Philip. *History of the Labor Movement in the United States.* New York: International Publishers, 1963.

Foner, Philip. *The IWW 1905–1911.* New York: International Publishers, 1965.

Frankfurter, Felix, *The Case of Sacco and Vanzetti.* Boston: Little, Brown and Co., 1927.

Fromm, Erich. *The Sane Society.* New York: Rinehart and Holt, 1955.

Fuccillo, Vincent and Jerome Krase. *Italian Americans and College Life: A Survey of Student Experiences at Brooklyn College.* New York: Center of Italian American Studies, 1975.

Fuchs, Lawrence, ed. *American Ethnic Politics.* New York: Harper & Row, 1968.

Galasso, Giuseppe. *Mezzogiorno medievale e moderno.* Torino: Einuadi, 1965.

Galli, Giorgio and Alfonso Prandi. *Patterns of Political Participation in Italy.* New Haven, Conn.: Yale University Press, 1970.

Gallo, Patrick. *Ethnic Alienation: The Italian Americans.* Cranford, N.J.: Fairleigh Dickinson University Press, 1974.

Gallo, Patrick, *Swords and Plowshares.* (Manhattan, Kansas: Military Affairs/Aerospace Historian Publishing, 1980).

Gallo, Patrick, ed. *The Urban Experience of Italian Americans.* New York: American Italian Historical Association, 1977.

Galtung, Johan. *Members of Two Worlds: Development in Three Villages in Sicily.* New York: Columbia University Press, 1970.

Gambino, Richard. *Blood of My Blood.* New York: Doubleday, 1974.

Gambino, Richard. *Vendetta.* New York: Doubleday, 1977.

Gans, Herbert. *The Urban Villagers.* New York: The Free Press, 1962.

Gerimino, Dante. *The Government and Politics of Contemporary Italy.* New York: Harper & Row, 1968.

Gerson, Louis. *The Hyphenate in Recent American Politics and Diplomacy.* Lawrence, Kan.: University of Kansas Press, 1964.

Glanz, Rudolph. *Jew and Italian: Historic Group Relations and the New Immigration, 1881–1924.* New York: KTAV, 1971.

Glazer, Nathan and Daniel P. Moynihan. *Beyond the Melting Pot.* Cambridge, Mass.: Harvard University Press, 1963.

Glazer, Nathan and Daniel P. Moynihan. *Ethnicity: Theory and Experience.* Cambridge, Mass.: Harvard University Press, 1975.

Gordon, Milton. *Assimilation in American Life.* New York: Oxford University Press, 1964.

Grasso, Pier Giovanni. *Personalita Giovaniti in Tranzione: Dal Familismo al Personalismo.* Aurich: Pas Yerlag, 1964.

Greeley, Andrew. *Ethnicity in the United States.* New York: Wiley, 1974.

Greeley, Andrew. *Why Can't They Be Like Us?* New York: E. P. Dutton, 1971.

Green, Rose Basile. *The Italian-American Novel: A Document of the Interaction of Two Cultures.* Cranbury, N.J.: Fairleigh Dickinson University Press, 1974.

Green, Rose Basile, *Primo Vino!* Cranbury, N.J.: A. S. Barnes, 1976.

Handlin, Oscar. *Race and Nationality in American Life.* New York: Doubleday, Inc., 1957.

Handlin, Oscar. *The Uprooted.* Boston: Little Brown, 1951.

Hay, Denys. *The Italian Renaissance.* London, Eng.: Cambridge University Press, 1961.

Higham, John. *Strangers in the Land.* New York: Atheneum, 1963.

Hughes, Stuart H. *Italy and the United States.* Cambridge, Mass.: Harvard University Press, 1965.

Iorizzio, Luciano, ed. *An Inquiry into Organized Crime.* New York: American Italian Historical Association, 1970.

Iorizzio, Luciano, and Salvatore Mondello. *The Italian Americans.* New York: Twayne Publishers, 1971.

Ianni, Francis A. J. *A Family Business.* New York: Basic Books, 1971.

Ianni, Francis A. J. *Black Mafia: Ethnic Succession in Organized Crime.* New York: Simon and Schuster, 1974.

Jemolo, A. C. *Church and State in Italy.* Oxford: Beachurd, 1960.

Jones, Maldwyn A. *American Immigration.* Chicago: University of Chicago Press, 1960.

Jouglin, Louis and Edmund Morgan. *The Legacy of Sacco and Vanzetti.* Princeton, N.J.: Princeton University Press, 1948.

Katz, Robert. *The Fall of the House of Savoy.* New York: Macmillan, 1976.

Kogan, Norman. *A Political History of Postwar Italy.* New York: Praeger, 1966.

LaGumina, Salvatore. *Vito Marcantonio: The People's Politician.* Iowa: Kendall-Hunt Publishing Company, 1969.

LaGumina, Salvatore. *WOP!* New York: Straight Arrow Press, 1973.

La Palombara, Joseph. *Interest Groups in Italian Politics.* Princeton, N.J.: Princeton University Press, 1964.

Levi, Carlo. *Christ Stopped at Eboli.* New York: Farrar, Straus & Giroux, 1969.

Lopreato, Joseph. *Italian-Americans.* New York: Random House, 1970.

Lopreato, Joseph. *Peasants No More.* Novato, Cal.: Chandler, 1967.

Mann, Arthur. *La Guardia: A Fighter Against His Times, 1882–1933.* New York: J. B. Lippincott Company, 1959.

Mann, Arthur. *La Guardia Comes to Power, 1933.* New York: J. B. Lippincott. Company, 1965.

Marchione, Margherita. *Philip Mazzei: Jefferson's Zealous Whig.* New York: American Institute of Italian Studies, n.d.

Mariano, John. *The Second Generation of Italians in New York.* New York: Christopher Publishing House, 1921.

Morrison, Samuel E. *Admiral of the Ocean Sea.* New York: Oxford University Press, 1940.

Moscov, Warren. *The Last of the Big Time Bosses: Carmen DeSapio.* New York: Stein and Day, 1971.

Musatti, Riccardi. *La via del sud.* Milan: Edizioni di Communita, 1955.

Mussamno, Michael. *The Story of the Italians in America.* New York: Doubleday, 1965.

Nelli, J. Humbert. *The Italians in Chicago, 1880–1930.* New York: Oxford University Press, 1971.

Nelli, J. Humbert, ed. *The United States and Italy: The First Two Hundred Years.* N.p.: American Italian Historical Association, 1978.

Novak, Michael. *Rise of the Unmeltable Ethnics.* New York: Macmillan, 1972.

Novotny, Ann. *Strangers at the Door.* New York: Bantam Books, 1972.

Odencrantz, Louise. *Italian Woman in Industry.* Fairfield, N.J.: Augustus M. Kelley Publishers, 1976.

Pansini, Anthony. *Machiavelli and the U.S.A.* New York: Greenvale Press, 1968.

Paulson, Belden and Athos Ricci. *The Searchers.* Chicago: Quadrangle Books, 1966.

Pisani, Lawrence. *The Italians in America.* New York: Exposition Press, 1957.

Prezzolini, Giuseppe. *The Case of the Casa Italiana.* New York: The American Institute of Italian Studies, 1976.

Redford, Robert. *Peasant Society and Culture.* Chicago: University of Chicago Press, 1956.

Renshaw, Patrick. *The Wobblies.* New York: Doubleday & Co., 1968.

Rolle, Andrew. *The American Italians.* Belmont, Cal.: Wadsworth Publishers, 1972.

Rolle, Andrew. *The Immigrant Upraised.* Norman, Okla.: University of Oklahoma Press, 1968.

Rosengarten, Frank. *The Italian Anti-Fascist Press.* Cleveland: Case Western Reserve University Press, 1968.

Rubenstein, Annette, ed. *Vito Marcantonio: Debates, Speeches and Writings 1935–1950.* Fairfield, N.J.: Augustus Kelley Publishers.

Russell, Francis, *Tragedy in Dedham.* New York: McGraw-Hill, 1971.

Salvadori, Massimo. *Italy.* Englewood Cliffs, N.J.: Prentice Hall, 1965.

Scarpaci, Jean, ed. *The Interaction of Jews and Italians.* New York: American Italian Historical Association, 1975.

Schermerhorn, R. A. *Comparative Ethnic Relations: A Framework for Theory and Research.* New York: Random House, 1970.

Schiavo, Giovanni. *Antonio Meucci: Inventor of the Telephone*. New York: Vigo Press, 1958.

Schiavo, Giovanni. *Four Centuries of Italian American History*. New York: Vigo Press, 1955.

Schiavo, Giovanni. *Italian American History*. New York: Vigo Press, 1949.

Schragg, Peter. *The Decline of the Wasp*. New York: Simon & Schuster, 1970.

Scotellaro, Rocco. *Contadini del sud*. Bari: Laterza, 1954.

Smith, Dennis Mack. *Italy: A Modern History*. Ann Arbor, Mich.: University of Michigan Press, 1969.

Smith, Dwight. *The Mafia Mystique*. New York: Basic Books, 1975.

Status of Italian Americans in the City University of New York. Italian American Center for Urban Affairs, 1976.

Suttles, Gerald. *The Social Order of a Slum*. Chicago: University of Chicago Press, 1968.

Tarrow, Sidney. *Peasant Communism in Southern Italy*. New Haven: Yale University Press, 1967.

Tomasi, Lydio F. *The Italian in America: The Progressive View*. New York: Center for Migration Studies, 1972.

Tomasi, Lydo F., and Betty Boyd Caroli. *The Italian Immigrant Woman in North America*. New York: American Italian Historical Association, 1979.

Tomasi, Silvano. *Piety and Power: The Role of Italian Parishes in the New York Metropolitan Area*. New York: Center for Migration Studies, 1975.

Tomasi, Silvano, ed. *The Religious Experience of Italian Americans*. New York: American Italian Historical Association, 1973.

Tomasi, Silvano, and Madeline Engel, eds. *The Italian Experiences in the United States*. New York: Center for Migration Studies, 1970.

Vecoli, Rudolph, ed. *Italian Radicalism: Old World Origins and New World Developments*. New York: American Italian Historical Association, 1972.

Viterbo, Michele. *Il sud e l'unita: genti del sud*. Bari: Laterza, 1966.

Whelpton, Eric. *A Concise History of Italy*. New York: Roy Publishers, 1964.

White, Theodore. *Breach of Faith*. New York: Atheneum-Readers Digest Press, 1975.

Whyte, William. *Street Corner Society*. Chicago: University of Chicago Press, 1955.

Williams, Phyllis. *South Italian Folkways in Europe and America*. New Haven: Yale University Press, 1938.

Williams, Robin M., Jr. *Strangers Next Door*. Englewood Cliffs, N.J.: Prentice Hall, 1964.

Yans-McLaughlin, Virginia. *Family and Community*. Ithaca: Cornell University Press, 1971.

Index